Constructing
World Culture

INTERNATIONAL

NONGOVERNMENTAL

ORGANIZATIONS

SINCE 1875

Constructing
World Culture

INTERNATIONAL

NONGOVERNMENTAL

ORGANIZATIONS

SINCE 1875

Edited by JOHN BOLI AND GEORGE M. THOMAS

Stanford University Press
Stanford, California
1999

Stanford University Press
Stanford, California
© 1999 by the Board of Trustees of the
Leland Stanford Junior University

Printed in the United States of America

CIP data appear at the end of the book

Acknowledgments

Our greatest debt is to our authors, both for the remarkable energy they have displayed in conducting their labor-intensive research and for their prompt and careful work through several rounds of revisions. On their behalf, we also wish to acknowledge the strong presence of John Meyer in more passages of the book than we can identify. As idea generator, mentor, research design consultant, statistical analysis coach, critical guide, and (for many of the authors) principal dissertation adviser, John has been a source of inspiration to us all. In his absence, neither this book nor most of the studies that comprise it would have ever seen the light of day.

For financial support at various stages of the project, we gratefully acknowledge funds supplied by the Swedish Social Science Research Council, the Emory University Research Council, and the Evangelical Scholarship Initiative. As usual, opinions expressed are those of the authors, not of the granting agencies.

We are especially grateful to the World Culture Research Group at Arizona State University for data coding and critical input, to Steve Miner for his work in the editing and preparation of the manuscript, and to Kristin Marsh for preparing the comprehensive bibliography and reformatting one difficult chapter. The first authors of each chapter also helped prepare the items for the index, a thankless task that we have well appreciated.

At Stanford University Press, both Laura Bloch and Muriel Bell have our gratitude for their interest, support, and helpful suggestions concerning the manuscript review process, final revisions, and production.

Finally, we owe a special and heartfelt thanks to Anthony Judge and the Union of International Associations. Mr. Judge was more than helpful in our correspondence with him about the Union's data-gathering process, and his willingness to share an electronic extract of the INGO database with us was a more than pleasant surprise. Without the remarkable efforts of the UIA, and the rich *Yearbook* that it has so faithfully produced for so long, most of the research reflected in this volume would not have been possible.

Contents

Figures and Tables

Figures

Tables

Contributors

Deborah Barrett is a postdoctoral fellow at the Carolina Population Center at the University of North Carolina at Chapel Hill.

Nitza Berkovitch is Assistant Professor in the Behavioral Sciences Department and Co-director of the Women's Studies Program at Ben Gurion University, Beer-Sheva, Israel.

John Boli is Associate Professor of Sociology at Emory University.

Colette Chabbott is Assistant Professor (acting) in the School of Education and Director of the Master's Program in International and Comparative Education at Stanford University.

Martha Finnemore is Assistant Professor of Political Science and International Affairs at George Washington University.

David John Frank is Assistant Professor of Sociology at Harvard University.

Ann Hironaka is a doctoral student in the Department of Sociology at Stanford University.

Young Soo Kim is Assistant Professor of International Studies at Soonchungyang University, Asan, Korea.

Teresa Loftin is a doctoral student in the Department of Sociology at Emory University.

Thomas A. Loya is a doctoral student in the Department of Sociology at Emory University.

John W. Meyer is Professor of Sociology at Stanford University.

Evan Schofer is a doctoral student in the Department of Sociology at Stanford University.

George M. Thomas is Professor of Sociology at Arizona State University.

Nancy Brandon Tuma is Professor and Chair of the Department of Sociology at Stanford University.

Constructing World Culture

INTERNATIONAL

NONGOVERNMENTAL

ORGANIZATIONS

SINCE 1875

Introduction

JOHN BOLI AND GEORGE M. THOMAS

Like other scholars in comparative-historical sociology and international relations, we have devoted much effort to understanding the workings of nation-state authority and citizenship, the formation and development of civil-society institutions, the operations of the interstate system, and the dynamics of global and international processes. Like others, we have been struck by the intense pace of change in the twentieth century, especially since World War II. Such developments as the apparent decline of nation-state sovereignty and citizenship, the rise of both transnational authority and intranational regionalism, the collapse of Communism and decline of Western hegemony, and the increasingly multipolar structure of the world have been so broad and were so poorly anticipated that we cannot but be awed.

These seemingly profound changes lose much of their dramatic force, however, when considered in larger historical and theoretical contexts. Shifts in world polarity are certainly not new; neither is the rise or fall of states, empires, or political economies. The most striking recent changes, if we are to believe the literature, are the "challenges to state sovereignty" and the "fragmentation" of nation-states. But these, too, are hardly unprecedented. Tensions in the symbiotic relationship between the nation-state and transnational cultural and organizational forces have characterized the modern world throughout most of this millennium. Much of the work we and our colleagues have undertaken in the past two decades has shown that the world-polity context that envelops the competitive state system has led to a mutual strengthening of states and transnational structures, very much contrary to the zero-sum imagery that often prevails in contemporary scholarship. Even more, these tensions have led to a remarkable degree of isomorphism among states and national societies.

In more general terms, in any relationship between actors and their environments mutually generative tensions commonly lead to similar actors pursuing similar goals. The fullest sketch of this line of argument as an explanation of state structure and national development is the 1987 work *Institutional Structure: Constituting State, Society, and the Individual*, of which the editors were coauthors along with John Meyer and Francisco Ramirez of Stanford University. That book has rightly been criticized for its lack of theoretical precision and empirical specificity in its analysis of the contextual effects of global institutions. We were acutely aware of these failings at the time and realized that our analysis could not move forward unless we could identify some of the "missing links" between global social construction and lower-level organization, policy, and mobilization.

One important missing link, we began to suspect, might be international nongovernmental organizations (INGOs). We had become aware of this burgeoning population of transnational associations through occasional use of the *Yearbook of International Organizations*, published by the Union of International Associations in Brussels, and we were puzzled by the paucity of scholarly studies of INGOs. They were treated as marginal, even epiphenomenal. The only types of INGOs that received much attention were those that had become prominent in the global public realm—such as Greenpeace, Amnesty International, the World Wildlife Fund, and the International Red Cross.

In the spring of 1988 the first editor of this volume systematically perused the *Yearbook* to explore the contours of the INGO population, confirming his suspicion that organizations like Greenpeace and Amnesty International were hardly typical INGOs. We soon recognized the enormous variety of these bodies, the richness of the information available about them, and the information's suitability for global historical analysis. In 1989 we began coding data from *Yearbook* volumes. As the contours of the data began to emerge, we became ever more convinced that INGOs had a powerful story to tell about the nature and operations of the world polity. Our endeavors eventually sparked a number of studies of different sectors of INGO activity, most of which are represented in this book.

As we tried to interpret the massive growth of INGOs, the range of activities they undertake, and the types of goals they pursue, we found that existing theories of global structures and systems left much to be desired. INGOs, and the world-cultural principles and models they embody, have very little presence in the dominant social-scientific approaches to international and global analysis. In international relations theory, the only objects worthy of study are states; this view characterizes functionalist, international-regime, and neoliberal institutionalist theories as much as it does the conventional realism and neorealism that have held the center of the field for so long. In sociology, state-competition and world-system theory similarly ignore INGOs, seeing states as central actors in networks of economic, political, and military power, but also, in the latter perspective, making much of the power and influence of transnational corporations. By contrast, the perspective developed in *Institutional Structure*, now often referred to as world-polity institutionalist theory, was already well primed to incorporate INGOs into its explanatory framework; indeed, the more we pursued our interest in INGOs, the more powerful this perspective seemed to become.

In adopting world-polity institutionalism in this book, we and our collaborators make two conceptual forays opening the way, we believe, to comprehensive analyses of global development that are well grounded in empirical reality and more satisfactory, in many respects, than other perspectives. The first is a Durkheimian leap of the sort that Mary Douglas articulates so well in her writings on the operations of cultural institutions. Our starting point is the universalistic (transnational, global) level of cultural and organizational formation that operates as a constitutive and directive environment for states, business enterprises, groups, and individuals. Arising out of Western Christendom and propagated via the processes and mechanisms analyzed so well in world-system and neorealist research, this transcendent level of social reality began to crystallize organizationally in the second half of the nineteenth century. After the vicissitudes of the two world wars, it has played an astonishingly authoritative role in shaping global development for the past fifty years.

Our second conceptual foray, best seen as the obverse of the first, is an insistence on problematizing the social units (states, corporations, groups, individuals) that other perspectives generally take for granted as the primary actors in global development. In this we find common ground with such growing movements among international relations scholars as the "constructivist" approach and the analysis of "epistemic communities," hesitant though these movements may be to depart radically from state-centric paradigms. For us, a fundamental question that must be addressed is not only how global actors go about their business but how and why they define their business as they do. At stake are the identities of these actors, the goals and purposes they adopt, the means they employ, and the causal logic they use to orient means to goals and purposes.

The approach taken here uses a world-polity response to answer the question of how global actors decide what their business is: to an ever increasing degree, all sorts of actors learn to define themselves and their interests from the global cultural and organizational structures in which they are embedded. Contemporary world culture defines actors of all sorts as rational, self-interested, and capable of initiative. These actors (especially corporations and states) are to find meaning and purpose through the pursuit of economic expansion and political power; through high-status consumption and self-development (individuals); through proper care and feeding of their populations (states); through technical progress (corporations, professions); and so on. Because the definitions, principles, purposes, and modes of action that constitute and motivate actors have come to comprise a global level of social reality, far-reaching isomorphism across actors is increasingly likely and observable. For the same reason, forms of conflict and modes for asserting distinctiveness are ever more stylized and standardized, though they may not be any less bloody or conflictual for that.

Conversely, in the familiar sociological dialectic given prominence in the work of Peter Berger, these global structures are maintained and transformed by the actors they constitute. World culture defines modern actors not as cultural dopes but as creative innovators who are the one and only source of change, adaptation, and restructuring in response to situational contingencies. Therefore these actors seek to expand their reach, fashion institutions after their own liking, reach cooperative agreements when their (globally constructed) interests so indicate, and engage in all the other high-adrenaline actions that state-centric, neorealist, neoliberal-institutionalist, and world-system theories put at the center of their analyses. Paradoxically, "agency" is a structurally constituted feature of the world polity, a characteristic that gives the modern world much of its extraordinary dynamism.

This theoretical approach guides all of our authors. In encapsulated form, they use it to address the following topics, with much historical detail and clearly specified bodies of evidence covering the period since 1875:

(1) Organizational dimensions of the world polity, that is, structures that embody, express, transmit, and transform world culture;

(2) World-cultural content, including principles and models that have dominated in specific global sectors and changes in these principles and models over time;

(3) Interactive effects between global cultural structures and actors embedded in those structures; and

(4) The sociology of global effects, with explicit concern for delineating

the mechanisms that link global processes to the identities and actions of various types of social units and actors.

If we are right in our approach, the structural isomorphism that characterizes actors, interests, and behavior in the world polity operates increasingly via "top-down" rather than "bottom-up" processes. It is the consequence of actors enacting cultural models that are lodged at the global level and linked in complex ways to other levels of organization, with increasing penetration of even the most peripheral social spaces. Much less often is structural isomorphism the result of rational choices by existentially given actors having inexplicably similar agendas, which is the implicit model underlying other perspectives on global change.

Most of the chapters in this volume touch only tangentially on the issue of conflict, the sine qua non of most social-scientific research. While it is the case that world-polity institutionalists need to give more systematic attention to strife and competitive conflict, the perspective does not suppose that globally driven cultural enactment entails harmony, peaceful relations, or reconciliation of interests. Quite the contrary: global enactment intensifies conflict and makes it more pervasive. Societies traveling diverse and weakly interconnected historical trajectories occupy varied ecological and social niches and, hence, have distinct or at least partly complementary interests. The increasing uniformity of societal interests within shared world-cultural goals and prescriptions implies that societies everywhere have increasingly similar goals and rely on increasingly similar resources. Uniformity at this basic level thus means that societies are much more likely to compete and struggle with one another than when they have different goals and rely on different resources. In addition, the principles of world culture promoted by INGOs in their role as "rationalized others" (as John Meyer aptly describes them) are themselves internally contradictory and conflictual (one example being the perennial contradiction between equality and liberty). Regrettably, a more harmonious world is not at all implied by the perspective developed here, be it at the societal, organizational, or individual level.

We are aware of the controversial nature of many of our claims. They go against the grain of habitual social-scientific thinking that sees actors as self-generative creators of the world, and we challenge this dominant view with some trepidation. We hope above all that the work described in this volume will stimulate rethinking of established perspectives on global development, perhaps prompting others to make the paradigmatic leap of recognizing the global level of social reality and its constitutive properties. A broad agenda has been opened up by the world-polity approach, and we allow ourselves the immodesty of suggesting that it offers one of the most fruitful fields of global investigation currently available to scholars.

Unlike most edited volumes, all of the chapters in this book work from a common theoretical perspective and are closely related to one another by a common orientation to empirical research. Some chapters explicitly evaluate empirical evidence that bears on the competing predictions of world-polity institutionalism in comparison with the other global perspectives. Other chapters concentrate mainly on world-polity theory, treating other perspectives more implicitly or in less detail. All chapters elaborate and empirically assess the distinctive reasoning and implications of the world-polity perspective.

Part I provides an overview of the INGO population. Chapter 1 is of central importance and should be read first, for much of its content is assumed but not explicated in other chapters. It provides an overview of the origins, development, and operations of the entire INGO population for the period 1875–1973, interpreted through the framework of world-polity institutionalism. We analyze INGOs as the primary organizational field in which world culture takes structural form, showing how INGOs help shape and define world culture as a distinct level of social reality. We also explore the substance and structure of world culture by a close analysis of the cultural principles by which INGOs are constructed and an examination of the distribution of INGOs across social sectors and over time.

Leaning heavily on Chapter 1, John Boli, Tom Loya, and Teresa Loftin examine participation in global organizations in Chapter 2, focusing mainly on INGOs but also comparing INGO membership structures to those of intergovernmental organizations (IGOs). Using several types of data regarding the countries in which members of INGOs reside, the chapter studies the distribution of memberships across types of countries (distinguished in terms of economic development, geographic region, dominant religion, degree of democratization, and other variables) and charts trends in membership distribution between 1960 and 1988. The analysis leads to reflections on the relative adequacy of functional, neorealist, neoliberal-institutionalist, world-system, and world-polity institutionalist theories for understanding the reach of INGOs in this period of rapid world development.

The remainder of the book, with the exception of the Conclusion, presents historical studies of distinct INGO sectors, most of them beginning with the origins of the sector in the nineteenth century and following its growth and intensification to the present. The chapters study both organizational expansion and substantive cultural content in their respective sectors, considering above all the role that INGOs play in developing and propagating world-cultural models, standards, discourse, and principles. The main target of INGO activity discussed in these chapters is the nation-state, which emerges from these analyses as a less dominant and self-directed actor than most scholars habitually assume. Another target is IGOs, which become both sites of intense INGO engagement and important factors affecting the INGO populations with which they interact. These chapters reflect exhaustive research into primary sources to identify the relevant INGO subpopulations and the key international conferences attended by INGO members. Many also involved laborious study of published documents about INGO operations and the voluminous proceedings and publications produced by international conferences. Some use advanced statistical methods, particularly event-history analysis, but they are written to minimize technical details so they will be accessible to a general audience.

Part II contains four studies of what we call "social movement" sectors. These are arenas involving high visibility in the global public realm and the mobilization of large numbers of people on behalf of purposes and values that movement members believe to be inadequately realized in existing institutions. In Chapter 3, David Frank, Ann Hironaka, John Meyer, Evan Schofer, and Nancy Tuma identify global institutional factors leading to the formation and growth of INGOs concerned with humanity's relationship to the natural world. They document changes in depictions of this relationship over the past century and show how these changes are reflected in the growth of environmental organizations, including both organizations that seek to preserve or protect nature and organizations that help drive the process of rationalizing the humanity-nature nexus. Along the way they improve our understanding of the significance of the United Nations Environment Programme and the first UN Conference on the Environment in 1972 for the formation of state environmental protection agencies.

In Chapter 4, Nitza Berkovitch traces the growth, decline, and resurgence of the international women's movement. She shows how the goals of the women's movement changed as world-cultural conceptions of women changed, moving from a conception of women as distinct from men and requiring special protection and consideration to a fully egalitarian conception after World War II. Women's groups' efforts with respect to individual states, the International Labor Organization (formed immediately after World War I), and UN organizations are important elements of her analysis. Her chapter offers some surprises to those who think they have a good grasp of the history of women's movements over the past century.

In Chapter 5 Young Kim follows the fortunes of Esperanto. The most successful artificial language, Esperanto was developed to serve as a universal medium of communication that would improve global and international harmony. In this more purely cultural sector, Kim develops an explanation for long-term patterns of Esperanto INGO formation. His analysis fits especially nicely with arguments developed in Chapters 1 and 2 on the importance of initially universal and diffuse world-polity organizations and the later relative decline of such organizations in favor of more specific, differentiated, and limited transnational structures.

In Chapter 6, Martha Finnemore studies one of the earliest and most successful of the global human rights movements, the International Committee of the Red Cross. Her concern is limited to the first phase of ICRC work, when its few but highly energetic members overcame tremendous odds to induce states to adopt humanitarian rules of war in the first of the Geneva conventions. Finnemore shows that functional and interest-related explanations have trouble explaining this development, while a world-cultural argument accords quite well with the way events unfolded.

The chapters in Part III deal with sectors that involve technical, socioeconomic, and scientific organization of the world polity. The sectors discussed in this portion of the book lie close to the core of world culture and involve much less controversy than those in Part II. They therefore are not well known and rarely receive much notice in the public realm. Chapter 7, by Tom Loya and John Boli, studies technical standardization, tracing the origins and growth of the two central INGOs in this sector, the International Organization for Standardization and the International Electrotechnical Commission. Through an analysis of the structure, operations, and memberships of these bodies, the authors show that standardization is a realm of essentially pure rationalization in which, contrary to state-centric and world-system theories, the power differentials of states and corporations have rather limited opportunity to influence outcomes. Their portrait of this extraordinarily comprehensive sector indicates that the technical homogenization process is already thoroughly global and highly institutionalized, even though it depends primarily on voluntary compliance with technical standards.

In their study of population policy, Debbie Barrett and David Frank (Chapter 8) study the shift from the nineteenth-century view of population growth as a vital component of national power to the strong postwar consensus that population control is necessary for economic development. The chapter shows that INGO conferences and discourse were crucial to this conceptual shift and eventually helped lead states to make population-control policy a standard part of their approach to societal management. Of particular importance here was the conceptual linkage that emerged between population control and national well-being, for earlier exhortations favoring population control for the general improvement of human welfare had been ineffective in evoking state action.

Chapter 9, by Colette Chabbott, surveys the field of development organizations in the postwar era. Chabbott describes the processes whereby development aid and advising became a transnational enterprise conducted by a burgeoning industry of INGOs closely tied to states and intergovernmental bodies. She identifies several phase shifts in the prevailing approach to development, from comprehensive planning and industrialization in the 1950s to sustainable development in the 1990s, and documents the expanding role of international and national nongovernmental organizations with each successive phase. In the process, she also shows how world-cultural images of the nature and role of the state in less developed countries have changed as part of the evolution of development discourse and organization.

Chapter 10, by Evan Schofer, studies the organization of science in professional associations. Schofer works with two subpopulations in this sector, strictly science-oriented INGOs and socially oriented science INGOs. Science-oriented bodies arose first, as science became a rationalized and professionalized arena, but socially oriented bodies have expanded rapidly in recent decades as science has been integrated into modern models of national development. Schofer then shows that scientific INGOs are especially important to scientists in peripheral countries and have helped motivate many states to engage in science policy.

Finally, in the Conclusion, John Boli reviews the detailed investigations in Parts II and III as part of his analysis of a central theoretical problem raised by the sectoral studies: How can INGOs exercise any sort of influence or authority in the world polity, given that they are resource-poor and lack coercive enforcement capabilities? Boli expands arguments in the first two chapters about the cultural properties and assumptions, deeply and widely embedded in world culture, that account for INGO authority and effectiveness. Building from the cultural foundation of the collectively defined sovereign individual, INGOs draw on a wide range of legitimations for their authority: the legitimated structures and procedures by which they operate, the legitimated purposes they pursue, and the cultural authority embodied in their members in terms of educational credentials, professional standing, moral charisma, and so on. With respect to IGOs, Boli shows that a somewhat different logic accounts for their authority because they have sovereign states as members, though there is a good deal of overlap with INGO authority legit-imations because IGOs, too, operate in a world in which legal-rational au-thority remains decentralized. In his analysis of three forms of INGO au-thority—autonomous, collateral, and penetrative—he argues that INGOs, IGOs, and states are engaged in complex processes of global governance in-volving a good deal of collaboration and mutual legitimation, though in many domains INGOs operate largely outside the formal authority struc-tures overseen by states.

All of these chapters develop theoretical reasoning about world political and cultural processes that operate through global and international organi-zations. Their theoretical claims are supported by detailed empirical studies that bring wide-ranging systematic evidence to bear on issues of world-polity organization, world-cultural content, the dialectical relationships between global structures and national and local actors, and specific processes linking the global with the local. We offer the book as a decided advance in world-polity institutional analysis and look forward to lively debate about its claims and findings.

Part One International
Nongovernmental
Organizations in the
World Polity

Chapter One # INGOs and the Organization of World Culture

JOHN BOLI AND GEORGE M. THOMAS

Much recent scholarship analyzes global structures and processes as a distinct level of social reality. In this work, the world is more than networks or systems of economic and political interaction and exchange; it has become a single "international society," or world polity (Meyer 1987a; Watson 1992; Bull and Watson 1984). This chapter advances the world-polity perspective on global change by examining the history, structure, and operations of international nongovernmental organizations (INGOs).[1]

Our world-polity approach brings to the forefront the institutional character of transnational development. Culture is increasingly global (Robertson 1992; Thränhardt 1992; Featherstone 1990; Lechner 1989; Hannerz 1987); a transnational "legal world order" operates with considerable autonomy from states (Weiss 1989; Berman 1988; Falk, Kratochwil, and Mendlovitz 1985; Weston, Falk, and D'Amato 1980); and world-cultural principles and institutions shape the action of states, firms, individuals, and other subunits (Boli 1999a; McNeely 1995; Meyer, Boli et al. 1997; Strang 1990; Thomas 1993). On numerous dimensions, then, the world polity is not reducible to states, transnational corporations (TNCs), or national forces and interest groups (Nettl and Robertson 1968; Mann 1986; Hall 1985; Thomas et al. 1987; Ashley 1992; Banks 1984; Thomas 1993).

We emphasize the importance of cultural or institutional frames, treating actors not as unanalyzed "givens" but as entities constructed and motivated by these enveloping frames (Jepperson 1991, 1992). The nature, purposes, behavior, and meaning of actors, whether individuals, organizations, social movements, or states, are subject to redefinition and change as the frames themselves change.

Empirical studies of nation-states find striking structural homology across countries in, among other things, education, women's rights, social security programs, environmental policy, and constitutional arrangements (Meyer et al. 1992; Bradley and Ramirez 1996; Strang 1990; Ramirez and Boli 1987a; Thomas and Lauderdale 1988; Abbott and DeViney 1992; Boli 1987b). These studies often argue that such homology derives from an overarching world culture, but they do not investigate that culture directly. They present little evidence about the structures by which world culture is organized, the processes by which it develops, or the mechanisms through which it affects states and other units.

Our research directly explores world culture by analyzing INGOs.[2] INGOs have proliferated spectacularly, from about 200 active organizations in 1900 to about 800 in 1930, to over 2,000 in 1960, and nearly 4,000 in 1980, but little systematic attention has been given to this domain of global organization. As we shall show, INGOs are transnational bodies exercising a special type of authority we call rational voluntarism. They employ limited resources to make rules, set standards, propagate principles, and broadly represent "humanity" vis-à-vis states and other actors. Unlike states, INGOs lack the rational-legal authority to make or enforce law. Unlike global corporations, they have few economic resources. We argue, however, that a culturally informed analysis of INGOs is necessary to understand key aspects of global development.

Our analysis can be distilled as follows. For a century and more, the world has constituted a singular polity. By this we mean that the world has been conceptualized as a unitary social system, increasingly integrated by networks of exchange, competition, and cooperation, such that actors have found it "natural" to view the whole world as their arena of action and discourse. Such conceptualization reifies the world polity implicitly, in the often unconscious adoption of this cultural frame by politicians, businesspeople, travelers, and activists, and explicitly, in the discourse of intellectuals, policy analysts, and academicians.

Like all polities, the world polity is constituted by a distinct culture—a set of fundamental principles and models, mainly ontological and cognitive in character, defining the nature and purposes of social actors and action. Like all cultures, world culture becomes embedded in social organization, especially in organizations operating at the global level. Because most of these organizations are INGOs, we can identify fundamental principles of world culture by studying INGO structures, purposes, and operations. By studying INGOs across social sectors, we can make inferences about the structure of world culture. By studying INGO promotion of world-cultural principles that they are centrally involved in developing, we can see how INGOs shape the frames that orient other actors, including states.

THE PROBLEMATIC OF WORLD ORDER FOR SOCIAL THEORY

The world-polity perspective, which makes the institutional aspects of transnational structures foundational, runs counter to more established approaches to global analysis. The latter, which we will refer to collectively as global neorealist perspectives, vary considerably in their emphases and explanatory models, but they share a metatheoretical style that can usefully be described as reductionist rationalism. For global neorealists, primordially given actors with well-understood needs and motivations create worldwide systems in the routine pursuit of their interests, and these systems operate to serve the interest of the actors that comprise them.

In sociology, state-competition (Evans, Rueschemeyer, and Skocpol 1985; Badie and Birnbaum 1983; Giddens 1985; Goldstone 1991; Skocpol 1979; Tilly 1975, 1992) and world-system (Wallerstein 1974, 1979, 1991; Chase-Dunn 1989; Smith 1980) theories reduce transnational structures to military or economic processes dominated by major world powers. For example, world-system theorists suggest that such worldwide phenomena as popular consumer culture and human rights discourse are ultimately explainable as capitalist domination or false consciousness.[3] Moreover, both state-competition and world-system theories hold to a functionalist conception of culture as little more than value orientations, and the well-known inadequacies of this conception make it easy for them to dismiss culture as irrelevant.

In international relations, classic realists (Morgenthau 1960; Aron 1984) depict the world as purely anarchic; only states and economic organizations matter internationally. "Neorealists" acknowledge that action takes place within a web of transnational institutions ("regimes," often organized as intergovernmental organizations, or IGOs), but they conceptualize these structures reductively as mere "networks of interdependence" (Jacobson 1979) that are controlled by the interest-oriented actors that create them (Krasner 1983a, 1985; Northedge 1976; Waltz 1979). While this perspective may acknowledge the stability and partial autonomy of IGOs, such properties are explained mainly in terms of "sunk costs" and organizational inertia (Krasner 1983b; Archer 1983).

What international relations theory refers to as "neoliberal institution-alism" attributes greater importance to international institutions, recognizing that they can affect state policies and interests, particularly those of weaker states (Keohane 1984, 1989; Stein 1993). Scholars of this view argue that conditions of interdependence at times convince states that they cannot manage or solve problems through first-order exchange, so they require and construct international norms and procedures. The resulting institutions are thus seen as functionally necessary for states, facilitating needed cooperation by providing information, reducing transaction costs, providing monitoring mechanisms, and generally reducing uncertainty (Keohane 1993; Diehl 1996; Weiss, Gordenker, and Watson 1996).[4] Nevertheless, neoliberal institution-alism is grounded in (neo-)realist assumptions: states are the paramount ac-tors, states rationally pursue self-evident interests, state cooperation is essen-tially voluntary and strategic. International institutions are reducible to state interests and cannot survive unless they are based on either hegemonic or shared interests (Keohane 1993). International institutions therefore are only the prescribed "principles, norms, rules, and procedures" (Krasner 1983b) that are formally built into IGOs by treaty arrangements. In short, for neorealists and neoliberal institutionalists alike, stability and change result from puta-tively rational, coherent states pursuing "natural" interests. These scholars recognize no order of social reality that transcends states nor any type of au-thority or actorhood but that of self-interested, rational states (Baldwin 1993).

The reductionist rationalism of these global neorealist perspectives has not gone unchallenged. International relations scholars of a poststructuralist or neo-Grotian bent (e.g., Burton 1972; Czempiel and Rosenau 1992; Wendt and Duvall 1989; Wendt 1992; Boulding 1990, 1991) sharply criticize the as-sumptions and narrowness of global neorealism. Some scholars give credence to transnational norms, various notions of a "world order," even a world cul-ture (Kratochwil and Ruggie 1986; Lapid and Kratochwil 1996; Murphy 1994). On the whole, though, neo-Grotians have been more normative than analytical, and they rarely conduct systematic empirical research with which to confront the dominant neorealisms. The debate between neo-Grotians and global neorealists has mainly involved epistemological and methodolog-ical polemics, often of an ad hoc character. Because both sets of perspectives are comprehensive, metatheoretically flexible, and rather vaguely specified, it is difficult to identify evidence that would allow one to choose between them in analyzing particular issues. Further, almost all of the debate has centered on states, the state system, and IGOs. Though studies of epistemic communities, international law, and transnational social movements (especially those focusing on environmentalism and human rights) are proliferating (Haas 1992; Otto 1996; Smith, Chatfield, and Pagnucco 1997; Wapner 1996), and some scholars see INGOs as important elements of an emerging "global civil society" (Boulding 1990), this material has yet to be incorporated fully in the debate.

In this chapter we push toward a more specified and evidentiary "neo-Grotian" analysis, beginning with an overview of our world-polity institutionalist perspective on world culture and organization. We then chart the development of the INGO population and document its close relationship with other aspects of world development. In the third section we identify five global cultural principles, embodied by INGOs, that are centrally involved in the constitution of the world polity: universalism, individualism, rational voluntaristic authority, rationalizing progress, and world citizenship. Our fourth section turns to the structuration of world culture, which we examine through the sectoral distribution of INGOs.

We end the chapter by showing how the analyses and case studies in the remaining chapters of the book fit into the theoretical and empirical framework we develop here. These chapters tell stories of the creation and development of world culture in international organizations. They document dimensions of global development in which INGOs formulate global issues, promote world-cultural principles by which those issues should be addressed, and prompt states to take action that is largely consistent with those principles. They show, in other words, how global structures and processes help shape and guide the definitions and behavior of less universalistic world-polity actors.

THE CULTURE IN WORLDWIDE INSTITUTIONS

Culture lies at the heart of world development. Technical progress, bureaucratization, capitalist organization, states, and markets are embedded in cultural models, often not explicitly recognized as such, that specify the "nature of things" and the "purposes of action." These cultural conceptions do more than orient action; they also constitute actors. People draw on worldwide cultural principles that define actors as individuals having inherent needs, emotions, and capacities, and they act in accordance with such principles. Worldwide constructs provide social identities, roles, and subjective selves by which individuals rationally organize to pursue their interests. World-cultural conceptions also define the collective identities and interests of such entities as firms, states, and nations, along with rational organizational forms that are to be adopted by such collectivities (Meyer, Boli, and Thomas 1987; Meyer, Boli et al. 1997).

In the context of these constitutive cultural principles and models, actors do not *act* so much as they *enact* (Jepperson 1991). But enactment does not entail mechanical recitation of highly specified scripts. Rather, actors actively draw on, select from, and modify shared cultural models, principles, and identities (Swidler 1986). Innovative enactment is especially common because world culture defines the exercise of agency via "self-directed" behavior as the successful model of action.[5] The enactment of cultural models thus represents broad homologies, with actors everywhere defining themselves in similar ways and pursuing similar purposes by similar means, but specific actions in specific contexts vary almost without limit.

In addition, the dialectical and internally contradictory character of the overarching cultural framework guarantees that variation and conflict, the preoccupations of the social sciences, are abundant and ubiquitous. Conflictual differentiation is especially likely because world culture is applied to a great variety of local situations, normally in selective and eclectic ways. Ambiguity and disarticulation (Sewell 1992; Wuthnow 1989) are thus general consequences as enacted routines reproduce not only actors but the cultural frame itself. By enacting general models in specific contexts, actors elaborate, modify, and transform the cultural framework as well.[6]

Most of the principles and models of world culture are shared primarily at the ontological or cognitive level; they are widely known and believed as inherent features of reality. Moral evaluations typically are far from consensual—values vary greatly, and moral judgment can become exceedingly complex—but ontological definitions of the nature of things are normally taken for granted. Regardless of one's attitude toward the large corporation, for example, one has great difficulty denying the social reality of Mitsubishi or Hewlett-Packard. Such cognitive ontology is rarely called into question because it forms the very foundation for action. It is composed of the assumptions we make about how things "truly are," for better and for worse.[7]

When we speak of culture as global, we mean this in two senses. First, definitions, principles, and purposes are cognitively constructed in similar ways throughout the world. The existence, general nature, and purposes of states, school systems, and TNCs are known everywhere. They are Durkheimian social facts, whether revered or reviled. Thus, even though many of the world-cultural principles we discuss are contested and generate considerable conflict, their reification is enhanced by the very contestation that challenges them.[8]

A second sense in which culture is global is that it is held to be applicable everywhere in the world. World-cultural models are presumed to be universally valid, usually by functional-imperative reasoning. The state is presumed necessary for order and coordination; therefore, France and Vanuatu must have states. Mass schooling is necessary for national development; therefore, Malaysia and Paraguay must have schools. Models that do not have general applicability are suspect unless they are conceptualized as special adaptations of general models. African development models may emphasize labor-intensive projects but their ultimate goals are still economic growth and rational social management.

In contemporary world culture, the dominant global actors are states, TNCs, and IGOs. These entities are defined as actors capable of wielding military, economic, and political power, and for the most part, they enact this conception well. Alongside the realpolitik networks formed by these actors, and intensely entwined with them, INGOs are much less well conceptualized actors whose primary concern is enacting, codifying, modifying, and propagating world-cultural structures and principles.

In speaking of world-cultural models that shape social reality, we recognize that competing models conflict in important respects. Yet the conflicting models and discourse that make global culture so dynamic nevertheless share fundamental conceptions regarding actors, agency, nature, technique, societal purposes, and much more. We also recognize that universal cultural principles may themselves generate conflict. For example, uniform conceptions of human purpose imply that actors have identical goals; they therefore are likely to compete for the same resources. Conflict intensifies when, for instance, peripheral regions are reorganized as progress-oriented societies. Their new, uniformly defined states may nationalize foreign industries, clash over territorial boundaries, or engage in other habitual forms of internal mobilization and interstate competition.

Dialectical processes of world-polity development thus generate struggles that would not arise in a less integrated world (Boli 1999a; Meyer, Boli et al. 1997). Although INGOs generally favor peace and harmony, they also foster conflict by helping to constitute the world polity. Simmel's insight is apt: conflict is also a form of interaction, and actors within the same cultural frame are likely to find more bases for conflict (and cooperation) than actors from barely intersecting frames.

A HISTORICAL OVERVIEW OF THE INGO POPULATION

The INGO Data

Since 1850 more than 35,000 private, not-for-profit organizations with an international focus have debuted on the world stage. Associations, societies, foundations, unions, committees, clubs, leagues, conferences, groups, federations, conventions—the range of designations is extraordinary. They include the Pan American Association of Ophthalmology, the International Exhibitions Bureau, the Commission for the Geological Map of the World, the International Catholic Child Bureau, the International Tin Council, and the Tug of War International Federation. Most are highly specialized, drawing members worldwide from a particular occupation, technical field, branch of knowledge, industry, hobby, or sport, to promote and regulate their respective areas of concern. Only a few, such as the Scout Movement, the International Olympic Committee, the International Red Cross, and the World Wildlife Fund, are widely known.

We have analyzed data on 5,983 organizations founded between 1875 and 1988. They constitute the entire population of INGOs classified as genuinely international bodies by the Union of International Associations in its *Yearbook of International Organizations*[9] (UIA 1985, 1988). We coded founding and dissolution dates, primary and secondary aims, type of membership, number of members, and type of dissolution.[10] Our population includes all nongovernmental organizations listed in the "Universal," "Intercontinental," and "Regional" sections of the 1988 *Yearbook*, along with those in the "Dissolved" section of the 1985 *Yearbook*. We omit the far more numerous NGOs of international orientation that are not international in membership and structure. They include a vast array of foundations, policy centers, religious bodies, research institutes, and the like.

Data Quality and Coding Issues

The UIA limits INGOs to not-for-profit, non-state organizations (TNCs and IGOs are excluded). They vary in size from a few dozen members from only three countries to millions of members from close to two hundred countries.[11] About half of the INGOs in our database have members from at least 25 countries, 20 percent have members from 50 or more countries, and only 11 percent have members from fewer than 8 countries.

Several features of the UIA's data-gathering process convince us that the data are adequate for meaningful analysis. First, the UIA has long had semi-official status as the compiler of information on INGOs and IGOs through ties with the League of Nations and United Nations (UIA 1985: 1654). Considered the definitive source of INGO data, it maintains continuous contact with over 13,000 organizations, including most of the active international organizations in our data set. Second, the UIA incorporates ever more information each year. Organizations are asked to identify other INGOs that have recently come to their knowledge, and UIA staff search newspapers, magazines, and journals to identify INGOs not present in the database. Even organizations that came to the editors' notice after they had ceased operations are included as dissolved bodies. Nineteen organizations in our database dissolved in the same year they were founded, 260 within three years of founding, and fully 502 within five years.

Third, the possibility that the quality of the data is better for recent years, so that rising INGO founding rates (below) would be partly artifactual, does not seem to be a serious concern. On the one hand, the magnitude of growth is stupendous: Even if as many as half of the INGOs founded in the early period have not been identified, the growth curve would still rise sharply. On the other hand, the history of the database suggests that only a small proportion of early INGOs have been omitted. The first INGO compilation in 1909 identified about 200 organizations, many of which were not international in scope. Our coding yielded 371 international organizations founded prior to 1909 (of 5,035 bodies with known founding dates). Of these 371, some 334 were founded after 1874. Hence, much more is now known about the early period of INGO formation than was known in that period itself.

No *Yearbook* is complete for the years immediately preceding its publication. We evaluated the length of the data-gathering pipeline by comparing the number of foundings identified in one edition of the *Yearbook* with those published in previous editions. Our analysis suggests that about 60 percent of all INGOs enter the *Yearbook* within five years of founding, while 80 to 90 percent enter within ten years and the remainder are identified within another five years. Proceeding conservatively, we have settled on 1973 as the last year for which the 1988 *Yearbook* provides complete data. None of our analyses looks any different if the end date is extended to 1980 or 1985, except that the founding rate for the extended period drops because many newer INGOs are omitted.

Measuring dissolutions poses a problem because many organizations never formally disband. The UIA classifies an organization as dissolved if it no longer responds to requests for information and no activity regarding it has been reported for five years. Our dates of dissolution are often taken from such phrases as "last reported activity 1948." In other cases dates of dissolution are more precise, especially if they involve mergers or absorption by other bodies.[12]

To classify the INGO population into sectors, we constructed a set of mutually exclusive and exhaustive categories from the organization titles and descriptions of aims in the *Yearbook*. Primary and secondary aims were coded independently by at least two coders. Inter-coder agreement was relatively low for each aim separately (about 60 percent), but reliability for primary and secondary aims taken together was high (about 90 percent). Agreement when we collapsed our 42 specific categories (Appendix Table A) into thirteen major sectors was higher still. Disagreements were resolved by group discussion, resulting in a set of formal criteria for establishing aims priority.[13]

Basic Historical Patterns

Figure 1.1 presents the founding dates of all (active and dissolved) INGOs and of only dissolved INGOs between 1875 and 1973.[14] Not-for-profit international organizing grew rapidly in the latter part of the nineteenth century, about ten organizations a year emerging during the 1890s. The population burgeoned after the turn of the century, reaching a peak of 51 foundings in 1910. The severe collapse after that point led to a low of 4 foundings in 1915. Swift recovery after World War I yielded a period of fairly steady growth followed by some decline during the 1930s that preceded another steep fall going into World War II. Following the war, international organizing exploded; by 1947 over 90 organizations a year were being founded, a pace that was maintained and even surpassed through the 1960s.

The founding pattern for subsequently dissolved bodies is similar, indicating a mostly steady rate of eventual dissolution punctuated by peaks of fragility for organizations founded just before each of the wars. About 70 percent of early INGOs eventually disappeared, but long-term viability increased markedly after World War I and still more after World War II. The great majority of INGOs founded after the war are still active. Analyses of dissolution in relation to life span suggests that this is not artifactual: if INGOs founded after World War II were as subject to dissolution as those from before World War I, a larger wave of dissolutions should be apparent for recent decades.

In Figure 1.2 we look at dissolutions as a percentage of the INGO population active at the beginning of each year. (The figure starts with 1906 because only seven recorded dissolutions occurred before that year.) After a rapid rise at the end of the first decade of the twentieth century, dissolutions

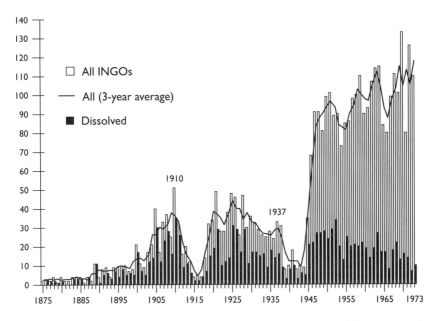

FIGURE 1.1. International nongovernmental organizations: Foundings of all and dissolved bodies, 1875–1973. SOURCE: *Yearbook of International Organizations* (UIA 1985, 1988).

peaked at almost 8 percent of the population (34 of 417 organizations) in 1913 before dropping to zero in 1917. The dissolution peak followed the peak of foundings by three years. Dissolutions rose into the 1920s to a fairly constant level until the crisis of the 1930s, when a second peak of over 7 percent was reached in 1936 (for 1936–38, a total of 113 organizations dissolved). World War II again reduced dissolutions drastically, and the rate of dissolution thereafter underwent a gradual decline. Note that the low rate of dissolutions after the mid-1950s prevailed while more INGOs were being founded than ever before.

INGO foundings and dissolutions thus match the general "state of the world" rather well, rising in periods of expansion and declining rapidly in times of crisis, with the declines beginning shortly before the outbreaks of the two major wars. This finding raises the issue of what these patterns tell us about world-polity formation. We approach this issue by examining (1) the relationship of INGO formation to other world-level variables and (2) the structure and operations of INGOs as world-cultural constructs.

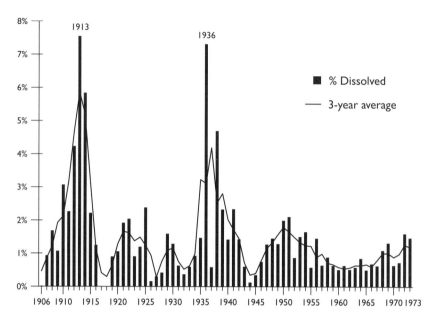

FIGURE 1.2.   Dissolutions as percentage of active INGO population, 1906–1973. SOURCE: *Yearbook of International Organizations* (UIA 1985, 1988).

WORLD DEVELOPMENT, INGOS, AND CAPITALIST AND INTERSTATE SYSTEMS

We have compiled an array of longitudinal world-level indicators, many of them normally accounted at the nation-state level but here summed to produce world-totals variables. Most of these variables are measured annually; a few are measured at twenty-year intervals.[15] Some reach back into the nineteenth century, while others are confined to recent decades. Many are not available for the war years 1914–1918 and 1940–1945.

The longitudinal correlations among these world-level variables, logged to eliminate skewness, are strikingly high. For the typical variables selected for Table 1.1, the great majority of coefficients are above .97, while a few are at .86 to .88. For example, world government revenue correlates .97 with world exports (103 years' coverage); world primary educational enrollment correlates .99 with the number of treaties; world energy production correlates .99 with world tertiary schooling. Even measures of military personnel and ex-

TABLE 1.1

Correlations Among Measures of Dimensions of World Development
(Time series data, nineteenth and twentieth centuries)

	Exports	Energy	Telephones	Primary education	Tertiary education	Urban population	Diplomat	Treaties	Rights
Government revenue	.97 (103)	.97 (49)	.87 (87)	.98 (103)	.99 (103)	.98 (103)	.99 (5)	.98 (5)	.99 (6)
Exports		.97 (49)	.86 (87)	.98 (103)	.99 (103)	.97 (103)	1.00 (5)	.98 (5)	.99 (6)
Energy production			.99 (49)	.98 (49)	.99 (49)	.98 (49)	—	—	1.00 (3)
Telephones				.89 (87)	.91 (87)	.92 (87)	.93* (4)	.88** (4)	.88* (5)
Primary educational enrollments					.99 (103)	.99 (103)	1.00 (5)	.99 (5)	.98 (6)
Tertiary educational enrollments						1.00 (103)	1.00 (5)	1.00 (5)	.98 (6)
Urban population (cities of 100,000+)							1.00 (5)	.98 (5)	.97 (6)
Diplomatic representation								1.00 (4)	.98 (5)
Treaties among states									.99 (5)
Citizen rights specified in constitutions									

NOTE: Variables are annual world totals. Figures in parentheses give the number of years for which data on the respective pairs of variables are available. Data for diplomatic representation, treaties, and rights are taken at twenty-year intervals. The endpoint for all other correlation series is 1973; most variables are missing for the world war years. All variables are logged to reduce skewness.

All coefficients are significant beyond the .001 level with the exception of: * $p < .06$, ** $p < .04$

penditures (not shown), which fluctuated sharply due to major wars, correlate at the .90 level or better with most other indicators.

This extraordinary covariation is extremely robust. When we use standardized measures, such as GNP per capita and energy production per capita, the coefficients diminish only slightly (.10–.15 units). Using the three periods demarcated by the world wars, we find that the intercorrelations have the same high magnitude for each period as for the entire series. Using different segments of the world economy based on country shares of world trade (see Boli 1987b), we find that the intercorrelations are above .90 (most above .95) within each stratum. When we divide the world into a more developed third and a less developed two-thirds, the same results obtain within each stratum.

These intercorrelations suggest that world development over the past century is all of a piece. Economies, states, constitutions, educational systems, communications, transportation, energy production, armies and weaponry, interstate relations—all have grown in lockstep. For the past hundred years, the world polity has operated as a singular whole.

Where do INGOs fit into this dense world structure? Table 1.2 shows correlations between the total number of INGOs founded each year and the indicators in Table 1.1. Again the figures are extremely high, mostly at about .90 or above. INGO foundings are less strongly related to a few indicators, notably military variables (not shown), but the basic conclusion is inescapable: the development of the INGO population is part and parcel of the general development of the world polity.

The strong covariation we have found in world-polity development is partly artifactual, but in a highly revealing sense. Only dimensions of social life that are deemed relevant to societal rationalization, as either indicators of progress or measures of problems like poverty or crime, are quantified with enough uniformity to generate world-level indicators. As properties of the rationalizing world polity, they are likely to correlate highly with each other. Aspects of social life that are not quantified or are not standardized in the world accounting system might correlate less highly, but their marginality to the official rationalizing project makes them unavailable. Data-gathering and its associated statistical manipulations are cultural practices that themselves tell us much about contemporary world culture (see Anderson 1983; McNeely 1995; Ventresca 1990).

These correlations would not be noteworthy in a world polity that was tightly managed by a world state; neither would they seem remarkable in a national society. In the absence of a world state, however, global neorealist

TABLE 1.2

Correlations Between International Nongovernmental and Intergovernmental Organizations and Measures of Dimensions of World Development
(Time series data, nineteenth and twentieth centuries)

	Government revenue	Exports	Energy production	Telephones	Primary education
Total INGOs founded	.89 (103)	.91 (103)	.87 (49)	.97 (87)	.93 (103)
Total IGOs founded	.94 (103)	.94 (103)	.90 (49)	.78 (87)	.92 (103)

	Tertiary education	Urban population	Diplomat	Treaties	Rights
Total INGOs founded	.93 (103)	.93 (114)	.89** (5)	.93** (5)	.81** (6)
Total IGOs founded	.93 (103)	.91 (114)	.96 (5)	.96 (5)	.93 (6)

NOTE: Variables are annual world totals. Figures in parentheses give the number of years for which data on the respective pairs of variables are available. Data for diplomatic representation, treaties, and rights are taken at twenty-year intervals. The endpoint for all other time series is 1973; most variables are missing for the world war years. All variables are logged to reduce skewness. INGO and IGO variables are logged five-year moving averages. See Table 1.1 for more complete labels of column variables.

The correlation between INGO foundings and IGO foundings is .83 (119 years).

All coefficients are significant beyond the .001 level with the exception of: ** $p < .03$

perspectives have trouble accounting for this degree of integration. It is not directly political, as state-competition theorists and strict neorealists might suggest, because not even hegemons have had the power to control world development so comprehensively. Neither is it directly economic, as world-system theorists might claim, since they argue that rates of development in different segments of the world economy must vary substantially. Steep stratification certainly persists among nation-states, but the covariation between world strata taken as aggregates is also very high (e.g., core government revenue is correlated .91 with periphery government revenue).

These high intercorrelations also are troubling to functionalist and neo-liberal-institutionalist arguments depicting an anarchic world driven by technological imperatives and large-scale problems to create global organizations (Mitrany 1943; Stein 1993; Axelrod and Keohane 1993). Like modernization theory, such arguments imply that high intercorrelations should also be found at the national level, but studies using nations as units report more moderate correlations (e.g., Meyer and Hannan 1979).[16] Like world-system theory, functionalism implies that structural variation should abound because national conditions vary so much, but homology is the rule.

More fundamentally, the perception of problems as global rather than national is not simply a technical matter. For example, pollution was almost certainly worse in the coal-burning nineteenth century than it is today, but a transnational environmental movement did not form at that time. What functionalist reasoning overlooks is the fact that technique and the definition of problems as technical in nature are themselves cultural processes (Ellul 1980).

World-polity development is more dialectical than global neorealist perspectives would have it. Global organizing proceeds in mutually reinforcing tension with the expansion of the nation-state system (Boli 1999a). INGOs began to proliferate during the heyday of nationalism and European imperialism; bringing the last "unclaimed" regions of the globe into the world economy and under the jurisdiction of states made the notions of "one world" and "one history" structurally compelling.

This dialectic is further evident in the effects of the world wars. The precipitous decline in INGO foundings after 1910 reflects the dominance of states for most of that decade, but the war also strengthened the conception of the world as a single polity and prompted expanded INGO (and IGO) efforts to organize the world polity. State efforts in this direction (the League of Nations and ancillary bodies), while ineffective in maintaining peace, helped further reify the world polity and world citizenship (cf. Giddens 1985). After a similar cycle in the 1930s and 1940s, a much broader discursive space for INGOs opened up as global technical and infrastructural resources increased exponentially. World-polity organizing jumped to a higher level than ever before just as the independent nation-state form was adopted by or imposed on the rest of the world.

The dialectic between world-polity and inter-state organization is also evident in the relationship between IGOs and INGOs. The shape of the growth curve for IGOs over the last hundred years is very similar to that of INGOs, although there are far fewer IGOs (Jacobson 1979; Jacobson, Reisinger, and Mathers 1986; Murphy 1994; Wallace and Singer 1970). IGO and INGO foundings are highly correlated (.83) over this period, and IGO foundings are highly correlated with other world-level variables (see Table

1.2). Global neorealist perspectives would interpret this relationship in reductionist and state-centric terms, perhaps arguing that, if not simply epiphenomenal, INGOs are generated indirectly by processes dominated by states and IGOs.

The evidence suggests instead a complex pattern of IGO-INGO relationships. First, INGOs can lead to the formation of IGOs and the expansion of IGO agencies and agendas. Many IGOs were founded as INGOs and later co-opted by states, including such major bodies as the World Meteorological Organization, the International Labor Organization, and the World Tourism Organization. Moreover, INGOs have often been instrumental in founding new IGOs and, as the chapters in this volume illustrate, in helping to shape IGO activities, policies, and agendas (see Charnovitz 1997 for a host of examples). Second, the creation of an IGO institutionalizes the related social sector at the global level; in a world of diffused formal authority, this legitimates the creation of INGOs in that sector. Third, old and new INGOs establish formal relations with IGOs; for example, thousands of INGOs have consultative status with UN agencies (Wiseberg 1991), over 900 with ECOSOC alone. Fourth, many IGOs engage relevant INGOs as providers of information, expertise, and policy alternatives, and states frequently rely on INGOs for help in conforming to IGO policies. Neither states nor IGOs relinquish their authority to INGOs, but their decisions can be heavily influenced by INGO experts and lobbyists even when such influence is resented or resisted. Despite resistance to, attempted insulation from, and conflict with INGOs, IGOs and individual states continue to call on INGOs in many situations.

Global neorealism clearly has problems accounting for these complexities. Straightforward state-centric reductionist rationalism implies that IGOs will always form before INGOs or that INGOs will emerge only in areas not organized by IGOs. Neither is the case. More sophisticated versions of global neorealism might argue, for example, that INGOs generally will follow IGOs and their agendas, or that the invasion of an INGO sector by one or more IGOs will lead to the dissolution or marginalization of INGOs. In any case, IGOs and states will easily insulate themselves from INGOs. Evidence showing such patterns would make our world-polity approach rather tenuous, but the massive growth of INGOs, their active leadership in many sectors, and their complex interactions with IGOs support our perspective and constitute serious difficulties for global neorealist perspectives.

Both IGOs and INGOs are products of a Tocquevillean world in which institutional structures endow diverse actors with the agency to mobilize and organize.[17] Various processes characterize IGO/INGO interrelationships—professionalization, mimesis, the exercise of authority based on scientific and technical expertise, and so on (Meyer, Boli et al. 1997; also see the Conclusion). At a practical level, their interrelationships represent a general process of mutual legitimation (Stinchcombe 1968). INGOs gain prestige by winning consultative status with IGOs, while IGOs gain by the involvement of diverse INGOs that lend IGO policies a nonpartisan flavor as reflections of world public opinion or putative technical necessity (Meyer 1994).[18]

Hence, strong covariation between INGO foundings and world-development indicators is of far-reaching substantive significance. World-polity organizations emerged in tandem with the universalization of the state; INGOs grew concomitantly with the incorporation of peripheral regions into the interstate system and world economy. Major wars have caused short-term declines but long-term intensification of world-polity discourse and organizing as INGOs have expanded in the interstices of power networks.

REGIONAL TRANSNATIONAL ORGANIZING

Figure 1.3 distinguishes two categories of organizations, those with an explicitly regional orientation and those of universalistic outlook.[19] Regional bodies, such as the European Federation of Biotechnology and the Arab Lawyers' Union, limit their membership by territorial or ascriptive criteria. Universal bodies are potentially all-inclusive—the *Association Zen Internationale* and the International Union for the Study of Social Insects, for example, which do not limit membership to any territorial or cultural segment of the world, even though their memberships may be concentrated in one geographic region.[20]

Figure 1.3 suggests that two quite distinct subpopulations of INGOs have been under formation over the past century. Universalistic organizations (56 percent of the total) reveal the long-term, dramatic waves of expansion and contraction. Regional bodies were few in number and were founded at a more even pace until after World War II, when they expanded enormously. From the later 1950s onward the two subpopulations grew about equally, more regional than universalistic bodies being founded for the first time in 1959.

Note also that foundings of universalistic bodies peaked right after World War II, the period of formation of the United Nations and many other major IGOs. After 1952 the curve drops to a considerably lower level. Here we see a gradual devolution in transnational organizing, the universalistic approach

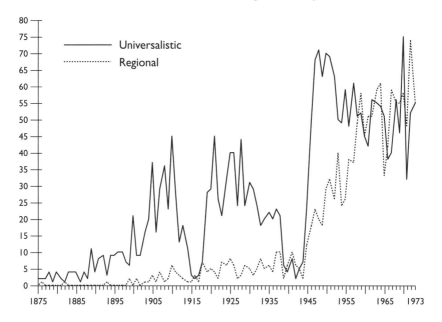

FIGURE 1.3.   Foundings of universalistic and regional INGOs, 1875–1973. SOURCE: *Yearbook of International Organizations* (UIA 1988).

that dominated the formative period being supplemented in recent decades by lower-level organizing with less ambitious scope and greater differentiation.

Thus, the great majority of INGOs founded before World War II were universalistic in character, whether their focus was medicine, science, world peace, industry, trade, or any other area. Like the upsurge of ethno-nationalism within states (Hechter 1975), a devolution of organizing to more particularistic levels is evident since the war. Various types of proto-polities at the regional level are under formation: geographic, religious, ethnic-linguistic-cultural, political, and combinations of these.[21]

All this makes good sense. Given the establishment of a firm world-polity foundation via extensive universalistic organizing into the 1930s, the increased incorporation of peripheral areas into the world polity, and the practical advantages of shared language, culture, and history as tools for mobilization with respect to the larger world, regional bodies became a favored organizing form. A seemingly simple and straightforward process, its result is a world polity of considerably more complex structure.

What this process shows is that the world-cultural frame is not a homogeneous, consensual order; neither does it drive a lockstep, homogenizing debilitation of mid-level organizations in favor of a global mass society. Rather, within the overarching frame, world culture authorizes and compels organization at diverse levels. Competing interests can be constituted and organized in many different ways, leading over time to the construction of transnational identities and spheres of action that institutionalize global differentiation. Hence world culture helps promote the formation of regional and subgroup identities within the larger polity, above all because the polity is formally decentralized. If the world polity were dominated by a world bureaucratic state, we would find more homogenizing efforts akin to those involved in state- and nation-building activity. We would also find formalized centralization among INGOs, with regional or local bodies mainly serving as extensions of their universalistic parent bodies. Instead, we find a variety of transnational identities that are less than universal, and these are typically viewed optimistically as building blocks of a global civil society in which the ideology of "unity through diversity" has become widespread.

This interpretation is supported by the more detailed analysis of regional INGOs presented in Figure 1.4 (using three-year moving averages to smooth out the trends). The upper half (Figure 1.4A) shows the number of foundings by region, while the lower half shows the percentage distribution of foundings across the five regions. Note first the steep decline in intercontinental bodies (geographic and cultural subpolities incorporating members from two or more continents) after World War I. Among the relatively few regional bodies founded before the war, about half involved such large subpolities; by World War II, almost no intercontinental bodies were being founded. Their resurgence came only after 1945.

Second, Europe dominated regional INGO foundings over the period. During the wars, however, few European INGOs were established; the bulk of INGO regional activity shifted to the Americas (mostly Latin America). The crisis of the 1930s was foremost a European phenomenon, while the founding rate for non-European regional INGOs actually increased until the middle of World War II. After the war other geographic regions began to enter the INGO population. By the 1970s, Asian and African INGOs were being founded in greater numbers than American ones, and Europe's share had fallen to its lowest level since the immediate postwar years.

One implication of these patterns reinforces the evidence given earlier about the close relationship between INGO growth and expansion of the state system: national independence seems vital to INGO activity. African and Asian INGOs were rare while these continents consisted mainly of

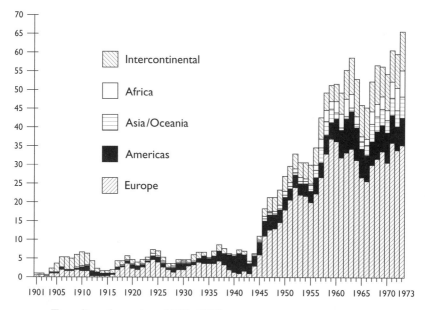

A.   Foundings by region, 1901–1973.

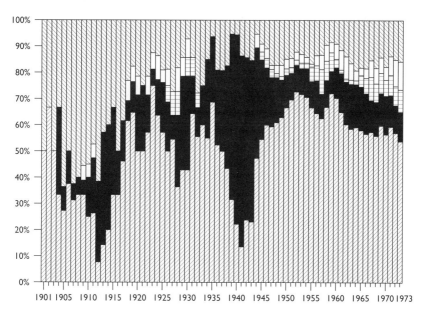

B.   Distribution of foundings by region, 1901–1973.

FIGURE 1.4.   Foundings of regional INGOs, 1901–1973. Regional
INGOs only, three-year averages. SOURCE: *Yearbook of International Organizations* (UIA 1988).

colonies; after independence, many regional INGOs emerged. Put another way, national citizenship seems to be a precondition for world citizenship (also see Chapter 2). The Universal Declaration of Human Rights as much as says so, insisting on the universal right of every person to have a nationality. Without a nationality one cannot be a full person, and less than full persons are unlikely to initiate or promote transnational organizing at the regional level. We see again the dialectic between the world polity and the state system at work.

INGOS AS ENACTORS AND CARRIERS OF WORLD CULTURE

Our findings to this point are consistent with nonreductionist sociological perspectives focusing on the cultural frames in which actors are embedded. INGOs are loci of transnational contextual knowledge. Sometimes they are experienced as only vague referential frames (a local Girl Scout troop normally has little contact with its parent INGO body), but the frame nevertheless defines the locally situated individual as someone who can, may, and should act globally. More generally, the INGO context supplies purposes and meanings of action, models for global organizing, forms of discourse and communication, and avenues for influencing states and other actors. The larger cultural reality is translated by individuals into specific forms and actions that reveal broad homologies.

Much of the content of this cultural framework can, then, be inferred from the characteristics and operations of INGOs, even though the culture enacted by INGOs certainly does not exhaust the category of all cultural elements that have worldwide character. How are INGOs constituted?

Almost all INGOs originate and persist via voluntary action by individual actors. They have explicit, rationalized goals. They operate under strong norms of open membership and democratic decision-making. They seek, in a general sense, to spread "progress" throughout the world: to encourage safer and more efficient technical systems, more powerful knowledge structures, better care of the body, friendly competition and fair play. To achieve their goals they emphasize communication, knowledge, consensual values and decision-making, and individual commitment.

To unpack the world-cultural elements upon which INGOs are constructed, we should first discuss the types of elements at issue. What we seek are the cultural assumptions, implicit or explicit, that make up the conceptual frame forming INGO purposes, structures, and operations. Some of these assumptions are (1) ontological: definitions of that-which-exists, that is, the basic elements of reality and the properties attributed to these elements. These assumptions define types of social entities (the individual, family, state, corporation, ethnic group . . .), the physical world or environment, the cosmos and its operations, spiritual reality, and so on. Other world-cultural assumptions are (2) epistemological or procedural: they identify the nature and sources of knowledge, the means to be used to generate such knowledge and apply it, and the forms of organization that are theorized as appropriate for the pursuit of collective goals. In counterpoint to these are (3) existential assumptions: cultural prescriptions regarding the establishment and expression of meaning, modes of dealing with mortality and theodicy, and avenues for the development and expression of collectivities and the individual self.

Rather than explore each of these types of cultural elements as such, we orient our analysis around what we see as five fundamental cultural themes reflected in the INGO population. These include universalism, individualism, rational voluntaristic authority, the dialectics of rationalizing progress, and world citizenship. As we proceed, we shall see that these principles embody ontological, epistemological, and existential cultural elements.

Universalism

Humans everywhere are seen as having similar needs and desires. They are capable of acting in accordance with common principles of authority and action, and they share common goals. In short, human nature, agency, and purpose are universal, and this universality underlies the many variations in actual social forms. Most INGOs are quite explicit about this: any interested person can become an active member, and everyone everywhere is a potential beneficiary of INGO activity.

Universalism is evident also in the breadth of INGOs' claims about what they do. Physics and pharmacology are presumed to be valid everywhere. Techniques for playing better chess are not country-specific. Red Cross aid will alleviate suffering in Africa as well as Asia. Across every sector, the purposes and means of action promoted by INGOs are assumed to be useful and meaningful right around the world.

A counterfactual argument reveals the importance of the universalism principle. A world not characterized by universalism does not coalesce as a singular polity; rather, it develops distinct sub-world polities (societies, civilizations, empires; see Collins 1986; Eisenstadt 1963). These interact with and respond to one another, but each understands the others as irrevocably and profoundly "Other," whether threatening, benign, or irrelevant. Joint mobilization with the Other in a mass organization pursuing shared goals and invoking common cultural icons is extraordinary to say the least. At the opposite extreme, a penetrative world state would thoroughly incorporate and regulate individuals and organizations. In this structure, universalism would prevail but it would be bureaucratically monopolized.

The present world polity lies between these two extremes. It is neither segmental or ad hoc, nor is it *etatisé*; legal-bureaucratic authority is partitioned among multiple states. The principle of universalism that INGOs embody remains culturally autonomous because INGOs operate in the interstices of this decentralized structure.

The universalism promoted by INGOs is not without self-contradictory effects. Robertson's (1994) "universalism of particularism" implies that world-cultural principles and bodies also encourage national, ethnic, and other local identities (Meyer, Boli et al. 1997), as suggested above with respect to regional INGOs. Indigenous peoples have "rights" to their own cultures and languages; states are to recognize national minorities and promote their distinctiveness. Universalistic structure and particularistic identity thus form a dialectical tension: each individual is a member of the universal human community, and each has rights to a variety of particularistic collective and individual identities. This dialectic was apparent at least as early as the eighteenth century, when doctrines of inalienable human rights were promulgated in the context of nationhood and state formation in France and the United States, and it has become quite complex in recent decades. Many INGOs project this ironic form of universalism in their concern for the rights of stateless peoples, regional identities, and particular categories of people (children, consumers, women, ethnic groups). Yet they do so in universalist terms: these categories deserve attention because they do not enjoy the same standing as more privileged categories.

Most INGOs, however, adopt the purer form of universalism that stresses the fundamental uniformity of all human actors. Scientific, technical, professional, medical, and business-related INGOs rarely allow much room for particularism, and they account for the great majority of all INGOs. We will return to this issue.

Individualism

Most INGOs accept as members only individuals or associations of individuals; the main exceptions are trade and industry bodies, which often have firms as members. Individualism is also evident in INGO structures. They use democratic, one-person one-vote decision-making procedures, they assess fees on members individually, and they downplay national and other corporate identities in their conferences and publications. In the worldview embodied by INGOs, individuals are the only "real" actors; collectivities are essentially assemblages of individuals. This ontological principle is greatly at variance with many local cultures, for which the family or lineage is the fundamental unit and individual autonomy is highly circumscribed.

The combination of universalism and individualism may undermine traditional collectivities, but it also strengthens the one collectivity that is truly universalistic: humanity as a whole, or, the world polity as a social unit. INGOs habitually invoke the common good of humanity as a major motivation for and goal of their activity, and the virtue of individual sacrifice for that common good is widely touted. The cultural dynamic at work parallels that characterizing national polities: as cultural constructs, the individual and the nation mutually reinforce each other. In recent times, this centuries-old dynamic has shifted to the global level.

Rational Voluntaristic Authority

INGOs activate a particular cultural model when they organize globally, debate principles, and attempt to influence other actors. This model holds that responsible individuals acting collectively through rational procedures can determine cultural rules that are just, equitable, and efficient, and that no external authority is required for their legitimation (Thomas 1989). Such "self-authorization" runs counter to Weber's analysis of authority as forms of domination because INGOs cannot dominate in the conventional sense. They have little sanctioning power, yet they act as if they were authorized in the strongest possible terms. They make rules and expect them to be followed; they plead their views with states or TNCs and express moral condemnation when their pleas go unheeded; they formulate codes of ethics and endow them with sufficient legitimacy to ensure that flagrant violators lose standing in the relevant community.

INGO authority is thus informal; it is cultural, not organizational. It is the agency presumed to inhere in rational individuals organizing for purposive action. Its basis can only be the diffuse principles of world culture, for it does not flow from any legal-bureaucratic or supernatural source.

Rational voluntarism is encouraged by the decentralized character of formal authority at the global level. If there is no world state, world authority must be constructed "from below." Thus, rational voluntarism is also practiced by states and TNCs at the world level. For example, because the doctrine of sovereignty implies that no state has authority over any other (Boli 1999a), collective action by states can occur only via rational voluntarism. This is why, like INGOs, most IGOs have resolutely democratic formal structures. It also helps explain why the legal-bureaucratic authority of states is brought into play to enforce INGO conceptions and rules, as we show below (also see the Conclusion).

Human Purposes: The Dialectics of Rationalizing Progress

The rational character of INGOs is evident in their epistemology—their purposive orientation, formalized structures, attention to procedures, and explicit goals. INGOs in science, medicine, technical fields, and infrastructure activities are engaged in purely rationalized and rationalizing activity; almost all others rely on science, expertise, and professionalization in their operations and programs. What they seek is, in essence, rational progress—not the crude nineteenth-century idea that steam engines and railroads will lead to heaven on earth, but the more diffuse and embedded concept of "development" that now prevails (Chabbott 1996; Clark 1991). This concept includes not only economic growth but also individual self-fulfillment, collective security, and justice.

At all levels, progress is assumed to depend on rationalization (Weber's instrumental or practical rationality, Ellul's [1980] technique). Rational social action and organization are the means to equality, security, comfort, the good life. Rational production and distribution (whether in the form of free markets, bureaucratic planning, or a mixture of the two) enable the achievement of collective purposes of all sorts. The scientific method, technique, monetarization, formalized accounting—these are the favored modi operandi. Not everyone "believes in" (that is, consciously values) the march of progress, and critics are sometimes highly vocal, but progress is built into worldwide institutions and the ideologies of individual and national development. We make progress *by definition* when GNP per capita rises or new social programs are implemented or stress-management seminars are offered by personnel departments.

Rationalization has, however, another face. A generative tension operates between the rational and the irrational that strengthens both simultaneously (Thomas 1989). The fundamental ambivalence toward reason that has characterized high culture in the West for so long has spread downward into everyday life and outward to the entire globe. The spread and intensification of rationalization desacralizes nature and society, a process Weber referred to as disenchantment. In its broadest sense this process not only excludes the spiritual from nature, it also strips transcendent personal value from everyday life. Simultaneously, however, disenchantment of the world endows the agents of rationalism with increasing substance and sacredness (Ellul 1973; Goffman 1959). To be rational, actors must be constituted as having internal processes and interests; the greater the rationalization of action, the more complex the internal subjectivities. But rationalistic models habitually result in the failure (or refusal) of actors to behave rationally; the greater the rationalistic demands, the greater the failure. This process leads to more elaborate theorizing about what is increasingly viewed as irreducible, primordial, irrational identities, selves, and cultures.

Rationalized actors are thus existentially constituted as having complex "nonrational" subjectivities that are more primordial than their exterior, objectified rationalities. À la Nietzsche, the construction of meaning becomes the province of a self-creating subject (an individual, a people); à la Sartre, the irrational becomes the arena of authenticity; à la Weber, the science of society is the grasping of these constructions. Consequently, this second face of rationalization results in obligatory development of the subjective self throughout the life-course (Berger, Berger, and Kellner 1973; Meyer 1987b). The result is widespread movements claiming to be anti-science (Snow 1959), anti-West, postmodern; decrying Western science, capitalism, and bureaucracy as imperialistic, dehumanizing forces against which authentic peoples must struggle to maintain their true, nonrational natures.

The rational/irrational tension thus generates conflict, but it also generates much rationalization as the irrational and subjective are channeled into rationalized activities and forms (e.g., revolution, UFO cults). Movements against Enlightenment rationalism pursue rational goals through rationalized means. Self-exploration and expression become stylized and organized within daily and weekly schedules rather than spontaneous or unplanned activities. Commodification and instrumentality creep in (transcendental meditation becomes a high-fee test-improvement technique). All this comes together in global organizations in such domains as sports, leisure, spirituality, therapies, and theoretical and applied psychology; in each of these domains, INGOs are abundant.

World Citizenship

The principles discussed so far jointly yield the construct of world citizenship. Everyone is an individual endowed with certain rights and subject to certain obligations; everyone is capable of voluntaristic action seeking rational solutions to social problems; everyone has the right and obligation to participate in the grand human project; everyone is, therefore, a citizen of the world polity. World citizenship is the institutional endowment of authority and agency on individuals. It infuses each individual with the authority to pursue particularistic interests, preferably in organizations, while also authorizing individuals to promote collective goods defined in largely standardized ways. World citizenship, as enacted by INGOs, is highly active, reflecting the decentralized and plebiscitarian world polity.[22]

World citizenship is strongly egalitarian. Individuals vary in their capacities, resources, and industry, but all have the same basic rights and duties. Correspondingly, only fully democratic governance structures are consistent with world citizenship. "Autocratic" tendencies are decried everywhere, and INGOs especially are to avoid them (Greenpeace and the International Olympic Committee have had legitimacy problems in this respect).

The source of world citizenship is the diffuse, abstract, universalistic cognitive framework of the world polity and world culture, but it is explicitly codified in well-known instruments, most prominently the Universal Declaration of Human Rights and related UN rights covenants that depict a global citizen whose highly expanded rights transcend national boundaries. States must ensure these rights for their citizens; national citizenship is the means whereby world-citizenship principles are to be realized. Yet states cannot be coerced into compliance with world-citizenship principles, for states are sovereign entities. Here INGOs fill the breach. Acting as the primary carriers of world culture, and as agents of many categories of individuals and peoples, INGOs translate the diffuse global identity and authority of world citizenship into specific rights, claims, and prescriptions for state behavior.

Consequently, we again observe that states sometimes act as agents of informal world-polity authority. World citizens must turn to national states for the protection of their rights, and INGOs back them up in the process. National identity and citizenship thereby become partly decoupled from states.[23] Individuals need not be national citizens to make claims on the state (Jacobson 1996; Soysal 1994); in many countries noncitizen residents have rights almost equivalent to those of citizens, for their humanness overrides the restrictions that national identity might imply.

The cultural principles represented by INGOs are also integral to the world economy and interstate system, but INGOs push them to extremes. Their discourse is often critical of extant economic and political structures, stigmatizing "ethnocentric" (non-universalistic) nationalism and "exploitative" (inegalitarian) capitalism. INGOs dramatize violations of world-cultural principles, such as state maltreatment of citizens and corporate disregard for the sacredness of nature. Such examples illustrate, we reiterate, the contested nature of these principles (Meyer, Boli et al. 1997); they are widely known but by no means uncontroversial.

INGO SECTORS AND THE SUBSTANCE OF WORLD-CULTURAL STRUCTURATION

We now turn to a sectoral analysis of INGO activity as a means of studying the structure of world culture. INGOs cover a broad range of activities that we have grouped into thirteen sectors. Figure 1.5 charts the distribution across these sectors for all INGOs active in 1988.

We interpret Figure 1.5 as a sectoral description of world culture. It suggests, first, that world culture is heavily "economic" in that not-for-profit bodies concerned with business and economic activity (industry and trade combined with tertiary economic organizations) account for about one-fourth of all active INGOs. But scientific knowledge and technique (medicine, the sciences, technical standards, infrastructure, and communications) are even more prominent, with just over a third of the total. In all, nearly 60 percent of INGOs concentrate on economic or technical rationalization.

This is the core of world culture: technical, functional, rationalizing, highly differentiated (some 2,400 organizations)—and peculiarly invisible. These bodies bring together physicists, radiologists, electronic engineers, bridge designers, manufacturers; they set standards, discuss problems, disseminate information, argue points of law, and write codes of ethics, but few of them are seen as important world actors (except, possibly, by their own memberships). The parallel with national organizations is plain: in most countries, only a handful of scientific, technical, or business associations are prominent in public discourse; most go quietly about their business of rationalizing and standardizing society in obscurity, but they are the most common type of association to be found.

A second implication of Figure 1.5 is based on the sports and leisure sector (more than 200 sports are organized at the world level). These INGOs sponsor the most visible rituals dramatizing the world polity (Boli 1999b), just as national and local sports dramatize lower-level polities. Sports competition has become a major source of identity and solidarity, combining

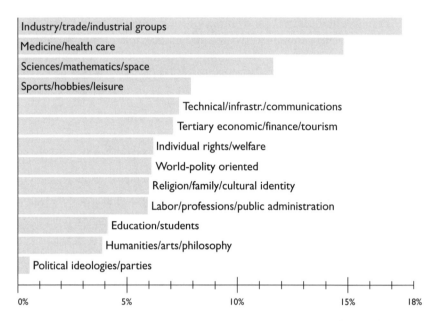

FIGURE 1.5.   Distribution of INGO population by social sector: Organizations active in 1988. SOURCE: Yearbook of International Organizations (UIA 1988).

neatly the devotion to individual development with the imperative of coordinated collective action in a highly rationalized and controlled situation. Sports are associated with the moral value of nations (Olympics medals and World Cup championships bring considerable prestige) and the moral virtue of individual excellence. Further, sports INGOs offer avenues for personal fulfillment in contexts that are claimed to contribute to world harmony. They thereby express and help shape the subjective axis of world culture, building and ritually displaying individual, national, and human moral value. Yet, obviously, sports and leisure are highly rationalized. INGOs both reflect this rationality and enhance it, by centralizing and standardizing rules, training methods, and measurement procedures.

Of special interest are two categories in the middle of the figure, individual rights and welfare INGOs and "world-polity oriented" INGOs. The former sector includes organizations promoting universal or, sometimes, particularistic group rights (for minorities, women, indigenous peoples), and charity and relief organizations. World-polity oriented bodies promote world peace, international law, world federation, a world language (most often, Esperanto), and environmental preservation. Each of these categories accounts for about 7 percent of the population.[24]

These less numerous sectors include many of the most prominent INGOs, especially environmental and human rights organizations, whose effectiveness depends on maintaining a high public profile. Amnesty International, for example, rallies "world public opinion" against states that violate universalistic human rights (Castermans et al. 1991; Jacobson 1982). Greenpeace emphasizes duties: world citizens must protect the natural world, which has certain rights to inviolability. As these examples suggest, INGOs that openly conflict with states for not conforming to world-cultural principles are likely to be controversial and, hence, well known (Willets 1982).

Finally, organizations promoting "primordial" social forms—religion, family, ethnic or cultural identity—account for about 6 percent of the INGO population. Most are religious bodies, often ecumenical.[25] Hence, neither the family nor ethnicity nor ethnic culture takes strong transnational form. Neither does politics, the smallest category of all.

The smaller sectors in Figure 1.5 (labor-professions-public administration, political organization and ideology, and religion-family-culture) are also sectors whose shares of total INGO organizing have declined during the past century. Relative decline should occur in sectors that are out of step with evolving world-cultural principles. This hypothesis seems applicable here: the individualism of world culture works against collectivist forms of transnational organizing (labor, family, religion, distinctive cultural identity).[26] The relative decline of these sectors indicates that individualism has become stronger since the early part of the twentieth century, when these sectors had their largest shares of the INGO population. On the other hand, current world developments indicate a resurgence of religious and cultural-ethnic identity, in part because identity-based collectivities are increasingly seen as endowed with the moral virtue of authenticity. So far, however, these trends have not led to an increase in INGOs in these domains.

The decline in political INGOs reflects, we think, the worldwide expansion of state authority (Boli 1987b), which has made politics ever more national rather than transnational. Coupled with a modest relative decline in educational INGOs, these trends suggest another hypothesis: organizational dimensions tied directly to state-citizen relations are relatively unlikely to generate transnational structures.

Much work is needed to understand the processes of world-cultural decline. Religion fits scientized world culture at least as poorly as labor fits in-

TABLE 1.3

Correlations Between INGO Social Sector Foundings and Measures
of Dimensions of World Development
(Time series data, nineteenth and twentieth centuries)

| | Typical non-declining sectors (eleven of thirteen) | | Declining sectors (two only) | |
	Medicine/ health	Sports/hobby/ leisure	Political party/ ideology	Labor/profs./ pub. admin.
Government revenue	.89 (103)	.88 (103)	.65 (103)	.76 (103)
Exports	.87 (103)	.90 (103)	.63 (103)	.78 (103)
Energy production	.94 (49)	.81 (49)	$-.07^{ns}$ (49)	.49 (49)
Telephones	.94 (87)	.92 (87)	.66 (87)	.80 (87)
Primary education	.88 (103)	.91 (103)	.63 (103)	.80 (103)
Tertiary education	.90 (103)	.92 (103)	.66 (103)	.80 (103)
Urban population	.90 (114)	.91 (114)	.61 (114)	.74 (114)
Diplomat	$.91^{**}$ (5)	$.92^{**}$ (5)	$.56^{ns}$ (5)	$.82^{*}$ (5)
Treaties	$.91^{**}$ (5)	.94 (5)	$.58^{ns}$ (5)	.97 (5)
Rights	$.84^{**}$ (6)	$.84^{**}$ (6)	$.53^{ns}$ (6)	$.71^{*}$ (6)

NOTE: Variables are annual world totals. Figures in parentheses give the number of years for which data on the respective pairs of variables are available. Data for diplomatic representation, treaties, and rights are taken at twenty-year intervals. The endpoint for all other time series is 1973; most variables are missing for the world war years. All variables are logged to reduce skewness. INGO and IGO variables are logged five-year moving averages. See Table 1.1 for more complete labels of column variables.

All coefficients are significant beyond the .001 level with the exception of: $^{*} p < .06$, $^{**} p < .03$, ns = not significant dividualism, but labor has declined more. Is this because the institutionalization of the International Labor Organization as a world center for labor policy (see Chapter 4) has inhibited further labor organizing (cf. Chapter 3 on such effects in the environmental sector)? Under what conditions might INGOs not in tune with world culture expand, in an attempt to alter world-cultural elements, rather than passively decline? Do some dimensions of nation-state authority promote, rather than hinder, transnational organizing? Such questions deserve detailed study.

The main rising INGO sectors are the two economic categories, industry-trade and tertiary economic bodies. These trends reflect the well-known globalization of economic relations and expansion of tertiary economic activities during this century. Other major sectors (medicine, science, technical and infrastructure organizations) have had fairly steady shares of the INGO population throughout our period.

Despite variations in long-term trends for the thirteen sectors, the INGO population is surprisingly unidimensional in its relation to world development. Table 1.3 presents correlations between sectoral-founding curves and world development measures (we include only two of the eleven nondeclining INGO sectors, since they all behave the same way). Most of the coefficients are very large, at the .85 level or better. Only the two declining sectors, labor/professions/public administration and political parties/ideologies, have more modest coefficients, but they too are quite high (.60 or above) except in a few instances. Even at this finer level of analysis, almost everything covaries with everything else, a finding that further supports our contention that INGOs reflect a global cultural framework undergoing tremendous expansion in the twentieth century.

CONCLUSION: INGOs AND THE CONSTRUCTION OF THE WORLD POLITY

Our analysis depicts INGOs as embodiments of universalism, individualism, rational voluntaristic authority, progress, and world citizenship. Individuals and associations construct rationalized structures with explicitly formulated goals, sometimes diffuse (world peace, international understanding) but usually highly specific and functionalist. The bulk of world culture that INGOs reflect and develop is oriented to intellectual, technical, and economic rationalization. Some smaller sectors, including human rights and environmental organizations, dramatize the failure of states to abide by world-cultural principles; others, particularly relief organizations, step in to heal the wounds caused by state conflict or breakdown; still others, sports and leisure above all, strongly reify the world polity through ritualized global events. The oppositional or emergency-catalyzed activity of human rights, environmental, and relief organizations makes them especially prominent in the world polity, while the more central rationalizing sectors are much less well known. Indeed, the latter sectors often are overlooked as global actors. Their highly rationalized universalism (especially in scientific and technical areas) is considered "neutral" and therefore unremarkable, despite the enormous effects they have on definitions of reality, infrastructure, household products, school texts, and much more.

Decentralized world authority among states both facilitates transnational organizing, because centralized barriers to rational voluntarism are weak, and forces transnational organizations to focus their attention on states. In mobilizing around and elaborating world-cultural principles, INGOs lobby and harangue states to act on those principles. In some sectors and with respect to some issues, INGOs clearly succeed in these efforts, inducing states to use their legal-bureaucratic authority to enforce INGO conceptions and rules. Thus, the chapters that follow show that under conditions yet to be specified, transnational organizations do shape the agendas and behavior of states.

More indirect effects of INGOs on states are evident in sectors where INGO-generated standards, methods, and models provide rationales and means by which states are able to meet their responsibilities. Berman (1988) offers a telling example in his discussion of international commercial law: rules made by the International Chamber of Commerce form the legal basis upon which national courts make decisions in disputes regarding trade contracts, bills of lading, and financial instruments. In another example, Jacobson (1996) argues that global human rights instruments allow states to develop and enact immigration policies. In such dimensions, states appear to be relatively passive, being "instructed" by international organizations about what they are and how they should behave (cf. Finnemore 1993 on science policy, and Haas 1992 on epistemic communities).

Our arguments and evidence raise four interrelated sets of issues that seem especially important and timely. First, we need to map the organizational dimensions of the world polity in more detail, both within world-cultural sectors and across nation-states and regions (defined in geographical, linguistic, and ethno-cultural terms). This work would include more specificity about foundings and failures as well as sectoral trends over time. Second, much could be learned by investigating the world-cultural principles and models that predominate in specific sectors, paying attention to how they have changed over time and their interrelations across sectors. Third, we need more study of the penetrative capacity of global processes, including theoretical and empirical work on the mechanisms by which global structures affect national and subnational institutions and actors.

Fourth, we find it especially important to develop a better understanding of the tensions and conflicts that operate between global cultural structures and the actors embedded in these structures. Two issues arise. On the one hand, we need to understand the generation and promotion of competing world-cultural models of social organization and action, such as Islamic fundamentalism (typically proffered as an alternative to individualistic Western materialism) and Asian familism (emerging as an alternative to both free-market libertarianism and welfare-state collectivism). On the other hand, we need studies that will move us toward a general theory about the conditions under which INGOs are able to take the initiative vis-à-vis IGOs, states, TNCs, and other less-than-global organizations. The rational voluntaristic authority of INGOs is demonstrably effective in some domains in some periods, but at this point we can say little about the factors that condition its effectiveness. In any case, the opportunity for INGOs to expand their role is greater than ever before, with respect to both influencing state policies and bypassing states altogether in seeking solutions to world-cultural problems (Spiro 1995).

The chapters that make up the remainder of this book represent initial efforts to address these and other issues raised by our world-polity perspective. They test and, we think, demonstrate the fruitfulness of this perspective for understanding the nature and workings of the contemporary world. In closely examining a range of world-cultural sectors, they study processes of sector formation, doctrinal development, interrelations with states and other actors, and the impact of INGOs on global and national development.

In some sectors INGOs take the form of social movements, which are the subject of the first four sectoral-study chapters. These chapters examine INGO-based movements that advance claims about the environment (Chapter 3), press for global action on women's issues (Chapter 4), attempt to institutionalize a world language (Chapter 5), and promote humanitarian norms in armed conflict (Chapter 6). In other sectors, INGOs are less commonly interpreted as movements and operate less visibly through more highly rationalized structures. The next four sectoral studies detail the emergence and operations of global structures for technical standardization (Chapter 7), population control (Chapter 8), development (Chapter 9), and science (Chapter 10).

Taken together, these sectoral studies reveal a common pattern that is more consistent with the neo-Grotian perspective of world-polity institutionalism than with the panoply of global neorealist analyses. The chapters show that the impetus for global action came, to a considerable extent, from the transnational INGO sector. As states entered the process, they responded not only to their own or societal interests but also to the global conceptions and principles promoted by INGOs. At times, states implicitly enacted global models and principles in the pursuit of national goals and state interests. At other times, states were more explicit agents of INGO authority.

The sectoral studies indicate that the long, conflict-ridden history of the symbiotic relationship between states and the transnational environment continues: the main organizational result of INGO influence is not the state's decline but its expansion via agencies and policies responding to global models. A complex web of interrelated actors emerges as local and national associations become involved in INGO activity while INGOs and other bodies conduct intense dialogue with states and IGOs. States also participate in global discourse, though they are often at a disadvantage because many influential experts ally themselves with INGOs. Power remains a state prerogative, but the impact of the world-cultural authority of INGOs is substantial. How this authority is structured and legitimated is discussed in the book's closing essay.

If a rational-legal world state should emerge, much of the INGO population is likely to be co-opted to staff its bureaucracy and fill formal positions as advisers on policy matters. So far, we believe, it makes most sense to think of the world polity as organized only by a world proto-state. A singular authority structure is lacking, states monopolize the legitimated use of violence, and states jealously guard their sovereignty. Nevertheless, the world as a proto-state has shared cultural categories, principles of authority, and universally constructed individuals who, as world proto-citizens, assume the authority to pursue goals that transcend national and local particularisms. More often than is commonly acknowledged, the resulting organizations prove to be effective. If they eventually are absorbed into a formal global authority structure, it may well be said that the road to a world state, whether welcomed or abhorred, was paved by the rational voluntarism of INGOs.

Appendix Table A: INGO Aims Categories Grouped by Social Sector

Medicine/health: Medicine, medical science; Health

Sciences/mathematics/space/knowledge: Natural sciences, mathematics, space, statistics; Economics, political economy, development, business; Social sciences, linguistics, geography; Documentation, libraries, information/knowledge management

Humanities/arts/philosophy: Literature, books, publishing, language; Philosophy, ethics, philology, other humanities; Art, visual arts, music, performing arts

Technical/infrastructure/communications: Engineering, technology, computers; Mass media, telecommunications, press, movies; Transportation; Water, seas, irrigation, dams

Industry/trade/industry groups: Agriculture, domestic science, forestry, fishing, mining, energy; Commerce, industry, general trade, sales

Tertiary economy/finance/tourism: Finance, stock markets, insurance, accounting, advertising; Services, tourism, architecture, detectives

Labor/professions/public administration: Labor organizations, unions; Professions, occupations; Public administration

Sports/hobbies/leisure: Sports; Hobbies, leisure, recreation

Religion/family/cultural identity: Religion; Family; Cultural identity, ethnicity, monuments, language

Education/students: Education; Students

Political ideologies/parties: Political ideology; Parties

Individual rights/welfare: Relief, charity, refugees, poverty; Social services, welfare, social work; Consumer protection, education; consumer unions; Women, men; Youth, children, socialization (except education); Elderly, retirement; Handicapped

World-polity related: Global identity, order, culture, world state; Peace, disarmament; Law, legal administration, law enforcement; General rights/rights discourse; Temperance, morality; Environment, conservation, animal welfare; International relations, military, diplomacy, treaties; Population control, migration, demography, housing

Chapter Two National Participation in
World-Polity Organization

JOHN BOLI, THOMAS A. LOYA,
AND TERESA LOFTIN

The preceding chapter in this volume analyzed the population of international nongovernmental organizations (INGOs) as the main organizational
arena of transnational cultural activity. The institutional theoretical framework developed there interprets the growth and structure of the INGO population as both reflecting and helping to generate world-cultural principles
and models. In this chapter, which should be read in conjunction with
Chapter 1, we move to a level of greater complexity and specificity by fore-
grounding the issue of national participation in INGOs.[1]

This chapter addresses three general questions: (1) Who participates in
these bodies? Are INGOs nothing but reflections of Euro-American domination in the world, or do they involve a diverse, genuinely worldwide set of
participants? (2) What do the patterns of participation tell us about the nature and structure of world culture, apart from what was discussed at the
more general level in Chapter 1? Do some dimensions of world culture evoke
more general global participation than others? If so, what accounts for the
differences in these patterns of participation? (3) What do these patterns tell
us about the explanatory usefulness of competing perspectives on world-
polity development? How much do the patterns corroborate or conflict with
neorealist analysis, functionalism, neoliberal institutionalism, world-system
theory, and world-polity institutionalist theory?

We begin with a discussion of the data and a review of important patterns
of global participation. We then turn to the theoretical implications of our
findings.

DATA

We employ three types of data regarding national participation in INGOs: memberships, referring to the countries of residence of INGO members; general secretariats, referring to the country in which organization headquarters are located; and regional secretariats, also referring to country of location. Memberships receive most of our attention.

Normally, INGO members are individuals, though in some cases they are associations; the latter, in turn, usually have only individuals as members, but some include companies or other associations. Our data on memberships are of three primary kinds:

(1) Longitudinal data covering the years 1960–1988, from the statistical tables included in the Union of International Associations' *Yearbook of International Organizations* (UIA 1960–1988). These data are aggregate figures using countries and territories as the units of analysis; they show the number of INGOs to which individuals or organizations from each country belonged in a given year. They are available for each of the four major categories of genuinely international INGOs (categories A through D, that is, federations of INGOs, universal INGOs, intercontinental INGOs, and regional INGOs) that were used by the *Yearbook* at the time. Our analyses use total figures for the four categories combined. For example, the data show that Kenyan residents (individuals and organizations) belonged to a total of 72 INGOs in 1960, but by 1988 that number had grown to 603.

Our longitudinal data end with 1988 because that is the year for which the detailed data set on the entire INGO population was coded (Chapter 1). While it would be desirable to include more recent data on INGO memberships, we could have extended the analysis only to 1991 in any case because the UIA dropped this classification scheme after that year. Hence, after the 1991 volume it was no longer feasible to identify a comparable set of genuinely international INGOs, as opposed to organizations with an international focus or orientation that were not themselves international in structure and operations. As we shall see, this limitation is hardly problematic, since INGO memberships are highly stable over time.

(2) Cross-sectional data from 1994 that we obtained as a direct extract from the UIA database, thanks to the gracious generosity of the Union of International Associations. The cross-sectional data use the individual INGO as the unit of analysis and indicate all of the countries from which each INGO draws its members. For example, the data identify the 70 specific countries in which members of the International Academy of Cytology

resided in 1994: Kenya, Nigeria, India, Belgium, Chile, and so on. From another angle, the cross-sectional data allow us to identify all of the specific INGOs to which Kenyan individuals and organizations belonged in 1994.

We have linked this INGO-specific membership data to the information coded about specific INGOs from the 1988 *Yearbook*, in particular the organizational sector and scope (universal vs. regional) of each INGO. The cross-sectional data represent 3,207 INGOs in the data set from the 1988 *Yearbook*, or about 72 percent of the 4,474 INGOs active at that time.[2] The mismatch in the years of the data, with country of member residence taken from the 1994 database but INGO characteristics coded for 1988, indicates the need for some caution in interpreting analyses of these figures. Again, however, because memberships are highly stable over time, this is only a minor concern.

Our cross-sectional data also include information on the location of INGO secretariats. We have both aggregate data from the *Yearbook* tables for 1988, with countries as the unit of analysis, and INGO-specific data from 1994, for INGOs in the data set for 1988. Of greatest interest are the locations of primary secretariats, that is, the headquarters or central offices of the organizations; we also use data on the locations of regional secretariats. The aggregate data indicate, for example, that Kenya was the site of 31 primary and 22 regional secretariats in 1988. Our INGO-specific data identify 24 INGOs active in 1988 whose primary secretariats were located in Kenya in 1994, along with 22 regional secretariats. Only about 23 percent of INGOs active in 1988 had regional secretariats; of these, 77 percent had only one regional secretariat, while another 9 percent had only two. The mean was 1.76 regional secretariats for all INGOs having any regional offices.

(3) Data on IGOs. Besides these INGO-related variables, we also have aggregate longitudinal data on IGOs, taken from the *Yearbook*'s statistical tables for the 1960–1988 period. Membership in IGOs is restricted to states, though some IGOs permit non-state political units (colonies, territories, protectorates, and the like) to join, usually as observers rather than voting members. While our analyses focus primarily on INGOs, we add revealing parallels and contrasts with the IGO findings that help us more fully understand the structure and development of world-polity participation.

WORLD-POLITY PARTICIPATION: INGO MEMBERSHIPS

Table 2.1 presents basic information regarding memberships in INGOs and IGOs from 1960 to 1988. The table shows the mean number of INGOs to which individuals or organizations from each country belonged, where "country" includes not only independent states but also colonies that eventually obtained independence and some territories, dependencies, and protectorates that did not. The overall growth in INGO memberships is spectacular: in 1960, individuals or groups from the average country belonged to 122 different INGOs; by 1988 the figure had risen to 485, a growth factor of 4.0 (1988 memberships divided by 1960 memberships). This was considerably faster than the total number of relevant INGOs (top row), whose growth factor was a little over two. Thus, while the INGO population was increasing rapidly, this measure of participation in INGOs was increasing almost twice as fast.

As the several sections of Table 2.1 reveal, increasing INGO participation was universal. We find it in all geographical regions of the world, across all levels of development, for old and new countries, for countries of every dominant religion (including local or folk religions), and for the six Communist countries classified by David Barrett (1982) as nonreligious. The overall growth factor of 4.0 is also almost universal as a minimum rate of growth; few of the categories of countries in Table 2.1 had growth factors much below the world mean, though a sizable number of categories had substantially higher growth factors.

A comparison of country averages within each classification dimension provides few surprises. Europeans participate in many more INGOs than any other region of the world; Africa and the mostly island countries of the Pacific/Oceania region participate the least. Individuals and groups from the richest quartile of countries participate in far more INGOs than those of the poorest quartile. For both of these dimensions, the highest category has memberships in about five times as many INGOs as the lowest category. Similarly, long-independent countries, which also are apt to be European and among the richer nations, have much broader memberships, and the conjunction of these factors helps explain why Christian-religion polities have broader memberships than those of other religions.

All of these differences were maintained throughout the period covered by the table: at both the start and the end of the period, national participation in INGOs was higher in Europe, in the most developed countries, in countries independent by 1800, and in Christian-religion countries. These findings are obviously consistent with the well-known fact that formal organizing on a transnational basis began in Europe, particularly in the core countries of Europe, and was structured around cultural forms and purposes derived in large part from Christian worldviews (Meyer, Boli, and Thomas 1987). One surprise, however, is that the highest religion category is Orthodox countries

TABLE 2.1
INGO and IGO Memberships, 1960–1988
(Means)

	1960	1966	1977	1988	Growth factor 1988/1960	N
Active INGOs	1987	2494	3539	4474	2.3	—
Active IGOs	154	199	291	309	2.0	—
A. INGO memberships						
All countries	122	181	260	485	4.0	199
World region						
Africa	34	76	121	264	7.7	55
Americas	103	152	224	395	3.8	49
Asia	82	129	201	407	5.0	40
Pacific-Oceania	37	60	95	218	5.8	17
Europe	342	478	641	1123	3.3	38
GDP per capita (quartiles)						
Lowest 25%	58	94	137	262	4.6	29–34
26–50th %ile	74	147	199	352	4.7	29–35
51–75th %ile	151	223	369	615	4.1	29–35
Highest 25%	463	614	749	1278	2.8	29–34
Period obtaining independence						
Before 1800	376	522	697	1232	3.3	21
1801–99	257	359	490	828	3.2	26
1900–44	252	360	504	889	3.5	20
1945–59	120	184	269	500	4.2	26
1960–75	17	52	103	240	14.1	61
1976–90	1	7	19	100	143.1	15
Not indep. by 1990	4	14	24	76	18.0	30
Dominant religion in 1980						
Catholic	165	240	333	596	3.6	76
Protestant	117	172	246	461	3.9	48
Orthodox	186	292	427	745	4.0	6
Islamic	46	86	146	313	6.8	42
Hindu-Buddhist	110	153	215	390	3.5	14
Atheist (Communist)	82	119	153	335	4.1	6
Indigenous or Chinese folk	60	113	212	479	8.0	6

TABLE 2.1 (*continued*)

	1960	1966	1977	1988	Growth Factor 1988/1960	N
B. IGO memberships						
All states	16	23	32	38	2.4	199
World region						
Africa	5	20	31	43	8.8	55
Americas	17	21	29	32	1.9	49
Asia	14	20	31	36	2.6	40
Pacific-Oceania	4	6	10	15	3.4	17
Europe	36	43	47	52	1.4	38

NOTE: Figures are rounded to integers.

SOURCES: GDP per capita from UN 1990, date of independence from Banks 1975, dominant religion from Barrett 1982, INGO memberships from UIA 1960–88.

(Greece, Yugoslavia, Bulgaria, Romania, Cyprus, and Ethiopia, in that order), averaging more than 50 percent above the overall country mean at each time. One reason for their prominence may be their geocultural status as "intersection" societies, linked to both Eastern and Western Europe and to both Europe and the Islamic world. On the other hand, Communist countries are notably low, reflecting their states' general restrictiveness regarding international contacts by their populations.

Growth Factors

The story becomes more complicated when we consider differences in growth factors across the categories of countries in Table 2.1. These differences are particularly important for understanding the theoretical implications of the table. Note that growth factors are inversely related to absolute levels of participation: they are highest for Africa and Pacific/Oceania (7.7, 5.8), for poorer countries (4.6, 4.7), for recently independent countries (14 or better), and for non-Christian religions except Buddhism (up to 8.0). In other words, those segments of the world that were relative latecomers to world-polity organizational activity have increased their participation considerably faster than the original "heartlands" of these organizations' memberships. Especially noteworthy are the large growth factors for categories that might be expected not to engage in much world-polity participation: Islamic countries (6.8), dependencies (18.0), and indigenous or folk religions (8.0).

These findings suggest that participation in INGOs has become a social imperative everywhere in the world polity. No matter how we slice the world, we find rapidly expanding participation in nongovernmental organizations. By 1988, residents of poor and peripheral countries were participating at levels approaching those of European countries in 1960, even though these peripheral countries were much less developed in 1988 than Europe was at the earlier time.

Table 2.1 leads to one of this chapter's central implications: world culture is increasingly global, decreasingly the provenance of the Europeans and Anglo-Americans, who dominated it in its early stages. This point is supported by figures for the proportions of total INGO memberships (by country residents): European countries accounted for over 54 percent of all INGO memberships in 1960 but only 44 percent in 1988, while Asia's share rose from less than 14 percent to almost 17 percent and Africa's share rose from less than 8 percent to 15 percent (the Americas' share was unchanged). Even if residents of peripheral societies are less active than Westerners in the INGOs to which they belong (an occasional claim that has never been evaluated), they likely have become considerably more active during this period of great growth in their memberships. They therefore play a growing role in developing INGO programs; promoting world-cultural principles, standards, and rules; and formulating world-cultural discourse at international conferences and conventions.

The trends indicated in Table 2.1 also suggest that the relative decline of Western participation in world-cultural bodies is likely to continue. World forums and ideology will become ever less the creature of the West, ever more the product of members from throughout the globe engaging in complex cultural construction from a variety of cultural backgrounds.

We can complement the overall findings of Table 2.1 with a look at particular countries with extremely high or low memberships and membership growth factors. The broadest patterns of membership for 1988 are displayed by residents of France (2,471 INGOs), Germany (2,406), and the quartet of Britain, Italy, Belgium, and the Netherlands (clustered near 2,250 INGOs); the next tier consists of Sweden, Denmark, Switzerland, Spain, and Norway (the United States occupies twelfth place). At the other end of the scale (excluding tiny island countries or territories), the countries with the narrowest membership patterns in 1988 are Cambodia, Equatorial Guinea, and Zimbabwe (all at only 47 INGOs), Albania (63), Laos (64), Namibia (74), and Afghanistan (78).

Turning to individual-country growth factors, we note that, first, of the many now-independent countries having no INGO memberships in 1960, those having the broadest range of memberships in 1988 include Malaysia (678 INGOs), Jamaica (434), Bangladesh (401), Zambia (388), and Trinidad-Tobago (367). Second, of those that had at least ten memberships in 1960, the highest growth factors are found for Saudi Arabia (38.0), Ivory Coast (22.3), the Congo (20.8), Senegal (19.6), and Benin (19.4), all of these having hundreds of memberships by 1988. Third, especially low growth factors applied to Vietnam (1.4), Burma/Myanmar (1.4), Cuba (1.7), Guyana (1.7), and Cambodia (2.0).

These extremes suggest additional inferences about the breadth of INGO memberships. For one thing, size makes little difference: Norway's 3 million people belonged to more INGOs than the United States' 240 million or Japan's 120 million. Two, peripheral countries that have broad memberships or large growth factors tend to be places with especially intense relationships with their former colonizers or mother countries: Jamaica with Britain, several West-African countries with France, the Congo with Belgium, Bangladesh with India and Britain. Three, the countries least involved with world-polity organizations are not only poor but, often, pariah states or places with deliberate policies of noninvolvement. This applies to Cambodia, Burma/Myanmar, Cuba, Albania, and Vietnam, and perhaps also to Afghanistan. Residents of these countries all had relatively few INGO memberships and quite low growth rates.

Finally, it is worth pointing out a few surprises in the data summarized in Table 2.1. Iranians belonged to 453 INGOs (68th place in the rank order, not far below the mean of 485); clearly, nine years of Islamic revolution had not led to withdrawal from world-polity organizations. Yugoslavia, the top Communist-dominated country, had 1,093 memberships (27th place), similarly indicating widespread participation in world-cultural activities. Nigerians held 764 memberships (slightly ahead of the Soviet Union), revealing extensive participation by a major black African country, while even remote Nepal had 215 memberships, up from only 17 in 1960, and Kuwait had 354, up from only 8. No impenetrable barriers to considerable world-polity participation exist, and participation is quite eager even in places where it seems unlikely.

IGO Comparisons

In the bottom panel of Table 2.1 we present comparable data on state participation in IGOs, for all countries and for world regions. The means are much lower because IGOs are far less numerous (just over 300 of comparable international scope by 1988), but we see a similarly rapid expansion of participation in these "official" bodies: countries in every region of the world except Europe at least doubled their IGO memberships, with the most peripheral countries (in Africa) expanding their memberships by the largest factor. By 1988, all regions except Pacific/Oceania had reached at least 60 percent of the European mean, indicating a much more universal level of general participation than ever before. The increasing density of world-polity participation is, thus, a quite general phenomenon, though it has proceeded at a faster rate among individuals and associations (in INGOs) than among states.

INGO Membership Stability

Despite the sizable variation in membership growth factors across categories of countries, overall INGO memberships are highly stable. Total INGO memberships in 1960 correlate .97 with total memberships in 1988, the two end points of our period; for any two consecutive points, the correlation coefficient is above .99 (logged versions of these coefficients are slightly attenuated). Further, the correlation coefficients for memberships in INGOs of different scope (universal bodies, intercontinental bodies, and regional organizations) are also quite high, falling only as low as .77 (for universal memberships with regional memberships in 1988). This stability further supports the inference that the trends observed in Table 2.1 have continued through the present and indicate ever greater universalization of world-polity participation in the future.

INGO SECRETARIATS

Secretariats are considerably more concentrated than memberships (Table 2.2). Europe accounted in 1988 for more principal secretariats (world headquarters) than the rest of the world combined (69 percent of the total). The same was true of the top economic quartile of countries (59 percent), while the oldest countries accounted for just under half of the total. We do not have longitudinal data on secretariats, but in all likelihood they, too, are more dispersed now than earlier, meaning that European concentration of INGO

TABLE 2.2
INGO Secretariats, 1988 (Means)

	Principal secretariats	Regional secretariats	N
All countries	22.4	6.2	199
World region			
Africa	3.7	2.4	55
Americas	15.7	6.0	49
Asia	8.0	3.9	40
Pacific-Oceania	4.2	2.4	17
Europe	80.9	15.9	38
GDP per capita (quartiles)			
Lowest 25%	2.1	2.3	34
26–50th %ile	4.3	2.9	35
51–75th %ile	8.4	5.0	35
Highest 25%	77.0	24.1	34
Period obtaining independence			
Before 1800	122.6	26.4	21
1801–99	37.2	11.0	26
1900–44	20.1	5.5	20
1945–59	9.3	4.8	26
1960–75	3.3	2.0	61
1976–90	0.5	0.1	15
Not indep. by 1990	1.4	0.5	30
Dominant religion in 1980			
Catholic	30.6	8.6	76
Protestant	34.7	7.1	48
Orthodox	6.3	3.2	6
Islamic	5.9	2.2	42
Hindu-Buddhist	6.9	5.6	14
Atheist (Communist)	2.0	1.3	6
Indigenous or Chinese folk	9.8	4.7	6

SOURCES: GDP per capita from UN 1990, date of independence from Banks 1975, dominant religion from Barrett 1982, INGO memberships from UIA 1960–88.

secretariat locations was even more extreme in 1960. On the other hand, in 1988 Europe accounted for a much lower portion of regional secretariats (49 percent of the total) because of the rise of substantial numbers of African, Asian, and Latin American regional INGOs. Nevertheless, the figures for total secretariats, principal secretariats, and regional secretariats are very highly intercorrelated (.94 or above; for logged versions of the variables, between .70 and .98).

The top locations for secretariats of both sorts are France (689 secretariats), Belgium (588), Britain (573), the United States (486), and Switzerland (354), which together accounted for about 47 percent of all INGO secretariats. Germany, the Netherlands, Sweden, Italy, and Denmark round out the top ten, all with at least 132 secretariats, followed by Norway, Canada, Australia, Finland, and Japan. This rank order suggests that INGO secretariat location is strongly related to national prominence in the world polity, but sheer size (in population or economy) is not the major determinant of prominence. By contrast, Communist-dominated countries were notably low. The highest was Czechoslovakia, with 21 secretariats (42nd place); the USSR had only 11 secretariats, in 62nd place, and China had only 3. The overall mean was 28.6 secretariats.

In regions other than Europe, the most prominent countries for primary and regional secretariats combined are Argentina (66, 17th place overall), Mexico (47), and Brazil (38) in Latin America; Kenya (53, 20th place), Nigeria (34), and Senegal (30) in Africa; Iraq (38, 26th place), Egypt (31), and Israel (27) in the Middle East; Japan (67, 16th place), India (57), the Philippines (40), and Malaysia (33) in Asia. Pariah or self-isolating nations, by contrast, were especially low: South Africa had only eight secretariats, Libya nine, Cuba five; no secretariats were identified in Albania, Burma/ Myanmar, Cambodia, North Korea, or Vietnam. Even minor peripheral countries like Cameroon (13), Fiji (11), and Guatemala (10) had more secretariats than these latter countries, though many other small or less developed countries had only a handful.

INGO MEMBERSHIPS AND NATIONHOOD

In Table 2.1 we saw that residents of older countries belong to a much broader range of INGOs than newer countries. Residents of the oldest cohort, countries that were independent by 1800, belonged to an average of 1,232 INGOs in 1988, while residents of newly independent countries (independent after 1975) belonged to only 100. However, growth factors for newer countries are noticeably higher than for older ones, even though few countries are close to the maximum number of possible memberships (France's leading figure of 2,471 memberships is 77 percent of the total possible, but only 15 countries' residents belong to as many as half of all INGOs). Meanwhile, memberships for colonial territories, though faithfully reported by the UIA, are exceptionally low. This raises the question of the relationship between independence and INGO participation: Is the formation of a national polity a prerequisite, as it were, for active world-polity engagement?

The data reveal a substantial impact of independence on INGO participation. Consider the twenty-one countries that became independent in 1960 and 1961, the peak point of African independence. In 1960, just before independence, their residents averaged only 23 INGO memberships, when the mean for all countries was 122. By 1966 their mean had jumped to 78, and by 1988 to 298 (about 62 percent of the all-country mean). Similarly, the thirteen countries obtaining independence between 1976 and 1983 averaged only 22 memberships in 1977, when most were still colonies, but by 1988 their mean was 102. This pattern emerges for all colonies that have gained independence in recent decades: their residents' INGO memberships increased sharply immediately after independence, at growth rates much higher than those for the overall population of countries.

What emerges here is a somewhat paradoxical inference. If we think of INGO participation as the activation of world citizenship (Heater 1990; Van Steenbergen 1994)—individuals enacting identities as members of humanity at large, engaged in voluntaristic, rational action to manage common human affairs and solve "problems without borders" (Boli 1998)—then we might expect that INGO memberships would not be affected by the transition from colonial to independent status. We find, to the contrary, that colony residents join relatively few INGOs before independence but begin participating avidly once they become national citizens. Hence, it appears that world citizenship is dependent on national citizenship: individuals are less likely to act as world citizens when they are not national citizens.

This inference underscores the fundamental importance attributed to the nation-state in contemporary world culture (Meyer, Boli et al. 1997). National identity is so fundamental that national citizenship is, as it were, a condition for the activation of world-polity citizenship. What at first glance seems likely to be a conflictual relationship—the connection between transnational identity and national identity—is, instead, a complementary one. National citizenship is a requisite part of the definition of the modern, active individual, with respect to world-level action as much as national or local action. In historical perspective, this makes good sense: it was not until the "age of nationalism" (Kohn 1962) in the latter part of the nineteenth century that citizens of European nations began to establish broad-ranging international organizations that would become the primary arena for world-cultural development and structuration. As is also evident with respect to the history of state sovereignty (Boli 1999a), the national and the transnational have developed in a relationship of mutually reinforcing tension rather than as a zero-sum game.

INGO SECTORAL MEMBERSHIPS

We have shown that the breadth of INGO memberships and secretariat locations is strongly related to such national characteristics as economic development and early independence. Analyses not shown in Table 2.1 show similarly strong relationships between INGO memberships and both country shares of world trade and the degree of democratization embodied in national political institutions. An easy way to summarize these findings is to say that residents of core countries are much more likely to belong to a wide range of INGOs than residents of peripheral areas. When we examine the breadth of INGO memberships across different sectors of the INGO population, the same findings emerge. Using the thirteen sectoral categories discussed in Chapter 1, ranging from medicine and health to industry and trade to world-polity organizations, the breadth of memberships in all sectors is strongly related to national wealth, prominence in world trade, early independence, and democratization.

Despite these strong general patterns, we find considerable variation in the degree of relationship between national characteristics and sectoral memberships. In some sectors, the differences in INGO memberships between highly developed, globally prominent national polities and their poorer, peripheral counterparts are enormous. In other sectors, the differences are much attenuated. Table 2.3 charts this variation in two ways. First, column 1 presents the coefficient of variation (the variance divided by the mean) for each of the thirteen sectors. These coefficients indicate the degree of dispersion of INGO sectoral memberships, controlling for the tendency of the variance to increase as the mean value of a variable increases. Second, columns 2 through 4 analyze variation across sectors in terms of three ranking variables: GDP per capita, share of world trade, and institutional democracy (sources are given at the bottom of the table). The columns compare INGO memberships of countries in the top portion of each ranking with countries in the bottom portion.

TABLE 2.3

Coefficients of Variation and Membership Ratios for INGO Sectors, 1994

	(1) Coefficient of variation	*(2)* GDP per capita ratio	*(3)* Trade share ratio	*(4)* Institutional democracy ratio
Sector				
Education/students	1.24	2.30	2.52	2.29
Religion/culture/ethnicity	1.32	2.61	3.09	2.72
Labor/professions/pub. admin.	1.27	2.83	2.50	1.64
Individual rights/welfare	1.36	3.19	2.98	3.11
World-polity oriented	1.38	3.43	3.33	3.12
Sports/leisure/hobbies	1.14	3.52	2.75	2.79
Tertiary economy	1.49	3.92	3.55	3.55
Technical/infrastructure	1.49	4.26	3.76	3.37
Mean, all sectors	1.53	4.49	3.86	3.68
Science/mathematics/space	1.68	5.10	4.23	3.82
Humanities/philosophy/arts	1.83	6.81	4.95	4.74
Medicine/health	1.78	7.25	4.33	4.39
Industry/trade groups	2.18	8.91	6.80	6.80
Political parties/ideology	2.01	17.0	4.36	7.45
Universal vs. regional bodies				
Universal INGOs, all sectors	1.34	1.77	1.01	1.46
Regional INGOs, all sectors	1.69	5.04	4.28	4.37

SOURCES: GDP per capita from UN 1990, world trade share from Banks 1975, institutional democracy from Gurr 1990, INGO memberships from UIA 1994.

NOTE: Spearman rank-order correlation coefficients (rho) for coefficient of variation and membership ratio rankings:

	Column		
	(2)	(3)	(4)
Column (1)	.90	.97	.95
Column (2)		.91	.96
Column (3)			.96

Column (1): Coefficient of variation = variance/mean
Columns (2) through (4): Ratios of the mean numbers of INGOs to which residents of categories of countries belong, dividing the mean for high-value countries by that for low-value countries on the respective variables.

GDP per capita compares the top quartile of countries ($n=34$) with the bottom quartile ($n=34$); world trade share compares the core (>3% of world trade, $n=11$) with the periphery (<1% of world trade, $n=140$); institutional democracy compares the top quartile of countries (Gurr scores of 9 or 10, $n=32$) with the bottom half (Gurr scores of 1 or 0, $n=67$).

The coefficients of variation in column 1 indicate the overall variability of the distributions of memberships in the different INGO sectors. They range from a low of 1.14 (the variance is only slightly larger than the mean) for sports/leisure/hobbies INGOs, to a high of 2.18 for industry and trade INGOs. For the first six sectors listed, education/students through sports and leisure, countries vary relatively little in terms of the numbers of such INGOs to which their residents belong. The sectors lower in the table reveal greater variability.

Columns 2 through 4 present what we call "membership ratios." They were calculated as follows. For GDP per capita, we ranked all countries from high to low, dividing the rank order in quartiles. We then divided the mean number of INGO bodies to which residents in the top quartile of countries belonged by the mean number of INGO bodies to which residents in the bottom quartile of countries belonged. The membership data come from our extract from the UIA database for 1994 but include only those INGOs whose sectoral category was available from our coding of the 1988 *Yearbook*.

Table 2.3 shows, for example, that residents of the richest quartile of countries belonged to 2.3 times as many education or student INGOs as residents of the poorest quartile. The membership ratio for education INGOs, with countries classified by GDP per capita, is therefore 2.3. For sports, leisure, and hobby INGOs, the membership ratio is about 3.5; for industry and trade groups, about 8.9. The richest countries' residents belonged to about 3.5 times as many sports and leisure INGOs as residents of the poorest countries, and about 8.9 times as many industry/trade INGOs.

The same sort of comparison applies to the rankings for world trade share and institutional democracy scores (columns 3 and 4). Residents of core countries (those engaging in 3 percent or more of world trade; see Boli 1987b) belonged to about 2.5 times as many education/student INGOs as residents of peripheral countries (those engaging in less than 1 percent of world trade). The corresponding membership ratio for sports/leisure/hobbies INGOs categorized by world trade share is 2.75, while for industry/trade groups it is 6.8. For institutional democracy, we compared the top quartile on Ted Gurr's (1990) index with the bottom 50 percent (variation in the lower half is small), finding that the ratio of education/student INGOs for the most democratic countries relative to the least democratic is about 2.3. Corresponding membership ratios for sports/leisure/hobbies INGOs and industry/trade groups are 2.79 and 6.80, respectively.

The rows in Table 2.3 are ranked from low to high in terms of the membership ratios for GDP per capita. This ranking is nearly identical to that for the other ranking variables (rank-order correlation coefficients are given below the main body of the table) and for the coefficients of variation. The separate columns thus present essentially the same information with only slight variations.

We read the columns in Table 2.3 as indicators of the degree of general institutionalization of the various world-cultural sectors or as indicators of the degree to which different sectors involve dispersed memberships and, hence, general world participation. Education/student INGOs consistently have the lowest membership ratios: residents of poorer, more peripheral, less formally democratic countries are relatively likely to join such organizations. This finding suggests that education is the most generally institutionalized sector of world-polity structuration. Even in the most marginal countries, many individuals learn of world-level educational organizations, recognize their importance, and become participants in their activities. Education is, then, rather uniformly constructed as a global enterprise.

The same applies to the other sectors with low membership ratios and coefficients of variation: religion and cultural/ethnic identity, labor and professions, individual rights and welfare, world-polity oriented bodies (promoting world unity, peace, international or world law, environmentalism, and the like), and sports and leisure INGOs are all especially universal, drawing members from the margins relatively frequently. At the other end of the spectrum, several sectors reveal much greater concentration of membership in the upper tier of countries: political party/ideology INGOs, industry/trade, medicine/health, and humanities and arts INGOs have especially high membership ratios and coefficients of variation. These sectors are much more the domains of Western, highly developed, more fully democratized nations.

The high membership ratios for industry and trade obviously reflect the dominance of the developed countries in the world economy; residents of countries that lack a given industry or commercial sector are unlikely to join the relevant bodies. Note, however, that three sectors in which the developed countries are similarly dominant in terms of resources, global corporations, and level of differentiation—medicine and health, science, and technical/infrastructural activities—have membership ratios only at about the mean for all sectors.

These patterns indicate that broader world-polity institutionalization is found in less formal and less resource-demanding organizational sectors, while greater concentration in the more developed and prominent countries obtains for more highly rationalized and resource-rich sectors. Religious, labor, professional, human rights, environmental, world-law, and world peace organizations are relatively common loci of participation for people from all types of countries. Organizations concerned with highway construction, biochemistry, philosophy, cytology, and machine-screw manufacturing have less widely dispersed memberships.

Some resource-intensive sectors are nonetheless more widely dispersed than one might expect. Education, which typically accounts for 8 to 10 percent of GNP in both more and less developed countries, is highly institutionalized in all nation-states (Meyer et al. 1992), so it is not surprising that educators everywhere are involved in global education organizations. Similarly, almost all countries have national health systems that involve the licensing of organizations and personnel, yielding relatively active participation in medicine INGOs by residents of less developed countries. More surprising are the moderate membership ratios for science and technical/ infrastructure INGOs, which on the face of it seem likely to be purely developed-country provinces. It may well be that the relatively few scientists and engineers who reside in poor peripheral countries are especially apt to join relevant INGOs, while their counterparts in developed countries may have a more national orientation. This would be consistent with Martha Finnemore's (1996) finding that poor and peripheral countries are surprisingly likely to have science policy agencies, as a means of establishing at least symbolic participation in the technical rationalization of their national polities.

Our final comment here concerns the sector of political parties and ideological organizations, which has the highest overall degree of concentration. Of course, Europe was the birthplace of transnational political movements (among parties and unions) in the late nineteenth century. The increasing identification of politics with nations in the twentieth century has undercut transnationalism in this domain; as Chapter 1 shows, the political party/ideology sector has declined sharply relative to other sectors. Other regions that achieved independence relatively late never developed much activity of this sort because it was already on the wane in the world polity as a whole.

Universal and Regional Membership Ratios

In the bottom two rows of Table 2.3 we present coefficients of variation and membership ratios for our two major classes of INGOs, universal and regional bodies (see Chapter 1). These results confirm the analyses above: the dispersion measures are much lower for universal INGOs, indicating a general drive to join these bodies that define their domain of action as the entire globe. Indeed, in column 3 we find an instance of full parity for universal memberships: the breadth of membership in universal INGOs is no greater for residents of the countries that dominate world trade than for residents of the weakest trading countries.

By contrast, the ratios are much higher for INGOs that restrict their scope to a single world region. The richest countries' residents belong to five times as many regional bodies as residents of the poorest countries, while residents of the most democratic countries belong to over four times as many regional INGOs as those of the least democratic countries. This disparity reflects above all the thickness of the European regional INGO network and the thinness of its African and Asian counterparts (Europe accounts for over half of all regional INGOs, Africa and Asia combined for only 13 percent). The Americas are, again, close to the mean in their regional INGO figures.

Multivariate Analysis of INGO Memberships

Our tables and discussion have identified a number of factors that are clearly related to INGO memberships. The obvious next step in the analysis would be multivariate regression analysis. Given the nature of the data available, cross-national panel analyses regressing INGO memberships (in, say, 1988) on independent variables measured at an earlier time, including the lagged dependent variable (1977 INGO memberships), would be a suitable model (see Meyer and Hannan 1979). We have conducted such analyses with an array of independent variables, including economic development, total population, school enrollments, percentage of world trade controlled, institutional democracy, book translations, and so on, logging all skewed variables to dampen the distorting effects of outliers.

We find, however, that the regression analyses are unstable because of high multicollinearity among the independent variables. Typically, the results change dramatically when various combinations of independent variables are employed. In some cases, a given variable, such as share of world trade, has strong positive effects in one equation but insignificant negative effects in another. We even find occasional reversals of effects for a given variable, a significant positive effect in one equation yielding to a significant negative effect in another.

The major source of multicollinearity is the array of high correlations between the lagged dependent variable and our independent variables. Table 2.4 gives some typical figures taken from one regression analysis, showing that five of the seven independent variables are correlated at .75 or higher with 1977 memberships. Other combinations of variables produce similar

TABLE 2.4

Correlations Between 1977 INGO Memberships and
Major National Characteristics in 1980

INGO memberships with:

Book translations	.76
Percentage of world trade	.88
GNP per capita	.80
Total population	.34
Govt. revenue/GDP	-.52
Institutional democracy	.76
Secondary education enrollment ratio	.78
	N=75

NOTE: For all coefficients, $p < .01$. All variables are logged except government revenue/GDP and secondary school enrollment ratios. The institutional democracy measure is the mean of Gurr's (1990) measure at five-year intervals for the period 1960–85.

correlation patterns, with the number of cases reaching as many as about 110 countries and territories.

Rather than treat this multicollinearity as a problem (after all, it does defeat the regression design), we find it substantively revealing. Cross-sectionally, INGO participation is closely related to economic development, educational expansion, participation in world trade, the importation of foreign culture, and institutional democracy. It is only weakly related to population size, and it is negatively related to state expansion (though only moderately so, the correlation coefficient usually falling to around -.3 in equations with 100 or more cases). We cannot reliably assess the impact on world-polity participation of each of the factors that are highly correlated with INGO memberships precisely because they form a more or less coherent "package" of traits, of which INGO membership is itself a constituent part.

Nevertheless, the instability of the regression coefficients indicates that none of these factors demonstrably affects membership growth over time. As we have seen above, membership growth is peculiarly universal, occurring among all categories of countries across numerous dimensions, and it is highest for countries that have low values on the traits that constitute the "package." With respect to theoretical interpretation, this is the single most important result of our analyses.

THEORETICAL REFLECTIONS ON NATIONAL INGO PARTICIPATION PATTERNS

Teasing out the implications of our data analyses for theoretical perspectives on global development requires some guesswork because most perspectives either ignore the INGO population or treat it as largely epiphenomenal. We therefore must read into the various perspectives our understanding of what they imply about national participation in INGOs. This somewhat hazardous exercise leaves us open to the charge that we have misinterpreted other perspectives. If so, we look forward to correction.

A brief summary of our findings regarding national participation in world-polity organizing comprises the following points. First, the global stratification structure is clearly reproduced in INGO participation. Residents of resource-rich, technically developed, older, formally democratic Anglo-European countries participate the most; residents of poor, less developed, newer, less democratic countries participate the least. Secretariat locations favor the former category even more than memberships. Second, while all sectors of the world, divided in a variety of ways, exhibit rapid growth in INGO participation, the rate of growth is inversely related to level of participation: residents of poor, less developed, peripheral countries have increased the breadth of their INGO memberships the fastest. Third, in consequence, residents of the periphery are more broadly involved in INGO activity than would be expected on the basis of the resources and networks available to them. These latter two findings probably also apply to secretariat locations, but our data do not allow us to demonstrate this.

Fourth, for each of the thirteen INGO sectors the patterns of participation again favor the richer, more developed, more democratic countries, but the degree of dispersion of memberships varies greatly across sectors. More resource-demanding, technical, organizationally elaborated sectors are mainly the provenance of the more developed countries; other sectors, especially education, sports, religion and cultural identity, individual welfare, and world-polity sectors, reveal more universal participation patterns. In addition, universal INGOs (organizations defining the entire world as their arena of action) reveal much greater dispersal of memberships than do regional INGOs, which are especially concentrated in Europe.

Functional-Rationalist Theories of Global Development

Most of the established perspectives on global development work from functional-rationalist assumptions. A number of perspectives in international relations theory have this character, including the self-designated functionalism of David Mitrany (1943) and successors (Jacobson 1979; Jacobson, Reisinger, and Mathers 1986); neorealism (Waltz 1979; Grieco 1993; Gilpin 1987; see Keohane 1986); and regime theory (Krasner 1983a, Young 1989) and its more generalized counterpart, neoliberal institutionalism (Keohane 1984; Murphy 1994; Baldwin 1993). These perspectives disagree sharply on some issues, but they all explain international organization and cooperation as the result of largely rational action by states pursuing self-interested goals. Functionalism and some versions of regime or neoliberal institutional theory invoke arguments about technical or functional necessity, claiming that international "governance structures" (Diehl 1996; Weiss, Gordenker, and Watson 1996; Charnovitz 1997), in which IGOs are the key players, emerge when "inherently" international or global problems arise—problems like air pollution, crowding of the electromagnetic spectrum, or expanding international air traffic. These problems are seen as "too big" for individual states and of such compelling magnitude that rationally behaving states realize they must be managed on an international basis (see also Young 1989).

Besides such functionally imperative cooperative arrangements, functional-rationalist theories posit that transnational organization also results from inter-state competition based on strategic action. States have strong incentives to create international structures to improve their clout in the world, particularly if they are strong (so they can displace costs of collective action to less central states) or relatively weak (so they can improve their bargaining position). Thus, for example, OPEC is explained as a means by which weak states could corner the world oil market and thereby command a greater share of world economic production. Similarly, strategic considerations lead states to form defense alliances of increasingly broad scope, to develop trade organizations that will lower tariffs, and to fund international monetary institutions that will help maintain the overall stability of global financial systems.

Much the same type of argument emerges in the work of Peter Haas (1992) and colleagues on "epistemic communities," in which experts, policy analysts, and bureaucrats in particular issue domains, such as food aid and the regulation of whaling, use their scientific and technical knowledge to dominate those domains. Epistemic community members are driven by the functional and technical requisites of global and national management; the organizations they dominate, both IGOs and INGOs, have specific, rationalized goals. Some members may see themselves as owing allegiance to particular nations, but others see themselves as transnational citizens (cf. Falk 1994) whose allegiance lies with humanity (global development) as a whole.

Another prevalent perspective, world-system theory (Wallerstein 1979; Chase-Dunn 1989), closely resembles these international relations theories, particularly neorealism, which insists that cooperative arrangements are bound to be relatively fragile and short-lived (an implication that is challenged in Cupitt, Whitlock, and Whitlock 1996). Core powers create international organizations to promote their interests, and they use these organizations to ensure their domination of lesser powers and of the world economy in general. The IMF and the World Bank are usually seen as prototypical examples in this regard (McMichael 1996). If core powers are not able to dominate the organizations, they neutralize them by refusing to provide resources or by shaping their agendas to preclude effective challenges to the existing order. Thus, international organizations are primarily vehicles for the extension and management of global capitalism, and they arise or are co-opted to deal with technical and functional problems related to capitalist development.

Though none of these functional-rationalist perspectives pay much attention to INGOs, their stress on the economic and technical dimensions of global organization, and their reduction of virtually all issues to matters of power politics or capitalist hegemony, lead to the following general predictions regarding participation in international organizations. First, INGOs should form primarily in economic, political, and technical arenas. Second, INGO members should come primarily from the developed countries, and especially from the major powers. Third, residents of the poorest countries of the world should be almost entirely uninvolved in INGOs. Fourth, these patterns should be reasonably stable. Exactly which countries' residents participate most actively in world-polity bodies will vary over time, as countries rise and fall in the world stratification order, but the dominance of the most powerful and most highly developed countries should be approximately constant.

Our discussion of the data above finds only partial support for these predictions. Certainly, the residents of powerful, highly developed countries belong to a wider range of INGOs than the residents of weak, poor countries. Such stratification is evident across all INGO sectors. However, the rapid growth of INGO memberships by residents of peripheral countries contradicts functionalism, neorealism, neoliberal institutionalism, and world-system theory. Participation is spreading to all sorts of countries, as Table 2.1 emphasizes, producing much broader memberships among residents of the periphery than their resources and tangible connections to world structures (via trade, telecommunications, and the like) would lead us to expect. This is why the membership ratios for numerous sectors in Table 2.3 are much lower than the disparities in wealth and global power among the world's countries; top-quartile countries have two, three, or four times the breadth of member-ship of bottom-quartile countries but their means for GDP per capita and share of world trade are typically ten to twenty times those of the poorest and most peripheral countries.

In addition, functional-rationalist theories have trouble accounting for the extremes of INGO involvement. At the high end, the small populations of the northern European countries are extraordinarily broadly represented in INGOs of all sorts, more than either of the two large-population economic giants of the world, the United States and Japan (cf. Jacobson, Reisinger, and Mathers 1986, on IGO participation). At the low end, it seems unreasonable to find the large population of Vietnam belonging to only 154 INGOs while the much smaller population of the remote, subsistence-economy Central African Republic belonged to as many as 159 INGOs. Vietnam may have been a pariah state in recent decades, but functional and power-political con-siderations lead one to believe it would be much more active in INGOs. Contrarily, why anyone in the Central African Republic would find a func-tional or political rationale for joining an INGO is not easy to explain.

A more fundamental problem for functional-rationalist perspectives has been discussed extensively in Chapter 1: the INGO population and, hence, INGO memberships, are more widely dispersed across social sectors than these perspectives can explain. Economic organizations (combining in-dustry/trade groups and tertiary economic organizations) make up the largest single segment of the INGO population, but they still are only about 25 percent of the total. Purely political organizations are, as we have seen, quite scarce and growing scarcer. Even with a very broad concept of global political economy, half or more of the INGO population would not fall in the category. Sports and hobbies, group identities, world law and peace, human rights, dance and ceramics, Esperanto and famine relief—the very existence of a great range of organizations is hard to explain in functional-ra-tionalist terms focused on power struggles among states or global capitalist competition.

World-Polity Theory

World-polity institutional theory improves on many of the inadequacies of functional-rationalist perspectives. This perspective recognizes the emergence and consolidation of global culture operating as an overarching level of social reality that takes concrete form in transnational organizations, both governmental and nongovernmental. INGOs are crucial to world-polity analysis, for they are the primary arena in which world-cultural conceptions of value, principles, standards, and norms are developed, codified, modified, and propagated. Participation in INGOs is participation in the ongoing elaboration of this all-encompassing cultural arena, and for most INGOs participation is explicitly universalistic and open. They welcome all interested people everywhere, under the expectation that new members will abide by basic world-cultural principles of cooperative voluntarism, democratic decision-making, acceptance of consensually agreed-upon rules, and reasoned settlement of disputes.

In short, participation in INGOs is the exercise of the rights and duties associated with world citizenship (Chapter 1; see also the Conclusion and Boli 1997). To understand INGO participation, then, we need to understand the processes involved in the activation of world citizenship. While rational and functional factors certainly are relevant, they cannot be the whole story. Some individuals and associations may be driven by perceptions of functional "needs" that require the action of world citizens, but if needs were the major issue, we would find much greater INGO participation than we do. (For example, environmental INGOs routinely imply that what is needed for effective environmental protection is global action involving literally everyone, but this "need" manages to induce only a tiny proportion of the world's population to join these organizations.) Many individuals and associations obviously see world-citizenship organizations as indispensable means of achieving rational goals, but the obvious weakness of INGOs in terms of resources, personnel, and legal authority suggests that rational actors would view them as too ineffective to accomplish much of value. (Hence the habitual complaining by INGO participants and officers that they never can attract enough members and money to make much of a difference in their areas of concern.)

Beyond functional rationality, we thus must consider world citizenship more on its own terms. Who is likely to act as a self-authorized, rational volunteer working to help organize widespread human endeavors or solve common human problems? What types of structural conditions in everyday life promote such world-citizen engagement? Thinking concretely, we suggest the following five responses to this question.

First, world citizens are likely to be people who know that INGOs exist—people who come into contact with the documents, activities, news reports, and conversations that indicate the reality, viability, and meaningfulness of INGOs. Such contact is more likely in national societies that are well integrated into world society in a variety of ways: economically, technically, linguistically; by means of extensive travel and tourism; in the orientations promoted by school curricula; by means of translations and student exchange. Trade, book translations, treaty participation, and tourism are all partial indicators of general national involvement in world-society sectors, and societies with a great deal of such involvement are likely to have broader INGO participation.

Second, world citizens are more likely to be people who have resources. People with telephones, typewriters or computers, money for foreign travel, and the cultural capital provided by higher education (active literacy, speaking skills, expert knowledge) are much better candidates for INGO participation than those who lack these resources. GDP per capita is a good indicator of the general level of resources available to a national population, and these resources engender world-citizenship activation quite apart from any rational or functional imperatives they may impose.

Third, world citizenship is more probable for people who are engaged in a social sector in which world-polity action has been established as an ongoing activity. INGOs have arisen across a spectacularly broad range of social arenas; they constitute a highly differentiated set of mostly rational, purposive organizations. The population of a national society similarly characterized by a highly differentiated organizational structure is eligible for membership in a much higher percentage of all INGOs than the population of a weakly differentiated society. Because a sizable portion of INGOs involve professionals, broadly defined, professional differentiation is especially important. Again, GDP per capita and similar measures may be the best available (if crude) indicators of societal differentiation, but their relevance from this vantage point is completely disconnected from resources or functional imperatives.

Fourth, world citizens would likely be people who have the habit (that is, live in a cultural milieu) of rational voluntaristic action. People in national societies with well-developed, formally democratic institutions and, even more, well-established practices of rational voluntarism across a wide range of organized activities, are good candidates for world-level engagement. Put another way, world citizens are more likely to come from cultural milieux structured around individualistic social theories and institutions that generate a dense "civil society" with a good deal of autonomy from the state (Seligman 1992). Gurr's (1990) institutional democracy measure is a plausible indicator of one major dimension of this characteristic, despite its uncertain relationship to actual practice. Even better would be a cross-national measure of the density of voluntary associations, but none is available despite the vast case-study literature on the topic (Wuthnow 1991). What this literature does suggest, though, is that civil society is on the rise throughout the world polity, even in such places as Islamic societies where civil-society traditions are weak or nonexistent (Ibrahim 1995).

Fifth, and in contrast to much of the above, world citizenship is likely to be a more compelling activity for people whose national identities and cultures are relatively weakly reified or incorporated in world culture but whose societies are subject to considerable penetration by the models, means, and values of world culture, and by the organizations that carry this culture. We can think of this factor in terms of a series of near-concentric circles. In its origins, history, and contemporary content, world culture is typified by various scholars as primarily (a) (Anglo-) American, (b) core-country dominated, (c) European and Anglo-American, (d) Western, or (e) developed-country dominated. In the residual category (f) lies the periphery, the South, the less developed world, whose contributions to world culture, past or current, are seen as minor. These societies are mainly recipients rather than originators of world culture, even though their role in world-cultural development is expanding rapidly (as shown in Table 2.1).

Because the value and significance of world culture have penetrated deeply in most places, members of societies outside the inner circles are especially highly motivated to participate in world organizations. They "know" that their societies are removed from the primary centers of global development and that they are mainly on the receiving end of world culture. They also "know" that developing links to world structures and world culture is a meaningful, desirable, even necessary enterprise, to avoid being "left behind" or "unable to compete."[3] This reasoning helps explain both the disproportionate INGO engagement of residents of middle-circle societies, such as the smaller European countries, and the unexpectedly high engagement and membership growth rates of outer-circle peripheral countries.

To summarize: as a matter of the activation of world citizenship, INGO memberships vary with the following national-society properties:

(1) Integration into global structures and processes.

(2) Productive and technical infrastructure and communications resources.

(3) Organizational differentiation and professionalization.

(4) Formal democratization and civil-society voluntarism.

(5) Marginalization in global development coupled with penetration by world culture.

Note again the apparent contradiction between the first three points, especially, and the last: for different reasons, residents of both highly integrated, resource-rich, differentiated societies, and residents of marginal, poor, undifferentiated societies, are likely to join INGOs. In the former case, INGO participation is a seemingly "natural" aspect of the general globalization of social processes. In the latter case, INGO participation seems more "artificial," with a larger proportion of participants having few rational or functional motivations to participate. An engineer in a poor African country is unlikely to be able to make much use of what he or she learns by attending a world engineering conference, but attendance is nonetheless meaningful as a signal of the engineer's and the country's eagerness to promote further incorporation of the country into global structures. Hence we find factors impelling broad INGO participation all across the board.

It is worth recalling that these factors have been at work in a world undergoing ever greater global structuration for many decades. Each of the factors has been increasing in intensity. This is why we find rapid INGO participation growth in all sorts of countries over our period. In simplest terms, INGO participation has become a central feature of social action virtually everywhere, with the exception of societies that are essentially "frozen out" of global participation (including those few closed societies that deliberately prevent such participation by their residents) and societies that are simply so poor that very few of their residents have the means to participate.

Much the same findings apply to IGO memberships. We conducted multivariate panel regression analyses of IGO memberships parallel to those for INGOs. These regressions reveal lower multicollinearity between the independent variables and the lagged dependent variable and thus more stable equations. The results reveal almost no significant effects for any variables: neither economic development nor world trade share nor state expansion nor population size appreciably affects IGO membership growth.[4] IGO memberships thus appear to be practically compulsory for states, as a means of establishing proper statehood and appearing engaged in the established array of state activities, regardless of national societal characteristics or the purportedly rational/functional justifications for IGO memberships. Like INGO participation, IGO participation has come to inhere in the very definition of the (world) actor, with remarkable uniformity everywhere.

CONCLUSION

The image emerging from our analysis of national participation in world-level organizations is that of a rapidly growing web of global links that envelop the world without regard for local topography and conditions. Residents of the more developed countries belong to a wider range of INGOs, but residents of the less developed countries are increasing the breadth of their memberships more rapidly. More resource-intensive or technically demanding activities especially engage residents of more developed countries, but activities of a more purely organizational or symbolic nature engender substantial parity in INGO participation. Given the trends since 1960, these patterns are likely to continue, producing ever greater parity in the breadth of INGO participation among residents of the countries of the world. If the trends do hold, we are likely to see substantial changes in world culture in the direction of greater variety of cultural models, more eclectic lifestyles, and more globally constructed debate and conflict.

The ubiquity and rising intensity of this global web is troubling for functional-rationalist theories of global development because so many of the participants in INGO activities have little "reason" to put their time and resources into such work. Little reason, that is, except that participation in global activities is becoming a central element of the definition of the modern actor everywhere in the world as global purposes become more important in orienting individual action. "Think globally, act locally" is therefore a somewhat misleading characterization of the modern prescription for actorhood. Rather, "think and act globally" is the emerging recipe, as the local itself becomes increasingly global (Robertson 1992; Meyer, Boli et al. 1997). With the increasing penetration of world culture and the increasing value associated with globally constructed knowledge, technology, popular culture, and ideology, even the very distinctions among local, national, and global action become hazy. In any case, the ongoing institutionalization of world citizenship via participation in world organizations is now so far advanced that such participation seems likely to continue to grow in the foreseeable future.

Part Two   Social Movement Sectors

Chapter Three # The Rationalization and Organization of Nature in World Culture

DAVID JOHN FRANK, ANN HIRONAKA,
JOHN W. MEYER, EVAN SCHOFER, AND
NANCY BRANDON TUMA

World society now contains a great deal of discussion, concern, and regulation with respect to the natural environment. We document a number of dimensions of the rise of this new world domain of activity and empirically explore the processes producing it, employing dynamic statistical methods.[1]

First, with descriptive data on environmental international nongovernmental organizations (INGOs), 1875–1990, we demonstrate the rise of the environment in world culture. During this period, environmental INGOs increased dramatically in number, members, resources, and linkages.

To explain this growth, we conduct an event-history analysis of the hazard rate at which environmental INGOs were formed after 1875. We find that INGO formation was spurred by the rise of a rationalized scientific discourse and further catalyzed by the creation of intergovernmental environmental organizations. We also find that INGO formation recently slowed as the intergovernmental environmental arena consolidated, favoring the growth of existing environmental INGOs over the birth of new ones. Finally, we find that the environmental INGO formation rate did not respond directly to global environmental problems, undermining the common functionalist imagery.

BACKGROUND

One of the profound changes of the twentieth century has been the expansion of the sense that society affects and is affected by the natural environment (Pepper 1984; Luhmann 1989). What were once thought to be bounded and divided entities—human society and nature—are now thought to be permeable and intertwined. The whole Enlightenment apparatus distinguishing nature from culture, the savage from the civilized, has been undermined.

What has progressively replaced the older separation is a more highly rationalized, complex, and dynamic vision. The human and natural realms are increasingly seen as interactive and interdependent. At the beginning of the twentieth century, the interconnections were narrow, depicting nature sentimentally—as a realm of Edenic innocence—or instrumentally, as a set of resources to be used for human benefit (Frank 1997b). But with advancing rationalization, the interconnections between humans and nature have grown thicker, more elaborate, and more integrated, such that now the very survival of Homo sapiens is thought to depend on the natural world. We are bound into a system of biospheric, geospheric, and hydrospheric processes (e.g., Stern, Young, and Druckman 1992). The notion of an ecosystem that includes human society has emerged (McIntosh 1976; Haraway 1989).

To provide just one example of the new understanding, it is now routine to imagine that human society depends on the integrity of an invisible gaseous mass called the ozone layer, which blocks invisible sunrays, which cause invisible damage to human bodies, which will cause—in some people, in the distant future—skin cancer. It is routine to further imagine that the preservation of this ozone layer depends on mundane human behaviors, such as restraint in the use of aerosol deodorants. Humans depend on the ozone layer, and the ozone layer depends on humans.

The systematization of human-ozone interconnections—the integration of invisible sunrays, imperceptible ozone, indiscernible aerosols, *and human society*—requires a sophisticated process of cultural imagination, and this is true regardless of whether one sees such interconnections as social constructions or as scientific facts. The relationships were pieced together over many decades, beginning in mid-century, with support from international bodies such as UNESCO and the International Council of Scientific Unions. The resulting multi-loop imagery is now taken for granted worldwide.

We believe the rationalization of the relationship between nature and humanity in this fashion underlies the proliferation of environmental discourse and activity in world society. This, rather than environmental problems per se, has driven social mobilization. To show that this is the case, we investigate the rise of environmental INGOs.

THE RISE OF ENVIRONMENTAL INGOS

In 1875, nature was almost invisible on the world agenda. There were virtually no conferences, no treaties, and neither intergovernmental nor international nongovernmental organizations focused on nature. Even the prescient admonitions of George Marsh ([1864] 1965)—who foresaw deforestation, desertification, wildlife extirpation, and more—generated little in the way of practical action (Lowenthal 1990).

By 1990, the situation had entirely changed. A plethora of conferences, treaties, and intergovernmental and international nongovernmental organizations dotted the global stage (Meyer, Frank et al. 1997), and the environment was, by all accounts, one of world society's preeminent issues (Chapter 1 of this volume; Forsythe 1991; Robertson 1992; Smith 1997).

Here we focus on one aspect of this explosion of activity: the rise of environmental INGOs. Environmental INGOs are here defined as those international associations that (1) have members from at least three countries and (2) are focused primarily on some aspect of nature. Our definition includes both organizations promoting the protection of nature and those promoting its rational exploitation, as well as those that promote the protection of human society from nature.

Early examples of environmental INGOs include the International Union of Forestry Research Organizations, formed in 1891, and the International Friends of Nature, formed in 1895. The interwar years produced the International Legal Institute for the Protection of Animals in 1929 and the International Council for Game and Wildlife Conservation in 1930. From the recent period there are the International Association for Impact Assessment, formed in 1981, and the International Society for Environmental Ethics, formed in 1989. The activities of these organizations vary, but they tend to focus on research, education, and advocacy, namely, identifying and publicizing environmental problems and then promoting their solution (cf. Luhmann 1989).

The rise of environmental INGOs in the world has many facets. We document organizational proliferation, broadening international participation, growing individual participation, swelling organizational resources, and surging interorganizational linkages. We illustrate each facet with data drawn from the *Yearbook of International Organizations* (UIA 1995). The *Yearbook* is indexed by keywords in organizational titles and descriptions. We used ten keywords (e.g., "nature," "environment") to construct an initial list of environmental INGOs, which we then pared to include only those having nature as a primary concern.

Organizational Proliferation

The first and perhaps most overwhelming facet of the rise of environmental INGOs between 1875 and 1990 was their proliferation, displayed in Figure 3.1 as a smoothed hazard rate, which essentially depicts the chances that the world will experience an environmental INGO founding in the next moment (Tuma and Hannan 1984). Our data record the founding of 173 environmental INGOs by 1990, with the first in 1882.[2]

Of course, our data represent only the core of the actual activity. Many other nongovernmental organizations are also, though more peripherally, involved in environmental activity. Some of these are international, though most are just internationally oriented; some are focused primarily on nature, though most have nature as one of many foci. Among this broad set, the Environmental Liaison Centre in Nairobi directly links 535 nongovernmental organizations to the United Nations Environment Programme (UNEP), and it maintains relations with 10,000 others worldwide (Trzyna and Childers 1992). At the 1992 Earth Summit in Rio, more than 1,400 nongovernmental organizations were officially represented (McCoy and McCully 1993).

The number of environmental INGOs did not increase steadily since 1875: there were three noticeable spurts. The first followed the end of World War II and the subsequent formation of the United Nations. The establishment of a multipurpose intergovernmental forum created favorable conditions for the proliferation of all kinds of world-oriented associations, including environmental ones (Chapter 1; Frank 1997b; Meyer, Frank et al. 1997). The second and third spurts occurred around the 1972 United Nations Conference on the Human Environment and the 1992 United Nations Conference on Environment and Development. The 1972 conference (attended by delegates from 113 governments) represented the first effort to mobilize the whole world around the environment. With the establishment of the United Nations Environment Programme, among other things, the conference laid the foundation for most of the international environmental activity that followed (Caldwell 1990; McCormick 1989). The 1992 conference (attended by delegates from 172 governments) refocused global attention on issues of the environment, gathering together the largest number of heads of state in history (McCoy and McCully 1993).

In short, the first notable facet of the rise of environmental INGOs between 1875 and 1990 was their proliferation over time. Their numbers have

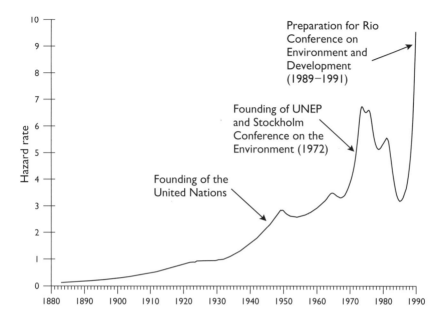

FIGURE 3.1.   Smoothed hazard rate of environmental INGO formation, 1880–1990.

increased substantially, especially in response to the structuration of a general intergovernmental forum and an environmental arena within it.

Broadening International Participation

Broadening and deepening international participation is the second facet of the rise of the environmental and international nongovernmental organizations on which we focus. To measure this, we counted the total number of nation-states that had members in each of twenty environmental INGOs beginning in 1911, the year for which data were first available.[3] To control for the expanding number of nation-states in the period 1911–1990, we only counted members from nation-states that were independent in 1911.

The increase was huge. In 1911, there were 13 country representations in our sample of twenty INGOs. In 1945, there were 73, and in 1972, there were 237. By 1990, the total number of country representations had risen to 543. Some of the increase follows from the fact that only a handful of our twenty environmental INGOs were in existence in 1911. As more INGOs were formed, the total number of country representations rose. But this mundane fact is related to a much more profound process: the environment became increasingly magnetic in world culture between 1911 and 1990, inspiring ever more INGOs and attracting ever more widespread adherence.

The results reported here are conservative in an important sense. We have included only members from nation-states that were independent in 1911. The period between 1911 and 1990 witnessed substantial growth in the number of independent nation-states (see Strang 1990). Were all of these included, the total number of country representations would be close to 1,200.

As seen in Chapter 2, persons who are not members of full-fledged nation-states are not likely to join INGOs. National citizenship serves as the basis for world citizenship. Thus, for example, the people of Zimbabwe, whose country won independence only in 1980, were very unlikely to join environmental INGOs until very recently.

As a result, participation in environmental INGOs at the beginning of the century was likely restricted to European countries. In 1925, 77 percent of the memberships in environmental INGOs were held by individuals or groups from European nation-states. By 1970, the figure had declined to 43 percent; by 1990, it had fallen to a mere 31 percent. Concomitantly, memberships from the rest of the world increased, first from the Americas and then from Africa and Asia.

Thus, the second facet of the rise of environmental INGOs in the period 1875–1990 was broadening and deepening international participation. Over the course of the twentieth century, a great many more memberships from a great many more countries were registered.

Growing Individual Participation

The third important facet of the rise of environmental INGOs was growing individual participation. To demonstrate this, we collected membership data for four environmental INGOs in 1985 and 1995 (UIA 1985, 1995; see Mitchell, Mertig, and Dunlap 1992 for comparable data on U.S. environmental associations).[4]

Individual memberships in three of the organizations increased substantially. The number of participants in the Fauna and Flora Preservation Society—one of the oldest environmental INGOs, originally intent on protecting nature in the British empire—increased about 50 percent, from 3,500 to 5,000. Memberships in the World Wide Fund for Nature (better known as the World Wildlife Fund), which is one of the largest environmental INGOs, grew an astonishing tenfold during this decade, from 570,000 to

5,200,000. Individual memberships in the International Society of Tropical Foresters—an INGO interested more in rationally exploiting than in protecting nature—increased by more than 50 percent over the ten-year period, from 1,300 to 2,000. Only memberships in the International Friends of Nature, an old and more sentimentally based environmental INGO, remained stable at 500,000 members.

Growth in individual memberships in these larger environmental INGOs may mislead one to believe that the average number of members per environmental INGO increased dramatically over time, but this may not be the case. New, small INGOs now pop up rapidly and routinely, probably keeping the overall average membership per INGO more stable than the data from the older and more established INGOs indicate.

Members were disproportionately from Western countries, especially those with liberal political traditions where citizen activism is legitimated (McCormick 1993; Jepperson and Meyer 1991). In the United States, millions of adults participate in environmental associations, many of which are international or internationally oriented (Mitchell et al. 1992).

But participation was not only from the West. Individuals and groups throughout the world organized and joined environmental INGOs. After the United Nations Environment Programme was formed in 1972, efforts expanded to catalyze citizen activism in the lesser developed countries, where popular perceptions have sometimes regarded environmentalism as a luxury from the outside. These efforts drew on an increasingly global normative framework asserting that individuals *should* be environmentalists. For example, to encourage the participation of Africans in the 1992 Earth Summit in Rio, the United Nations Nongovernmental Liaison Service provided travel and other funds to African nongovernmental organizations (McCoy and McCully 1993).

Similar outreach efforts were made by the environmental INGOs themselves. For example, the World Wide Fund for Nature has made participation by locals one of the main criteria for awarding its conservation grants, and the organization recently announced a five million dollar conservation training program for individuals in developing countries, called Education-for-Nature.

Over time such efforts bore fruit, and individual memberships in INGOs diversified while they were growing. This, along with continued expansion in the West, contributed to the third facet of the rise of environmental INGOs: a growing number of individual memberships.

Expanding Organizational Resources

Concomitant with the above is a fourth facet of the rise of environmental INGOs: expanding organizational resources. Whether measured as the size of the staff or the size of the budget, the world's environment INGOs enjoyed a massive infusion of resources between 1875 and 1990.

To show this in the most recent period, we collected data on budget and staff size for the period 1968–90 for three environmental INGOs. The changes were striking. Between 1968 and 1990, the budgets of the World Wide Fund for Nature, the International Union for the Conservation of Nature, and the International Council for Bird Preservation all increased nearly a hundredfold. Staff size also grew tremendously, at least tripling in the 22-year period.

The pool of resources likely affects organizational performance. It allows environmental INGOs to dramatize the global environment more effectively: identifying problems, proposing solutions, mobilizing support, and pressuring both national and intergovernmental bodies for policy reform.

Surging Interorganizational Linkages

The fifth facet of the rise of environmental INGOs was the growing number of interorganizational linkages. Over time, formal connections among environmental INGOs increased greatly, as did connections between environmental INGOs and environmental intergovernmental organizations (IGOs). Linkages also thickened between environmental INGOs and the wider population of INGOs and IGOs.

Figure 3.2 depicts interorganizational connections in 1965 and 1995 for two large environmental INGOs: the International Union for the Conservation of Nature, first formed in 1913 and reorganized in 1948, and the International Council for Bird Preservation, formed in 1922 (UIA 1965, 1995).[5] The increases are pronounced.

In 1965, the International Union for the Conservation of Nature and the International Council for Bird Preservation had only one common connection: both had consultative status with the Council of Europe. By 1995, their common linkages had increased to fourteen, including many important IGOs and INGOs. Simultaneously, both the International Union for the Conservation of Nature and the International Council for Bird Preservation forged an increasing number of formal relations independent of each other. In 30 years, the International Council for Bird Preservation doubled its con-

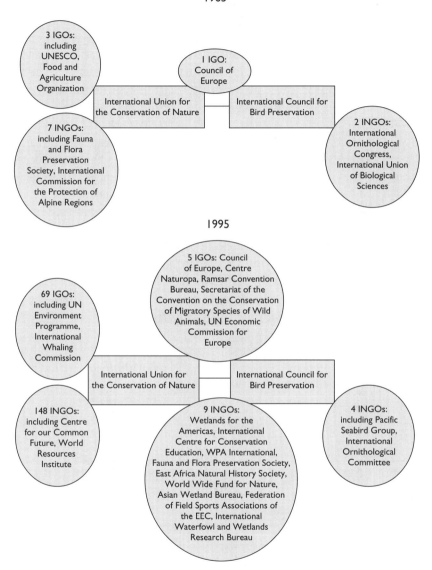

FIGURE 3.2. Interorganizational linkages for two environmental INGOs, 1965 and 1995.

nections from two to four; the International Union for the Conservation of Nature increased its connections more than twentyfold, from 3 IGOs and 7 INGOs to 69 IGOs and 148 INGOs.

The data suggest the formation of a distinct, hierarchically organized environmental sector in world society (Scott and Meyer 1991; Meyer, Frank et al. 1997). Interrelations among all kinds of international environmental organizations increased. The International Council for Bird Preservation, for example, forged an elaborate set of linkages both to INGOs in its subsector (birds) and to general environmental INGOs and IGOs.

On the other hand, the boundaries of the sector appear to be highly permeable. This is demonstrated by the formal linkages that the International Union for the Conservation of Nature, one of the most central organizations, established with various organizations outside the environmental domain, including those focused on health, agriculture, the economy, and population. The International Union for the Conservation of Nature maintains official relations with the African Development Bank, the International Planned Parenthood Federation, and the World Health Organization, among others. This network suggests that the environment has become institutionalized in world culture. To demonstrate appropriate concern, all kinds of international organizations now seek ties with the largest and most central environmental INGOs.

Thus, the fifth facet of the rise of environmental INGOs was a proliferation of interorganizational linkages. Relations both within the environmental arena and to a broader set of world organizations increased dramatically.

FACTORS UNDERLYING THE RISE OF ENVIRONMENTAL INGOS

Overall, environmental INGOs experienced an astonishing ascent between 1875 and 1990. We now focus on one facet of this larger phenomenon—the increasing number of environmental INGOs—in considering explanations of the processes whereby the general rise occurred.

Most analysts have seen the rise of the environment in the world culture as being driven by a functional process: mounting worldwide ecological devastation (e.g., Stern, Young, and Druckman 1992; Caldwell 1990). We propose a broader perspective that emphasizes the institutional conditions under which worldwide ecological devastation—amenable to and in need of concerted global management—can be experienced and known (Pepper 1984; Luhmann 1989; Taylor and Buttel 1992; Frank 1997b; Meyer, Frank et al. 1997).

In particular, we argue that the environmental INGO formation rate rose in response to (1) the expansion of rationalized discourse around nature; and (2) the creation of "official" environmental intergovernmental organizations.[6] By contrast, we argue that the formation rate contracted in response to the consolidation of the official intergovernmental arena and the subsequent routinization of environmental activities (Frank 1997b; Meyer, Frank et al. 1997).

These relationships are contingent, first, on the *statelessness* of the world polity (Meyer 1994). Were a world state in existence, the process would be expected to devolve from central authority rather than be built up from popular discourse and association. Second, the relationships are contingent on the existence of a pervasive *world culture*, which provides the basic elements of meaning and organization necessary to assemble (rather than impose) global institutions (Robertson 1992; Meyer 1994; Boli and Thomas 1997).

The first task here is to explicate each piece of our argument. We begin with discourse centering on nature.

Rationalized Nature Discourse

The rise of a rationalized discourse around nature promoted the formation of environmental INGOs. With rationalization, nature was stripped of its local idiosyncrasies and imbued with an ever wider array of functional utilities susceptible to human management (Weber 1946). As nature's functions accumulated, human efforts to coordinate activities around the environment became increasingly possible and desirable, and concerns about the environment became central in world culture. The creation and expansion of a world science system played a crucial role in this process. It established a frame in which all sorts of environmental issues could be seen as universally significant and in which many policy activities could be seen as useful.

Observation of any element of nature reveals the rationalizing trend. Songbirds were discovered not only to sing but also to play a vital role in the forest ecosystem, protecting trees from predatory insects. Buffalo were discovered not only to make good steaks but also to prepare the soil for wild grasses. Even the lowly mussel turned out to be an important source of food (for muskrat, waterfowl, humans); revenue (their shells stimulate pearl formation in oysters); and medical information (mussels are peculiarly resistant to tumors). Furthermore, mussels filter river water, acting as a built-in river sanitation system (Chadwick 1995). The movement was toward rationalization rather than sentimentalization: a panoply of functional interdependencies—a web of life—was discovered and elaborated.

Early on, rationalized discourse was distilled in nongovernmental organizations. There arose not only talk about nature but also expert bodies self-designated to do the talking (Meyer and Jepperson forthcoming). The initial stages of rationalization took shape in environmental INGOs to (1) protect nature on sentimental grounds (for example, the International Friends of Nature, formed in 1895); and (2) exploit nature on instrumental grounds (for example, the International Union of Forestry Research Organizations, formed in 1891). Such organizations represented an advancing sense that humans could and should assert secular control over a useful environment. However, in these early years nature's theorized utilities were narrowly instrumental and, to a lesser extent, sentimental (Pepper 1984; Haraway 1989; Kates, Turner, and Clark 1990; Dunlap and Mertig 1992).

With increasing rationalization, nature's utilities dramatically expanded in both intensity and scope. Scientists proposed the existence of "ecosystems," in which the very survival of human beings depended on the integrity of the natural environment. The ecosystem model represented rationalized discourse par excellence. It depicted universal, lawlike, and highly consequential interrelations between human society and nature. Thus, the ecosystem model—whether regarded as truth or social construction—provided easy building blocks for environmental INGOs, such as the Asian Ecological Society, formed in 1977, and the International Association for the Protection of the Environment in Africa, formed in 1990.

The transition toward increasingly broad rationalization can be demonstrated empirically by dividing environmental INGOs into those with narrow sentimental and resource foci and those with a broad ecosystemic focus. We used organizational titles and statements of aims from the *Yearbook of International Organizations* (UIA 1995) to make such a division. The results appear in Figure 3.3. Clearly, the narrowly rationalized sentimental and resource organizations appeared much earlier, foreshadowing the ecosystemic organizations to come (Frank 1997b). Furthermore, when the broadly rationalized ecosystem INGOs did appear, they proliferated much more quickly than their sentimental- or resource-oriented predecessors.

Of course, the differences between sentimental, resource, and ecosystemic INGOs can be overemphasized. These are not three distinct types of organizations as much as they are three points on a continuum of rationalization. In the early stages, sentimentalization set boundaries around the entity "nature," establishing it as a realm of purity and innocence. Once bounded and defined—once conquered in both the cognitive and technological senses—nature was discovered to be useful for human society, first narrowly as a resource

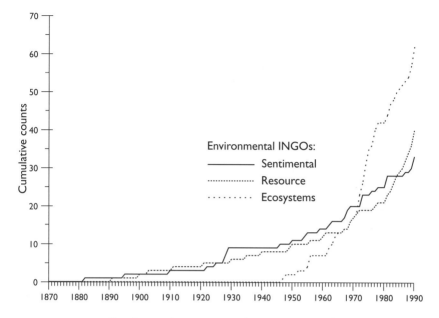

FIGURE 3.3.   Sentimental, resource, and ecosystems INGOs, 1870–1990.

and later more complexly as an ecosystem. Viewed as a resource, a forest should be cut for timber only as fast as it can regenerate; otherwise, the capital stock will be depleted. But viewed as an ecosystem, many additional factors need to be considered, including the impact of deforestation on various species of flora and fauna, carbon dioxide production and global warming, soil erosion and desertification, and so on (cf. Freudenberg, Frickel, and Gramling 1995).[7]

The important point is that nature became increasingly rationalized over time and, as a consequence, acquired increasing functional utility to human society. Thus the rationale and legitimacy for forming environmental INGOs increased. To restate this point as a hypothesis:

> 1. The rise of a rationalized discourse around nature should increase the rate at which environmental INGOs are formed.

Creation of an Official Intergovernmental Environmental Arena

The creation of an official intergovernmental environmental arena, which began after World War II, further spurred the formation of environmental

INGOs. The designation of central and official nodes in the world polity, expressly devoted to the global environment, catalyzed further associational activity.

The intergovernmental environmental arena consists of coordinated nation-state activities around nature. Typically such activities are initiated by international conferences and treaties and routinized in intergovernmental organizations, such as the International Whaling Commission, established in 1946, and the United Nations Environment Programme, established in 1972 (Frank 1997b; Meyer, Frank et al. 1997).

There are both diffuse and specific mechanisms through which the creation of the official intergovernmental environmental arena encouraged environmental INGO formation. Diffusely, the intergovernmental arena legitimated and provided a target for associational activity. Before governmental involvement in environmental matters, environmental INGOs were relegated to the status of social-movement outsiders, lacking entrée to the official interstate polity (Tilly 1978). Thus, INGOs were often stymied in their efforts to coordinate intergovernmental agreements around the environment (see Hayden 1942). Environmental INGOs lacked legitimacy themselves and they lacked a consolidated target. Therefore their formation rate was depressed. Once an official forum was structured, by contrast, INGOs received both legitimacy and a defined set of actors to supplicate. Under these conditions, the INGO formation rate increased.

More concretely, intergovernmental activities directly facilitated the formation of environmental INGOs by making resources available. Intergovernmental conferences, treaties, and organizations often designated roles and funds explicitly for environmental INGOs. For example, at the United Nations Earth Summit in Rio in 1992, nongovernmental organizations were granted official accreditation, which gave them access to national delegations as well as the right to propose draft treaties and influence negotiations. As noted earlier, more than 1,400 associations registered at the Rio summit (McCoy and McCully 1993; for other examples see Haas, Keohane, and Levy 1993). The role of nongovernmental organizations in Rio was further cemented in Agenda 21, an Earth Summit plan to achieve environmentally sustainable development by the twenty-first century. Chapter 27, paragraph 6, of the Agenda, "Strengthening the role of NGOs," states:

> With a view to strengthen the role of nongovernmental organizations as social partners, the UN system and Governments should initiate a process, in consultation with NGOs, to review formal procedures and mechanisms

for the involvement of these organizations at all levels from policy-making and decision-making to implementation. (Quoted in McCoy and McCully 1993: 30)

Clearly such developments positively affected the formation and activity of environmental INGOs. Thus our second hypothesis:

> 2. The creation of an official intergovernmental environment arena should increase the rate at which environmental INGOs are formed.

Consolidation of the Official Intergovernmental Environmental Arena

Over time, the consolidation of the official intergovernmental environmental arena, especially following the creation of UNEP in 1972, had the effect of crystallizing the whole domain, slowing the rate at which new environmental INGOs were formed. The idea is not that the INGO formation rate declined (although see Nadelmann 1990) but that it decelerated, with existing environmental INGOs becoming larger and more interconnected.

The *creation* of the intergovernmental environmental arena and its *consolidation* are, of course, closely related. But as population ecologists have clearly established, the fluid conditions of the early period (creation) and the more fixed conditions that emerge later (consolidation) have starkly different consequences for organizational formation (Hannan and Freeman 1989).

Before the creation of the official arena, environmental INGOs had a diffuse goal: mobilizing the public at large. The amorphousness inherent in such a project engendered a proliferation of associations. When the official intergovernmental arena first arose, the incentives and resources available to form associations greatly increased and even more environmental INGOs appeared. But with the consolidation of a discrete set of official actors that exercise semiformal jurisdiction over environmental matters, the goal stabilized and narrowed, encouraging a parallel consolidation among environmental INGOs.

The process has taken many specific forms. For example, some intergovernmental organizations, such as the International Organization for Standardization (see Chapter 7), have allowed environmental INGOs access to their decision-making commissions, sometimes even with direct participation. But the access has been limited, and it has tended to be granted only to the large, established environmental INGOs. This has created an incentive structure favoring the growth and interconnection of existing environmental INGOs rather than the establishment of new ones.

The idea here draws on a common sociological finding at the nation-state level: more centralized states are accompanied by more centralized social movements, with fewer and larger associations (see Nelkin and Pollak 1981). Accordingly, as the environmental arena consolidated and centralized, particularly in the United Nations Environment Programme, the population of environmental INGOs should have done the same, producing fewer but larger INGOs.

The data presented on the rise of environmental INGOs demonstrate exactly these trends. The major environmental INGOs experienced big increases in membership and significant expansions in interconnections. And the proliferation of environmental INGOs recently decelerated. Thus, we posit a negative effect on the formation rate of environmental INGOs as expressed in a third hypothesis.

> 3. The consolidation of an official intergovernmental arena should decrease the rate at which environmental INGOs are formed.

We evaluate these ideas in the empirical analysis that follows.

METHODS AND DATA

To test for the expected relationships, we employ event-history analysis, which captures independent variable effects on the limiting probability per unit of time that an entity (in this case the world polity) will experience an event (Tuma and Hannan 1984). The event at hand is the formation of an environmental INGO. The event is recurrent, such that the dependent variable is the transition rate from an organization count of N to $(N + 1)$. We use a constant-rate model, which assumes that the transition rate depends not on any inherent characteristics of time but rather on the time-varying independent variables.

To measure the rise of a rationalized discourse around nature, we used the cumulative number of science-oriented INGOs, based on data from the *Yearbook of International Organizations* (see Chapter 10).[8] Scientists are the main professional agents of the rationalization of nature, playing pivotal roles in imbuing nature with functional purposes.

To measure the creation of an official intergovernmental environmental arena, we used two measures. One is a dichotomous variable for the years surrounding the two major United Nations conferences on the environment, the first in Stockholm in 1972 and the second in Rio in 1992. These two conferences produced charters, action plans, and international environmental treaties. No forums in history generated more intergovernmental activity around the environment.

The second measure of an official intergovernmental environmental arena is the yearly foundings of intergovernmental environmental organizations, based on data from the *Yearbook of International Organizations* (UIA 1989). We used the same criteria to select environmental IGOs that we used to select environmental INGOs.

To measure the consolidation of the intergovernmental environmental arena, we used a dichotomous variable for the post-1972 period, following the formation of the United Nations Environment Programme.[9] UNEP is the master environmental IGO, taking some measure of responsibility for the whole environmental domain.

Finally, we included a measure of environmental degradation induced by industrialization, to test the functionalist alternative hypothesis that environmental INGOs were formed in direct response to increasing resource scarcity and environmental despoliation. We created a factor score from two measures of industrialization, correlated at .96: the natural log of anthropogenic carbon dioxide emissions (Keeling et al. 1989; UNEP 1991) and the natural log of chlorofluorocarbon emissions (Council on Environmental Quality 1991).

RESULTS

The results of the analysis, estimated using the RATE program (Tuma 1992), appear in Table 3.1.[10] All three of the hypotheses received strong support. The effect of the measure of rationalized discourse is positive and significant, as expected. The result lends support to the notion that the redefinition of nature, such that it is increasingly conceived in terms functional to human society, drives the rise of environmental INGOs.[11] Less rationalized formulations, depicting a rude and savage nature, or even an inert and Edenic one, would provide less fuel for INGO formation.

The two measures of the creation of the official arena also have positive and significant effects, demonstrating that the rise of formal nodes in the world polity devoted to the environment spurs additional associational activity. With the designation of these nodes, environmental INGOs gain legitimated purpose and goals, and this promotes INGO formation.

And, finally, the measure of the consolidation of the official arena has a significant negative effect, substantiating the contention that the consolidation of environmental activity in designated intergovernmental organizations slows the formation rate of environmental INGOs.[12] Some routinization

TABLE 3.1

Event-History Analysis of the Hazard Rate of Environmental
INGO Formation, 1875–1990

Variable	*Indicator*	*Parameter and standard error*
Rationalized discourse	Cumulative number of science INGOs	0.013** (0.002)
Creation of official arena	Years around the United Nations Conferences on the Environment (Stockholm) and Environment and Development (Rio)	0.504* (0.197)
	Yearly foundings of environmental IGOs	0.210** (0.033)
Crystallization of official arena	Post-UN Environmental Programme period	-0.744* (0.320)
Degradation	Greenhouse gas and chlorofluorocarbon emissions factor	-0.106 (0.133)
Constant		-1.066** (0.188)

Chi-square improvement over baseline: 217.75**
N=173 environmental INGOs (two-tailed tests)
*p < .05, **p < .01

clearly occurs in the environmental domain, and international mobilization slows down accordingly.

Note also that the functionalist hypothesis receives no support in the analysis. What matters in the formation of environmental INGOs is not environmental degradation per se, but rather discussion and organization concerning this degradation.

CONCLUSION

The twentieth century has witnessed a profound transformation in the relationship between society and the natural environment. From an initial point of radical separation, expressed in purest form by Enlightenment writers, society and nature have become increasingly intertwined such that the well-being and survival of each is now seen to depend on the other.

This transformation in the relationship between society and nature, indeed, the very idea that such a relationship exists, can in part be traced to the activities of environmental INGOs. Over the past century such organizations have grown, proliferated, and formed ever deeper and more complex interlinkages. Concomitantly, environmental INGOs have spurred increased concern with and regulation of the natural environment in world culture.

States, as many other chapters in this volume indicate, are responsive to changes in world culture. Thus, one implication of the rise of a world environmental sector is that nation-states, especially those tightly linked to world culture, ought to have become "environmentalized" over time. The number of nation-state-level environmental laws, bureaus, and ministries should all have rapidly increased, and preliminary evidence indicates that this is the case (Frank 1997a; Meyer, Frank et al. 1997). It is clear, for example, that nation-states created national environmental ministries in preparation for, and in the wake of, the first United Nations Conference on the Environment in 1972 (Meyer, Frank et al. 1997). Similarly, it is clear that techniques to protect the environment, such as the Environmental Impact Assessment, were adopted throughout the world only after receiving the blessing of both environmental INGOs, such as the International Union for the Conservation of Nature, and environmental IGOs, such as the United Nations Environment Programme (Hironaka 1996).

The overall picture is striking. INGOs participated in a world-level rationalized discourse around nature long before nation-states were interested, and they now play an active role in maintaining the international environmental sector. Driven partly by INGOs, the environment has moved from invisibility in world culture to centrality, and it now appears to be rather well institutionalized—a routine concern requiring little justification or defense by those active in the environmental arena.

Chapter Four

The Emergence and
Transformation of the
International Women's
Movement

NITZA BERKOVITCH

At the closing session of the World's Congress of Representative Women, Rachel Foster Avery, a leader of the American women's suffrage movement, declared:

> What the International Council of Women may come to be is for the future to decide, but we hope that the plan . . . may materialize in a permanent Congress of Women, composed of delegates from all civilised nations . . . throwing the influence of united womanhood in favor of better conditions for humanity, better educational opportunities for all children, and in favor of that equality between man and woman. (Quoted in Spencer 1930: 13–14.)

Rachel Avery's statement was intended to inspire women to join the International Council of Women, created a few years earlier, in the pursuit of ambitious goals: the general betterment of the world and improvement of the social position of women. The means to be used included the formation of an organizational basis for international cooperation among women's associations, clubs, and societies from the "whole civilised world." This approach was typical of the period—a period in which the emerging world polity was made up mainly of transnational movements for moral purity and social reform that generated numerous international organizations formalizing the movements as permanent social actors.

The International Council of Women was soon followed by many other women's transnational organizations. During the twentieth century, and especially after World II, as part of the intensification of world-polity cultural and political structuration, women's organizations proliferated throughout the globe. By the 1970s, women's groups from the Third World began playing a major role within the movement, introducing new issues, shifting its agenda, and changing its priorities. By 1985, there was a total of about 170 women's international organizations in operation.

All these international women's organizations (WINGOs) constitute what I refer to in this chapter as the international women's movement. This is not to say that it has been unified or homogeneous. A continuously changing "collage" is a suitable metaphor for this complex web of organizations. The composition of this web and the relations between its parts keep changing as new, often divisive issues emerge and new commonalities are achieved. This changing character, mode of operation, and agenda can best be accounted for by considering the global context in which the movement operates. It is not a mere aggregate of national women's movements, nor it is an expression of one hegemonic power. Though regional interests and perspectives do play a role, the mode and scope of their influence are determined, to a large degree, by prevailing conceptions of the structure and role of the international community in any given period. At the same time, I argue that women's groups are not only products of their wider environment but also shapers of that environment. These groups were significant players in the changing world-cultural conceptions about what could and should be done regarding women's issues. They took the lead in putting women's status and rights on the agenda of intergovernmental organizations; via these IGOs, they helped put women's issues on the agenda of nation-states. Thus, by using a world-polity perspective I attempt to explore the mutual interplay between the women's movement and the context in which it operates, that is, how it both reflects world culture and structure and helps shape them. I show how an investigation of WINGO discourse and action can inform us not only about how women's issues became a global concern but also about transformations of the world polity from the mid-nineteenth century to the present.

The women's movement grew in three chronological stages, which correspond to stages in the transformation of world-polity culture and structure: the formative period, the interwar period, and post-1945 developments. The formative period was marked by low but definite levels of world organizing and a spirit of social reform and moral internationalism. Women's organizations broadened the platform of early transnational movements to include "correcting wrongs done to women," the inferior status of women being one of many such "wrongs." A diffuse tension between moral reform and equality

is evident, with equality subordinated to moral concerns: social and moral regeneration was the main mobilizing strategy, while women's equality, focused
mainly on political rights, was conceived as a means of purifying society:
"Give women the vote and see what will be the result" (Johnson and Johnson
1909: 153–54).[1]

In the second period, besides the proliferation of nongovernmental organizations of all sorts, the first broadly inclusive intergovernmental organizations were established. The formation of the International Labor Organization and the League of Nations led to an increase in the level of formalization and cooperation within the women's movement while also intensifying
conflicts internal to the movement. Toward the end of the period, after re-
peated efforts and despite much resistance, the advocates of world action regarding the status of women managed to make women's equality a part of the
official agenda of these bodies.

In the postwar period, universalism and human rights became the dominant elements within world culture. The United Nations was the main car-
rier of these elements; the ILO adopted this orientation as well. The mandate
given to official world organizations was widened to include developing general models as guides for nation-states regarding appropriate treatment of
their citizens. These systemic changes, coupled with massive growth in world
organizing, opened new arenas for the women's movement. Whereas in previous periods women's organizations stood alone in promoting women's
rights, now world "official" organizations joined the campaign, which later
was coupled with "development." All this has helped further rationalize the
world polity and give it more coherence, while also creating space for new divergence to emerge, in this case between women's movements from the developed world and those of developing countries.

THE FORMATIVE YEARS: THE EMERGENCE OF WOMEN'S
TRANSNATIONAL REFORM MOVEMENTS

The late nineteenth century was marked by social and moral reform movements that swept Europe and the United States. They differed from movements in earlier times in that their missionary zeal envisioned not just reform
of their own societies but the creation of a transnational moral community.
Women carved out their own pieces of this moral agenda and helped develop
a new method of pursuing it—international cooperation on social matters by
means of formal organizations. Seeking improvement of the "lot of woman-

hood" as part of a wider vision of a better world, women began to play an active role in bringing about desired changes. While cooperating with men, they also brought something new to the world scene: international organizations either headed by women or composed exclusively or mainly of women.

The earliest attempts to organize women from different countries took place in the 1850s. Carried out in the name of a vaguely specified notion of world peace, they were short-lived (Evans 1977; Boulding 1977, 1992). But the last two decades of the century witnessed the rise of more solid and widespread organizing attempts by women that resulted in the creation of twelve international nongovernmental organizations by 1900 and, by the eve of World War I, 22 such bodies.

Some of these organizations, such as the International Council of Women (founded in 1888), started initially as women-only organizations; some were mixed-gender but dominated by women, like the International Abolitionist Federation (founded in 1875); some split off from mixed organizations while others, such as the International Socialist Women's Secretariat (founded in 1909), gained autonomy within male-dominated organizations. They also differed in orientation (Boulding 1992). Some were religious, like the World Young Women's Christian Association (founded in 1894); others were cultural, such as the General Federation of Women's Clubs (founded in 1890). But they were all inspired by the spirit of internationalism of that period, coupled with strong dedication to social and moral reform. For the first time, the issue of wrongs done to women was formulated as a social problem that should be rectified through global action. Examining the early efforts of international women organizers reveals the ways in which women contributed to emerging world social sentiments. Both cooperation and conflict characterized these varied movements, with each emphasizing a different aspect of women's emancipation and operating in different organizational and ideological contexts.

I use one central issue—women's suffrage—as a lens to examine how the spirit of the period shaped the women's movement and made it into a mobilizing force. By the late nineteenth century, suffrage associations were active in many countries (Offen 1987: 366–73). Attempts to foster international linkages began around the turn of the century. The demand to grant women political rights was entwined with a larger agenda and constructed as a means for higher ends (on this "expediency theory," see Kraditor 1981). Women's equality as such was a rather weak ideology, but it gained strength when depicted as a means of improving the community and society.

The interaction between the International Council of Women (ICW) and the International Women Suffrage Association (IWSA) illustrates important features of the early women's movement. Whereas the IWSA demanded equality using mainly "natural rights" terminology, socialist women and World Woman's Christian Temperance Union (WWCTU) activists emphasized the general betterment of society to be achieved by granting women the right to vote. All these organizations saw international cooperation as a necessary form of action, without which their goals could not be obtained. Collectively they played a dynamic role in the emerging organizational infrastructure of the world polity and its expanding agenda.

The Suffrage Movement

The idea for an international effort on suffrage was first raised in 1882 at a meeting in England organized by "friends of women suffrage" in honor of Elizabeth Cady Stanton and Susan B. Anthony, leaders of the National Women's American Suffrage Association of the United States. Nothing came of the idea for five years, until it was again raised at an annual meeting of the Association. Whereas all agreed that international action was needed and that an international congress was the next appropriate step, a controversy arose over its purpose. The older "pioneer" suffragists urged that the congress should be limited to the advocacy of equal political rights, while the younger generation preferred a wider agenda. The latter could endorse suffrage only because they recognized the ballot as a means to larger ends (Sewall 1914). De-emphasizing suffrage turned out to be the only strategy that could induce a wide range of women's organizations (reformers, trade unionists, and professionals) to participate in the congress (Sewall 1914; Spencer 1930). The broader strategy prevailed.

The International Congress of Women, finally convened in Washington in 1888, was attended by representatives from England, Scotland, France, Norway, Denmark, Finland, India, and Canada. At that congress the International Council of Women was established. It was planned as a permanent body that would function as an umbrella organization for all women's associations, clubs, and societies. Its political functions were, however, minimized, the congress achieving consensual endorsement only for "an organized movement of women [that] will best conserve the highest good of the family and of the state" (Sewall 1914: 19). The demand for suffrage disappeared and was not included in the constitution.

The Washington gathering provided a stage for enacting the idea of universalism as embodied in international action. The guiding idea was that "universal sisterhood" was both a result of women's subordinate position "everywhere" and a mobilizing idea for efforts to rectify the situation:

> However the governments, religions, laws, and customs of nations may differ, all are agreed on one point, namely, man's sovereignty in the State, in the Church, and in the Home . . . Such a Council will impress the important lesson that the position of women anywhere affects their position everywhere. Much is said of a universal brotherhood, but for weal or for woe, more subtle and more binding is universal sisterhood. (Sewall 1914: 8)

The constitution of the ICW provided for the affiliation of national Councils of Women only. In its first five years only the American Council became a member, but by the eve of World War I some 21 national councils had joined. Most of the national councils were moderate-feminist. They included associations concerned with such matters as philanthropy, religion, industry, moral reform, education, art, literature, and science. Suffrage was only one among many issues (Spencer 1930; International Council of Women 1966). The ICW's most important function, apart from instigating the formation of national councils, was satisfying "those who were anxiously concerned to see so large an undertaking, entirely officered by women, carry out its business in a business-like way" (Evans 1977: 251).

In the meantime, the idea of a federation of national suffrage associations was not abandoned. For that purpose, in 1902, representatives from England, Australia, Canada, Norway, Sweden, Germany, Russia, Turkey, Chile, and the United States convened in Washington. Two years later, in 1904, the International Alliance of Women for Suffrage and Legal Citizenship (currently known as the International Alliance of Women) was established (Woman Suffrage in Practice 1913). The declaration of principles presented at the founding congress in Berlin exemplified the Enlightenment rhetoric that was the basis of their action. The declaration describes men and women as equally free and independent members of the human race, equally endowed with intelligence and ability, and equally entitled to the free exercise of their individual rights and liberty (Whittick 1979: 32). Though dominated by the "justice argument," "expediency theory" played a role in their discourse as well. Giving women the vote was meant to correct injustices done to women as well as to benefit society as a whole. A report published in 1913 (Woman Suffrage in Practice 1913) stressed the various positive consequences that were apparent in those countries in which women had gained the suffrage (e.g., lower death and infant mortality, better education legislation).

Also in 1904, the ICW finally passed a suffrage resolution and formed a standing committee on women's suffrage. These moves prompted the formation of national sections of suffrage organizations (Schreiber and Mathieson 1955) that joined previously existing bodies affiliated with the new International Alliance. In 1911 another international suffrage organization was founded, the Catholic Women Suffrage Society (now St. Joan's International Alliance). Very quickly, the International Alliance of Women for Suffrage and its 26 national sections became the leading force in the campaign for political rights for women. Working with the ICW, they held international meetings, served as a nexus for establishing contacts between different national feminist movements, and helped feminist societies get started.

The suffrage organizations sometimes cooperated and sometimes came into conflict with other women's organizations. Their relations with socialist women's groups most clearly demonstrate the tensions within the early international women's movement.

Socialist Feminism

Beginning in the 1890s, an open and assertive feminist movement began to develop within international socialism. As part of the first internationally organized political movement, feminist socialists had access to the arena provided by the organizational infrastructure of the First and Second Internationals (Boxer and Quataert 1978). The largest groups were in Germany, the United States, and Austria, but there also was activity in Italy, France, Russia, Scandinavia, the Netherlands, Australia, South Africa, and Argentina. The figure most identified with this international socialist women's movement was Clara Zetkin, the leading woman in the German Socialist Party, which in turn was the leading party of the Second International (DuBois 1991).

Socialist feminists had an uneasy relationship with both socialist men and feminists outside the socialist movement (Tax 1980). They differed from the suffrage movement in their approach to voting rights. Zetkin argued that "electoral rights without economic freedom are neither more nor less than an exchange without currency" (quoted in Bell and Offen 1983: 90), and she and her comrades objected to the demand made by the suffrage movement to extend the vote to women "on the same terms as men." Because the right to vote was often restricted to property owners, this formulation benefited the wealthier classes only (Tax 1980). Similarly, the emphasis of the feminist movement on married women's right to property seemed irrelevant to women from the working class. Another dividing issue was labor legislation for women, favored by the socialist feminists but of little concern to middle-class suffragists. After World War I, this became an acute conflict.

Socialist men were not favorably inclined toward their feminist sisters. The Working Women Association was expelled from the First International (1864–1867) on the grounds of subversion, mainly because all feminist efforts were suspected of bourgeois tendencies. All contact with feminist groups not associated with the socialist movement was banned (Meyer 1977; DuBois 1991). In addition, the official policy of the Second International, backed by resolutions adopted by the women's circles, forbade any cooperation with bourgeois groups.

The feminist socialists not only competed with the suffrage movement, they also imitated it by trying to establish organizational autonomy as a force within the socialist movement. The results were highly consequential. Zetkin believed that to have an impact on the socialist agenda a separate organizational structure for women, both within the German party and at the international level, should be established. She initiated a separate women's bureau run by women and designated it to act as an interim center for women's activities between conferences (Honeycut 1981). The First International Conference of Socialist Women, attended by members from fifteen countries, was held in conjunction with the 1907 International Socialist Congress (Evans 1977). The principles that were affirmed by the Conference had historic significance: first, all Social Democratic parties must be firmly committed to suffrage for all men and women; second, there must be no cooperation with bourgeois feminists (Evans 1977). This was the first time an official statement and a resolution to join in the reformist struggle for unrestricted female suffrage were adopted by women socialists (Tax 1980). Zetkin proposed a similar resolution to the full Congress of the International, declaring that "wherever a struggle is to be waged for the right to vote, it must be conducted only according to Socialist principles, *i.e.*, with the demand for universal suffrage for both men and women." In spite of opposition from the Belgian and Austrian delegates, the resolution passed. In addition, the congress voted to set up an independent women's secretariat with Zetkin as its head (Sowerwine 1987).

Thus, the results of the feminist socialists' efforts was the commitment of the international socialist movement to the suffrage cause. Consequently, socialists joined the campaigns for women's suffrage in numerous countries.

The Temperance Movement

The suffrage movement had much easier relationships with the World Woman's Christian Temperance Unions (WWCTU). The singular possessive form ("woman's") used in the title was chosen deliberately: "The women of the World's WCTU are as one woman, one heart, one soul, on one purpose intent, the protection of the homes of the world, by the annihilation of the traffic in intoxicating drink, opium, and other narcotics" (quoted in Staunton 1956).

This was the first and largest single constituency supporting the ballot for women (Giele 1995). Many of the women activists within the suffrage movement were mobilized from the ranks of the WWCTU (Tyrrell 1991); a good many of them had experience in the antislavery movement. Though appealing to a different constituency (the upper-middle class rather than the poor), applying different methods (political activities rather than charity and community work), and diverging on some issues (Giele 1995), the two movements maintained cooperative working relations.

A typical transnational reform movement of the late nineteenth century, the temperance movement was a sort of international Puritanism inspired by religious and moral concerns. It was active in the United States well before women took the lead; in the 1850s women had been refused permission to speak at a number of temperance conventions run by men. By the 1870s, however, an effective women's temperance movement was under way, leading to the founding of the Woman's Christian Temperance Union in 1874. Temperance associations and national unions were soon organized in other countries as well.

Operating with almost missionary zeal, the WCTU made internationalism an integral feature of its platform and activities (Tyrrell 1991). In 1876, women from several countries attending the International Temperance Congress in Philadelphia met to initiate an International Women's Temperance Union. In the early 1880s, during a visit to San Francisco, Frances Willard, the leader of the American union, was horrified by the "opium dens side by side with the houses of shame" she saw there, and she determined to take vigorous action (Stanley 1983: 11): "We must be no longer hedged about by the artificial boundaries of States and Nations, we must utter, as women, what good and great men long ago declared as their watchword—'The whole world is my parish.'" (quoted in Staunton 1956: 8).

Willard initiated a petition addressed to all heads of state asking them to join in a campaign to set a standard of purity and total abstinence. This idea was the crystallizing force for the founding of the international body. Four women members were commissioned to travel the globe, spreading the idea of organized action against alcohol and setting the foundation for a coordinated network of national organizations. By the time of the first international convention, in 1891, 86 unions in 26 countries were in operation (Stanley 1983).

Temperance women saw political equality and the good of the family as one and the same goal. The "rum curse" was perceived as a major cause of moral degeneration and the ruin of homes and families; activities to prohibit drinking, in the name of "protection of the home and community," depended on a successful struggle for women's suffrage. "Prohibition, Woman's liberation and labor's uplift" were the "blessed trinity of the movement" (Stanley 1983: 23). The rhetoric of the movement interwove images of women as victims—the deserted wives of drunken men—and women as powerful actors—crusaders on an evangelizing quest (Epstein 1981). Their mission depended absolutely on political rights for women: "It is the right, and ought to be the purpose of every woman of this country to demand every ounce of power which will enable her to do for her children the very best and noble service" (Gordon 1924: 170).

THE INTERWAR PERIOD: LOBBYING FOR EXPANSION OF THE WORLD AGENDA

The world polity after World War I differed markedly from that of the previous period. Earlier dreams of establishing permanent international cooperative bodies were realized with the creation of the League of Nations and the International Labor Organization (ILO), which ushered in a new phase of world-polity construction. The League and the ILO, both created at the Paris Peace Conference of 1919, constituted the first stable organizational basis for inter-state cooperation (Myres 1935; Haas 1964; Northedge 1988; Archer 1992). They opened a new arena for women's mobilization by offering a central world focal point that theretofore had been lacking. In so doing, they changed the context in which women's organizations operated, consequently provoking changes in their modes of operation as well. Their main effort now targeted the newly created international bodies.

By turning their attention to the new world bodies, women's organizations conferred legitimacy on them and thus helped institutionalize their centrality. At the same time, the degree of organization and cooperation among women's groups increased. Many women's organizations moved their headquarters to Geneva to facilitate contacts with the various bodies of the League, while others established specialized bureaus expressly to deal with the League (Whittick 1979). In addition, a new type of organization emerged, the multi- or supra-international organization consisting of representatives of a number of international organizations. For example, in 1925 the Joint Committee of Representative Organizations was founded (Lubin and Winslow 1990), and in 1931 ten of the largest women's groups formed the Liaison Committee of Women's International Organizations. Members of the Committee established close contacts with high officials in the League Secretariat, cooperating with the League on various welfare-related and other activities (Miller 1994).

The increased global mobilization of women within the formally organized global arena sharpened tensions within the international women's movement. Bitter conflict emerged between those who supported action on behalf of women's equality and those who favored laws that gave women special protection, especially in the area of work. Both camps focused their efforts on getting the League and ILO to take action on women's issues, but with quite different emphases.

The League's limited mandate did not allow women's issues to be considered in full; regulation of the relationships between states and their respective citizens was not included in its jurisdiction. Instead, the League concentrated on regulating relations among states. Individual "rights," a construct that had mobilized social movements for more than a century, were not considered an international concern that could be regulated by international standards. It was only through a sustained effort lasting almost two decades that women's international organizations were able to place the heart of their social concerns, the legal status of women, on the League's agenda.

The exclusion of the issue of women's rights from the League's jurisdiction was explicitly stipulated by officials during the Paris Peace Conference. Facing continuous pressure from women's organizations, however, and after much hesitation and deliberation on the part of the politicians, Conference officials agreed that "women's organizations could be heard," but only "by commissions occupying themselves especially with questions touching on women's interests" (Whittick 1979: 70). The women's delegation to the Conference presented seven resolutions covering moral, political, and educational issues (Whittick 1979: 71–72). For the most part, they were ignored.

Three of the issues brought forth by the women's movement were the nationality of married women, the equal rights treaty, and women's employment rights. The campaigns around these issues demonstrate various features of the crystallizing world polity, especially the unresolved issue of the jurisdiction of its central organizations.

Women's Nationality

One of the issues raised by the women's delegates at the 1919 Conference appeared again in the 1930s—the issue of the nationality of married women. In 1930, a League Conference for the Codification of International Law was held in the Hague. International women's groups wanted the conference to adopt the principle that "every woman, whether married or unmarried, shall have the same right as a man to retain or change her nationality," and to draft an international convention on the matter. To do so, they organized a nongovernmental joint conference attended by delegates from 35 countries (International Council of Women 1966: 60). Besides holding a political demonstration, the conference established an international committee of women and sent memoranda to governments, the League, and the chairman of the Codification Conference (Bussey and Tims 1980). The Conference responded by merely urging governments to embody the principle of equality between the sexes in their laws regarding nationality. This response was unsatisfactory; the campaign continued. In 1931, petitions from women's organizations were delivered to the League Council to submit a report and appoint a committee of women to consider the issue. Another measure taken was a well-coordinated protest action in Geneva, initiated by the International Alliance of Women for Suffrage. Also, an intensive telegram campaign was launched during League Council meetings (League of Nations 1931).

To facilitate contacts with the women's movement, the League created the Women's Consultative Committee on Nationality, comprised of representatives of eight women's international organizations (League of Nations 1935a). Yet the League still avoided taking positive action. It responded to a series of proposals submitted by the Women's Committee by requesting countries to provide information on the effect of their nationality laws on the status of women (League of Nations 1933). The Committee also suggested that League action was unnecessary by pointing out that, in 1933, the Organization of American States had adopted a Convention on the Nationality of Women in which signatory states agreed that "there shall be no distinction based on sex in their law and practice regarding nationality" (Inter-American Commission of Women 1974). The only concrete result of the women's groups' effort on the nationality issue was the announcement in 1935 by the League's Assembly that the Pan American Convention was open for signature for all states who were members of the League (Miller 1994). No further action was taken.

Despite the League's reluctance to act, the symbolic significance and organizational implications of the events surrounding the issue of nationality law should not be underestimated. This was the first time an official international body discussed matters concerning equal rights for women, and the issue had been placed on the League's agenda only because of the persistent activity of international women's groups.

Equal Rights and Employment Rights for Women

Whereas most women's organizations cooperated on the nationality law campaign, controversy arose regarding the campaign for an equal rights treaty. The idea for such a treaty originated in Britain in 1926, was communicated to American feminist groups, and was then picked up by various women's international organizations (Miller 1994). For more than a decade the issue divided the international women's movement, the conflict intensifying when some groups launched an extensive effort to get the League to draft a treaty. The controversy revolved primarily around the issue of labor legislation under development by the ILO, especially several measures regarding women's employment. The women's organizations that supported an equal rights treaty opposed many provisions of the ILO legislation because it placed restrictions on women in the name of "protection." Those who objected to the treaty saw the labor legislation as promising a major improvement in women's working conditions.

What gave the issue its urgency was the economic crisis of the 1930s. All countries that experienced the Depression adopted laws or administrative measures that either prevented married women from taking jobs altogether or set quotas for women. The "back to the home" movement clearly jeopardized women's claims to a right to work.[2] Massive mobilization of international women's groups to fight this reactionary worldwide trend included efforts to get the ILO as well as the League to take a stand in favor of women's right to work. In light of the grave situation, an international treaty that expressly affirmed equality of rights between men and women in all areas of life, including economic activity, seemed imperative for many of the women's groups.

The League responded officially by putting the issue of women's rights on its agenda in 1935 and again in 1937. It addressed "the question of the status of women in all its aspects" but remained reluctant to take any action

(League of Nations 1937a). The official report stated that the League expressed appreciation for the "strength and extent of the movement for the removal of differences in the legal position of the sexes" and "sympathy was felt for the ideas underlying this movement" (League of Nations 1938a: 178). But, in the very same paragraph, barriers to meaningful action were specified. One argument was that differences among countries prevented the homogenization of national legislation. A second and more frequently voiced objection was the limited jurisdiction of the League to act autonomously. A general consensus supported the idea that "the status of women was so essentially a matter of domestic jurisdiction" that it lay outside the appropriate field of action of the League (League of Nations 1937a).

The only League step regarding equal rights was taken in 1937 when, spurred by the Liaison Committee of Women's International Organizations, the League decided to conduct a "comprehensive survey of legal status enjoyed by women in the various countries of the world" (League of Nations 1937b). Framing the study as preparation for an international convention, the Assembly decided to set up a committee of experts to work closely with representatives of women's organizations and legal scholars to produce a plan for the domain and geographical scope of the survey (League of Nations 1937b). The study that eventually resulted was not, however, as comprehensive as planned. Relatively few countries responded to the instruments distributed by the committee, and the outbreak of the war prevented publication of the report.

Whether the League might indeed have drafted an international treaty under other circumstances is uncertain. In any case, the fact that women's status was considered to be an issue worthy of thorough study by an official international body represented a major change in the global approach to women's issues. Its precedent-setting significance was acknowledged not only by women's organizations but also by the chairman of the League: "Even as it stood, the programme of work is vast. . . . Nothing of the kind had ever before been attempted on such scale" (League of Nations 1938b: 180).

Women's INGOs as the Impetus to ILO Action

The ILO had a more authoritative mandate than the League: It was charged with setting international standards that participating states would incorporate in their national legislation (Morse 1969; Johnston 1924; Foggon 1988). The ILO thus was authorized to generate world models of labor and labor relations and oversee their implementation, while the League followed the principle of minimum interference with the authority of sovereign states. The ILO's guiding principle was "social justice," balancing the rights of labor with those of employers; however, its initial interpretation of social justice did not include the notion of equal economic rights for women. Still, the very creation of this organization shaped the scope and content of the international women's groups' efforts, in the same way that the League's appearance did. Both the ILO and the League, since their inception, became a focus of attention and target for lobbying efforts. Yet women's groups had better success with the ILO, eventually managing to get it to start framing much of its activity in terms of "women's rights."

Under the terms of the 1919 Treaty of Paris, the First International Labor Conference, to be held in Washington, made no provision for women delegates. In response, to ensure that women's interests would be considered and represented, the National Women's Trade Union League of America decided to call an international congress of working women to meet immediately prior to the labor conference. Two goals were paramount: developing an international policy that gave special consideration to the needs of women, and promoting the appointment of working women to organizations whose actions affected the welfare of women (Waggaman 1919; Foner 1980). The significance of the Women's Congress, attended by delegates from seventeen countries, became clear early on, when some of the delegates to the ILO Conference came to greet the congress (First Convention 1919). This first international meeting of women trade unionists was followed by a second meeting in 1921, at which the delegates established the first permanent international organization of women's trade unions, the International Federation of Working Women (Foner 1980; Waggaman 1919). Lubin and Winslow (1990) argue that lobbying efforts by these women helped induce the ILO to make an important concession to women workers—inclusion of the "principle that men and women would receive equal pay for work of the same value" in the constitution of the ILO (Article 41).

The International Federation of Working Women actively participated in debates regarding women's labor legislation. They concentrated on improving women's working conditions through protective laws and expanding maternity provisions, while the suffrage organizations, supported by the many professional organizations that emerged in the interwar era, promoted equal pay for women. Women's groups had expressed divergent views in earlier periods, but the differences of opinion gained new meaning in the changed transnational context. With the opportunity to present their demands to the relatively authoritative ILO, and the possibility that their action would have tangible and lasting consequences, women's organizations found that controversies became less abstract and more acute.

The conflict was sharpest between women trade unionists promoting protective labor legislation and organizations such as Open Door International for the Economic Emancipation of the Woman Worker. Open Door, founded in England in 1926, had as its sole goal the defeat of the protective policies promoted by the ILO. It declared a "total war" against the ILO and its "sex-based" legislation, demanding an international convention on equal pay for "work of equal value." "An international organization" was needed "that would be in a position to combat its [the ILO's] attack on women workers" (Open Door Council 1929). Open Door tried to employ economic equality and economic rights as the mobilizing issues for the international women's movement in the same way that suffrage had been before the war. However, their extreme opposition to all protective measures conflicted with the agenda of the majority of the women's organizations of the time.

The ILO ignored Open Door and its like, promoting and implementing labor standards consistent with the position of the working women's movement. As early as its first session, held in 1919, it had drafted two conventions prohibiting women's nighttime employment and employment shortly before or soon after childbirth (ILC 1919). In succeeding years, these measures were gradually extended and elaborated (Lubin and Winslow 1990; Berkovitch forthcoming). However, the ILO scrupulously avoided instructing states to equalize the status of women and men workers.

In the mid-1930s the ILO was at last induced to join the "equality" campaign. As with the League, the impetus came from a study, this one initiated in response to requests made by women's organizations directly to the League. The League asked the ILO to examine "the question of equality under labor legislation." The ILO in turn described the study as being undertaken "with a view to satisfying a request made by several women's occupational associations, to develop to the greatest possible extent its studies of the question of the actual economic position of women workers as shown by the facts" (ILO 1935–36: 189).

By the late 1930s, the principles of equality in employment in general, and equal pay in particular, were voiced increasingly forcefully in official forums. In a 1936 meeting of the Conference of American States, in Santiago, Chile, those states that were also members of the ILO adopted a resolution regarding equal pay (ILO 1936: 45–46). In 1937, the International Labor Conference adopted its first resolution on the matter, declaring that "it is for the best interest of society" that, in addition to political and civil rights, women should be granted full rights at work equal to those of men (ILO 1937: 146). In 1939 a more explicit resolution was adopted. This was a major milestone. The ILO announced that its role was not only to protect "our working womanhood," as had been declared in 1919, but also to raise the status of women while recognizing "the importance of the principle of equality of pay" (ILO 1939: 95).

These declarations of principle, coming only in the late 1930s, represent the first direct action by the ILO and the League to promote women's rights. They signaled that women's status was constituted as a legitimate world-polity concern, a "problem" that could and should be addressed at the global level. This set the stage for the postwar era, in which women's rights became a prominent issue of global development.

THE POSTWAR ERA: ARE WOMEN'S RIGHTS HUMAN RIGHTS?

Further far-reaching changes emerged in the world polity of the postwar period, so numerous that I cannot list them all. I confine my analysis to three interrelated developments: the emergence of the United Nations system, accompanied by an increasingly dense official IGO network that, unlike the League, has a charter for greater penetration in states' affairs; the expansion of human rights ideology, including women's rights; and the linking of the status of women to the concept of development, the latter taking place mainly though the United Nations Decade for Women.

The UN System and the IGO Network

The creation of the United Nations greatly intensified world-polity structuration, inaugurating an era in which supranational organizations are vested with the authority to set international standards for nation-states with respect to a wide range of social concerns. The limited actions of the League of Nations and ILO were replaced by authoritative directives to states to adopt specific measures on behalf of their citizens (Farer 1988), including women. Many new international bodies, official and private, emerged to deal with women's issues; numerous international declarations and conventions have been adopted, and reports and studies regarding women's issues could fill a library (Armstrong 1982; Donnelly 1986; Forsythe 1991; Gibson 1991).

This is not to say that this was the first time the international community became engaged in social issues. As I indicate elsewhere (Berkovitch forthcoming), the League of Nations had established an elaborate organizational

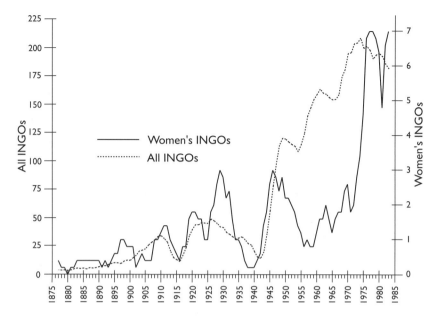

FIGURE 4.1.   Foundings of all INGOs and WINGOs, 1875–1985 (five-year moving averages). SOURCE: UIA (various years).

apparatus to deal with social and humanitarian concerns. However, early on the focus was exclusively on groups of displaced persons such as minorities, refugees, political deportees, and women and children transported across borders for purpose of prostitution. The novelty of "human rights" ideology stems from its focus on individual rights that are independent of the person's citizenship status. The concept of human rights implies that world-polity organizations are invested with the authority to issue instructions for nation-states regarding how to treat their own inhabitants (see Conclusion).

The broadening agenda and authority of world-polity organizations were intertwined with rapid organizational proliferation. The number of IGOs increased immensely after the war, to a total of several hundred (Jacobson 1984: 47–53). Even more impressive is the proliferation of INGOs of all sorts (see Chapter 1) and of specifically women's international organizations (WINGOs; see Figure 4.1). Organizational expansion brought about thickening formal and informal ties among IGOs and INGOs, and women's organizations have been very much involved in these cooperative relations. In 1980, for example, women's organizations had a slightly higher average number of official linkages with IGOs (9.4) than the average for other INGOs (9.2; calculated from Jacobson 1984, Appendix B). In 1985, six of the 34 INGOs that had official authorization to communicate directly with the various commissions of the UN Economic and Social Council were WINGOs (UN *Yearbook* 1985).[3] Women's organizations have been shaped by the new context while also helping to form the context themselves. New arenas for action have emerged; new issues and modes of action have become common; the interplay and mutual influences between the women's movement and official world organizations have intensified.

Human Rights and Women's Rights

What made it possible for women's issues to come to the fore as never before was the emergence of human rights as a global cultural complex. The UN Charter was not only the preeminent statement of the doctrine of human rights; it was also the first international instrument containing a wide-ranging sex-equality provision as part of that doctrine. A group of feminists working with the Inter-American Commission on the Status of Women (established in 1928) was largely responsible for the provision's inclusion in the Charter; this same group also sparked the establishment of the UN Commission on the Status of Women, first as a Sub-Commission of the Human Rights Commission, then (in 1946) as one of the six full-status commissions of the Economic and Social Council. At least until the 1970s, the Commission was the central policymaking body in the UN for all questions regarding women (Reanda 1992), and it prompted the ILO to develop an equal-pay policy.

As I show below, the hesitancy of the ILO to deal with women's employment rights in the interwar period yielded, following World War II, to a much more activist and decisive approach. In a series of major documents capped by two international conventions, the ILO made the principle of equality between men and women a major plank in its global platform. The split over this issue, which had caused much rancor within the women's movement earlier, disappeared. Both socialists and trade-unionists, as well as professional and bourgeois organizations, joined forces in the campaign and initiated various organizational activities, such as setting up committees of experts to gather information and produce position papers (ILC 1944, 1947; Lubin and Winslow 1990: 60–61).

The quest for world equal-pay policies began in earnest in the second (1948) session of the UN Commission on the Status of Women, which adopted a series of resolutions regarding women's rights and urged the Economic and Social Council to take "urgent action" on the issue of equal pay (UN *Yearbook* 1947–48). Meanwhile, the women's section of the World Federation of Trade Unions proposed as an item on ECOSOC's agenda the "question of the principle of equal pay for equal work for men and women workers." Four women's organizations (the Co-Operative Women's Guild, the Women's International Democratic Federation, the Liaison Committee of Women's International Organizations, and the Women's International League for Peace and Freedom) prepared and submitted statements that accompanied the proposal.

As a result, in 1951 the ILO adopted the Equal Remuneration Convention (ILC 1951), the first multilateral treaty that both focused exclusively on women's rights and directed states to take positive action to equalize the status of women and men. Previous international documents that addressed the principle of equality specified "sex" among other criteria without explicitly discussing gender equality, while earlier documents that focused on gender equality were mainly expressive declarations of principles.

Six years later a much more comprehensive convention was adopted, the 1958 Employment (Discrimination) Convention (ILC 1958). By 1991, the 1951 and 1958 conventions had been ratified by 112 and 110 countries respectively, making them two of the most broadly ratified ILO conventions (ILC 1992). These activities, initiated in the previous era by global women's organizations and endorsed in the postwar era by intergovernmental bodies, have been the driving force, in large degree, behind the adoption by states of the principle of equality in national employment legislation (Berkovitch forthcoming).

Development Ideology

During the 1970s, the discourse of women's rights encountered that of development. This encounter was the result of the most significant event in global organizing on women's issues: the United Nation's Decade for Women (1976–1985). The Women's Decade coincided with the Second United Nations Development Decade, during which development started to dominate global discourse and activity (see Chapter 9). The two events melded into each other in the sense that a core dimension for grappling with women's issues became the concern for "incorporating women into development"; women's issues came to the fore in many development documents and projects. Framing women's issues in the context of development brought about qualitative and quantitative changes on both national and international fronts.

It led to an intensification of world activity on women's issues that in turn had an enormous impact on nation-states, while it stimulated the establishment of women's movements in many countries (see, for example, the special [1985] issue of *Women's Studies International Forum*) and led most governments in the world to create an official state agency for the promotion of women's issues (Stetson and Mazur 1995). Women's issues became a state concern.

Before discussing these interrelated developments, I should note that the catalyst for the Decade for Women is believed to have been a women's organization, not any of the UN bodies. Hilkka Pietila, who was herself involved in some of the activities she documents, refers to "an oral tradition in the UN family" that identifies the Women's International Democratic Federation (WIDF) as the source of the proposal for an International Women's Year (Pietila and Vickers 1990). As observers on the UN Commission on the Status of Women, the WIDF's president and a number of other WINGO leaders drafted a proposal that the Commission recommended to the General Assembly. Despite initial resistance, the Assembly eventually endorsed the idea in 1972, proclaiming 1975 as International Women's Year (IWY) with the themes of equality, development, and peace (also in Whittick 1979).

In 1975 the World Conference of the International Women's Year was held in Mexico City. One hundred and thirty-three states participated, endorsing two major documents: the "Declaration of Mexico on the Equality of Women and Their Contribution to Development and Peace" and the "World Plan of Action for the Implementation of the Objectives of IWY." The conference designated the 1976–1985 period as the UN Decade for Women. Representatives from 145 countries attended the 1980 Mid-Decade Conference in Copenhagen, convened as a "mid-point review of progress and obstacles in achieving the goals of the Decade," and adopted a Programme of Action. The end of the Decade was marked by the 1985 World Conference to Review and Appraise the Achievements of the UN Decade for Women, held in Nairobi. Drawing representatives from 157 countries, the conference adopted a document titled "The Nairobi Forward-Looking Strategies for the Advancement of Women" (UN *Yearbook*, 1975, 1976, 1980, 1981).

As mentioned before, it was during the Women's Decade that the status of women was linked to the development of their countries. As a result, both the form and content of global organizing has changed. Official bodies and the international women's movement shifted their focus from legal standards and international law to concrete projects, further organizational expansion, greater research efforts, and network enhancement to coordinate these numerous endeavors (Ashworth 1982; Pietila and Vickers 1990; Reanda 1992).

Within the new framework, elevating women's status and achieving equality between the sexes were conceptualized as necessary conditions for full national—economic and social—development. Women were now considered important human resources essential to comprehensive rationalization. Eradicating discrimination was an integral part of the global plan to improve the well-being of national societies and of the world as a whole (Berkovitch 1995). "Human rights" as a leading concept lost its prominence, though it did not disappear. Thus, for example, the sweepingly broad Convention for the Elimination of All Forms of Discrimination Against Women (adopted by the General Assembly in 1979) incorporates, side by side, the principles of abstract social justice and a more "instrumental" principle of development. In 1982, a commission under the same name was established to monitor the Convention's implementation (Jacobson 1992). By 1990, this convention had been ratified by 101 countries, one of the highest rates of ratification of any UN convention.

Prior to the Decade, most official activity regarding women took place within the United Nations Commission on the Status of Women, which had adopted an "equality" and "human rights" orientation. During the Decade, under the influence of the "development" sector, women's issues diffused throughout the UN system. New, autonomous UN organizations appeared, including the UN Development Fund for Women (1976) and the International Research and Training Institute for the Advancement of Women (1979). Many of the UN regional economic commissions established units for "women in development." Various UN specialized agencies, such as the Environment Programme and Population Fund, incorporated the "women's component" into their documents, projects, and organizational structures (UN *Yearbook* 1985). By 1990 there were about 70 designated units ("focal points") for women's issues within the UN system (Pietila and Vickers 1990). Decade for Women activities were not restricted to UN-affiliated bodies; other IGOs mobilized as well. For example, the Organization of African Unity and the EEC endorsed the International Women's Year and initiated action in the prescribed direction (Taubenfeld and Taubenfeld 1983). These examples could be multiplied manyfold.

WINGO Proliferation and Complexity

At the same time, the organizational base of the international women's movement has expanded and diversified its activities. WINGOs of many kinds grew rapidly in number. This growth was part of the general increase in INGOs, but its specific pattern was shaped largely by specific events that pertain to women. Figure 4.1, contrasting the frequency of founding of all nongovernmental organizations with that of women's organizations since 1875, reveals that, until the 1950s, the pattern of WINGO founding was similar to that of all INGOs: gradual growth but sharp declines during the wars, with rapid recovery in the interwar period and after World War II. However, WINGO founding declined during the 1950s and 1960s while INGO founding exploded. Only in the 1970s did WINGO founding take off, with the major turning point occurring in 1975. More than a third of all WINGOs were formed during the Decade for Women.[4] Hence, it was not until women's issues became prominent on the "official" world agenda, specifically via UN-initiated activities centered around the three World Conferences for Women, that the WINGO curve accelerated to match the general increase in INGOs. It was also during the 1970s that the first women's organizations for development were founded and veteran organizations added "development" to their mission statements.

Deborah Stienstra (1994) analyzes the type of organizations that were founded during the decade and finds that a new type of women's international organizations emerged: a more feminist, grassroots organization that was more of a network than a formal "organization." This type has no members in the conventional sense and lacks a bureaucratic infrastructure. Many of these new organizations drew their main constituency from Third World countries and formed an integral part of the development sector.

Some of the new women's organizations were formed by UN agencies, such as the Women's Feature Service founded during the 1975 conference by UNESCO and UNFPA. But the majority were motivated by or established in conjunction with the INGO world conferences that took place parallel to the official UN events. I can mention, for example, the International Women's Tribune Center, founded in Mexico City in 1976; the Arab Women Feature Service founded in 1980; and International Women's Rights Watch, founded in Nairobi in 1985. These meetings indeed inspired much of the growth and changing agenda of the international women's movement.

The NGO conferences were organized and attended by representatives of women's groups from all over the world: 4,000 participants at the 1975 IWY Tribune in Mexico City, 7,000 at the 1980 NGO Forum in Copenhagen, a remarkable 14,000 at the 1985 Non-Governmental World Conference of Women, Forum '85, in Nairobi. The NGO conferences conducted workshops, discussion groups, lectures, and informal gatherings, bringing national and international women's groups together to make connections, initiate joint projects, and exchange ideas, in addition to forming new organizations (Pietila and Vickers 1990; *For the Record, Forum '85* 1985).

While the NGO conferences were extraordinarily rich and complex (Ashworth 1982; Basch and Lerner 1986; Eisler and Loye 1985; Cagatay, Grown, and Santiago 1986; Tinker and Jacquette 1987; Papanek 1975; Bunch 1987), two of their most important consequences can be stated simply: they fostered a sense of "global sisterhood" (as mentioned in many of the accounts), while they also provided an arena in which different groups (re-)discovered the wide gaps separating them. "Global sisterhood" became a widely shared identity, but the meaning and implications of this identity were constantly contested. Women from all parts of the globe, including many from Third World countries, took part as responsibly authorized world citizens, but this very inclusiveness produced arenas of disagreement.

The presence of women from the Third World brought to the forefront issues that were new to the Western feminist agenda and lexicon. At the 1975 (Mexico) and 1980 (Copenhagen) conferences, battle lines were drawn between First and Third World feminists over what constituted a feminist issue and what were legitimate feminist foci and goals. The Mid-Decade Meeting in Copenhagen was the most conflict-riddled, with Western women pillorying clitoridectomy and similar practices as violations of human rights while women from Africa and the Middle East, where these practices are common, resisted this characterization and the uses made of it. "Third World women felt that as First World women promoted the issue, it seemed to establish a hierarchical relationship to their Third World sisters through intellectual neocolonialism" (Gilliam 1991: 218; see also Giorgis 1981 and Brennan 1989). Other dividing issues were apartheid and Zionism. Women from the developing countries argued that the oppression that resulted from these two regimes was an integral part of oppressive sexism. First World women denounced this argument as a "politicization" of women's issues and preferred to focus on what they defined as women's issues alone.

The issue of development, as much as it sparked new organizing and thickened the women's movement, also added another line of controversy and deepened the North/South divide. Beginning with the Decade, and intensifying during the 1980s, feminist scholars from the South started challenging the ways in which development has been defined and practiced by Western scholars and experts and by the international aid agencies. This critique was interwoven with a strong criticism of Western-style feminism that portrayed Western feminists as the saviors of Third World women, who were seen as passive victims of their circumstances (e.g., Marchand and Parpart 1995;

Sen and Grown 1987). This new approach resulted in new organizations (AAWORD and DAWN) and a new type of scholarship, written for and from the perspective of the women of the South.

Learning the lesson from the previous conferences, the 1985 Nairobi Conference was less conflictual and more cooperative in spirit and in action. First, women of color from the North and women from the Third World were much more visible than previously. Second, the agenda broadened to include issues that concerned women from the South alongside more traditional Western feminist issues (see various articles in *Signs*, 1986, no. 11). Still, the new form of cooperation did not assume any notion of universality, nor did it erase old divisions and controversies. Rather, this new type of feminism that emerged during the 1980s—"postcolonial feminism"—assumes "difference" but aims at fostering different forms of coalitions among the various groups of women (Mohanty 1991; Johnson-Odim 1991). Coalition-building became the new focus of much of the international women's movement. The NGO Forum of 1985 Conference was one of the main triggers for this shift, while it also provided a prime arena for its realization. Thus, these world gatherings helped shape the women's movement, mapping its internal conflicts and setting the parameters for divergence and controversy within a framework of shared value commitments.

SUMMARY

The story of "united womanhood" must be understood within the larger framework of the changing world polity. The existence of the international women's movement as such, its huge conferences, its plethora of documents and resolutions, and its ubiquitous lobbying visibly enact the concept of transnationalism and thus boost our tendency to see the world as a single global social system. As Roland Robertson (1992: 107) notes: "Indeed this is one among many movements and organizations which have helped to compress the world as a whole." Thus, the international women's movement did not only reflect world culture but also helped shape its content and structure.

What started in earlier periods as moral crusades led by women's groups eventually culminated in highly legitimized and rationalized actions enacted by official world bodies on behalf of women. Around the turn of the century, the women's movement, being part of the transnational reform movement, reflected and reinforced the emphasis on moral reform and universalism. However, these early groups also promoted elements of equality, rights, and suffrage. One way of resolving the tension between the notions of individual rights and moral regeneration was subsuming the former in the latter. The international women's movement promoted women's rights as a necessary condition for enacting and bringing about desired changes in society. However, in the early period there were no world bodies to act on behalf of women.

With the establishment of the ILO as a global organization with the mandate to set international standards, the women's movement found a central target for its advocacy of the principle of equality alongside the principle of "protection," with growing tension between the two principles. The League of Nations also helped shaped the mode of action and agenda of the women's groups when it became the focus for their lobbying efforts for and against an international equal rights treaty. However, it was only after World War II, when world-level organizing intensified and a more authoritative world center was established, that the principle of equality began to guide world activities regarding women. The changing agenda of the ILO regarding women's employment is striking. The sole focus on protective legislation was widened to include binding standards on equality in employment. Nation-states joined the campaign, and the majority of them revised their national labor codes to be consistent with the new spirit of women's rights.

In the 1970s another layer was added: an instrumental discourse of development that brought with it further rationalizing and organizing of world activities on women's issues. The encounter between the two discourses shaped much of the activity and spirit of the UN Decade for Women (1976–1985). The international women's movement began to operate in a much more complicated environment, with more options but also more constraints. Thanks to the initiatives of women's organizations, regular world women's conferences were held both during the Decade and after, the latest in Beijing in 1995.

The three UN conferences indicate a great deal about the worldwide construction of women's issues. First, official world organizing and activities regarding women's issues have expanded tremendously in comparison with previous periods. Second, the effects are not limited to the international level. Nation-states put "women" on their agenda, altering existing laws and establishing official bureaus and departments to deal with women's issues. Third, world-cultural ideas about women have penetrated developing countries as well, leading to the emergence of women's movements in almost every country in the world.

All the while, the international women's movement has expanded in size and transformed in content and composition. It became truly global as it grew to incorporate women from the Third World, with their specific concerns and perspectives. This process, however, was not unproblematic. Rather, it was accompanied by rising tension between women from the South and women from the North. This shows that, in contrast to conventionally held wisdom, transnational movements in general and the women's movement in particular cannot be reduced to the interests of one hegemonic region. National and regional factors can affect international organizing agenda, but, as I have shown all through this chapter, the wider context affects, to large degree, the legitimacy and effectiveness of international organizing (see also Barrett 1995b). Once international organizing emerges and gains a degree of legitimacy and operational capacity, however, new organizational dynamics are set in motion that reshape the wider context itself.

Women everywhere have been integrated into the ongoing global campaign. The international women's movement has emerged as a visible and viable global force. The overarching result is, indeed, a reconceptualization of feminism as

> a movement of people working for change across and despite national
> boundaries, not of representatives of nation states or national govern-
> ments . . . we must be global, recognising that the oppression of women
> in one part of the world is often affected by what happens in another, and
> that no woman is free until the conditions of oppression of women are
> eliminated everywhere. (Bunch 1987: 301)

Chapter Five Constructing a Global Identity:
The Role of Esperanto

YOUNG S. KIM

Despite much recent talk of global society and world culture, the cultural formation of globally embedded identities has received little scholarly attention.
Social scientists have treated global identities primarily as natural byproducts
of postwar socioeconomic development (Croce 1993; Hannerz and Löfgren
1994; Peterson 1993; Wallerstein 1990), and most studies have focused on
the impact of global interdependency on national identities. In this chapter I
examine efforts to build a global identity as an intentional process of cultural
construction involving individuals acting autonomously to create a medium
for world citizenship: the planned universal language of Esperanto.[1]

Individual initiative to create planned languages for global use was the
earliest form of self-conscious organized effort to construct a global identity.
These early movements hoped to fashion one human society by linking all
individuals across different societies, thereby transcending nation-states.
Their ideology reflected what one could describe as a unitary-humanity
model, or one-worldism. Esperanto was the most successful of these movements, though it obviously never became the dominant language of communication between speakers of disparate tongues (a distinction assumed by
English, especially as the language of business), and it never accounted for a
large portion of the population of international nongovernmental organizations (INGOs). Many international organizations rhetorically activated the
unitary-humanity model that the Esperanto movement had helped crystallize, but rapid differentiation of the INGO population produced mostly specialized, technical, and practically oriented bodies for whom pure global-

identity formation was secondary at best. Moreover, because the nation-state prevailed as the primary world actor, national identity proved to be more durable than early enthusiasts of Esperanto imagined, and the task of building a global community of commonly tongued individuals proved more daunting than they had hoped.

Recently, however, globalization processes and discourse have begun to downplay the centrality of the nation-state in some respects, thereby encouraging more diffuse cultural movements and organizational elaboration. This trend, though still modest, has given new life to one-worldism based on direct individual efforts at global cultural integration.

As this overview indicates, globalization processes and the emergence of global society should not be regarded as constituting a monotonic or singular historical transformation. Global identity formation is only partly a consequence of growing webs of international interaction; it is also a cultural product based on intentionally mobilizing interaction and organization, and the success of such mobilization has varied over time. The pattern of early growth, relative decline, and modest new growth of the Esperanto movement raises several questions that I address in this chapter: What global conditions accelerate or hinder the construction of a global identity fashioned through a planned universal language? How do changes in the transnational environment affect autonomous efforts by individuals to construct a new identity of global reach?

Esperanto INGOs embody direct individualized action in line with a unitary-humanity model, as distinct from the more instrumentally rational, scientized, and technical action of most other INGOs. Given that the Esperanto movement has been an active and purposeful effort to construct and spread the notion of global society and global identity, in my analysis I take into account the interactive effects between these two realms of world discourse and organization—the Esperanto movement and all other INGOs.

GLOBAL SOCIETY AND GLOBAL IDENTITY

Figure 5.1 presents the pattern of foundings of Esperanto INGOs from 1905 to 1984, along with the density of this sector (the number of organizations active at any given time). Note the flurry of Esperanto activity at the beginning of the century and the paucity of foundings thereafter. The slow founding rate between 1915 and 1955 yielded a slowly growing population of INGOs, but a more vigorous growth rate emerged in the last two decades, particularly in the 1970s.[2] The central issue to be addressed, then, is the

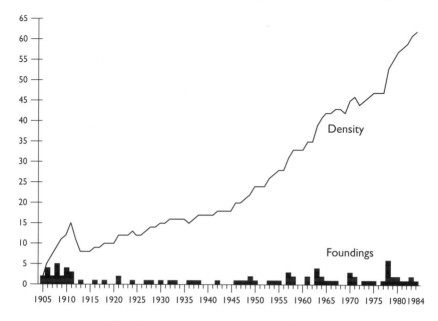

FIGURE 5.1.   Foundings and density of Esperanto INGOs, 1905–1984.
Density is the number of organizations active in each year.

problem of explaining the rising and falling rates of Esperanto INGO foundings over time. Why did these bodies first appear, and why have they appeared in greater numbers in some periods than in others?

Evolution of Global Society

Unlike recent globalization activity, early global conceptualization occurred
in the absence of an institutionalized organizational frame. It began with the
classical Greek notion of cosmopolitanism, a form of cultural idealism
seeking to transcend the constraints of traditional locales, and reappeared in
various guises throughout Western history. Abstractly conceived cultural fusion was the projected vision, but this vision was largely disconnected from
mechanisms of institutionalized rules or organizational structure (Sorokin
1957; Spengler 1932; Melko 1995; Bainbridge 1985; Carden 1969; Parsons
1964).

From the mid-nineteenth century on, however, global or one-world efforts turned to more structured forms, among them the cognitive orientation
that underlay planned languages like Esperanto. Rather than imagining a fic-

tive community that surpassed national boundaries, cosmopolitans envisioned that a common language would promote global citizenship by offering a means of acquiring and heightening individual attachment to world society and preventing problems caused by miscommunication in translations between languages. The notion of global community was concretized by bringing together social actors in distant areas who belonged to different societies. Integration, both geographically and culturally, would be achieved on the basis of a shared global identity.

Cultural integration of this abstract, generalized form was seriously challenged by two factors: the emergence of more differentiated, specialized, and functionally oriented global organizations, and the expansion of states as the loci of responsibility for societal management. Most of the proliferating INGO population in the twentieth century consists of organizations pursuing specific rationalized goals of rather narrow scope. They focus on practical, often highly technical issues related to well-defined problems, rather than the much vaguer goals of world harmony and cooperation that motivate Esperanto organizations (Chapter 1). While these goals are usually linked rhetorically to one-worldism and global peace, the latter concerns clearly take a back seat to functional specificity. Hence, one-worldism has lost some of its legitimacy because of its abstract comprehensiveness, even though the general expansion of INGOs legitimates global organizing in general and expands its resource base. Figure 5.1 shows a decline in foundings of Esperanto organizations after 1911, an indication that this direct form of transcendent cultural organizing was no longer so attractive. More rationalized forms had begun to dominate the process.

At the same time, state responsibilities and capacities with respect to society were on the rise (Boli 1987b). At the global level, the centrality of the state was institutionalized in the League of Nations, United Nations, and other IGOs that emphasize collective state action to manage transnational issue areas (Gilpin 1987; Skocpol 1985; Tilly 1985). The centrality of the state, even while nongovernmental organization was accelerating rapidly, meant that globalization as a purely cultural matter, disconnected from state authority and action, also lost some of its legitimacy (Evans 1995; Held 1989). Moreover, state expansion reinforced the close link between nation and culture, making national languages both more uniform and more intensely reified. All this meant that the organizational growth of Esperanto and other planned languages declined relative to the INGO population.

In recent decades, another shift has occurred: to some extent, discourse and theorizing about world society has moved away from the nation-state as the dominant global actor in favor of a revitalized unitary-humanity or one-world model. We see this shift in such areas as human or women's rights (Chapter 4 in this volume; Boli 1987a; James 1994), world sociopolitical regimes and governance structures (Held 1991; Krasner 1983a; Murphy 1994), and environmentalism (see Chapter 3), where global structures have begun to loosen the strong grip of national states on their associated societies. Consequently, Esperanto movements have enjoyed a period of resurgence (Figure 5.1). In addition, the differentiation of INGOs has led to parallel differentiation among Esperanto organizations, so their one-worldism is now wrapped around more specific and rationalized endeavors.

In sum, Esperanto and similar movements elaborated a form of one-worldism that more specialized technical INGOs continue to activate in a secondary way, while the growth of these rationalized INGOs has provided organizational forms and social spaces advantageous to Esperanto groups. Partly complementary, these two types of INGOs are also locked in tension because specialized INGOs support a world cultural environment in which rationalized and differentiated means/ends logics sit uncomfortably with the unmediated individualistic one-worldism of Esperanto.

Formation of Global Identity

Individuals can build identities as members of ethnic, religious, or other types of groups that have common characteristics and myths (Meyer and Rowan 1977; Razak 1995; Van de Veer 1994). They can also consciously construct identities to be shared and recognized by members of disparate groups that lack a common heritage. Modern societies are based on complex multidirectional interactions, and different types of identities are constructed through different types and levels of interaction (Alund 1991; Rogers and Kochunny 1994). A global identity is one among many identities available to individuals because global action and interaction facilitate the formation of identities that comprehend humanity as a whole (Butora and Butorova 1993; Hannerz 1992; Mongardini 1988; Robbins 1992). The solidarity involved can assume global dimensions without relying on common physical characteristics or history (Blanc, Basch, and Schiller 1995; Friedman 1992), or such commonalities can be constructed by creative interpretation of disparate lines of historical development.

Similarly, the global cultural frame in which global identities are embedded does not require a universally shared set of values and physical traits distinct from those of national cultures. Global culture and identity need not, and usually do not, replace national cultures and identities. The global cultural and institutional framework also legitimates nations and national identities as inherent elements of world society (Meyer, Boli et al. 1997), even though much of the ideology behind global identities sees national identity as problematic for the solution of many human problems. What makes global identity possible and likely is the presence of this global institutional framework, which is evident in a wide array of social activities. In education (Huefner, Naumann, and Meyer 1987; Meyer et al. 1992; Ramirez and Boli 1987a), human rights doctrines (James 1994; Kaganas and Murray 1994), welfare programs (Chang and Strang 1990; Thomas and Lauderdale 1987), ministerial structures (Jang 1995; Kim 1995), and many other areas (including those studied in other chapters in this volume), globally institutionalized processes provide foundations upon which global identities can be built.

Hence, though national variations in culture, language, and historical experience are considerable, in many dimensions the institutional elements that construct social life are the same almost everywhere. The primary action entities are individuals, organizations, and states; basic mechanisms for pursuing progress include development strategies, school systems, and science; basic purposes include economic development, personal achievement, and so on. In the same way that world society can be conceptualized as a set of institutionalized organizations (Chase-Dunn 1989; Wallerstein 1974), global culture constitutes an institutional environment for the units of world society (Meyer and Rowan 1977; Ramirez 1987; Thomas and Meyer 1984). Global culture is expressed in many different institutional forms that do not rely on a homogeneous physical frame (Lévi-Strauss 1966; Meyer, Boli, and Thomas 1987) but nevertheless provide fertile soil for the growth of all-encompassing identities.

Attempts to create a planned international language are a prominent example of modern efforts to establish a global identity. Consider the corresponding development of national languages. One of the more powerful driving stimuli for modern nationalism was the adoption of the vernacular for administrative purposes in European states (Anderson 1983; Hobsbawm 1990; Wallerstein 1974). In conjunction with the spread of printing, this change created a unified field of exchange and communication. Citizens of a given state gradually became aware of the many people in their language group and saw themselves as part of an imagined national community based in part on their distinctive but shared language (Anderson 1983; Wuthnow 1989).

Planned languages for international communication were intended to operate similarly, mobilizing diverse segments of international society to act in unity, transcending political and cultural boundaries. The artificiality of the process does not distinguish it from national-identity formation, though global interaction is clearly less intensive than interaction at the national level.[3] The deliberate construction of national languages was often driven by states, but at the world level such a mechanism has not been available. Esperanto INGOs were therefore the result not of state action but of the dedicated efforts of individuals deliberately bypassing states. From its inception, the Esperanto movement was embedded in a cultural arena that both championed the state and had begun to question the wisdom of state domination, and Esperanto INGOs came down on the side of global rather than national identity formation.

GLOBAL IDENTITY AND ESPERANTO

Birth and Initial Growth of Esperanto

While nothing is known for certain about when the first planned language appeared, since the seventeenth century several hundred artificial languages have been created (Large 1985). The first prominent effort was "Volapük," invented in 1880 by Johann Martin Schleyer, a Catholic priest. Schleyer's rationale and motivation for creating the language were not markedly different from those of other internationally minded individuals of the time. He strongly believed that the scientific and technological development of the nineteenth century had created a need for a verbal tool that would unite people with different linguistic origins, thereby avoiding conflicts caused by miscommunication.

> Thanks to railways, steamships, telegraph and telephone, the world has shrunk in time and space. The countries of the world are in effect drawing closer to one another. Thus the time for small-minded and fainthearted chauvinism is forever over. Humankind becomes daily more cosmopolitan and increasingly yearns for unity. The amazing universal postal system is an important step toward this splendid goal. With respect also to money, weights and measures, time zones, laws and language the brothers and sisters of the human race should move toward unity. (Quoted in Janton 1993: 13)

Despite some grammatical difficulties and its extended alphabet of thirty-eight letters, Volapük rapidly became popular within the European middle

TABLE 5.1

Growth in the Esperanto Movement, 1890–1918

Number of:	1890	1895	1900	1905	1909	1914	1918
Local clubs	3	8	26	308	1,447	1,800	1,200
Journals	1	1	3	36	91	118	35
Books published	28	88	123	211	133	2,700	2,900

SOURCE: Large 1985: 85.

class, especially among intellectuals. Ten years after its introduction, some twenty-five periodicals were being published regularly and roughly three hundred Volapük societies (local organizations) had formed. At the same time, textbooks teaching Volapük appeared in twenty-five different languages (Janton 1993). Because of Schleyer's extreme intolerance toward suggestions for improvement, however, Volapük did not develop further, and schisms eventually wrecked the movement.[4]

The impressive success of Volapük, especially during its earlier stage, inspired a young Polish doctor named Lazar Ludwik Zamenhof to publish a booklet in Russian in 1887 about his own planned language, Esperanto. From this beginning, seven years after the birth of Volapük, Esperanto grew rapidly and received widespread positive reactions, which encouraged Zamenhof to continue his work energetically (see Table 5.1). Two years after his initial book, Zamenhof published *Dua libro de l'Lingvo Internacia* (*Second Book of the International Language*) and the first Esperanto magazine, *La Esperantisto*. *La Esperantisto* was a great success and was followed by other periodicals that further increased the popularity of Esperanto. Another cornerstone of Esperanto's success was the Esperanto dictionary, the first edition of which appeared in 1894 with translations for five major European languages. In 1903, an anthology brought together previously published articles, lectures, stories, poetry, and prose in both original and translated form. In 1905, a more complete version of the sixteen-rule Esperanto grammar was published, along with a revised edition of the 1894 dictionary (Janton 1993).

Enlivened by their initial successes, Esperantists worked diligently to spread the new language to distant lands. In 1905, the first World Congress of Esperanto brought together local Esperanto groups from twenty different countries, more than six hundred participants in all, to celebrate the popu-

TABLE 5.2
Esperantists in Non-European Countries in 1928

Country	Number of Esperantists
Japan	6,903
United States	4,845
Brazil	1,182
Australia	1,087
Argentina	445
Uruguay	416
China	393
New Zealand	324
Palestine	252
Cuba	207
Other	5,621
Non-European total	21,675
European total	109,680

SOURCE: Forster 1982: 24.

larity of Esperanto. The World Congress of Esperanto became an annual event, and the number of participants grew each year. In 1914, a total of 3,739 participants registered for the Paris Congress, although it was canceled because of the outbreak of the war. The Congress resumed in 1920 and continued annually until 1940, resuming again in 1946 after World War II had ended.

The Esperanto movement during the early period was not limited to Europe. Although the majority of early Esperantists were Europeans, the language also gained great popularity on other continents. As Table 5.2 shows, a significant portion of world Esperantists were non-European, with high concentrations in Japan, the United States, Brazil, and Australia.

Esperanto was not created as a substitute for local languages; rather, "it exists to serve as an additional second language for the purposes of international communication" (UEA 1981a: 1). From its inception, its advocates promoted Esperanto as a tool for achieving peace and harmony in international society. Zamenhof inspired the movement with a particular kind of idealism, emphasizing the progressive and evolutionary potential contained within an international language simply by virtue of its internationality. He presented Esperanto as a new and important factor necessary for transformation of the social order to create a better world, and he called for cooperation in the struggle to bring this about. He argued that knowledge and usage of Esperanto would raise the social consciousness of individuals and groups and bring them together on the basis of their common humanity. Thus, Esperanto addressed eminent aspirations of the human race and sought to mobilize these aspirations. At the same time, it offered concrete rewards in the sense that those who learned the language and participated in its congresses could feel that they were contributing to human progress toward peace and harmony. In sum, the language motivated individuals to take action with respect to far-reaching concerns regarding international relations and world development (Janton 1993).

During the first and the second World Congresses, Zamenhof preached this ideology vigorously. Esperanto soon came to be recognized for its ideological underpinnings and potential usefulness, and these qualities are evident in contemporary Esperantism as well. Currently, a prominent goal of the Esperanto movement is to include Esperanto as an official language used by both governmental and nongovernmental international organizations (UEA 1979).

International Esperanto Organizations and the Universal Esperanto Association

Foundings of international organizations intended to promote the use of Esperanto (Figure 5.1) are a major indicator of the growth of the Esperanto movement and mark its development as a formally structured part of world culture. Of course, the logic of Esperanto's genesis made most of the official activities of Esperantists decidedly international from the very beginning. However, it was not until nearly two decades after the initial introduction of the language that the first formal international organization was founded. Zamenhof initially insisted on controlling the movement rigidly, especially in linguistic matters, so he resisted the establishment of a formal organization that would act as a ruling body. Nevertheless, the use of Esperanto eventually escaped Zamenhof's control, and so too did the movement. Thus, only in 1905 did the first Esperanto INGO, Akademio (the Academy), appear, formed during the first World Congress.

The Academy was more of a "Language Committee" in its functions and characteristics than a conventional INGO that governs and provides guidelines for various official activities. Three years later, the first conventional Esperanto INGO, the Universal Esperanto Association (UEA, *Universala Esperanto-Asocio*), was founded. With Zamenhof's support, the UEA was quite successful in gaining recognition from local Esperanto groups. It began with eleven local groups that elected delegates to the UEA; participation by other local organizations grew significantly faster than anyone had anticipated. The UEA still acts as an umbrella organization that provides guidelines for the contemporary Esperanto movement, and all currently active Esperanto INGOs are collective members of the UEA.

Because they focused heavily on international issues such as global peace and brotherhood, early Esperanto INGOs generally had broad missions, trying to deal with a variety of issues using Esperanto. Later, however, Esperanto INGOs became more specialized, emerging in many different social arenas (among them chess-players, photographers, radio amateurs, mathematicians, and bicyclists; see note 2). These twin lines of development can be understood as outcomes of two different logics. Because the idea of a unitary human society, which was so central to the early Esperanto movement, was adopted by other international organizations and became a prominent INGO model, the Esperanto movement could piggyback on the proliferation of such organizations. At the same time, however, INGOs began to appear in new social arenas with ever increasing frequency, and Esperantists were stimulated to organize in many of these new sectors as well.

Despite the specialization of Esperanto INGOs, the basic aims and goals of these organizations have remained consistent over time. The goals of the UEA, approved by the World Congress in 1908, were as follows:

(a) The goal of the Association is the facilitation of relations of all kinds between speakers of different languages and the creation of a strong link of solidarity between the members.

(b) UEA is neutral in relation to religion, politics, and nationality.

(c) The sole official language is Esperanto, such as it is defined by its literary and scientific vocabulary.

(d) The members are individuals, *i.e.*, a member joins the Association directly, and not through his local group or national society.

(e) In places where this is possible, one of the members is a delegate (his address appears in the Yearbook) and he voluntarily fulfills various practical services for the members who turn to him. (Forster 1982: 155)

Compare these with the present aims of the UEA, which are similar to all other contemporary Esperanto INGOs.

The aims of the UEA are:

(a) to spread the use of the International Language Esperanto;

(b) to take action to solve the language problem in international relations and to facilitate international communication;

(c) to facilitate every kind of spiritual and material relationship among people, despite differences of nationality, race, sex, religion, politics or language;

(d) to cultivate among its members a strong feeling of solidarity, and to develop in them understanding and esteem for other people. (UEA 1981b: 5)

Descriptions of early Esperanto INGOs indicate that the movement initially gained support more from professional groups than from the general public. For example, many early organizations, such as the International Esperantist Scientific Association (1906), the Esperantists Association of Doctors (1906), and the World Association of Esperantist Teachers (1908), were based in a professional field. Since World War II the Esperanto movement has diffused into more diverse sectors. The International League of Homosexual Esperantists (1977), the Esperantist Go League International (1979), and the International Association of Handicapped Esperantists (1983) exemplify this diversity.

QUANTITATIVE ANALYSIS

Hypothesis Framework

By studying the founding process of Esperanto INGOs, we can identify factors that affected the formation of this type of global identity construction. On the one hand, because Esperanto INGOs are a subset of the larger INGO population, they should reveal a founding pattern similar to that of the entire population. On the other hand, because of early Esperanto INGOs' extreme and explicit form of one-worldism that was much less technical and rationalized than the purposes adopted by most other organizations, a tension between Esperanto INGOs and the larger population can be expected. My quantitative modeling will thus focus in part on delineating the pattern of foundings of Esperanto INGOs and showing how this pattern is related to the foundings of other INGOs.

In line with established methods in the study of organizational foundings (Hannan and Freeman 1989), the unit of analysis in this study is not the individual organization but the population of organizations—the entire set of Esperanto INGOs. Correlatively, the properties of the external environment in which the population is embedded are of central importance. The population of international organizations exists and operates at the global level, so we need information at the same level to evaluate its development. I therefore will use indicators that represent various characteristics of the world society in which the Esperanto INGO population is embedded.

Globally institutionalized discourse concerning Esperantism and the Esperanto movement is an important feature of the environment that we can use to explain the foundings of Esperanto INGOs. When Esperanto INGOs and the notion of global identity were relatively new and unfamiliar to world society, it was difficult for Esperantists to mobilize the necessary personnel and resources to found additional Esperanto INGOs. However, as more Esperanto INGOs were founded and their activities received greater recognition in world society, it became easier to mobilize resources. The increasing intensity of institutionalized discourse regarding Esperantism and Esperanto INGOs can be measured by the number of all active Esperanto INGOs (the population density) in each year. The increasing density of Esperanto INGOs is thus expected to have a positive effect on the founding rate of new Esperanto INGOs.

Note that I predict a positive relationship between density and the founding rate of Esperanto INGOs throughout the entire period of analysis (1905–80). This prediction differs from what most organizational ecologists claim regarding organizational founding processes (Freeman and Hannan 1983; McPherson, Popielarz, and Drobnic 1992; Ranger-Moore, Banaszak-Holl, and Hannan 1991). According to conventional arguments, the founding rate of new organizations has a positive effect only during the beginning of the population's life cycle, owing to the increasing social legitimacy of new organizational forms. Once legitimacy has been established, organizational density begins to affect new organizational foundings negatively. This reversal reflects increasing competition among organizations within the common niche in which the necessary but limited resources on which they depend are located. During the process of forming organizations, therefore, the life of each organization is strongly influenced by three important factors: available niche width in the situated community, possible competition among similar organizations in the population, and the number of other active organizations in the population.

As Charles Perrow (1979) notes, however, it is not clear that we can apply the same notion of competition to all organizational populations. In the Esperanto case, niche capacity may not be particularly limiting if the boundary of the surrounding niche is for practical purposes not finite. In this situation, social carrying capacities are large enough to remain unfilled for long periods of time and may even expand along with the growth of the organizational population. One can argue that world society has a much wider carrying capacity than that of a single national society and that, at least for the period under consideration, its limits have not been approached. In other words, international society has many resources that can be discovered and used by various mobilizing movements. This multiplicity of resources prevents severe competition among actors, especially when the activities of these movements are not motivated primarily by financial interests. At the same time, if an available niche can be expanded in a short period of time, competition among organizations within the population will be less intense than where a fixed niche width prevails. Consequently, in world society the growth-favoring legitimation effect may well overwhelm growth-inhibiting competition effects. This reasoning leads to my first hypothesis:

> 1. The number of active Esperanto INGOs positively affects the founding rate of Esperanto INGOs.

Using a similar line of reasoning, I suggest that the number of active Esperantists in the world is an indicator of the social recognition of Esperanto and the Esperanto movement. It is difficult to define the term "Esperantist" precisely because individuals vary in their ability to speak and write Esperanto as well as in their level of interest in the Esperanto movement, and I cannot measure directly the total membership of the movement. Instead, I use as a proxy the number of participants in each World Congress, which represents the time-varying intensity of the Esperanto movement. Despite the fact that Congress participants vary considerably in their levels of language skills and commitment, it is quite certain that they are active Esperantists. In addition, this indicator's range covers the entire period of Esperanto INGO history because the first Esperanto INGO was founded as a direct result of the first World Congress, in 1905.

Similar to the density arguments, I expect that, as the total number of active participants increased over time, the niche width available to Esperanto INGOs grew, making more resources available to Esperantists to start new Esperanto INGOs. From this line of argument I have the following hypothesis:

> 2. The number of participants in the annual Esperanto World Congress positively affects the founding rate of Esperanto INGOs.

Turning more directly to the global environment's effects on Esperanto INGOs, two relevant global factors are the volume of world trade and the density of the entire INGO population. Trade is a form of interaction that requires some minimum level of recognition of a shared cultural framework among actors (Wallerstein 1974). Trade clearly was important to the early formation and spread of transnational culture and institutions; it was a principal mechanism integrating world society and helping, largely unintentionally, to form an incipient global identity. During the early period of great increase in world trade (prior to World War I), therefore, trade could make a significant contribution to one-worldism and associated organizing. However, as other forms of global interaction became prevalent (especially through the expansion of INGOs and IGOs), international trade may have become less crucial for integrating world society and therefore less related to the founding rate of Esperanto INGOs. This argument thus suggests that the emergence of global society and global identity resulted in part from the increasing density of economic interaction, though it leaves open the possibility that other types of global interaction have increased in importance relative to economic interchange. As a working hypothesis, I use a straightforward application of world-system theory envisioning a constant effect of world trade over the period:

3. Growth in world economic interaction, measured by the total amount of exports, positively affects the founding rate of Esperanto INGOs.

International nongovernmental organizations represent another important type of interaction among actors at the world level. As discussed in Chapter 1, long-term global interaction cannot be organized in the absence of institutionalized cultural elements, and INGOs can reasonably be interpreted as indicators of both the content of global culture and the density of global collective interaction. INGOs represent a stable, long-term form of interaction, with relatively low organizational mortality rates (in part because they are driven less by monetary concerns than are typically shorter-lived business organizations). For the most part, INGOs are voluntary organizations open to all individuals interested in the particular issues they address. They function at the global level as primarily cultural "advocacy groups" that transcend the usual scope within which political and financial interests operate, and they can survive lean times simply by contracting in size and scope.

As suggested earlier, we can distinguish three phases in the relationship between diffusely oriented Esperanto INGOs and the large majority of

INGOs that have more rationalized and specialized forms. In the first phase, before World War I, Esperanto organizations provided one of the few forms that directly attempted to develop or strengthen global identities. Subsequently, as other INGOs began to organize various global sectors, the dominant INGO model became more rationalized, with a more formal organizational structure and a more specialized set of practical goals. In the third phase, after World War II, the opening up of global discourse facilitated a resurgence of Esperanto INGOs. At issue in this progression is not competition over resources so much as competition among contrasting models of legitimate form and purpose. Because Esperanto INGOs favored the model of diffuse goals and relatively low rationalization, I hypothesize that growth of the total INGO population has decreased the Esperanto founding rate. Though the upturn in the founding rate in recent decades suggests that this negative effect occurred only during the interwar period, viewing the different types of organizations as distinct cognitive models suggests that this tension may have lowered the rate to some extent in all periods.

> 4. Growth in rationalized transnational cultural interaction, measured by the number of active INGOs in all fields, negatively affects the founding rate of Esperanto INGOs.

Finally, the impact of the world-society environment on INGO formation should be considered historically as a matter of changing conditions during different periods. Three periods, plus the punctuating events of the world wars, are significant in this context. The early period, again before World War I, was especially conducive to the founding of INGOs of a diffuse, one-worldist orientation. I therefore expect to find that the founding rate of Esperanto INGOs was highest between 1905, when the first such INGO was formed, and 1914. After the war, global society entered a new phase in which the League of Nations constituted the first worldwide organization explicitly designed as a supranational body transcending individual state authority, albeit to a modest degree. Relative to this new world "center," individual nation-states were conceived as somewhat less autarchic in wielding their power. Put another way, states became subunits of world society to a greater extent than previously. Because this "new world order" was based on official agreements among state authorities, however, this arrangement likely dampened Esperanto INGO formation, which is based primarily on civilian interactions decoupled from formal state authority. Thus the interwar years (1920 to 1938) should have a lower founding rate of Esperanto INGOs, and in my analysis I enter a dummy variable for these years to evaluate this effect.

During the world wars themselves, meanwhile, Esperanto INGOs found it difficult to maintain their operations (as was the case for all sorts of international organizations). States assumed massive control of their societies and monopolized resources for war-making needs. Naturally, it was not easy for Esperantists to initiate new activities during the wars; neither was it easy for them to maintain international communication. For these reasons, a dummy variable is used to capture the years of world war (as modified slightly for data considerations: 1913–19, 1939–44), and I expect its effects on the founding rate of Esperanto INGOs to be negative.

The period used as the benchmark for my analysis is the postwar years, 1945 to 1980. During this period, as part of the general expansion of global interaction in the UN system—among IGOs, in world trade and international relations, and so on—INGOs were formed at higher rates than ever before. They became a standard vehicle, widely implemented, for the organization of activities at the world level. Within this environment that was favorable to INGOs in general, Esperanto INGOs also benefited. Greater recognition in national societies and abundant resources from the rapid economic development that followed the war meant that the Esperanto movement could expand more rapidly than earlier. At the same time, specialized Esperanto INGOs diffused into social sectors that previously had lain outside the Esperanto movement. Thus, independent of other variables, the Esperanto INGO founding rate in the postwar period should be higher than in earlier periods. To summarize, we have:

> 5. The founding rate of Esperanto INGOs was higher during the postwar era than in earlier periods, while the lowest founding rates occurred during the world wars.

Statistical Methods

Regression models based on the Poisson process are commonly used to study the founding rates of organizations (Barron 1992; Hannan and Freeman 1989; Johnson, Kotz, and Kemp 1992; Koch, Atkinson, and Stokes 1986). A normal Poisson regression model, however, is based on the oversimplified assumption that the founding rate is independent of the history of previous foundings (Matsunawa 1986).[5] If the rate at which new organizations appear in the population follows a Poisson process strictly, therefore, the founding rate would be a constant determined solely by factors external to the population of organizations itself.[6]

Actual organizational founding processes rarely fit this constant-rate assumption. Rather, the founding rate fluctuates significantly across periods because of the contagion effect among founding events: as soon as a founding occurs, the probability of future foundings occurring in the same period changes. The probability of the next founding grows as the number of previous foundings increases and the time interval since the previous foundings decreases (Barron 1992; Cox and Isham 1980; Hannan and Freeman 1989). To allow the founding rate to vary, then, it is necessary to incorporate the notion of variability in terms of both density dependence and changing environments. This allows us to explore the effects of measured independent variables in a loglinear model stated as follows;

$$\rho(t) = \exp(\alpha N_t + \beta X_t + \rho_p)$$

where $\rho(t)$ is the founding rate at time t, N_t is the density of Esperanto INGOs at time t, and X_t is the set of independent variables that includes the variables that test my five hypotheses: the density of all INGOs, total world exports, and dummy variables for the different periods whose changing properties are hypothesized to affect Esperanto foundings. Finally, ρ_p is a set of period-specific effects.[7] Using this model, I can determine if the founding rate varies in response to (1) the changing density of Esperanto INGOs and that of all other INGOs, (2) levels of international economic interaction, and (3) sociopolitical shifts across historical periods.

Four hierarchical models were tested to allow for comparisons of the effects that different sets of independent variables have on founding rates; they also allow me to evaluate overall model fit. The fit of each model is reported in terms of G^2; changes in G^2 across models can be tested with the chi-square statistic (Hannan and Freeman 1989). Comparisons of overall model fit allow me to determine which type of international activity has made the greatest contribution to the increasing density of the Esperanto movement and, thus, to the diffusion of this form of global identity construction.

Results

Regarding the first two hypotheses, Models 2 and 4 of Table 5.3, and Model 1 to a degree, show that, as predicted, the density of Esperanto INGOs and the number of participants at Esperanto world congresses have consistent and significant positive effects on the founding rate of Esperanto INGOs. These results indicate that it became easier to found Esperanto organizations as the movement became better known and recognized (Hypothesis 1) and as the number of active Esperantists increased (Hypothesis 2). Both of these

TABLE 5.3
Poisson Regression of Esperanto INGO Founding Rate, 1905–1980

Variables	Model 1	Model 2	Model 3	Model 4
Esperanto density	-.0017	.181***		.180***
	(.0088)	(.053)		(.069)
Participants in congress	.0004***	.0003**		.00024*
	(.0001)	(.0001)		(.00012)
LN (total export)		-1.385*		-1.553*
		(.741)		(.824)
LN (INGO density)		-1.721***		-1.392**
		(.303)		(.585)
World Wars			-1.481***	-.477
			(.522)	(.683)
1905–12			.783***	.600
			(.261)	(.750)
1920–38			-.775**	.260
			(.337)	(.531)
Constant	-.585**	16.689***	.228	15.839**
	(.249)	(5.543)	(.151)	(7.129)
df	2	4	3	7
χ^2	94.459	52.002	72.909	50.125
G^2	95.204	63.489	78.537	60.738
ΔG^2		31.715		2.751[a]
				17.799[b]

* $p < .10$, ** $p < .05$, *** $p < .01$
[a] ΔG^2 between models 2 and 4
[b] ΔG^2 between models 3 and 4

factors made it easier for Esperantists to mobilize social resources to start additional INGOs. More broadly, these results indicate that the increasing density of ongoing global discourse concerning one-worldism has increased the spread of global identities.

Counter to Hypothesis 3, Models 2 and 4 show that international economic interaction (measured by world exports) has significant negative effects on the Esperanto INGO founding rate. Note that this negative effect applies to the founding rate; it does not indicate that the number of Esperanto foundings actually decreased (they did not) but that the rate of foundings decreased relative to the rising level of world trade. This finding indicates that, unlike what world-system theory implies, the emergence of a global identity is not a simple byproduct of the increasingly dense economic exchange achieved in this century. Rather, this result supports the notion that global citizenship and a global identity of the sort encapsulated in the Esperanto movement are constructed by intentional individual activities not closely linked to economic interests and interdependence.

For Hypothesis 4, Models 2 and 4 in Table 5.3 show that the density of the entire INGO population had a negative effect on Esperanto INGO foundings, in line with the prediction. The broad and diffuse approach of early Esperanto INGOs, aiming to solve diffuse problems in international relations and improve general international communication, appears to have been a liability as more specialized and rationalized INGOs of all sorts became common. However, the dummy variables representing distinct periods and, hence, changes in the world-polity environment, do not have consistent effects across the models. Model 3 contains patterns that we would expect from Figure 5.1: negative effects during the world wars and the interwar period and a positive effect for the earliest period. These period effects, however, are significant only when other variables are not controlled. When additional variables enter the equation (Model 4), the effects of the dummy variables for the different periods disappear. This result indicates that the founding rate of Esperanto INGOs has not fluctuated as a matter of simple period effects when the latter are made statistically distinct from substantive variables. The variables identified in Model 4 seem to capture the changes in world-polity conditions that are relevant to Esperanto INGO formation. When controlling for these variables, the founding rate of Esperanto INGOs is surprisingly steady even when subject to "punctuating" events such as the world wars and the founding of the League of Nations.

DISCUSSION AND CONCLUSION

I have investigated two major issues regarding the formation of global culture and the emergence of global identity: (1) the historical process of creating a global identity through Esperanto INGOs, and (2) the relationship between the growth of Esperantism and the world-polity environment. With respect to the first issue, I argue that Esperantism and the Esperanto movement should be interpreted as an effort to build a global vernacular that encompasses human societies and identities throughout the world. This effort was not intended to replace languages, administrative authorities, and cultural identities at the national level. Rather, it was designed to provide a transcendent basis for cooperation and common identity at the global level even as national differences persisted. In the absence of centralized political and cultural authority in world society, the Esperanto movement helped generate an ideological framework of one-worldism that has been utilized and adopted by other actors, especially other INGOs. Esperanto has had a substantial rate of growth for nearly a century, proliferating into new domains and extending to somewhat unconventional areas.

The analyses reported here suggest that Esperantism has endured and grown largely independently of economic activity and period-specific factors. They further suggest that, like other organizations, Esperanto INGOs have grown in part as a function of the number (density) of all existing Esperanto INGOs, indicating that Esperantism became a self-reinforcing movement that was able to draw on its own success for further expansion and proliferation.

Another important finding is the negative impact that increasing total INGO density has on the founding rates of Esperanto INGOs. We cannot reasonably infer that this effect is due to competition over resources because it does not apply generally to the INGO population, but it does point to the complexity of the relationship between organizations and their environment. During the early stages of global cultural formation, Esperanto INGOs were a major source of a one-worldism framework of global consensus and identity. The formation of other INGOs made this framework more implicit as most INGOs activated more specialized and instrumental versions of global identity and organization. In the process, it appears that Esperanto INGOs and their nonspecialized, generalist, unitary-humanity model lost ground, at least in relative terms.

Overall, then, we do not find a linear history of the rise and spread of this form of global identity. Esperanto INGOs provided an early model of global identity and organization based on individual action. In some respects this model was very successful and was picked up by other INGOs, but it gave way to an explicit focus on highly specialized and instrumental goals and organizations. Esperantism and the Esperanto movement helped make it possible for citizens of global society to express new, comprehensive ideologies in a new cultural framework, but the organizations they helped spawn became more differentiated and instrumentally rational than the typical early Esperanto organization.

Esperanto has hardly become the preferred mode of communication among all the peoples of the world, as its originator and many adherents hoped. Thanks to centuries of British imperialism and American economic predominance, English is the world language *par excellence* and it is likely to remain so for the foreseeable future. In this sense Esperanto is a failure, regardless of the many Esperanto INGOs that have flourished and the millions of individuals who have made Zamenhof's creation their own. Yet the Esperanto movement has certainly helped reify the world polity and foster the expansion of global identities. Its means have been far less than adequate to create a genuinely universal language, but it has helped spread universalism nonetheless.

Contemporary global culture and global identity thus should not be understood solely as involving scientific, technical, and economic networks of interdependence among national and other actors, important though these may be. They also in part are outcomes of intentional collective action that transcends interdependent units of less than global scope.

Chapter Six Rules of War and Wars of Rules:
The International Red Cross and
the Restraint of State Violence

MARTHA FINNEMORE

International relations scholars have tended to think of war as anarchic competition in a Hobbesian state of nature. In war, above all other situations, we should be able to treat states and soldiers as self-interested utility-maximizers simply because in times of war the most basic survival interests are at stake. War should be a hard case for cultural and institutional explanations of behavior because interests are so clear and so vital.

In fact, however, war is a highly regulated cultural institution whose rules have changed over time. Inter-state war could not even be conducted if survival were the only or paramount concern of soldiers and other individuals because it is in war that the requirements of state survival and personal survival directly conflict. Soldiers may not fight without some other social or cultural value such as comradeship, honor, nationalism, or political ideology. It is social and cultural values that give war a purpose, that define its meaning and make it worth fighting. Further, social rules and cultural models govern the *way* in which states and soldiers fight. Notions of chivalry and codes of conduct for the warrior are as old as war itself. Some of these norms clearly contribute to fighting efficiency and survival interests—norms of unit solidarity, for example. Other rules of war are less easily understood outside a larger social and normative context, for example agreements to cease hostilities in recognition of religious holidays.

Rules of war, like many other features of social life examined in this volume, have become increasingly globalized and transnationalized. In this chapter I examine the origin and spread of one core component of the global rules of warfare, the Geneva Conventions.[1] The Conventions specify a variety of humanitarian protections for both wounded soldiers and noncombatants that warring states must guarantee. Signatories to the Conventions agree to provide these protections even to soldiers and civilians of the states with whom they are at war.

The Geneva Conventions have more signatories than the United Nations has members. This near universal acceptance is not surprising given the universalization of the state as a political form (Meyer, Boli et al. 1997). As states have spread across the globe, the most basic rules of state intercourse governing basic state functions have spread with them—rules of diplomacy, diplomatic immunity, treaty-making, and war. What is more surprising is that an INGO should play an important part in the spread of rules of warfare. Warmaking is, after all, a defining prerogative of the state. It is the most conspicuous and consequential exercise of the state monopoly over violence, and militaries have traditionally been shielded from civilian interference to a much greater extent than other parts of the state apparatus.

In fact, however, war was one of the first demonstrations of strength by an INGO in the defense of world-cultural principles. The first Geneva Convention, signed in 1864, was not a state-sponsored initiative. It was drafted and "sold" to states through the efforts of a nongovernmental group of citizens that later became known as the International Committee of the Red Cross (ICRC). The principles championed by this group and subsequently embodied in both the Conventions and the Red Cross movement (as the ICRC and its associated national organizations are called) are world-cultural principles. They emphasize the need to protect the worth and dignity of the individual even when this is most difficult and costly for states. They emphasize universalism, in applying the principles even to the wounded in enemy uniforms. They emphasize voluntarism and rationalism in formally organizing private relief societies to provide these protections. They emphasize world citizenship in their claims that all states and all humanity must come under the Red Cross umbrella.

This chapter examines how the ICRC drafted and persuaded states to adopt the first Geneva Convention. The chapter begins with a discussion of why the humanitarian principles championed by the Red Cross are interesting theoretically. The practical importance of these principles is fairly obvious; conformance to humanitarian principles makes the world a safer and more pleasant place to live. However, humanitarian principles challenge central notions of sovereignty and traditional understandings about the organization of international politics in important ways.

As part of this discussion I identify three explanations for the Conventions suggested by more traditional approaches to state behavior that take interests for granted and ignore cultural effects. I then present an account of the origins of the Geneva Conventions that looks for evidence to support these explanations. I find little such evidence. The alternative explanation I develop focuses on the role played by a few morally committed individuals and the organization they built, the ICRC, in promulgating and transmitting these world-cultural models.

Since its founding in the mid-nineteenth century, the ICRC has tried to protect individuals from suffering caused by state violence in four ways: (1) it has sought to ensure humane standards of treatment and neutrality status for noncombatants, particularly medical personnel, the wounded, and civilians; (2) it has sought to provide aid to and facilitate the return of prisoners of war; (3) it has sought to provide humanitarian aid to non-state forces during civil conflicts; and (4) it has sought access to and humanitarian treatment for political prisoners. Its primary means of accomplishing these goals have been the establishment of national relief societies (what are now the national Red Cross societies extant in most countries), and the establishment of international treaty guarantees concerning each of these four areas of humanitarian behavior (what are now known as the Geneva Conventions).

ICRC efforts in each of these four areas of humanitarian concern were contested by states at the time they were proposed as an infringement on state warmaking powers or sovereign rights. Each has now been established with some degree of normative authority in the system. The research question in this chapter is, then: How did these principles become established?

My analysis focuses on the role of the ICRC in establishing and codifying the first of the four types of principles mentioned earlier: principles concerning standards of treatment and neutrality status for noncombatants, particularly the wounded and medical personnel. Historically this was the first area of interest of the ICRC; indeed, it was this issue that inspired the creation of the Committee. Subsequent efforts to establish concern for other principles within the ICRC have been strongly colored by the general worldview and moral code elaborated in this early period of its history.

HUMANITARIAN PRINCIPLES AND INTERNATIONAL RELATIONS THEORY

The fundamental difficulty with asserting humanitarian principles in a world dominated by states is that humanitarian values are premised on a worldview not easily accommodated within the principles and rights associated with state sovereignty. In a state system, the unit of concern is the state; individuals are recognized and categorized only in their relationship to the state, primarily as citizens or aliens. By contrast, the humanitarian worldview asserts that individuals have status and worth *independent* of their relationship to states. By asserting that human beings have rights and value simply by virtue of their humanity, humanitarians create a set of normative claims that compete with the claims made by states. They assert that states do not have unlimited rights to pursue and defend their national interests; rather, that pursuit must be tempered by respect for the well-being of individuals. Thus, to the degree that humanitarian claims succeed, they constrain states, circumscribing their sovereignty and free exercise of power.[2]

The humanitarian claims of the International Committee of the Red Cross are of special significance because they have focused on the aspect of state power most central to the essence of sovereignty itself—the state use of violence. It is precisely the control over use of arms that states guard most jealously. In the classic Weberian definition, the defining element of the state is its monopoly on the legitimate use of force within a given territory (Weber 1968: 56). ICRC claims for protection of individuals from the effects of state violence are claims that the exercise of that essential monopoly must be limited.

Claims like that of the Red Cross, that states must restrain their use of violence in wartime, should be particularly difficult for humanitarians to establish. War is presumably a time when states' vital interests, even survival, are at stake. One would not expect policymakers or generals to take on burdens making protection of those vital interests more difficult. But they do. Compliance with ICRC requirements that states provide enemy wounded with medical treatment equal to that provided for their own soldiers is one example. From a realist perspective there is no good reason to give treatment to someone in an enemy uniform who needs medical attention. That person might yet be dangerous, and even if the combatant is not a threat, why should a self-interested state invest scarce resources in aiding an enemy?

Hypotheses

Without resorting to cultural arguments, one can develop three strong explanations of this behavior. First, states might be prompted into humane treatment of enemy wounded and medical personnel by a process of reciprocity. They treat and repatriate enemy wounded in the hope that their wounded will be similarly treated and returned. This hypothesis presupposes that states have reason to place significant value on their wounded. They could do so for two reasons, each of which suggests a further cause for states' interest in the wounded.

States might care about the wounded for purely instrumental military reasons: They want their trained soldiers back to fight another day. It would, after all, be much cheaper and easier to reintegrate veterans than to train raw recruits. Alternatively, states might care about humane treatment of the wounded for domestic political reasons. Following the logic of Immanuel Kant (1963 [1795]), one might expect the democratizing forces at work in Europe in the nineteenth century, when the ICRC was founded, to represent powerful constraints on leaders of democratic states to protect their citizen-soldiers from harm. Establishment of humanitarian laws of war and of relief societies to aid the wounded would offer those leaders powerful political tools to legitimate their governments and might lead democratic states to push for international treaty protection for soldiers wounded in war.

The following analysis will show that, while all of these factors may have played some role, none is sufficient as an explanation of the formation of the ICRC and the ratification of the first Geneva Convention. Early applications of the Geneva Convention in wartime were unilateral, undermining the reciprocity argument. Military and medical technology in the 1860s was such that the wounded were unlikely again to be fit for combat at any time during the conflict (if, indeed, they were ever fit again), undermining the utilitarian argument. Finally, the earliest and most enthusiastic supporter of the Red Cross and the Geneva Convention was Prussia, one of the least democratic states in Europe. Britain, perhaps the most democratic, was one of the most recalcitrant.

In addition to failing on the facts, all of these explanations suffer from misidentification of the underlying impetus for these events. These explanations identify states as the prime movers behind the origins of the Convention. However, the ICRC and the Convention were not state initiatives. They were the product, not of *state* action, but of action by private individuals and an INGO. Individuals, not states, formed the organization that in turn drew up the Convention and persuaded states to adhere to it.

ORIGINS OF THE INTERNATIONAL COMMITTEE OF THE RED CROSS AND THE FIRST GENEVA CONVENTION

The catalyst for the founding of the International Committee of the Red Cross lies in the experiences of one individual, Henry Dunant.[3] Dunant (1828–1910) was a Genevese-Swiss banker who, for a combination of personal and professional reasons, happened to be in Lombardy in 1859 during the Italian wars of independence.[4] Immediately following the engagement between French and Austrian forces at Solferino on 24 June, Dunant arrived in the nearby town of Castiglione to find thousands of wounded soldiers from both sides flooding the town, with virtually no medical care in sight. At that time, the French army marched with less than one physician per thousand men; its artillery did not have a single doctor. The situation among the Austrians was no better. There were no medical supplies or equipment; even food and water were scarce.[5]

Confronted with this scene of chaos, Dunant could have fled. Instead, he threw himself into relief work—cleaning wounds, dispensing water and food, canvassing the local community for whatever supplies could be had. These events had a profound effect on Dunant and prompted him to publish an account of his experiences entitled *A Memory of Solferino* (1986 [1862]). In addition to providing a lively and detailed description of Dunant's experiences, the book contains a proposal for change, a remedy for the horrors Dunant encountered. Dunant proposed that relief societies staffed by qualified volunteers be set up to care for the wounded in wartime. Further, he proposed that these volunteer relief societies be officially recognized in an international agreement. Building an organization in peacetime, Dunant argued, was the best way to ensure adequate care for all wounded personnel after hostilities had broken out (Dunant 1986 [1862]: 115–28).

Dunant published his work at his own expense and sent copies to members of ruling families, influential politicians, philanthropists, and newspaper publishers. The book was an instant success. It went through three printings in the first four months, attracted notice in most of the influential newspapers of Europe, and became a subject of conversation in the *salons*.[6] Dunant received a flood of correspondence from readers, among them author Victor Hugo; philosopher Ernest Renan; peace activist Frédéric Passy; Surgeon-General Bertherand; Prince Alexander of Hesse, the king of Holland, the grand-duke of Baden; Marshall Randon, the French minister of war; Ferdinand de Lesseps, the celebrated builder of the Suez Canal, and Florence Nightingale (Gumpert 1938: 104; Boissier 1985: 40–43; François 1918: 119).[7]

Among those impressed by the book was a lawyer and fellow citizen of Geneva, Gustave Moynier. Moynier was chairman of the Geneva Society for Public Welfare, a private institution devoted to philanthropy and social progress. After reading *A Memory of Solferino*, he sought out Dunant and proposed that the Society for Public Welfare take up Dunant's suggestion for the formation of relief societies. At the Society's next meeting a committee of five men was set up to investigate Dunant's proposals. These five shortly became the International Committee to Aid the Military Wounded, which would later be called the International Committee of the Red Cross.[8]

The original five members of the Committee were Moynier and Dunant; General Dufour, commander of the Swiss army and former military instructor of Louis Napoleon; and two physicians, Louis Appia and Theodore Maunoir. Appia was a military physician of wide experience who had been near Solferino at the same time as Dunant. Maunoir was a civilian surgeon whose recommendation for the position seems to have been the great respect he commanded among his peers.

After two initial meetings, the Committee decided that the best way to achieve its goal of creating relief societies in each country was not to try to do this themselves but to convene an international congress of interested and influential delegates from each country who would return home and implement Dunant's proposals (ICRC, Aug. 25, 1863).[9] Anticipating resistance to their plan from military commanders, who had already expressed reservations about the notion of volunteers cluttering up battlefields and confusing military operations, the Committee decided at its first meeting that relief societies must gain official government recognition and be made subject to the orders of military commanders. This meant that participation by philanthropists was not sufficient; the conference had to attract delegates from governments, particularly from military commands.[10]

To ensure attendance by delegates from as many countries as possible and to ensure that those delegates were sufficiently influential in their home countries to launch relief societies successfully, the committee undertook what would now be called a publicity campaign to interest possible participants in their project. As Maunoir put it, it was necessary to "maintain an *agitation*, if one can put it that way, so that our views will be adopted by everyone, high and low, from the sovereigns of Europe to the people, themselves" (ICRC, Feb. 17, 1863).

In fact, the strategy adopted for this *agitation* was largely a top-down approach. The Committee would first contact the government and others in power to ensure their support for the formation of a national relief society. Once in place, the national society would be responsible for publicity for its cause in that country and for the development of mass support for the project (ICRC, Feb. 17 and Mar. 17, 1863).[11]

Dunant became the principal executor of this *agitation* among elites. He began by attending a session of an international statistical congress in Berlin, the fourth section of which was concerned with comparative health and mortality statistics and was attended overwhelmingly by civilian and military doctors. In addition to an address to this section of the congress, Dunant made personal contact with scores of delegates, promoting his ideas and inviting them to attend the upcoming conference in Geneva. By the end of the conference he had provisional acceptances from representatives of Sweden, Denmark, Hannover, Bavaria, Mecklenburg, Prussia, Spain, and Italy.[12]

Dunant then traveled to Potsdam and was received by King Wilhelm I and Crown Prince Frederick as well as the Prussian minister of war, the court physician, the army physician, and the minister of the interior. While in Prussia, Dunant also made contact with the official representatives of Russia, Spain, Saxony, Bavaria, and Norway, each of whom promised to take up Dunant's cause with their respective governments. He later traveled to Saxony and secured support from the king there, then to Vienna, Bavaria, Darmstadt, Stuttgart, and Karlsruhe. He wrote letters to Lord Grey, Britain's minister of war, and to France's commissary-general, Baron Darricau, who persuaded Louis Napoleon to allow him to send a representative to the Geneva conference.[13]

The Conference of October 1863 in Geneva

Dunant's efforts paid off. Attendance at the Geneva conference surpassed his and the Committee's expectations. Thirty-one delegates responded to the invitation from sixteen countries and three philanthropic societies. Represented were Austria, Baden, Bavaria, Britain, France, Hannover, Hesse, Italy, the Netherlands, Prussia, Russia, Saxony, Spain, Sweden, Switzerland, Württemberg, the Order of St. John of Jerusalem, the Neuchâtel Social Science Society, and the Society for Public Welfare of the Canton of Vaud (Boissier 1985: 70). Virtually all of these governments had been contacted personally by Dunant. Most of the representatives were military physicians, usually heads of the military medical corps of their countries.[14]

Prior to the conference, the Committee had drafted a convention for the assembled delegates to consider which contained details of the organization of relief societies. After some discussion and amendment by the delegates, the proposals considered were the following. Each country was to establish a national relief society whose mission would be to provide aid to the war wounded, regardless of nationality. The societies were to be private organizations, staffed by volunteers and funded by private donations.[15] They were to seek recognition from national governments and could act in armed conflict only when invited to do so by the national military. All volunteers were to wear a white armband with a red cross so that they could easily be identified. In addition, neutral status was extended to all medical personnel, including volunteers from both relief societies and the civilian population at the battle site, as well as to the wounded themselves.[16]

These provisions did not sail through the conference unopposed. The French and the British, in particular, rejected the very concept of volunteer relief societies. Neither wanted to see civilians on the battlefield meddling in what should properly be military affairs. The French distrusted the competence and integrity of these volunteers. They did not believe the societies would ever be able to adequately supply themselves with food, clothing, and medicines amid the difficulties of war. Civilians suddenly thrown into the chaos and horror of battle were unlikely to perform effectively; they would be paralyzed by the sight of blood and unable to survive the privations of war. Protecting these civilians would thus become one more strain on an army already engaged in combat. Further, the French delegate voiced fears that the relief societies would attract volunteers from the lower classes who could not be relied upon for orderly conduct or to refrain from plundering the dead and wounded.

The British objection was simply that these societies were superfluous in the British army. Following the horrors of Crimea and the efforts of Florence Nightingale, the British military medical services had been completely overhauled and much expanded. They were now fully adequate, the British claimed, to care for military wounded in any conflict and did not need civilian assistance to accomplish their task. In the British view, care for military wounded was a state obligation. If other states copied the British reforms, the Committee's relief societies would not be necessary.

The principal supporters of the Committee's proposals were the German states, particularly Prussia, which took exception to the British position, arguing that it made no economic sense for the state to maintain a standing medical corps large enough to meet all military eventualities. Further, it was pointed out that in Germany there was a long tradition of the Knights Hospitalers, a noble order of unquestioned integrity, providing voluntary aid to the war wounded without undue interference in military affairs or collapse under the strain of battle (Boissier 1985: 73–76; Gumpert 1938: 128–30; ICRC 1954: 386–87).

In the end, the Prussian arguments, supported by other German states, swayed the delegates and the conference voted unanimously to adopt the Committee's proposals. The Conference was adjourned and the delegates went home with two tasks: to start the work of setting up relief societies in their respective countries, and to persuade their governments to accept and sign an international agreement recognizing (1) the neutrality of military and relief society medical personnel, civilian volunteers, the wounded, hospitals and ambulances; and (2) some uniform emblem to distinguish these personnel, hospitals, and ambulances.

Early Attempts to Found Relief Societies

Relief societies were formed quickly in Württemberg, Oldenburg, Prussia, and Belgium but by March of 1864 it was clear that the societies were encountering serious opposition in important European states. In the Netherlands, the society was rejected because relief of the war wounded was regarded as a state responsibility (Boissier 1985: 89). The Austrians argued that they already had a relief society, the Austrian Patriotic Society for Aid to Wounded Soldiers, War Widows, and Orphans.[17] Efforts to form a Russian society were thwarted by the minister of war, Milutine, who refused to allow volunteers onto the battlefield. The British continued to oppose the founding of any such society on the grounds that their War Office had already taken on this responsibility and was carrying out these duties effectively. The French minister of war, Marshall Randon, also continued his opposition to the societies. Only after Dunant spent several months in the *salons* of Paris pushing his cause and eventually gained an audience with Napoleon III (by using a letter of introduction from Dufour, who had once been Napoleon's teacher) was Randon circumvented and the society's proponents given official state sanction (ICRC 1954: 386–87).[18]

The 1864 Geneva Convention

To implement the second part of the Conference's resolutions, the Committee began drafting an international agreement in which neutrality status and a distinctive emblem were explicitly recognized. There was no precedent for a diplomatic convention of this kind. Previously, laws of war had been based solely on customary usage and, to a lesser extent, on legal opinions. The Committee's initiative was the first step in constructing a treaty-based law of war (Boissier 1985: 113).

To obtain signatures for the new convention, the Committee persuaded the French and Swiss governments to sponsor an international conference at which states would hammer out details of the treaty and formally accept it. Many states were not enthusiastic, as their earlier treatment of the relief society proposals suggests. However, in the end, a group of seventeen states, very similar to the group of states attending the 1863 conference, convened in Geneva in August of 1864.[19]

The principal provisions of the Convention agreed upon by the delegates were as follows.

Ambulances, military hospitals, medical personnel, and the administrative, transport and quartermasters' staff which supports these will all have neutral status.[20]

In the event of enemy occupation, these neutral personnel shall have the right to continue to carry out their functions. When they choose to return to their units, this return shall be facilitated by occupying forces.

Hospital materials captured may be retained by the occupying forces; ambulances may not.

Inhabitants of the country who provide aid to the wounded shall be respected and remain free. Generals of belligerent powers have a duty to notify these inhabitants of the neutrality such humane conduct will confer.

Wounded and sick combatants shall be collected and cared for. Those recovered, if unfit for further service, must be repatriated. Those fit for service shall be repatriated on the condition that they not take up arms again for the duration of hostilities. Evacuation parties conducting these repatriation operations shall be neutral.

Personnel, hospitals, and ambulances enjoying neutral status shall wear the emblem of neutrality, a red cross on a white background.

Not all delegates had been sent to the conference with full powers to sign the agreement. Consequently, only twelve states signed at the close of the convention on August 22, 1864: Baden, Belgium, Denmark, Spain, France, Hesse, Italy, Netherlands, Portugal, Prussia, Switzerland, and Württemberg. By the end of 1866, however, twenty states had signed. By 1868, Russia and the Vatican had as well. Thus, within four years, virtually every state in Europe was a signatory to the Convention, along with some of the most important extra-European states—the United States and Turkey.[21]

EARLY APPLICATIONS OF THE GENEVA CONVENTION IN WARTIME

The first test of the Geneva Convention came in 1866, when fighting broke out between Prussia and Austria over control of the German Confederation.

At this time, only Prussia was a signatory to the Convention; Austria had continually refused to accede despite intercession by the French ambassador on behalf of the Committee.[22] The Prussian response in this case was to apply the Convention unilaterally, despite Austrian refusal to return captured Prussian doctors. Similarly, Italy, a signatory to the Convention, applied its provisions unilaterally when it joined Prussia in the attack on Austria (Boissier 1985: 182–86). The other early conflict in which one side was party to the Convention and the other was not was the Sino-Japanese War of 1894. In that case, too, the Japanese chose to apply the protections of the Convention unilaterally.[23]

The Franco-Prussian War (1870) was the first conflict in which both parties were adherents to the Convention. What was notable in this case was the way in which both used compliance or noncompliance as a propaganda tool in the war. The very fact that the Convention was so used indicates the degree of normative authority it carried in international public opinion.[24]

Overall, the Prussians were better able to observe the Convention than the French simply because the French relief societies were too few and too disorganized to do their job. The French societies had not been able to publicize the meaning of the red cross armband and neutral status for medical personnel adequately among the military ranks and civilian population. Several ICRC and relief society workers from neutral countries complained of being treated as spies by French unfamiliar with the Convention. Not surprisingly, the Prussians were quick to publish these and many similar stories.

Later conflicts posed important issues for the Committee, with the result that the scope of the Convention's protections for individuals in wartime gradually expanded. The Balkan Wars (1875–78), in which Herzegovina, Bosnia, and Bulgaria rebelled against the Turks, are especially notable as precedent-setters. First, they raised the question of applying the Geneva Conventions in cases of civil war. Initially, the Committee announced that these protections applied only in inter-state, European conflicts. Later, however, it changed its mind, stating that humanitarianism is a "profession of faith" and a "moral code"; it cannot, therefore, be optional in some cases and compulsory in others.[25]

This conflict was also the first case in which Red Cross principles—principles the Committee had hitherto understood as "Christian" in nature—were applied outside the Christian West. One result of this was to clarify the universal scope of Red Cross humanitarian claims on states; *all* states could and should conform to Geneva principles, which were compatible with all religious beliefs.[26] Hand in hand with this, however went a concession to religious and cultural diversity—the admission of the Red Crescent as an alternative symbol for humanitarian relief societies.[27]

Finally, the Balkan Wars provided the first case in which civilian refugees were explicitly recognized as victims of war and eligible for Red Cross protection. Rather than simply being a Society to Aid the War Wounded, the Red Cross had now expanded its mandate to provide relief for all suffering caused by what it called "man-made disaster."

THE RED CROSS AND MILITARY MEDICINE

During the first twenty years of the ICRC's history, military medicine underwent some remarkable changes which were both consequential for and caused, in part, by the Red Cross itself. Enumerating the qualities needed for volunteer relief work in 1867, ICRC Committee members Moynier and Appia emphasized respectability and impartiality; they said nothing about medical knowledge (Boissier 1985: 316). Neither did Dunant in his initial call for creation of the relief societies.[28] And, indeed, given the state of military field medicine, further qualifications were hardly necessary. It did not require extensive training to teach volunteers to hold a patient down on the operating table while his leg was being amputated, the saw still dripping with blood from the previous operation. Neither was it difficult to learn to wash a wound with water from the local stream or to apply already-used lint and bandages. Certainly this was the extent of Dunant's own activities at Solferino, and little had changed by the time of the Franco-Prussian War.

By the 1880s, however, such methods were no longer tolerated. The work of Louis Pasteur had made sterilization routine practice in military hospitals. Surgeons increasingly demanded trained nurses and medical orderlies to safeguard the hygiene of their patients and carry out increasingly complex procedures. In fact, it was very often Red Cross personnel who introduced these changes into military hospitals.

The resulting change in mortality rates was extraordinary. In the Serbo-Bulgarian War (1885), only 2 percent of the 6,000 wounded Serbians died. Hospital gangrene all but disappeared. The amputation rate plunged and the success rate of those amputations rose.

In addition to changes in medical technology, two changes in weapons technology also influenced the change in mortality—the introduction of steel-jacketed small caliber bullets and the repeating magazine. The military advantages of these innovations were clear. Reducing the caliber of the bullet from 11mm to 7mm allowed soldiers to open fire at a range of 2,000 meters.

The repeater system increased the rate of fire from four shots per minute to twenty.

The medical consequences were at least as great as the military consequences. Greater firepower increased the number of wounded but it also changed the character of the wounds. The narrower, high-speed bullet penetrated with greater force, but paradoxically, also caused less lethal damage. With greater velocity, these bullets did not lodge in the body but penetrated completely and created relatively small holes where they entered and left. Infections became less common with fewer gaping wounds. Excessive hemorrhaging and bone shattering became rare. The need for amputations decreased.

As a result of all this, the relationship between the wounded, military hospitals, and the army changed. In the 1860s, the wounded were a military write-off. With the existing state of military medicine, the number of wounded who could be saved at all was not large; the proportion of those who would be fit for duty within the duration of the conflict was negligible. By the mid-1880s, military hospitals were recycling troops back into the army in significant numbers. Thus, by the time the military and medical technology combined to make protection of the wounded a material asset to armies, the Red Cross movement and the Geneva Convention were already firmly established. However, at the time states were making the decision to adhere to the Convention and found relief societies, the military utility of treating the wounded was negligible.

AGENCY, CONTESTATION, AND WORLD-POLITY PERSPECTIVES

The foregoing analysis makes clear that none of the three hypotheses about why states would agree to provide humanitarian aid to enemy wounded provides a sufficient explanation for the success of the International Committee of the Red Cross in promulgating the Geneva Convention. Unilateral application of the first Convention undermines arguments about reciprocity as states' chief motive. Early support for ICRC activities from less democratic states, like Prussia, and recalcitrance by the most democratic state, Britain, undercut Kantian expectations that democracies responding to mass publics are the probable source of this innovation internationally. Technological innovations in munitions and medicine do not coincide well with the timing of state adherence to the Conventions and formation of Red Cross societies. The societies were promoters of military medical change, not results of it.

All of these arguments miss the real causal forces at work by focusing on states as the important actors. What is essential to the origin of the ICRC and the Geneva Convention is the role of a few morally committed private individuals—individuals without government positions or political power—and the elite networks they were able to use to build a transnational organization. Neither of these has received much attention from international relations scholars.[29] The state-centric analysis dominating the field has made it difficult to recognize that private individuals with no formal political standing might have significant influence.[30] Further, realism's rejection of morality as a significant force in world politics provides few tools for understanding either people like Henry Dunant or the widespread ethical convictions he harnessed.[31]

A world-polity perspective that emphasizes the cultural and institutional frameworks in which war is fought provides an explanation for what would appear to be anomalous, other-regarding behavior from a realist, interest-maximizing perspective. War *is* its rules. It is the rules of warfare that give the practice meaning, that distinguish war from murder and soldiers from criminals. The cultural frame and the social values embodied in that frame give people reasons to fight and die. They also dictate appropriate manners in which to conduct war.

As was discussed in the opening chapter of this volume, however, world-polity scholars have had little to say empirically about the process by which these rules are constructed. Research in this vein has tended to be correlational studies in which cultural causes are inferred from the isomorphism predicted by world-polity theories (see Chapter 1). There is little agency in this research program, nor is there much discussion of contestation about the content of world-cultural models.

The case study in this chapter sheds light on both agency and contestation. It highlights the importance of transnational, nongovernmental organization in bringing about change in world culture, but it also points to the importance of individuals in the formation of these INGOs. Dunant was a world-cultural "entrepreneur" whose action was not power seeking or utility maximizing, as most conventional social-theoretical perspectives would expect. Indeed, Dunant spent all his limited funds on his Red Cross project, leaving him in impoverished obscurity for decades before he was finally located by a curious admirer and awarded the Nobel Peace Prize.

Dunant's action does not make sense in any consequentialist framework. His action makes much more sense when understood as the product of a "logic of appropriateness."[32] The discussions surrounding the adoption of the Geneva Conventions and subsequent compliance were not about interests and advantage. They were discussions about duties, responsibility, and identity. They were discussions about appropriate and necessary behavior. Dunant framed his appeal in terms of responsibilities of Christian gentlemen and civilized nations. Leaders justified decisions to sign and comply on the basis of religious and moral duties borne by civilized nations. Citizens embraced the Conventions for similar reasons.

Agency in this case is driven not by interest, conventionally understood, but by a cultural model of Christian charity and humanitarian duty constructed by Dunant and his colleagues from existing cultural principles and applied in new ways to the conduct of war. Conflict over whether the ICRC model would prevail was a matter less of interest than of appropriateness. It was a cultural conflict to determine world-cultural rules. Each side in the debates surrounding it appealed to different cultural norms and models to support its views. Those opposed to the Convention emphasized rational values of effectiveness and efficiency and the legitimate security-providing functions of the state. They argued that the Convention's requirements would put too much strain on militaries in difficult situations, that private volunteers on the battlefield would be ineffective at aiding the wounded and would create problems for military commanders. They did not argue that the humanitarian measures proposed were undesirable. However, they did argue that these concerns needed to be accommodated within and subordinated to state sovereignty, military effectiveness, and the state's supreme authority in warmaking.

The codification of Red Cross principles into international law is best understood as the result of competing world-cultural principles, not competing interests. Many of the chapters in this volume emphasize the mutually reinforcing nature of these principles, but there is no reason that these principles should always or even often be in accord. World-cultural models may combine principles in paradoxical ways or may be the focus of overt conflict among principles. In this case, we see world-cultural principles in conflict at the heart of the state, that dominant world-cultural actor imbued with legitimate and rational political authority (Meyer 1987a). As was illustrated in this case, world-cultural valuation of the state as the possessor of a legitimated monopoly on coercion conflicts with concern for the dignity and well-being of individuals in important and obvious ways. Models of state sovereignty also conflict with voluntarism, as evidenced by the debate over whether private relief societies could be allowed onto the battlefield, which previously was the exclusive domain of the state.

The victory of humanitarian principles over claims for state control in

1864 can be seen as an early episode in a much larger pattern of cultural contestation between states and individuals over the past 150 years. Subsequent normative battles for human rights in the twentieth century have invoked similar principles of individual worth and universal humanity to protect people from state violence of all kinds. Increasingly, the humanitarian claims have won. This by no means implies that states now are weaker than they were in the nineteenth century. On the contrary, state power and state penetration of all areas of life have increased. But the realms in which legitimate state power, particularly state violence, may be exercised have been redefined by challenges from these world-cultural humanitarian principles. Thus, to understand state action and how it changes over time, we must understand the world-cultural context in which it occurs.

Part Three Technical, Scientific, and Development Sectors

Chapter Seven **Standardization in the World Polity: Technical Rationality over Power**

THOMAS A. LOYA AND JOHN BOLI

Standardization affects virtually every commodity and productive process in daily life, from the mundane to the esoteric.[1] International standards determine credit card thickness (0.76 mm), photographic film sensitivity (ISO ratings), the tensile strength and thread pitch of screws, the symbols used on automobile dashboard controls, the dimensions and discharge duration of batteries, the phase-alignment of AC current in overhead power lines, the output of ultrasonic devices for dentistry and obstetrics, and the measurement of BAUD rates for electronic information transfer, to name a few from the immense horde of possible examples. In all, the International Organization for Standardization (officially known as "ISO") has published over 9,000 sets of standards and over 500,000 standards-related documents. Its companion body, the International Electrotechnical Commission (IEC), has published more than 3,000 sets of standards comprising 100,000 pages of text.

For more than 80 years, global standardization organizations have been steadily and energetically at work promoting the construction of a uniform built environment. Part of the dense web of international nongovernmental organizations (INGOs) that has emerged in the twentieth century, their work is highly technical, strongly rationalized, and ubiquitously consequential. Through the production of standards, they homogenize the technical base and consumer products of the world to a degree unimaginable even a hundred years ago.

Remarkably, the global standardization sector and its consequences are invisible to almost everyone affected by them. They are studied by specialists in the manufacturing and scientific areas they regulate, and by analysts of business and organizational development (e.g., Fox 1992b, 1993; Thayer 1994; and Mahoney and Thor 1994), but even their very existence is largely unknown outside rather narrow circles. Social scientists have not considered this sector as a sociological or political problem worthy of much study; our literature search yielded few articles that touched on the subject, except for case studies of particular standardization issues that have become relatively prominent internationally (e.g., Cowhey 1990, Salter 1993, Fels 1992, and Genschel and Werle 1993; the formation of the European Academy for Standardization [EURAS 1994] and such conferences as the SCANCOR/ SCORE Seminar on Standardization held in Sweden in the fall of 1997 indicate that this neglect is coming to an end).

In this chapter we want to heighten awareness of the global standardization process via an analysis that moves beyond the concerns of existing articles with the practical problems and pitfalls of standards implementation (Brock 1975; Crane 1979). Technical standardization is a domain of activity whose structure, operations, and self-proclaimed rationales are highly revealing about global social organization. The unique characteristics of standardization shed light on such issues as the constitution of world authority, world-cultural conceptions of human purposes, and the limits of coercive power in a decentralized global polity. In short, these organizations are a constitutive part of world society. An analysis that treats them as such can teach us much about that transcendent level of social reality.

A variety of research methods were used to support this analysis. We mailed a request for detailed information concerning origins, structure, operations, affiliations, and numerous other organizational characteristics to all 75 member bodies of the International Organization for Standardization (ISO, discussed below), following up with a second request three months later. After reviewing materials from 47 standardization bodies, we selected and coded key data for analysis; in this chapter, however, we use these materials only illustratively.

Second, extensive information concerning key aspects of ISO's organizational structure and operations, which is unavailable in compiled form elsewhere, was obtained from ISO and other global standards organizations. Third, we contacted individuals occupying a variety of positions in standardization organizations for in-depth interviews, both in person and via the Internet. We asked them to reflect on their experience with respect to specific aspects of the structure, operations, history, and internal dynamics of global standardization organizations. Their participation in this research is ongoing.

Departing from customary practice, we begin empirically, with a sketch of the origins, structure, and operations of the global standardization sector. We then discuss this sketch in relation to prominent perspectives on global development—world-systems theory à la Immanuel Wallerstein (1974; Wallerstein and Hopkins, 1980); state-competition and neorealist theory à la Charles Tilly (1992), Anthony Giddens (1985), Theda Skocpol (1979), Kenneth Waltz (1979), and Joseph Grieco (1993); regime analysis, or neoliberal institutionalism (Keohane 1984, 1993; Baldwin 1993) in international relations theory; and world-polity theory as developed by George Thomas et al. (1987; see also Boli and Thomas 1994 and Meyer, Boli et al. 1997). We argue that neither world-systems theory nor state-competition/neorealism nor neoliberal institutionalism can adequately account for the standardization sector—global standardization is not reducible simply to the workings of the capitalist world economy or the interests of states. We offer instead, in the last section, a more fully theorized analysis of the sector from the world-polity perspective, linking what we learn about standardization to recent advances in research about the general issue of world-level organization. This perspective accounts more fully for the distinguishing features of global standardization organizations and their activities.

ANALYTICAL DESCRIPTION OF THE GLOBAL
STANDARDIZATION SECTOR

Emergence and Structure

The earliest roots of standardization organizations lie in the late nineteenth-century period of increasingly large-scale capitalist enterprise and rapid technological innovation. Entrepreneurial capitalists of the 1880s and 1890s drew upon a variety of ideologies in founding the organizational progenitors of the national standardization institutes; elements of capitalism, nationalism, modernism, and socialism are evident in the founding accounts. In the United States, General Electric's Schenectady, New York, standardizing laboratory[2] was founded largely because of the efforts of a socialist German émigré engineer, Charles Proteus Steinmetz (1865–1923). Prior to his advocacy of socializing technical activities for the needs of industry, GE had little interest in sponsoring standardization research and was skeptical of its value, preferring instead to concentrate on buying patents on new electrical inventions (Teich 1989: 31). In Germany, the electrical innovator and entrepreneurial capitalist Werner Siemens (1816–1892) resolved to construct a standard measure of electrical resistance (the "Siemens unit"). He believed that "the country which first realizes [standards] will thereby attain a great advantage over other countries. . . . There is a danger that here again England and France will gain precedence of us." His concern for Germany's global ascendancy led him to found the government-supported Physikalisch-Technische Reichsanstalt to further standardize the measurement of electricity (Teich 1989: 33).

England's early concern for standardization centered on electricity's critical importance to public welfare, as electrical energy was clearly a marketable commodity and "there was an overriding need for its accurate measurement with instruments conforming to recognized standards" (Teich 1989: 35). However, the technical problems associated with unleashing the transformative potential of electricity and the considerable degree of international technical interchange led to a broader discourse among engineers about standardization issues.

The idea of establishing a permanent body to organize regular congresses of technical societies emerged among engineers in 1904, at the fifth International Congress of Electricians (the first Congress took place in 1881). Earlier international electricians' congresses were concerned especially with the measurement of electrical resistance (leading to the 1893 agreement in Paris upon the "international ohm"), the lack of which was "the major obstacle to the technical and commercial utilization of electricity" (Teich 1989: 32). The International Electrotechnical Commission (IEC), founded in 1906, was the outgrowth of the modernizing project envisioned by these internationally oriented technical intellectuals. Between 1906 and 1908 the IEC's statutes were developed by representatives of thirteen European nations and the United States; its work was under way by 1911. The IEC's founders were not merely enthusiasts of the harnessing of electrical power, nor were they apolitical technicians or representatives of entrepreneurial capitalists; their collective goals encompassed but were not limited to any one of these perspectives. Rather, they were in effect socializing on an industry-wide basis a critical aspect of technical innovation. They expressed in their founding documents their global vision of technological pacification: the IEC was to "provide the electrical industry of the world with the permanent [organizational] machinery . . . for the continuous study of the problems for international unification and standardization . . . and to promulgate international recommendations representing an international consensus" (Marcel 1949: 559).

The IEC's standardization domain was the rapidly growing field of power generation, radio communication technology, and basic electrical devices. It developed standards for the measurement of electrical voltage and current, international units such as the hertz (the unit of frequency), an international technical vocabulary, and the standards for all early radio equipment. By 1939 representatives from 27 nations were full participants in the IEC, including all European countries and such non-European countries as Argentina, China, Japan, the USSR, Egypt, and India. In 1948 the IEC relocated to Geneva. Currently it has 47 member bodies, which are national committees "fully representative of national interests . . . of . . . countries officially recognized by the United Nations Organization (UNO)" (IEC 1993c: 7).

The process of global standardization in non-electrical technical fields began in 1926 with the founding of the short-lived International Federation of National Standardizing Associations (ISA), which concentrated on mechanical engineering. Most European and many non-European countries had formed national standards associations between 1907 and 1926, but before the ISA appeared only the IEC was active in international standardization. The ISA did not survive the war (it dissolved in 1942), although some standardization projects were maintained between 1944 and 1946 by the newly formed UN Standards Co-ordinating Committee.

ISO was founded in Geneva in 1947 as a fresh start by representatives of 25 national standardizing associations, about half of them from developed countries. ISO's domain is industrial production standardization, from textiles to photography to furniture finishing. Currently, ISO has 76 national member bodies, twenty corresponding members, and four subscriber members, the last two categories having limited rights and privileges. ISO and the IEC have become deeply intertwined, having a common set of rules and procedures, sharing some personnel, and occupying the same building.

The geographic scope of international standardization has expanded steadily since its inception. At present, nearly one hundred national standards bodies representing the vast majority of the earth's population carry out the project of producing and distributing global standards. Figure 7.1 provides an overview of the structure of the global standardization sector. Below the regional level we include only a few sample organizations and connections because a complete representation would be far too complex to capture in one figure.

For most of its history, the development of standardization was strictly a global and national process. Newly formed national bodies often began participating in ISO as associate members; when they developed the organizational capacity to meet its membership requirements, they applied for full membership rights. Early national standardization bodies were voluntary technical associations that later developed ties with their respective govern-

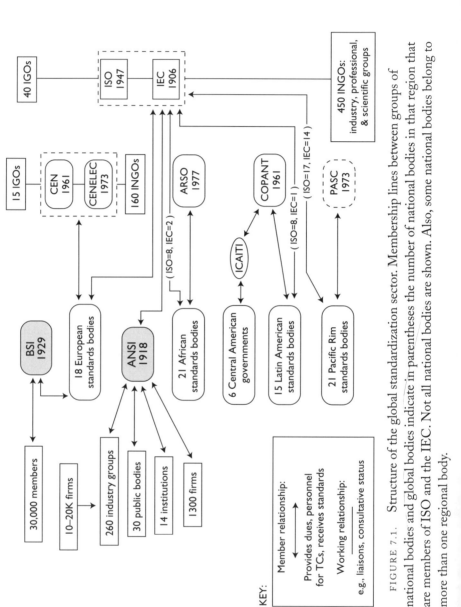

FIGURE 7.1. Structure of the global standardization sector. Membership lines between groups of national bodies and global bodies indicate in parentheses the number of national bodies in that region that are members of ISO and the IEC. Not all national bodies are shown. Also, some national bodies belong to more than one regional body.

ments, but national bodies in the less developed and newly independent countries have been created primarily by government directives or as government ministries. At present, about 70 percent of the national bodies are governmental or quasi-governmental, while the remainder are private bodies. Regardless of their legal status, they are required by both the IEC and ISO to represent all national standardizing interests—firms, scientific communities, governments, and consumers—and must be evaluated as having that representative status by the unanimous vote of ISO/IEC Council member bodies in order to be admitted.[3] Newly independent countries account for virtually all of the membership growth of global bodies since 1950. This growth is also, in part, the result of a recent development in the global standardization sector—the emergence of regional standards bodies.

Regional standardization began in 1959 with the founding of CEN, the Comité Européen de Normalisation (see Figure 7.1). Later entries include the pan-American body (COPANT, founded in 1961); the Arab Organization for Standardization (AOSM, 1967); CENELEC, another European body that is a regional version of the IEC (1973); the pan-African ARSO (1977); and a Pacific Rim body, PASC (1973). Regional standards bodies see themselves as promoting the intensification of regional trading, though not at the expense of larger markets; they also seek to prevent the de facto domination of global standardization by Europe's CEN and CENELEC. European standards bodies currently have great prestige and influence at the global level, attributable to their extensive resources, their high rate of standards publication, the large share of ISO and IEC administrative burdens they shoulder, and the intensity of European regional integration. While they are leading standardizing bodies, they nonetheless actively promote and support the global bodies. Many countries that are not members of global bodies have ties to regional bodies, allowing them to participate, if marginally, in the public discourse on global standardization. With the exception of the European bodies, regional bodies do not develop standards but are only vehicles for regional coordination, yet even CEN "aims at the closest possible alignment between European and world standards" (CEN 1993). Indeed, they are often referred to as harmonization bodies.

The emergence of regional bodies prompted a wave of foundings of national standards bodies in their respective regions; these new national bodies quickly sought membership in the global organizations. COPANT sees such development as a primary aim—to "promote creation of, and coordinate, national associations." Though they typically have close working relationships with global bodies, regional bodies cannot be members. Normally, regional bodies adopt and promulgate global standards; they avoid formulating regional interests in opposition to the global bodies. Though the relations between national, regional, and global standardization organizations are complex, the important point is that authority to coordinate international standardization appears to be increasingly lodged in the global-level organizations, regardless of the individual contributions or influence of lower-level entities.

The global standardization sector is much broader than the standards bodies themselves. Though a precise estimate is impossible, probably tens of thousands of organizations are involved worldwide. At the world level, ISO has liaisons with some 450 INGOs, from the International Association for Cereal Science and Technology to the International Information Centre for Terminology, as well as working relationships with 40 intergovernmental organizations (IGOs) and consultative status with a dozen agencies of the United Nations. Regional bodies have similar connections; for example, CEN maintains relations with 160 regional INGOs.

At a lower level, the connections between national standards bodies and firms, industry groups, governmental departments, and individuals are extremely dense. For example, the membership of the American National Standards Institute (ANSI) includes approximately 1,300 corporations, about 260 technical professions and industry groups, 30 governmental agencies, dozens of universities, several towns, and even a few foreign companies. Canada's national standards body (CSS) lists 8,000 members; Japan's (JISC) 11,000 members; and the United Kingdom's BSI a staggering 23,000 members. For each of these, many members are associations that themselves have thousands or tens of thousands of members. The structure of the global standardization network that emerges here is almost incomprehensibly complex; indeed, even many participants have a fuzzy and incomplete image of their place in the whole.

It is also at the national level that we see the most variation among standardization organizations. For example, they vary in the type of members allowed: while some, such as Sweden's SIS, are virtually restricted to the largest national industry associations, others like the United Kingdom's BSI allow all types of entities, including individuals, to be members. They also vary on such characteristics as the number of mandatory national standards issued, the nature of the rationalized accounts they give of themselves,[4] whether they issue certification marks, and the degree of their autonomy from national governmental supervision. Despite such interesting points of differentiation, it is important to recognize that on the whole they are remarkably similar.

National bodies are compelled to be virtually isomorphic with each other as a prerequisite for membership in global bodies. Exceptional bodies such as the United States' ANSI (a loose, disjointed federation) and Japan's JSS (a secretive and rigidly hierarchical organization) are under overt international pressure as well as pressure from their member firms to become more like other national bodies, and they are apparently responding to this pressure (Egan and Zito 1995).

Resources

In terms of resources a peculiar fact appears: given the scope and ambition of the global standardization project, ISO and the IEC are small organizations. ISO has 155 full-time staff, the IEC about 120. Regional bodies vary in size from 75 full-time staff (CEN) to ARSO's 24 and COPANT's mere 4 paid staff. The bulk of standardization work is done voluntarily, its costs borne by the member organizations: member firms in national bodies furnish and support the experts who comprise the technical committees (TCs) and subcommittee (SC) secretariats, the conveners of the many working groups (WGs), and the WG delegates who actually develop standards. Just in ISO, volunteers serving as TC and SC secretariats equal a full-time staff of about 500 persons; *in toto*, more than 30,000 individuals are active in the standardization sector at the global level alone.

These experts are empowered not as representatives of their firms or countries, but as impersonal technicians who must put the universalistic purposes of standardization first. The British Standards Institute (BSI) describes the necessary qualities of technical committee members as follows:

> Not only must the right people with the right expertise be found to form these committees, they must be willing to impart that knowledge for the good of the industry as a whole. Employers must also be committed—it is they who allow these key members of staff the time and resources necessary to fulfill their responsibilities. (BSI 1994b: 5)

Individuals carrying out the standards project thus work within a unique framework: they continue to be paid by their employers, but they must not attempt to advance their employers' interests. For example, one of the U.S. delegates to the IEC's Technical Committee 77 (TC 77), which deals with electromagnetic radiation's disruptive effects on electronic devices, is employed by Digital Equipment Corporation (DEC) but represents all affected U.S. industries, from movie theaters to elevator manufacturers, including DEC's fiercest competitors. Furthermore, when a delegate is elected secretariat of a TC or SC, the secretariat must "maintain strict neutrality and distinguish sharply between proposals which it makes as a member body and in its capacity as secretariat" (ISO 1985). Individual standards developers thus wear several hats at once: employee, expert technician, and global homogenizer. Their activities are highly circumscribed by the technical demands of the various problems associated with standardization and further rationalized by the voluminous ISO/IEC directives issued to Technical Committee members.

Membership fees provide the bulk of the budgets of standardization bodies.[5] National standards bodies supply 80 percent of the operating expenses of ISO, the remainder deriving from the sale of subscriptions and publications.[6] Membership is not just ritualistic or prestige-endowing—it is required for participation in the development of standards, and only members and subscribers have access to the technical documents that define the standards. In this sense, membership is voluntary more in theory than in practice. Firms generally feel obligated to become members in order to improve their access to global or regional markets, professional groups feel they must join to keep up with world technical development, and so on. The existence of the global bodies, and the increasing participation of national standards bodies, have created a clear imperative to join for any country wishing to engage in international trade or enjoy the fruits of modern technology. Thus the membership base of ISO and the IEC has been steadily expanding.

Operations: The Production of Global Standards

Figure 7.2 diagrams the central operations of ISO, the IEC, and representative national standards bodies with respect to the generation of standards.[7] Working our way through the figure, we outline the procedures whereby standards are defined and adopted in global standards bodies, as well as the mechanisms for implementation of the standards once adopted.

Worldwide standards originate among the experts of the Working Groups of a Subcommittee or Technical Committee of the IEC or ISO; no other formal mechanism is permitted. Industry associations typically submit a formal statement of need for a new standard through their national committee to a joint ISO/IEC committee, which then assigns the task to a TC of either organization, or in some cases creates a new TC. The work is then distributed among any number of working groups. An extensive division of labor has developed to meet the growing complexity of technical development, and subordinate bodies are authorized to create ever more subordinate

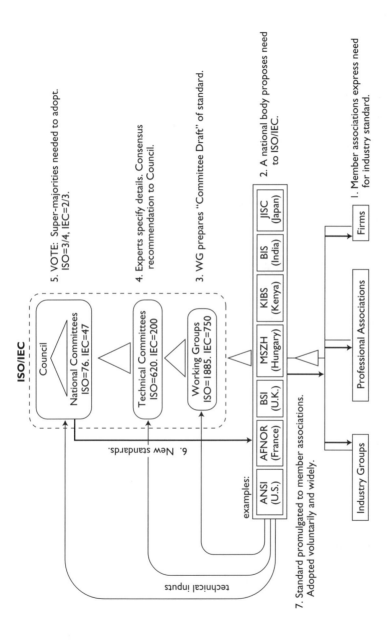

FIGURE 7.2. Procedures for generating international standards.

bodies as technical needs require. Thus, Figure 7.2 indicates that ISO has 179 TCs overseeing 620 TC subcommittees, which in turn coordinate 1,885 SC working groups. Affected industries, consumer groups, and various other concerned parties have informal input to WG meetings, but only national member body delegates may participate in the drafting of a standard.

Individuals of widely recognized technical expertise are nominated by or volunteer through the national bodies for positions on these committees. WG delegates meet three to four times yearly but conduct most of their work at a distance (increasingly via e-mail). Since the Subcommittees and Working Groups of every TC assemble only once every three years at plenary meetings, there are no single meetings at which all organizational levels and segments are represented. The bulk of standardization work takes place in the Working Groups, with the Subcommittees and Technical Committees serving primarily to coordinate and collect the efforts of WG delegates. If a WG cannot agree on a particular technical proposal, a Task Force of a few members is created for the purpose of gathering more technical information and data. This additional data is brought back into the Working Group and used to influence and convince others to adopt or reject the proposal. After a period of development the WG agrees upon a committee draft, which is circulated to all national standards bodies for comment. It is incumbent upon the WG to carefully review and, if possible, accommodate all national member body comments on the committee draft. Finally, the committee produces a Draft International Standard (DIS), which is again circulated to all national standards bodies, who then have six months in which to vote on it (via mail). Three responses are permitted: an unqualified positive vote, abstention, or a negative vote. Negative votes must be justified, and only technical arguments are acceptable justifications; political or economic arguments justifying a negative position are invalid.

Though TC members are officially delegates of their national committees, they are charged to develop standards without taking national concerns into account. The technical environment and extraordinary expertise of all members virtually eliminates nontechnical factors from the standards production process (for example, that a delegate might attempt to delay or direct the development of a standard to protect some national interest is practically unheard of). Though WG delegates may try to garner their colleagues' votes for or against a committee draft, their efforts at persuasion must revolve in every instance around technical matters.

The standardization organizations themselves are off-limits to particularistic influence as well; Article 11 of the ISO constitution warns that "each member . . . shall respect the international character of the responsibilities of the Central Secretariat staff and shall not seek to influence them in the discharge of their responsibilities." According to informant Frank Loya, political maneuvering is extremely rare and instantly detected. The only acceptable nontechnical issue ever raised in the development of a standard is the possibility that its adoption will inadvertently erect a trade barrier.

Final votes on Draft International Standards are adopted with super majorities of the general assemblies (full members only); a two-thirds majority in the case of the IEC and a three-quarters majority in ISO. CEN goes even further, requiring consensual adoption of standards.[8] Once adopted, however, standards are not obligatory as far as ISO and the IEC are concerned. While the standards bodies expend much effort in disseminating new standards to member firms, consortia, and individuals through national standards bodies, ISO's constitution states that "decisions . . . shall constitute only recommendations to the members, each member remaining free either to follow or not to follow them" (ISO 1985: 4). Some national standards bodies with close state ties have the authority to require compliance within their countries, but the preferred means of *global* standardization is universal voluntary compliance, a principle that thoroughly infuses the standardization sector. The logic of the sector is quite simple: the character of the standards and the nature of the processes by which they are generated—universal, consensually derived standards of unimpeachable technical merit—are themselves sufficient rationale for their adoption. Add to that the compulsion of market competition, and coercive mechanisms are entirely unnecessary in the increasingly integrated world economy. As the BSI notes, "pressure to conform has never been stronger" (BSI 1994a: 1).

Purposes

Do standardization bodies define their goals in narrowly technical terms? Hardly. Rather, the goals are emphatically social. The BSI sees standards as safeguards of everyday essentials: "Our homes are more comfortable places to live in, our appliances more reliable and our children's toys and playgrounds a great deal safer—thanks to the existence of standards" (BSI 1994b: 4). ISO claims that standards lead to "improved health, safety and environmental protection and reduction of waste," along with "enhanced product quality and reliability at a reduced price" (ISO 1993: 4). Indeed, standardization is routinely portrayed as the rational means to solve some of humanity's most serious problems. IEC general secretary Anthony Raeburn opened the 1992 annual report by quoting Nietzsche: "It is our future that lays down the law of our today" (IEC 1993a). He then went on to detail the ambitious "Rotterdam Masterplan" to accelerate, improve, and modernize the efforts of the IEC to serve the growing needs of technical standardization into the next century, with a special focus on less developed countries moving toward industrialization. A pragmatic utopia, not just an inchoate world of technical marvels, is the implicit ultimate vision.

As dutifully rational organizations, the standards bodies have a clear causal theory of how their work accomplishes these broad goals. The main link between standards and global progress is the removal of technical (nontariff) barriers to world trade. Unrestricted exchange is the key to the improvement of living standards, health, and safety, first because it promotes the flow of goods and technologies generated in one place but useful in another, second because it increases the economic efficiency of competing firms and therefore total human wealth and resources.

The latter point—benefits to participating firms—receives particular attention. First, conformity to standards is presumed to reduce information and transaction costs between economic partners, as "standards regulate every aspect of the manufacturing process—materials, dimensions, performance, codes of practice, test methods and terminology" (BSI 1994b: 3), thus simplifying and clarifying contractual relations. Second, standardization shifts some of the costs of rationalization from the firm to the system. Third, for member firms standards are "strategic tools . . . to gain access to the future markets of the world" (AFNOR 1994). Quick compliance with new standards gives firms a competitive edge over laggards. Finally, the rapidly expanding ISO 9000 certification process requires extensive internal and external review and assessment of the firm's production and management procedures, the result of which is supposed to be better economic performance. Industry journals abound with "success stories" of firms whose ISO 9000 certification purportedly has resulted in higher credit bond ratings, improved customer satisfaction, better stock control, and expanded markets. Tens of thousands of firms worldwide have qualified for ISO 9000 certification (the United States is a laggard in this respect),[9] and since January 1992, all European Union corporations require it of their trading partners (see Timbers 1992 and Walgenbach 1997).

Another purpose activated by standards organizations is political in nature—or, more accurately, antipolitical. As we have seen, these bodies resolutely resist becoming vehicles for the interest-maximizing action of firms, states, or ideological blocs. ISO/IEC voting procedures ensure that domination by narrow interests is difficult: each country has only one vote, no country has veto power, votes are unweighted (except in CEN), and only technical negatives are permitted. The secretary-general of ISO is prohibited from seeking or receiving "instructions from any member or from any authority external to the Organization" (ISO 1985: 7–8). This structure is designed to activate transcendent purposes oriented around global progress. Helping promote such commitment among individuals, firms, and associations is itself a central purpose of these organizations.

Rationality in Standardization

The rationality of the standardization process is apparent at many levels. For the individual firm, adherence to global standards is rational because failure to comply is believed to disqualify a commodity for trade in global markets. For national economies and states, participation in the standardization process is rational both for effective action in the market and for increased capacity to import products from abroad. Beyond these motivational logics, we find that the standardization process itself has been intensely rationalized. The standards bodies strongly emphasize their commitment to greater efficiency in their work. Standards are rationally produced and managed, and they are transformed into commodities that are advertised and sold. The metrics for rationalization are numerous: the IEC boasts that "production of pages of standards has increased very considerably in the past five years" and goes on to document the rising rate of thousands of pages of standards produced, the decreasing average time to develop standards, the falling cost per standard developed, and other measures common among firms producing more conventional commodities (IEC 1993a: 4). BSI advertises their "best selling standards" and promotes the advantages of membership in BSI even to individuals, who can access BSI's standards reference library with 600,000 documents, sign up for a monthly CD-ROM service with the latest standards, or shop from BSI's "unrivaled stock of British, European and international documents" (BSI 1994a: 2). Similar measures of increasing efficiency are present in publications from most other standards bodies; commitment to rationality in standards production is ubiquitous.

ALTERNATIVE PERSPECTIVES ON GLOBAL STANDARDIZATION

Keeping this review of origins, structure, operations, and purposes in mind, we next turn to alternative theories of world development. Our aim here is to assess the theories in terms of their capacity to account for the standardization sector.

World-System Theory

Christopher Chase-Dunn's useful review of world-system theory stresses the reproduction of core-periphery structures and relations of inequality through the interaction of four processes: "power-block formation, state formation, unequal exchange, and class struggle" (Chase-Dunn 1989: 238). Though fundamentally economic, these processes depend heavily on state action: economically determined class alliances (power blocs) construct and use relatively strong core states to secure advantages in global markets and maintain unequal exchange. Extreme stratification in the world economy is inevitable as long as it remains capitalist, for the reproduction of core-periphery inequalities is both sought by capitalists and imposed on them by the competitive nature of the system. Mobility in the system is possible, but systemic change is prevented by the operations of the system itself.

Many dimensions of world stratification appear to fit this argument: compared to peripheral countries, core countries have far higher levels of economic production, capital accumulation, military power, technical research and development, trade, and much more (Bornschier and Chase-Dunn 1985; Amin 1977; Meyer and Hannan 1979). The core does dominate the periphery, though not as directly as in the heyday of European imperialism, and arguments about the subjugation of such world-level bodies as the IMF and the World Bank to the interests of international capital are plausible (Petras et al. 1981; Pfister and Suter 1987). Even the United Nations's structure reflects core domination in that three of the five permanent members of the Security Council are major core countries.

Given the importance of standardization to the integration of the capitalist world economy, and to the mobility of capital that world-system theory insists is crucial to the perpetuation of capitalism, the global standardization sector ought to reflect the same sort of core domination we find in other domains. Core countries should dominate standardization organizations, and the interests of core states in maintaining exploitative relations with peripheral and semiperipheral zones should be reflected in their operations.

World-system theory also identifies the site of likely counterhegemonic challenges to the capitalist core: the semiperiphery. As the "weak link" between dominators and the dominated, semiperipheral countries are most likely to mobilize their resources sufficiently to become upwardly mobile in the system (Germany and the United States in the nineteenth century) or to build a semi-autarchic subsystem that limits and controls its ties to the capitalist world (the Soviet Union and Communist bloc). These attempts are often led by the state, either directly (e.g., state-directed industrialization) or through the successful use of military force or coercive social policy (Rubinson 1978; Wallerstein 1979).

The implication for the standardization sector is that semiperipheral countries should resist core-dominated standardization efforts. Upwardly mobile semiperipheral countries might refuse to join capitalist-dominated standardization bodies, they might establish competing standards organizations within an autarchic subsystem and develop their own sets of standards, or they might work within the standards bodies to mobilize non-core countries against the capitalist center.

Are these implications of world-system theory consistent with what we have shown regarding the transnational standardization sector? Some problems are at once evident.

The first and most fundamental problem with this perspective is that standardization happens at all. If global capitalism is a sort of Darwinian competitive process, successful firms should develop competing sets of technical standards and try to impose their respective standards on the markets they compete to control. This occurs routinely, in the early phase of the emergence of a new industry, but very quickly we find industry associations arising to homogenize standards, often quite voluntarily (e.g., Fox 1992a). The result is an industry standard. The dominant rationales for voluntary industry standards are usually economic: the total market will be greatly enlarged if buyers have a simple information structure to deal with, prices will be lower because of the efficiencies generated. But global standardization elevates the criteria of rationality to a level beyond that of competing capitalists: what is sought is system rationality, which is defined in terms quite different from narrow industry interests. All interested parties must be represented in the standardization process through their national member body delegates, and firms must then either adopt the new consensual global standard or risk market exclusion.

The world-system perspective could counter that the combination of competitive and cooperative relations among firms is neither new nor necessarily contrary to capitalist rationality; Harry Braverman (1975) accounted for the origin of this combination in the need for industry-wide coordination at the national level during two world wars and its later institutionalization to serve capitalists' long-term interests. However, this argument overlooks the fact that industries or firms, as such, do not publish or impose standards at the global level. Furthermore, while firms may have an interest in supporting their delegate-employees in the creation of what is essentially a public good, this support is also constructed as a moral obligation among those involved in global standardization, and the expenses can be considerable, while the benefits are often dubious.[10]

The same arguments are offered to explain why firms and states support global standardization—the market will be larger, trade opportunities will be enhanced, efficiency will increase. But this argument cuts both ways. A larger market creates opportunities for existing firms to expand, but a homogenized market in which proprietary standards have been eliminated also offers much easier terms of entry to new firms. As is now well recognized, late entry can be advantageous, especially for firms backed by mobilizing states in countries with low wages and protective trade policies (Milbank 1994; Voss 1994). From the point of view of established firms in core countries, standardization is at best of ambiguous utility; at worst, it constrains firms from realizing the full benefit of innovation and costs sunk in research and development. For example, global standards that supersede a company or industry-wide *de facto* national standard impose much greater costs on those most heavily invested in it, namely, the largest firms of the core countries.[11]

World-system theorists might also propose that the standardization sector is nothing but a rubber-stamp parliament for dominant transnational corporations. If, for example, IBM adopts a computer cable end-fitting standard to suit its internal production designs, it would then get ISO to accept its standard and force other manufacturers to follow suit. Participants in ISO activity say that such practice is increasingly rare. As IEC general secretary Anthony M. Raeburn observed: "The imposed *de facto* standard has been shown to not work in today's environment. The corporate standard has no place in the global market" (IEC 1993b: 9). Occasional attempts to promote a design favoring a single corporation, whether deliberate or inadvertent, are immediately countered, according to a key informant:

> If a new delegate advances the narrow interests [of their employer] over
> general interests, others will speak right up, and point out that "well,
>   that might be good for your company, but that's not what we're doing
> here . . . " New members often need to learn about such differences.
> They think they are arguing a purely technical matter, and they'll put
> their foot in their mouths. Someone will take them aside, show them the
> difference.

Indeed, large U.S. corporations and industries have been notably unsuccessful at having their particular interests accommodated in standards production (see note 9), because of the weak federal structure of U.S. standardization organizations, no government direction whatsoever, and little coordination among firms. Many of our informants observe that the United States, the home of some of the most powerful transnational firms, is a laggard in almost every respect in the standardization sector. According to one standardization consultant:

> American corporations, as a matter of policy, have avoided complying to any kind of standards. They've been able to sell their products anyway, and assumed this would continue. Now their buyers insist on certification to IEC safety standards and the company is years away from a redesigned product. . . . Many American firms are behind the 8-ball. The dates for conformity to a number of different types of standards were set back in 1987, then again in 1990. They went into effect in 1995 and 1996. Companies are just now, [9] months after certification marks became obligatory to sell products in Europe, saying "What is this standard?" "Where does it come from?" "How do I get a mark?" They're way behind.

Alternately, core countries could dominate standards development by their command of the largest portion of the world's highly trained and most-experienced technical experts. Thus, the current unequal distribution of technical expertise between core and periphery would ensure that core interests are privileged and the dependent technical development of the periphery maintained. There is some substance to this position. First, core countries hold 80 percent of all TC secretariats, and 60 percent of TC secretariats are held by the United States, England, France, Germany, Sweden, and Russia. There are large, statistically significant differences ($F = 45.36$) between the mean number of TC and SC memberships maintained by countries of each world-system zone: while peripheral countries maintain an average of 102 SC memberships, for semiperipheral countries the mean is 288 and core countries average 555 subcommittee memberships. Second, the firms and states of peripheral countries cannot support as many delegates to global bodies as can core countries, and core countries often "pack" working groups with their delegates so they will have greater input into standards development. Even so, our informants indicate that secretariats have neither sufficient opportunity nor authority to direct outcomes, and their administrative obligations are quite heavy.[12]

In the final analysis, regardless of whether core delegates outnumber peripheral delegates, have greater technical expertise, or hold more positions of authority, draft international standards are voted on by all member bodies, and regardless of who drafts them they must meet the basic criteria for all global standards. There is little evidence that administrative dominance can be parlayed into benefits for core countries. According to one working group facilitator, "In the end, technical matters can all be decided upon. Scientific, technological knowledge is everywhere the same . . . and at the end of the day, you generally go out and get a beer."

A final problem for world-system theory in this dimension is the absence of global capital from the standardization sector. Transnational capitalists (banks, investment firms, market traders) are conspicuously missing. They are not members of ISO or the IEC, and they are rarely members of national standards bodies either individually or collectively (as associations). International industrial associations, which might conceivably serve as vehicles for the articulation of capitalist interests, do not typically set standardization agendas for their member firms. Perhaps standards bodies are under structural pressure to promote the global interests of capital, but evidence for such pressure within standardization bodies is lacking, and the mechanisms by which it might be brought to bear would have to be extraordinarily indirect.

A second major problem for world-system theory is the egalitarian structure of the standards bodies. As we have shown, they go to great lengths to put all actors on an equal footing, and they require consensus or near consensus in their decision-making processes. ISO (not an acronym but the Greek-derived prefix for "equal") grants its members the right to be represented on all technical committees they deem of interest, and "in these committees qualified representatives of industry, research institutes, government authorities, consumer bodies and international organizations from all over the world come together as equal partners in the resolution of global standardization problems" (ISO 1993: 8). The IEC adds that "consensus among all stakeholders is required to ensure a level playing field for the world's trading nations and industry" (IEC 1993b: 3). While Chase-Dunn or Wallerstein might object that an "equalizing" measure like freer trade resulting from standardization works to the advantage of the technically advanced and politically powerful countries, a bit of counterfactual thinking shows the weakness of such an objection. If capitalist core interests dominated standardization, we should find much more inegalitarian structures and processes in this sector. The last thing we would find is such thoroughgoing commitment to technical rationality as the sole determinant of standards. Of course, it may be that the technical superiority of core-based firms allows them to dominate the formally egalitarian and rationalistic structures of the standards bodies, but our informants did not support this view and they offered counterexamples against it. We have yet to turn up evidence in its favor.

Third, the prediction of resistance by countries outside the core fails because resistance of any sort is so hard to find. After World War II the Soviet Union seized Eastern Europe to protect itself from the capitalist core, yet it was a founding member of ISO and has always participated cooperatively in it. Russian was adopted as an official language of both ISO and the IEC (along with English and French), an indication of semiperipheral assertiveness perhaps but hardly of an attempt to build an alternative institution. All of Eastern Europe has been active in ISO from the beginning; ISO never attempted to exclude Communist countries, as one might expect if it were truly capital-dominated. ISO and IEC principles exclude partisan politics from considerations of membership and operations, and the organizations seem to have lived up well to those principles.

On the whole, world-system theory is uncomfortable with the notion of transnational cultural or institutional structures that cannot be reduced to the interests of powerful, competing actors or explained as unambiguous expressions of global inequalities resulting from the capitalist mode of production. While there is little doubt that the core countries maintain a dominant presence, this is inevitable considering the current unequal distribution of technological and productive capacity. Furthermore, while world-system theory may explain some effects of global standardization, it cannot account for the distinctive structures, procedures, and ideology of global standardization organizations. Chase-Dunn (1989: 344) does propose that "the growth of international organizations . . . will eventually result in a world state" that will open possibilities for coordinated struggle to create a just moral order on the global level. The key here, however, is the term "state." He gives no credence to non-state structures that lack coercive power or the possibility of resorting to armed force, yet that is exactly the character of the global standardization sector.

State-Competition/Neorealist/Neoliberal Institutionalist Theories

While they might make strange bedfellows in some respects, state-competition theorists such as Tilly (1985, 1992), Giddens (1985), Skocpol (1979; see also Evans, Rueschemeyer, and Skocpol 1985), realists and neorealists like

Raymond Aron (1984), Waltz (1979) and Grieco (1993), and neoliberal institutionalists like Robert Keohane (1986; Axelrod and Keohane 1993) share
a common theoretical frame quite different from that of world-system
theory. For them, the world is fundamentally structured by the system of
competing states. States operate in a capitalist economic context, but their
behavior is mainly self-interested, and they have a good deal of (variable) autonomy from economic actors. For strategic reasons, states may elect to form
cooperative arrangements with other states, but these are motivated by bal-
ance-of-power considerations and stronger states normally dominate weaker
ones in such arrangements (cf. the work on international regimes by Krasner
1983a, Keohane 1984; see also the articles in Baldwin 1993). Even strong
forms of cooperation that become institutionalized in international organizations are seen as ultimately reducible to the interests and relative power of
states (Krasner 1983b; Keohane 1993).

In short, these theories view states as truly sovereign, rational, advantage-
seeking actors. Transnational arrangements are strategic and temporary, and
states are inherently unwilling to yield their sovereignty to transnational organizations by granting them taxation or military powers. Whatever exists
beyond the nation-state is therefore completely at the mercy of states or
simply too insignificant to matter much in the development of the state
system and global economy. (Indeed, transnational bodies are often either ignored or barely mentioned by state-competition theorists; Tilly's [1992]
"grand statement" is a prime example.)

Giddens (1985) is quite explicit in his rejection of a transnational level of
social reality, insisting on the "low level of governability" of world society
caused by its lack of a sufficient "degree of organizational integration" (p.
322). Like world-system theory, his analysis is consistently reductionist, but
he substitutes states for capitalists, or the state system for capitalism, as the
major actors of world development. Beyond the level of states, nothing of
substance is to be found.

The state-competition/neorealism perspectives are even more uncomfortable than world-system theory with the global standardization sector. States
are only minor players in standardization, strong states are not dominant
characters, and the plot of the play involves much less competition and conflict than the perspective predicts. Further, state competition and neorealist
theories suggest that states would promote a variety of sets of standards and
find it extremely difficult to compromise about them. We find variety in some
particular areas, such as the different television technologies of North
America, Japan, and Europe, but they are too exceptional to constitute evi-

dence of general competition regarding standards. Standardization is a resolutely cooperative venture.

Neoliberal institutionalism appears at first glance to have better prospects of accounting for the standardization sector. This perspective predicts interstate cooperation when multilateral institutions would lower transaction costs, promote mutually beneficial gains, and serve common interests. Exactly how these fiercely competitive states are to solve the free-rider problem that makes it irrational for any state to underwrite the initial costs of organizing cooperation (Olson 1965) may remain an unsolved problem in this theory, but the theory does help explain the durability and effectiveness of international regimes once they are established. At the risk of being redundant, however, we stress again the virtual absence of states in the global standardization sector: the largest and most active national standards bodies that make up ISO and the IEC are private associations, states have only indirect representation even where standards bodies are quasi-state organs, and firms typically resist state interference at all levels of the standardization process.

Any state-centric theory thus has great difficulty with this sector. If state-competition/neorealism theories were applicable to standardization, we would have more competition about standards, more state participation, and domination by strong states over weak ones. World-system theory and neoliberal institutionalism produce essentially the same predictions, though the latter is more willing to accommodate cooperation. We find a largely contrary pattern: technical rationality dominates over power. Reductionist views are therefore inadequate. We need to consider the transnational standardization sector on its own terms, as a transcendent level of social organization. That is what the world-polity perspective attempts to do.

STANDARDIZATION AS A WORLD-POLITY PROCESS

The global standardization project constitutes a highly institutionalized sphere of world-level collective action; the global standards bodies that direct this project operate at a level beyond that of firms, states, or countries. Their rules of nonpartisanship make all of "humanity," not portions of humanity identified by nationality, race, religion, or any other invidious distinction, the target beneficiaries of their activity (ISO and the IEC even symbolize this principle by operating out of neutral Switzerland). Their members include individuals, firms, industry and professional groups, and government agencies from all parts of the world, and these members see themselves as participants in a unitary, coherent, necessary, and practically inevitable process.

The global standards project is also highly rationalized, both in the social theory that motivates action (standardization contributes to a broad range of desirable human purposes) and in the procedures employed (the rules for producing and adopting standards, the concern for efficient standards production, the commodification of standards and efforts to disseminate them). This emphasis on rationality is, indeed, a central tenet of the project; in an unrationalized world, it would never have emerged in the first place. In short, like other INGOs, standardization organizations are built on world-cultural conceptions of universalism, rational progress, and egalitarianism (see Chapter 1). They conceive science and technique as impersonal and ubiquitously applicable. They conceive rational analysis and organization as crucial to— and to a large extent, even coextensive with—human progress. They conceive their work as promoting the realization of deliberately chosen goals. They further conceive all humans everywhere as having the same basic needs (for comfort, convenience, safety, and so on) and assume that these needs can best be met by uniform, standardized technologies.

This analysis implies that the standardization sector is part of "world society" (Meyer, Boli et al. 1997), the transcendent level of social reality that encompasses regional, national, and subnational levels of social construction. World-cultural principles are directly embodied and given expression by standards organizations; indeed, standards bodies are an important, albeit rather small, segment of the organizational structure that institutionalizes world culture. They also, of course, help to define and shape world culture through their action at the global level.

The standardization sector displays several noteworthy characteristics. First, it embodies the principles of universalism, rationality, and homogenization to an extreme degree. It insists that technical considerations alone determine standards, as in ISO's provision that dissenting votes must be backed only by technical arguments. It adopts a single, uniform set of standards in each technical area rather than a set of options among which firms and professionals might choose. It homogenizes the technical infrastructure of the world in a notably tautological way: because the standardization sector exists, subunit actors at all levels must promote its ever-expanding reach and effectiveness.

Given the pressures of the competitive world economy, a paradox emerges here. The standards bodies champion voluntary participation and rational decision-making, and they have far too few resources to impose their standards on lower-level organizations, but the standards they adopt become obligatory and are routinely enforced by states, industry groups, and individual firms. These lower-level actors find it virtually impossible to reject standards because doing so is seen as irrational—they would be limiting their access to world markets and technologies to a fatal degree.

This observation indicates a second important characteristic—the extraordinary degree of authority exercised by these bodies, despite their lack of resources. That they are indeed authoritative can be illustrated by further counterfactual thinking. Independent bodies challenging their sectoral monopolies do not arise; since ISO's formation, no other body has attempted to wrest control of standardization from it, and the IEC has monopolized standardization in electrical domains since its inception. Similarly, factions from within standards bodies do not break away to proffer themselves as alternatives, and even very large firms operating in new technical fields quickly accede to global standardization norms. A devolution of organizational structure is apparent in the emergence of regional standards bodies, but that too has failed to produce challenges to the authority of the global bodies. The latter monopolize the standards-setting process, and actors at all levels find it "natural" to abide by the standards they produce.

Third, the basis of the standards bodies' authority is essentially social-contractarian: voluntaristic action by rational actors in a frame of universal knowledge and principles generates standards for behavior (informal "laws") that reason obligates the actors to accept (see Power 1997). This is neither charismatic nor patriarchal authority; neither is it legal-rational domination (à la Weber), for standards bodies are not capable of imposing their standards by formal law or military force. Instead, their authority derives from the truth presumably embodied in science and technique, from the righteousness presumably embodied in the principles of governance by which the standards bodies operate (equality, fairness, nonpartisanship), and from the presumed self-interest of the lower-level actors that comprise them (see Conclusion).

Though states often now create national standards bodies and impose some global standards locally via regulatory agencies, our historical sketch makes it clear that states have always played a relatively restrained role in global standardization. Neither ISO nor the IEC is a treaty organization. States are not permitted as members. National standards bodies may be closely tied to states, but internally they are dominated by non-state entities, especially firms, industries, and professions. States are largely passive and secondary members of standards bodies, acceding to the authority associated with technical expertise and the universalistic knowledge systems grounding that expertise.

This structure amounts to a complex web of mutual legitimation (cf.

Stinchcombe 1968). Individuals, firms, and associations legitimate national bodies through the theory of rational voluntarism; national bodies legitimate the global bodies by making the latter transcendentally inclusive and by bringing the authority of their respective states into the structure. The global bodies in turn legitimate national bodies by subjecting them to evaluation in accordance with universalistic, technically based criteria for admission and retention of membership, and they legitimate the technical experts who do the bulk of their work by the very act of selecting them for TC membership.

In short, we find a remarkable fusion of private (rational-voluntaristic) and public (bureaucratic) authority throughout the standardization sector. Most ISO member bodies are closely tied to states, but many of the most important national bodies are private (including ANSI and the BSI). Within national standards bodies, membership includes mostly private entities (firms and individuals) but also numerous public or quasi-public bodies—governmental agencies, industry associations organized to deal with the state, professional groups whose members are licensed by the state, and so on. Public authority is therefore present at many levels, but the sector is driven by private actors motivated by both private and public concerns.

The fact that the standardization sector so thoroughly fuses public and private authority in a structure of global reach and consequence implies that more than just a world "society" or "culture" is in operation here. What we infer is the outlines of a world polity—an all-embracing, complex social unit with a well-defined central authority structure that coordinates action at all levels of social organization. In lieu of a world state, which would monopolize military force and constitute the locus of legal sovereignty in the entire world, we find standardization organized as a specialized central structure whose authority is restricted to a single (albeit increasingly broad) domain, that of technical development and production. All other actors are subordinate to this authority structure and their particularistic objectives are prevented from shaping the outcomes of its decisions.

Thus, when Giddens (1985: 341) states that "the increasing social integration of the globe does not betoken an incipient political unity," he is trapping himself in too limited a concept of the polity. A world state is not necessary for global authority to be concentrated, rationalized, and effective. The standardization sector constitutes an alternative model—not coercive, not powerful, not even recognized as such except by those directly involved in its operations. Yet, as we have shown, the sector is eerily state-like in its effects, but based on a very different theory of rational, voluntaristic authority from that normally embodied by states.

Global standardization is part of a much more general process of transnational organizing that has institutionalized world-cultural principles and practices as world-polity phenomena (see Chapter 1). Both the IEC and ISO were founded during periods of rapid transnational organizing. The IEC was part of the first major wave of INGO formation, from the 1890s until just before World War I, that made voluntaristic transnational organizing a regular feature of world-polity development. ISO was part of the explosive period of transnational organizing following World War II, when INGO formation leapt to entirely unprecedented levels. That regional standardization bodies did not appear until the 1950s is also consistent with INGO trends: while regional bodies were rare before World War II, from the 1950s onward they have proliferated rapidly.

The INGO population is a variegated collection of organizations. As Chapter 1 shows, about a third of these bodies are engaged in the domains of relatively pure rational knowledge production and technical development (12 percent in the sciences and mathematics, 15 percent in medicine and health, 7 percent in standardization, infrastructure, and communications). Another quarter are essentially economic organizations—industry and trade groups, finance and tourism associations, and the like—while about 6 percent are professional associations or labor unions. The standardization sector is closely tied to all these areas, which together account for about 65 percent of all INGOs (1988 data). It also maintains close ties with a number of international sports organizations (5 percent of all INGOs) but is not linked to other categories, such as individual rights and welfare bodies, educational organizations, and INGOs concerned with world peace or environmental protection.

In many of these sectors, a number of INGOs resemble the global standardization bodies. Seismologists have their International Association of Seismology and Physics of the Earth's Interior, cytologists their International Academy of Cytology, architects their International Union of Architects; these bodies operate in accordance with rational-voluntaristic principles to set standards, debate ethical questions, disseminate techniques, and so on (UIA 1994). Most sectors are more highly differentiated than the standardization arena, however, with numerous world bodies that, while not exactly competing with each other, certainly do not exhibit the unitary coherence and organizational dominance of the IEC and ISO. In addition, states are explicitly excluded from most INGOs, at all levels. States have their own world bodies, the IGOs, to which INGOs link themselves via consultative status, but the world-cultural principles of properly constituted authority favored by INGOs generally denigrate the coercive and power-oriented principles of state actors. For most INGOs, states are seen as intrusive, even illegitimate interlopers in their domains.

In several respects, then, the standardization sector is unique. Authority is voluntary and rational, as with other INGOs, but it is much more centralized and effective than in most other sectors. States are not excluded—private and public authority are fused—but the role of states is carefully managed to lock them into subordinate status. Principles of technical rationality and universal science are activated in highly purified form, beyond the level of other sectors except those in the pure sciences, and their purity in this respect is an important underpinning for their authority vis-à-vis states and their member organizations and individuals. In sum, the standardization sector displays traits shared with much of the world-polity-constructing INGO population, but it pushes them to a higher level of purity and effectiveness than has been achieved in other sectors.

CONCLUSION

The global standardization sector is structured around principles derived ultimately from images of a world polity undergoing construction as a single societal unit. While such capitalist ideologies as the value of competition between firms and the necessary pursuit of profits are legitimated in the standardization project, they are circumscribed by a meaning structure that is not reducible to the world economic system. These elements of capitalist ideology are subordinated to larger "goods" of a peculiarly universalistic and technical sort, the ultimate goal being the welfare and comfort of the human species and, as a necessary component of this goal, the health of the planet and all its life-forms.

The principles of the standardization sector are also irreducible to the global system of states locked in competition for political, military, and economic domination. States take a back seat in both structure and process, and the deadly competitive struggle between states is not permitted to shape the products of global standards organizations.

When Giddens asserts the lack of organizational structure necessary to make world society governable, he overlooks the fact that, as the standardization sector demonstrates, INGOs are actively generating this condition of governability. When Chase-Dunn (1989) dismisses "culture" as essentially epiphenomenal and irrelevant to world-system development, he is neglecting the key role of cultural principles in the constitution of world authority by non-state actors. What INGOs achieve is a peculiar form of authoritative management—they assemble the resources required to give world-cultural principles credibility and effectiveness, and they embody those principles sufficiently well to make them effective in shaping social practices (cf. Wuthnow 1987).

The result, in the standardization sector, is a built environment that is homogenizing in its base at an extraordinary pace. This does not mean that the built environment necessarily must look the same everywhere in the world, but it does mean that it will work the same way everywhere. The uniformity engendered by standardization is deep and far-reaching, but it is also subtle. It reduces fundamental differences and provokes the intensified reification of superficial differences: varied facades attract much attention, but underneath they are hardly distinguishable. The process is much like the homogenizing capacity of national cultures, which reduce the cultural base of ethnic differences while provoking the mobilization of remnants of those differences as superficial symbols of a disappearing past (cf. Steinberg 1989). The phenomenon is not new. Alexis de Tocqueville (1966 [1836]) identified it 160 years ago during his travels in America: nothing produces a more conformist model of society than rational voluntarism undeflected by the whims of coercive power. What is new is that it has shifted to a higher level, and it may well be paving the way for the creation of a world state (Boswell 1995; Meyer, Boli et al. 1997).

Chapter Eight Population Control for National
Development: From World
Discourse to National Policies

DEBORAH BARRETT AND DAVID JOHN FRANK

This chapter documents the ascent of population control as a global concern,
first in world culture and later in national policies.[1] We distinguish three
main issues: the changing *content*, the increasing *density*, and the *diffusion* of
population-control discourse and activity.[2]

We demonstrate the relationship between conditions in the world polity
and the *content* of population-control discourse by comparing the total and
relative numbers of international conferences that emphasize different population-control models over time. Our argument is that the content of international population-control discourse has changed in step with changes in
the wider global institutional environment. Thus, pronatalism, which promotes population growth for national strength, dominated in the imperialistic
pre–World War I period; eugenics, which promotes population management
for national purity, dominated in the nationalist, corporatist interwar period;
and neo-Malthusianism, which promotes population control for national and
individual development, has dominated in the recent nation-state period.

The legitimacy of the content of the population-control discourse in
world society has, in turn, influenced the *density* of population-control system discourse. In particular, density rose with the consolidation of population-control models that directly linked population control to national interests. Density has also been affected by the overall expansion of the world
polity. We demonstrate both effects by charting the total number of international population-control conferences over time.

Finally, the content and density of international population-control discourse have influenced the *diffusion* of national-level population policies. The linkage of population control to national interests suggested the benefits of a national-level policy. In addition, the increasing density of a nationally oriented population-control discourse, and its attendant institutionalization in the global arena, set forth a policy model for states to adopt. By comparing the timing of international conferences and national policies, we show that national policies emerged from a discursive regime that first redefined the meaning of "population" in world culture.

INTRODUCTION

In the late nineteenth and early twentieth centuries, the discussion of population control was largely taboo in the public domain. Matters relating to sexuality were confined mainly to the inner world of the family, to be discussed privately, if at all, between men and women. What few explicit norms existed were religious in origin and recommended the bounty of unfettered reproduction.

Indeed, to the limited extent that population was related to any broader collective good, and thus a public issue, the emphasis was on stimulating birthrates. Large nation-states were thought to be strong nation-states, militarily and economically. Demographic data fed countries' concern with numbers, as illustrated with this quotation from a French patriot: "As Germany since 1891 has twice as many births (1,903,106) than France (908,859) it is fatal that in 14 years she will have twice as many conscripts. Then this nation which hates us will devour us! The Germans say it, they print it, and they will do it."[3] Even as recently as the 1960s, most governments wanted to boost national fertility.

Against this climate of pronatalism, altruistic crusaders for population control began to organize in Europe and the United States. They gained legitimacy from association with the field of demography and by playing on fears that urban poverty, overcrowding, and rapid immigration threatened the body politic. This emerging class of population experts held international conferences and founded international organizations, at which they proclaimed scientific theories and humanitarian manifestos about the deleterious psychological, genetic, and economic impacts of unregulated population growth.

By the late 1960s, the admonitions of population-control advocates had taken hold: the meaning of population had been radically transformed in world culture. Population had become a routine matter of public interest, and population growth had become more liability than strength, more national problem than solution. Poverty, disease, environmental despoliation, and inequality between the sexes were all seen to follow from "overpopulation." These new understandings, the first inklings of which were already apparent in the nineteenth century, have been distilled in an array of world- and national-level activities.

To explore the processes underlying the transformation of the meaning of population in the world polity, we address the content, density, and diffusion of population-control discourse and activity. Most theorists have assumed that all three of these are functionally related to world-population growth (see, e.g., Warwick 1979; Mauldin and Lapham 1985; Livi-Bacci 1994). We contend that important global institutional factors (i.e., definitions and organizations of entities) are also at work (see Thomas et al. 1987).

The overall picture we draw charts the world-cultural movement from population *growth* as national benefit to population *control* as national benefit. The path was forged by a world population-control discourse that increasingly incorporated the interests and authorities of nation-states. Early on, the carriers of the population-control discourse were mainly international social-movement organizations (cf. Smith, Pagnucco, and Romeril 1994). But as the discourse itself incorporated states and citizens, intergovernmental and governmental organizations became increasingly involved and produced a proliferation of national population-control policies.

INTERNATIONAL POPULATION-CONTROL CONFERENCES AND NATIONAL POLICIES

The empirical grounding for our argument comes from a systematic analysis of international conferences and national policies on population control. Conferences are forums where ideas are shaped and disseminated, where experts present theories for world betterment. To investigate these ideas, we used a comprehensive list of population-control conferences. Such a list was constructed from a Library of Congress database, pertinent secondary sources, various lists of meetings, and conference proceedings themselves.[4]

To be included, conferences had to meet two criteria. First, they had to be explicitly international, defining their actions as relevant to the world at large. This was judged by the titles and stated aims of the conferences and the organizations hosting them. Second, the main topic of the meeting had to relate directly to some aspect of population control. All conferences that clearly advocated a population-control regime were included, as were international scientific meetings on demography and genetics, which importantly contributed to the scientific basis of policies. However, medical meetings on population (physiology, diseases, etc.) that did not directly discuss population control were excluded.

Whenever possible, the content of population-control conferences was coded directly from the published conference proceedings and papers.[5] This information was supplemented by the proceedings of later meetings and from various reports and newspapers put out by nongovernmental and intergovernmental organizations,[6] such as the League of Nations, the International Labour Organization (ILO), the United Nations (UN), the World Health Organization (WHO), and the United Nations Education, Science, and Culture Organization (UNESCO).

National policy represents "state-sanctioned ideology" (Wuthnow 1987: 177). Data on two types of national policy were collected: eugenics-based sterilization policies and policies intended to decrease national fertility rates. We argue that these policies were shaped by the vagaries of international discourse. In the interwar period, when the acceptability of eugenics programs in scientific circles was high, countries began considering legislation intended to abate the reproduction of "criminals" and the "feebleminded." Data on the adoption of such policies were provided by reports from international eugenics conferences as well as a systematic survey of two journals on eugenics.[7]

Since World War II, national population-control policies have been strongly supported in international conferences. In the mid-1960s, the forward-looking, precautionary step for leaders of developing countries came to be the adoption of policies to curb fertility growth rates. Our data represent the year each country adopted such a policy. To be included, governments must have an official statement with an operative part intending to reduce population growth through changes in fertility rates (migration is not included). Because population control became a major concern, data were collected by UN organizations. We also supplemented UN data with various other sources.[8]

THE CONTENT OF INTERNATIONAL POPULATION-
CONTROL DISCOURSE

To explore the issue of content, we studied transformations within and between three population-control models: neo-Malthusian, eugenics, and individual choice.[9] First, we describe the main outlines and changing aspects of each model. Then, we compare both the total number and the proportion of international population-control conferences propounding each model over time. The idea is to look at both the overall and the relative emphasis given to the different discursive streams.

Our argument is that population-control discourse is embedded within a wider global-institutional environment, changes in which generate changes in that discourse. We demarcate three historical periods—pre–World War I, the interwar years, and post–World War II—with broadly different global-institutional conditions.

In the pre–World War I period, the world polity was centered in Europe and organized mainly by a latticework of bilateral diplomatic relations. The period was marked by an imperialism at once exploitative and paternalistic. The European powers measured their strength in terms of military prowess, which translated into colonial domination. During the interwar period, the world polity expanded beyond Europe to include all independent nation-states, which won formal membership in the spate of new intergovernmental organizations, such as the League of Nations, founded at the time (see Chapter 1). Attention shifted from empire building to national rebuilding, especially in war-ravaged Europe, and this new self-absorption inaugurated what Hobsbawm called the "apogee of nationalism" (1990: 131). Following World War II, liberal principles—introduced by the victors and enshrined in the United Nations—set universalistic frameworks for membership in the world polity and its organizations and rendered all nation-states juridically equal. The emphasis on formal equality underscored gross economic inequalities, and increasingly nation-states became focused on economic development as the standard measure of national strength. Simultaneous with all of these developments was the rising centrality of science (see Chapter 10).

Our argument is that these changing global-institutional conditions constituted broadly different discourses on population control. To demonstrate shifts *between* models, international population conferences were coded by their main themes: neo-Malthusianism, eugenics, and individual choice. Themes were counted if they were elaborated upon in the opening speeches and included in conference papers. The categories are distinct and were easily discernible. Many conferences contained more than one theme and hence were counted more than once. We also describe the changes *within* each model that changed its acceptability within a dynamic world context.

No international conferences espoused pronatalist views, despite the predominance of these views on the national level. While governments coveted large population size for their own strength, they were flatly against popula-

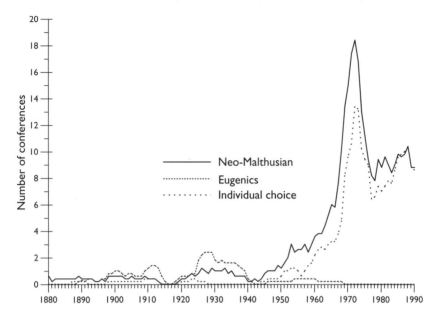

FIGURE 8.1.   International population-control conferences, 1880–1990, by model of population control (five-year moving averages).

tion expansion in other countries, and thus no international cooperation existed.

Figures 8.1 and 8.2 illustrate the extent to which the three population-control themes have appeared in conferences. The first figure shows their numerical representation in international activity over time, emphasizing the dramatic increase in conferences in the more recent period. The second figure depicts their relative representation: the percentage of activity, at any given moment, pertaining to each of the three themes. This depiction clearly demonstrates the reassertion of neo-Malthusian language after World War II, the brief dominance of eugenics in the interwar period, and the attention to individual choice issues in the contemporary period.

Neo-Malthusianism

The main idea of this model, derived from Malthus (1803), is that world population will inevitably increase faster than the food supply, resulting in war, famine, and disease, unless population growth is checked. Malthus himself asserted that the check on reproduction must come from moral restraint,

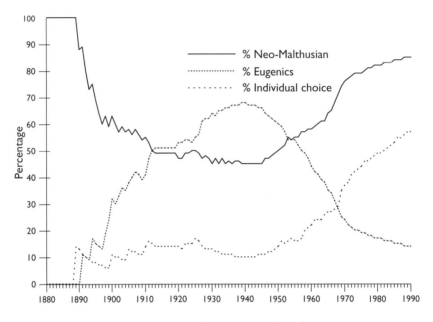

FIGURE 8.2.   International population-control conferences, 1880–1990: Percentages of each theme over time (five-year moving averages).

but the neo-Malthusians propose a more radical solution: contraception. They claim that, among other things, the deliberate restriction of family size increases the standard of comfort for parents, eliminates prostitution and abortion, and reduces overcrowding, alcoholism, crime, and war.

In the pre–World War I period, neo-Malthusian arguments about global population and food supply appealed to and drew legitimation from the imperial paternalism prevalent in Europe: it befit the core powers to bear some responsibility for the world's well-being. Thus, the neo-Malthusian model catalyzed some mobilization. However, the model faced two major liabilities. First, it promoted solutions in terms of global optima and individual preferences rather than in terms of national interests, thus failing to counteract the dominant pronatalism of the European empires. The neo-Malthusian argument subordinated countries to the world collective good and relied on the benevolence of countries to weigh the collective impact of self-interested actions. Thus what countries stood to gain from population control—world peace—rested on national sacrifice and the presumption that other countries would similarly comply. Rather than pursuing its own immediate military interests, each of these countries was to "lower its birthrate if it desires to be admitted into the company of honest folks who accept the principle of fair competition, but object to the introduction of a host of unfortunates into the world who make civilization impossible and can only be ruled over by military despots."[10] But as long as national and international population interests conflicted, cooperation remained unlikely.

The other major obstacle facing the neo-Malthusian model was its promotion of contraception, which earned the model the opposition of the Roman Catholic Church and medical professionals alike. The following quotations from mainstream medical journals illustrate how some physicians' views resonated with religious objections to birth limitation:

> Surely there is something radically, vitally wrong with the man or the woman who opposes the divine mandate, "Increase and multiply," and who would like to see fewer children born into the world.[11]
>
> The hideous vice and crime which marks the prevention and destruction of the product of conception must be abhorrent to every right-thinking man and woman . . . and nothing can ever give it the garb of respectability.[12]

The combination of these factors, as Figures 8.1 and 8.2 show, meant that the neo-Malthusian model dominated what international population-control discourse there was, but that this amount was extremely small.

Support for the neo-Malthusian model declined further during the interwar years. The prevalent nationalism was even less receptive to world-level arguments about population and food supply than the imperialism of the previous period had been. War losses made the notion of population reduction more unacceptable to governments interested in rebuilding national strength. In an effort to restore credibility to population theory, advocates emphasized the scientific side. The International Neo-Malthusian Congress, based on the "utility and rights of parents to limit the size of their families," gave way to the meetings of the International Union of Scientific Investigation of Population Problems, "to consider in a purely scientific spirit the problems of population." Thus discourse shifted from pleas to reduce birthrates to the "objective" study of population trends, which led sometimes to recommendations of eugenic reform and even increases in birthrates. Figures 8.1 and 8.2 indicate relatively less attention given to the neo-Malthusian model during the interwar years.

It was not until the model was infused with national development ideology in the post–World War II period that neo-Malthusian arguments finally took off, as is clear from Figure 8.1.[13] Until this time, arguments about population limitation were considered detrimental to national economic and military strength. During this period, national economic development—codified in per capita measures (such as gross national product per capita)—became the dominant interpretive grid to mark the strength and progress of nation-states (Ferguson 1990). Economic development was seen to depend on the "fertility transition," in which birthrates declined, and this in turn was seen to depend on population control, especially in the less developed countries (Coale and Hoover 1958). The neo-Malthusian discourse quickly shifted to include the new understandings, emphasizing the relationship between national population and national economic resources as they had once emphasized the world population and world food supply. Thus, for the first time, *decreasing* population size came to be seen as directly beneficial to the nation-state, the central policy actor in world society.

This fomented a great upsurge in the total and relative number of international conferences extolling population control from a neo-Malthusian point of view, as Figures 8.1 and 8.2 reveal. A dramatic peak occurred in the late 1960s when the discourse directly reflected central international concerns. Numerous new and already existing population organizations focused on neo-Malthusian themes. Most significantly, the United Nations began participating in and hosting international conferences on population control issues. In 1967, the international community formed the United Nations Fund for Population Activity (UNFPA) to strengthen international action in population programs. Throughout the post–World War II period, the neo-Malthusian model has continued to be the dominant frame for the ascendant issue of population control, even as the model has evolved to include the effects of overpopulation on the global ecosystem and, more recently, the empowerment of women (Crane 1993; Hartmann 1995).

Eugenics

The eugenics model bypassed the contentious issue of population quantity in favor of population quality. From the eugenics point of view, the main goal of population control was to improve the genetic pool of inherited qualities by preventing the unfit from procreating and by encouraging the multiplication of better stocks.

In the pre–World War I period, eugenics benefited from its scientific aspects and from its correspondence with the imperial order: the superior genetic endowment of the Europeans entitled them to act as trustees over the "backward" races. Most notable were the International Meeting on Race Hygiene in 1911 and the first International Congress on Eugenics in 1912. Eugenics themes outpaced neo-Malthusian concerns by World War I in both absolute and relative terms, as Figures 8.1 and 8.2 attest.

The eugenics model burgeoned in the highly nationalistic interwar period, as seen in Figures 8.1 and 8.2. At its most prominent, eugenics accounted for nearly 70 percent of all meetings, averaging about two international meetings a year. As nations turned inward to rebuild after World War—especially in Europe—the issue of population quality rose to the fore. Governments sought scientific assessments of optimal genetic combinations. Eugenics talk permeated the population conferences, attracting scientists (and some government representatives) from nearly every nation-state. Eugenic topics infused other professional conferences, such as the International Institute of Anthropology, which devoted one of its four divisions to eugenics. Even the League of Nations, slow to involve itself with issues outside international relations, mentioned eugenics in passing.[14] The eugenics model dominated international population-control discourse during the interwar years.

During World War II, however, the detestable use of eugenics by Nazi Germany turned the global tide against this model. At the formative meeting of the UN Food and Agriculture Organization (FAO), for example, a prominent demographer explained, "The whole weight of scientific evidence today" indicates that most interpretations that ascribe genetic factors to intelligence and other differences among races and nations "are fallacious and that one should be extremely cautious in resorting to this hypothesis, even tentatively" (Frank Lorimer, in Schultz 1945: 59). Figures 8.1 and 8.2 reveal that virtually no international eugenics conferences have been held since 1945. Except for a few papers on genetic research, the UN has avoided this area altogether.

The new spirit fostered in opposition to the flagrant disregard for human rights during the war also helped reify liberal notions of individualism and national development in the world polity. This liberal model was codified in normative international agreements such as the UN Charter and the Universal Declaration on Human Rights. World society valued the sovereignty and development of nation-states and individual citizens. Under this model the eugenics approach is clearly invalidated because it denies the basic sacredness of all individuals and denies the potential of those declared unfit, which universalistic individualism especially champions (giving us all the "disabled" and "disadvantaged" movements of recent decades).

Individual Choice

This model emphasizes neither the overall quantity nor quality of populations but rather individual reproductive choice. The basic idea is that individuals, especially women, can be limited by their familial roles and hindered by too many children. Liberation entails personal control over reproduction, and this requires contraception.

In the prewar period, the model's emphasis on contraception—and more generally its separation of sexuality from procreation (Giddens 1992)—caused the individual choice model to come under concerted attack from church and medical leaders. Furthermore, unlike the neo-Malthusian and eugenics models, the individual choice model did not benefit from a scientific basis— its authority was strictly moral. Between these liabilities and the fact that individual-level arguments did not mesh well with the imperialist thinking of the day, the individual choice model received little international attention in the pre–World War I period, as Figures 8.1 and 8.2 attest. Still, it was a subordinate theme at the International Neo-Malthusianism Conferences, where having small families was considered not only prudent but the right of husbands and wives.

In the interwar period, the individual choice model faced even worse odds. The extreme nationalism of the period clashed sharply with the idea of granting individuals unfettered control over their own reproductive decisions. Although contraception gained acceptability in countries with strong liberal individualist traditions, in the international arena birth control was regarded as destructive. Instead, population conferences focused almost entirely on eugenics or "scientific" research on demographic trends. Even the small number of vocal feminists who had advanced radical individual choice rhetoric before the war now looked to the science of eugenics for legitimacy. At the 1930 International Birth Control Conference, for example, former individual choice activist Margaret Sanger reported with pride that the scientific had triumphed over the personal: "All theories, all propaganda, all moral and ethical aspects of the subject were left in abeyance—practically forgotten—in the unanimity of cool, scientific conviction that today contraception as an instrument in racial progress is on the way to be reliable and efficient and may in the very near future be perfected" (Sanger and Stone 1931: xiii). Figures 8.1 and 8.2 demonstrate extremely little interest in the individual choice model during the interwar years.

All of this changed after World War II. Previously, advocates of individual choice in reproduction had faced an arduous struggle to promote their view as a national or world goal, because prior to World War II collective interests were not widely regarded as aggregates of individual ones. However, World War II saw the triumph of the liberal powers and their vision of world society as built on democratic nation-states and sovereign individual citizens. Thereafter, international population conferences became more likely to emphasize the individual. Because of its controversial nature, however, birth control talk based on rights rhetoric was not accepted outright but only as a secondary, albeit important, component of national economic development. People had the right to make an *informed* choice about the number and spacing of their children, and the relevant information included the population density and economic resources of their country. These rights were proclaimed concomitant with campaigns (especially in developing countries) to convince people of the value of small family size.

Figures 8.1 and 8.2 show how individualism rose later and parallel to the neo-Malthusian model in the post-1945 period. Organizations that began with pure individual rights language (the IPPF in particular) quickly incorporated more acceptable rhetoric about national economic development. Most international conferences broached rights language only after population discourse was secured under the rubric of national economic development. Individual rights rhetoric, which began to permeate all areas of UN activity in the 1970s, also became a component of its population-control-for-development programs and has continued and expanded to the present day. Individual choice, particularly as it relates to women's rights and empowerment, is now a commanding model in international population-control discourse.

In the postwar world polity, individual rights not only became compatible with but definitionally linked to neo-Malthusianism. The shift to individual choice and neo-Malthusian thinking stems from the crystallization of the definitive model of a national society based on individuals and personhood, managed by an active central authority structure, and devoted to progress. The individual choice and neo-Malthusian models are really two sides of the same coin, especially since economic development was itself individualized at that time (per capita measures replacing the corporate measures of earlier times, such as total population, total industrial production, miles of railroad track). The expansion and sacralization of citizenship—the conjunction of the individual and the nation—have legitimated these development-centered models of population control.

The main point is that international population-control discourse is established in a changing global institutional environment, from which it draws

TABLE 8.1

Global Institutions and Population Control During Three Periods

	Pre–World War I	*Interwar years*	*Post–World War II*
Organization of the world polity	Bilateral diplomatic relations among European powers	League of Nations	United Nations
Character of world culture and international relations	Age of Empires: competitive empires focused on expansion of colonial domains	Age of Nations: competitive nations focused on rebuilding organic national communities	Age of States: competitive states focused on economic development of nation-states and individuals
Dominant world population discourse	Pronatalism: population growth for military and economic strength	Eugenics: population purification for improved national communities	Neo-Malthusianism: population control for the progress of nation-states and individuals
Subordinate world population discourse	Neo-Malthusianism associated with turn-of-the-century idealism, eugenics associated with empire	Scientized population discouse	Individual choice closely aligned with neo-Malthusianism and national development
Illegitimate world population discourse	Individual choice associated with radical individualism and and sexual immorality	Individual choice associated with antinationalism	Eugenics associated with fascism and Nazi Germany

meaning and legitimacy, as well as organizational support. Our argument is summarized in Table 8.1.

THE DENSITY OF POPULATION-CONTROL DISCOURSE

Besides the changing *content* of international population-control discourse, there has been a marked increase in its *density*. Between 1880 and 1990, there was a total of 428 conferences, as shown in Table 8.2.[15] Among the earliest meetings to address population control were the International Congress on Hygiene and Demography (1884) and the International Genetics Conference (1899).[16] Later conferences included the International Neo-Malthusian

TABLE 8.2

International Population Control Conferences, 1880–1990

Decade	Number of conferences	Cumulative count
1881–1890	7	7
1891–1900	6	13
1901–1910	7	20
1911–1920	7	27
1921–1930	19	46
1931–1940	19	65
1941–1950	17	73
1951–1960	33	106
1961–1970	83	189
1971–1980	139	328
1981–1990	100	428

Conference (begun in 1900), the International Eugenics Conference (1912), the International Congress for Studies on Population (1931), International Planned Parenthood Federation meetings (1946), the World Congress of Fertility and Sterility (1953), the World Population Conference (1954), and the Pan-American Assembly on Population (1965). In recent years, at least a handful of population-control conferences have been held every year.

We argued earlier that *density* has increased with (1) the rise of population-control models that explicitly incorporate the primary actors in international society, nation-states (see Barrett 1995a and Meyer, Boli, and Thomas 1987). This has meant that international population-control discourse has flourished most when it has embraced the most basic assumption underlying international society: that nation-states are the sovereign and primary legitimate actors in world forums. This link has depended on the compatibility of population rhetoric with larger societal emphases. When tethered to nation-state interests in the interwar years, eugenics thrived. The emphasis on nation-state interests and responsibilities in postwar discourse caused an explosion in neo-Malthusian and, later, individual choice rhetoric.

The dramatic proliferation of discourse in this later period is also a result of (2) the consolidation of the world polity both culturally and organizationally (see Meyer forthcoming, Robertson 1992, and Chapter 1 in this volume). The rise and elaboration of the world polity has involved the establishment of an increasingly meaningful "international" realm, in which general and abstract issues, relevant to all the world's nation-states and individuals, are discussed and activated. The consolidation of the world polity has also provided concrete resources and a target for international mobilization. Thus, the targeting of the nation-state in the discourse, and the expansion of international organization, led to a dramatic proliferation of activity. To highlight these effects, we discuss the density of international population-control discourse during our three historical periods.

Before World War I, population size was equated with national strength, and population increases were thought to enhance military power and economic capacity. Any population excesses in Europe were encouraged to spill into the colonial territories. Within the colonies, population growth was valued as labor supply for industrial expansion. It was therefore nearly impossible to present fertility reduction as beneficial to nation-states. Moreover, the world polity at this time lacked much formal organization. No general-purpose intergovernmental organizations, with authority over the whole domain of international activity, yet existed.[17] The fragmented and decentralized world polity thus provided a target ill-suited to international mobilization. Attempts to promote "world" benefits of birth limitation fell on deaf ears.

As a result of the dominant pronatalist discourse and fragmented world polity, only a small number of population-control conferences were held before World War I, as Table 8.2 attests. A few international nongovernmental organizations tried to present population control as a condition for world peace. Aided by European paternalism, organizations arranged meetings among Europeans and referred to them as "international" and "world" congresses. But this idealistic movement, directed at an abstract world audience, could scarcely overcome deeply entrenched ideas about the benefits of a large population or the illegitimacy of interfering in the private realms of sexuality and procreation.

During the interwar years, a more direct link between national interests and population control was forged in international discourse. Compatible with the extreme nationalism of the period, eugenics gained considerable strength. Eugenics sought to improve the store of inherited human characteristics. It was directed chiefly at discouraging propagation among the "unfit" and encouraging it among those with desirable traits. The eugenics model offered nation-states a means of improving the quality of their citizens. Numerous governments considered various eugenics-inspired policies.

Population-control advocates also focused on another scientific formulation of population: a population "optimum" for national well-being. However, devising an acceptable plan was problematic because countries valued large population for themselves but feared growth by their neighbors. Any international plan implied compromise, unlikely to appeal to governments without safeguards in place to prevent noncompliant countries from multiplying. The notion of a population optimum was introduced at international meetings and even before the League of Nations but remained too abstract to be applied to practical politics.

Concomitantly, the formation of the League of Nations after World War I—an intergovernmental organization aimed at enhancing peace for all the countries of the world—provided a broader world organizational forum than had ever before existed. Both eugenics and neo-Malthusian advocates appealed to the League of Nations to bolster their cause by claiming that their population strategies would reduce the likelihood of international warfare. But the League was beholden to its sovereign national members, who still considered population size a primary measure of national strength. The League of Nations committees, fearful of overstepping their charter, directly sponsored only one population-control meeting, to consider the role of population from a scientific vantage point.[18]

With the rise of eugenics and a center, however weak, of the world polity, there was a rise in the number of international population-control conferences during the interwar years, as indicated in Table 8.2. International nongovernmental organizations for population control tried unsuccessfully to devise acceptable scientific (neo-Malthusian) plans that would appear sensitive to national needs and relevant to the newly formed intergovernmental organizations. Given the lack of support in the world polity and the League's narrow focus on security issues, the rise in international population-control conferences during the interwar years is significant.

After World War II, emerging discourse explicitly posed population control as beneficial to individuals and nation-states. The harbingers of this argument were members of an increasingly prestigious group of demographers. Successfully distanced from birth control propaganda and the discredited field of eugenics, demography gained the reputation of an objective and apolitical science. From their empirical studies came recommendations that resonated with the world's newly intensified focus on development. As early as the mid-1940s, demographers claimed that population control could facilitate national and individual development. They explained that the "population transition" that had occurred in Europe with modernization (in which high birthrates and widespread poverty gave way to low birthrates and increased prosperity) would have to be fostered in the less developed countries. The benefits of promoting the demographic transition were clear: national economic development and increased individual living standards. This became the dominant rhetoric of international nongovernmental organizations after World War II. In the late 1960s, for example, World Bank director-general McNamara, among other prominent spokespersons, referred to high rates of population growth as "the greatest single obstacle to economic and social development."

At the same time, the world polity experienced a stunning expansion of its legitimate domains and its organizational agents, sparked by the founding of the United Nations in 1945. The agenda of the new intergovernmental bodies expanded well beyond interstate security issues to include the betterment of the nation-states and individuals of the world. This broadened agenda paved the way for the UN community to consider the improvement of the welfare of its members as a legitimate objective in its own right. UN and other scientific organizations began accumulating cross-national population statistics, thereby providing scientific evidence for the notion that reduced birthrates fostered national development. International treaties in the 1950s set up demographic training centers and population censuses to collect population data. In the UN Development Decade of the 1960s, it was asserted as fact that population growth hampered development efforts. Demography then acquired the status of a technique at the service of development, and an induced reduction in population growth rates became an essential development strategy.

As a result of the emergence of the population-control-for-national-development discourse and the overall expansion of the world polity, the number of international population-control conferences soared after World War II to close to 300. Two international nongovernmental organizations were responsible for a significant number of these: the International Planned Parenthood Federation and the International Union for the Scientific Study of Population. When the UN and its affiliate organizations began hosting international conferences and collaborating with various nongovernmental organizations, the number of international meetings multiplied even further. A dense community of organizations and conferences developed. Increasingly, meetings were sponsored by several organizations working together. More and more organizations formed around population issues and began hosting and participating in international meetings. In addition, all sorts of organizations became more likely to incorporate population issues into meetings on other topics. Conference activity reached a peak in the late 1960s and early 1970s. This coincided with the 1966 United Nations Declaration on Population, which was signed by 33 countries and claimed that population growth constituted an important global problem; the founding of the United Nations Fund for Population Activities in 1967; and the 1974 United Nations Plan of Action, which urged all nation-states to adopt population-control policies. As population control became institutionalized on the world agenda, activity then leveled off (see Frank 1995 and Nadelmann 1990, for other examples of institutionalization).

Two general conclusions may be drawn. First, international population-control discourse and activity—here measured by international conferences—has increased as nation-states have been incorporated as the direct authorities over and beneficiaries of population control. Second, international population discourse has increased with the general centralization of world-polity organization. Together these two factors have made population control a significant domain of discourse and activity in world culture.

THE DIFFUSION OF POPULATION-CONTROL DISCOURSE AND ACTIVITY

Catalyzed by changing *content* and increasing *density*, population-control discourse and activity experienced a striking *diffusion* between 1880 and 1990. It extended (1) from a social-movement to an intergovernmental base; and (2) from the international to the national level. Given the world polity's cultural saturation and lack of a statelike center, this is the expected process (see Meyer 1994 and Robertson 1992). Shared understandings—in this case, around the problems of unfettered reproduction—were distilled in international discourse and carried by nongovernmental organizations, which act as the main social-movement carriers. International nongovernmental organizations in turn organized international conferences and proposed international treaties, increasingly involving intergovernmental organizations and national governments. Finally, the accumulation of official world concern generated policies at the national level.[19]

From Social Movement to Intergovernmental Base

The first relevant dimension of diffusion occurred when population-control discourse extended from a social-movement to an intergovernmental base. This happened as the changing content and rising density of population-control discourse increasingly implicated nation-states.

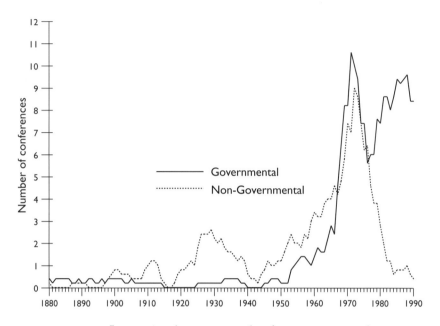

FIGURE 8.3.   International governmental and nongovernmental congresses, per annum from 1880 to 1990 (five-year moving averages).

The earliest international population-control conferences were initiated by *national* nongovernmental organizations in Europe. At these conferences, the first *international* nongovernmental organizations were founded. These international organizations then served as the bases for further international activity.[20]

With the accumulation of international social-movement activity—especially of the sort directly targeting nation-state policies—population control began to find fertile ground in the intergovernmental arena. To examine the shift from international nongovernmental to intergovernmental activity, the 428 population-control conferences were coded by whether or not they received governmental endorsement. They were counted as governmental if they were directly supported by international governmental organizations or national governments, or were attended by official state representatives. Each conference was counted only once.

Figure 8.3 displays the results. Clearly, international nongovernmental organizations hosted the great majority of international population-control conferences through the mid-1960s. Then the UN adopted the neo-Malthusian population-control-for-national-development model, and population control became institutionalized on the intergovernmental agenda. Once governmental organizations became involved, most conferences came under their sponsorship and nongovernmental organizations became consultants and participants in UN-sponsored activities. Some of these organizations had seen themselves as proxies for UN agencies (e.g., the International Planned Parenthood Federation as a proxy for the World Health Organization), eager to hand over the reins once UN bodies finally assumed responsibility for population control.

From Intergovernmental Discourse to National Policy

The second relevant dimension of diffusion occurred when population-control discourse and activity extended from intergovernmental discourse to national policy. As before, this happened as the changing content and rising density of international population-control discourse increasingly implicated nation-states and, more proximately, as population control became institutionalized on the intergovernmental agenda. International conferences were engaged in population-control discourse long before countries adopted these ideas as policy.

Moreover, we argue that national population policies emerged from the current international discourse. Even the earliest international conferences often concluded with resolutions urging governments to adopt particular population policies. At the Fourth International Neo-Malthusian Conference, for example, which met in Dresden in 1911, delegates called for the attention "of all Governments to the evil results arising from the great pressure of population in all long civilised countries as regards poverty, unemployment, overcrowding and race deterioration, and [hoped] that they will give the most earnest attention to this matter with a view to reducing the birthrate, especially among the poorer and less capable classes" (Malthusian League 1911: 82).

International discourse preceded and predicted two "waves" of national population policy. The early wave of eugenic sterilization laws was inspired by international eugenics discourse.[21] Before World War II, eugenics organizations and conferences set forth a variety of recommendations for national policy. In 1914, for example, the American Eugenics Society published a "recommended federal law" that prescribed "eugenic sterilizations for all inmates of federal hospitals, reformatories and charitable and penal institutions" as well as "defective immigrants." International conferences advocated

eugenics policy years before any country adopted national eugenics sterilization policy. The United States was first in 1907, when Indiana adopted a
policy requiring inmates of state institutions, deemed "unfit for procreation"
by a commission of three surgeons, to be sterilized. The next earliest states
were Washington, California, Connecticut (in 1909); Nevada, Iowa, and
New Jersey (1911); New York (1912); and North Dakota, Michigan, Kansas,
and Wisconsin (1913). By the late 1930s, 37 states had enacted eugenics sterilization policies.

While international eugenics meetings increased in the interwar period
(see Figures 8.1 and 8.2), national governments began considering eugenics
policy. During the 1930s, representatives from more than 50 countries attended international congresses where eugenics measures were discussed and
applauded as progress. In 1929, Denmark adopted a sterilization policy to
"benefit the community" by preventing the transmission of hereditary diseases, including "feeble-mindedness" and mental disorders. Germany followed in 1933, Norway in 1934, and Sweden in 1935. Support for eugenic
policies as a means to preserve the nation-state is reflected in the comments
of an American professor at the 1935 International Population Conference:
"Adolf Hitler . . . has been able to construct a comprehensive racial policy of
population development and improvement that promises to be epochal in
racial history. It sets the pattern which other nations and other racial groups
must follow, if they do not wish to fall behind in their racial quality, in their
racial accomplishment, and in their prospects of survival" (Clarence G.
Campbell, in Harmsen and Lohse 1936: 602).

By the end of the 1930s, twelve countries had adopted similar eugenic-
based sterilization policies, and another dozen or so were seriously considering them (Barrett 1995b). If eugenics discourse had continued to gain popularity, other countries most likely would have heeded policy advice to improve the quality of their stock. The horrific practices of Nazi Germany,
however, ensured the worldwide delegitimation of the eugenics model.

A more recent wave of fertility control policies was inspired by neo-
Malthusianism. Intergovernmental support for population control took form
in a steady stream of conferences and international treaties beginning in the
late 1960s. An international community of demographers defined and organized population control as part of the formula for national advancement,
and nation-states quickly took notice. As neo-Malthusians adopted the population-control-for-national-development stance after World War II, national policies to alter population rates increased dramatically. As of 1950,
not one country had a policy to reduce population growth. India adopted the

TABLE 8.3
National Population-Control Policies, 1946–1990

Year	Number of policies	Cumulative count
1946–1950	0	0
1951–1955	1	1
1956–1960	1	2
1961–1965	10	12
1966–1970	14	26
1971–1975	17	43
1976–1980	7	50
1981–1985	6	56
1986–1990	15	71

first, in 1951, amid much attention from the international demography community.

In the mid-1960s, however, when international neo-Malthusian discourse reached a peak (see Figures 8.1 and 8.2), governments began to adopt policies to curb their growth. In 1966, heads of state from 33 countries signed the UN Declaration on Population that proclaimed population growth an important global matter. The more the ideology took hold in the world, the more likely countries became to adopt antinatalist policies. The UN World Plan of Action in 1974 recommended that all countries adopt appropriate population policies in accordance with their economic and demographic conditions. This neutral and abstract language was aimed at developed and developing countries alike, but "developing" countries were seen as the appropriate candidates for population-control policies. The rate of policy adoption increased in tandem with world discourse on the counterproductivity of rapid population growth. Table 8.3 shows the dramatic increase in policies to control population growth, from 2 in 1960 to 71 by 1990.

CONCLUSION

This chapter argues for a focus on the history of international discourse and activities to understand local activity. It shows that what finally was codified as state policies and programs was initiated years earlier in the form of discussions among experts in international meetings. The international discourse on population that brought forth ideas for policy consideration had a pattern and momentum that merit examination in their own right. The content and volume of international population discourse reflected changes in world conditions that provided expanded mechanisms for international cooperation and defined what constituted appropriate discourse. The ideas that were later embraced by national governments were tossed about in international forums until a model emerged that could link the control of population to both national and international aims.

Our findings underscore the centrality of nation-states as units of action and accounting in the world polity, and of states as responsible authorities in their respective societies—as conventional theories of global development assume. At the same time, we find that the adoption of alternative population policies was in no way an automatic response to demographic conditions; rather, countries had to be taught that population regulation was in their national interest.

Because pronatalism had been embedded in traditional world ideology, the legitimacy of contrary population policy ideas required a global paradigmatic shift in the significance of population for the state. This shift came about through the rationalization and scientization of population by nongovernmental actors in international arenas and the eventual success of these actors in linking population issues to world and national objectives. In the interwar years, eugenics models were promoted internationally and adopted nationally because they were promoted as a means for wartorn nations to improve the quality of their citizenry. This scientized argument complemented rather than competed with existing pronatalist values.

The adoption of population-control policies, however, relied on an overhaul of the meaning of population size before unpopular neo-Malthusian theories could become compatible with national goals. This trend was not simply a "natural" reaction to large or growing populations. China and India, for example, have long had large populations, yet neither adopted a policy to restrict growth until after World War II. Before this time, the problem of "overpopulation" was virtually unthinkable. Many nineteenth-century European countries had much higher population density than some developing countries today, yet their numbers were celebrated as means for territorial expansion, colonization, and military strength. It was not until the ascendance after World War II of a new international gauge of national strength, measured in per-capita economic terms instead of sheer numbers, that neo-

Malthusianism became a plausible basis for national policy. Governments, particularly those in poor, populous countries, then learned that a central component of development not only involved but relied on the control of population growth.

International conditions also influenced global world acceptance of different population paradigms. The advocacy of eugenics models by scientists in the interwar years led a dozen countries to adopt eugenics policies, but the rapid consolidation of the world polity after World War II engendered a much more dramatic response to the new version of Malthusianism. When population control became appropriate to UN goals of economic and social development, the results were spectacular: population-control policies were adopted in developing countries, and in many developed countries, worldwide.

Chapter Nine Development INGOs

COLETTE CHABBOTT

> The emergence in underdeveloped countries of this common
> urge to economic development as a major political purpose,
> and the definition of economic development as a rise in the
> levels of living of the common people, the agreement that
> economic development is a task for government . . . all this
> amounts to something entirely new in history.
>
> Gunnar Myrdal, *Economic Theory and Under-Developed Regions*

Since the end of World War II, a distinct community of organizations has
emerged in high-income countries to promote "development" in the low-income countries of Africa, Asia, and Latin America. Individual nation-states,
national social movements, and intergovernmental agreements played a role
in the creation and growth of these "international-development" organizations. This chapter focuses on the role that one type of development organization—international nongovernmental organizations (INGOs)—plays in
institutionalizing world culture about international development and in
broadening the exercise of rationalistic voluntary authority in the world
polity.[1]

This chapter proceeds from an institutionalist perspective. Macro-institu-
tionalists working in the social construction of knowledge tradition (Thomas
et al. 1987) propose that, over time, global culture constitutes various recipes,
scripts, rules, and frames of reference that define and constrain the repertoire
of potential action and discourse for nation-states. As examples of this global
culture, they point to an increasing reification of both the nation-state and
the individual in international agreements. They suggest that rationality has
become the most valued motivation for both the nation-state and individual
behavior, and that science-based progress has become the highest good.

I use macro-institutionalist insights to interpret the emergence of a rationalized discourse and international activity around "development" in the
twentieth century. Specifically, I argue that the emphasis on science-based
progress and on individual human rights in international-development dis-

course derives in part from the work of INGOs in the nineteenth and early twentieth centuries. I analyze how realist Cold War concerns and the ambitious, though underfunded, mandates of specialized UN agencies in the last half of the twentieth century provided the impetus for increasing interaction between intergovernmental organizations (IGOs) and nongovernmental organizations (NGOs) around development discourse. I argue that an organizational-level institutional process—professionalism—helped to operationalize this development discourse in ways not entirely consistent with the Cold War concerns of some of its major funders. Specifically, I suggest that international-development professionals have used their concerns—distinct from those of their funders—to carve out a larger role for INGOs in the world polity over time.

My approach represents a departure from much of the mainstream literature on international development, which focuses on cross-national variations in aid giving and receiving as a reflection of power-oriented interstate competition, core dominance, and U.S. hegemony in the postwar period. I argue not that these factors are unimportant but that there is remarkable consistency across many different types of organizations, despite funding bases in countries with different positions in the world system.

This argument is consistent with but on a different level than that of David Lumsdaine (1993). Lumsdaine argues that social movements and the rise of the welfare state, driven in large part by moral concerns, created a constituency, precedents, and momentum for foreign aid legislation in many different countries in the last half of the twentieth century. In contrast, I focus on how some of the same ideas, meshed with the peculiar conditions of service of many international-development professionals, shape the way those professionals choose to interpret and carry out that legislation. Examining cross-national variations in light of these consistencies is beyond the scope of this chapter, though in my conclusion I make a few suggestions for future research along these lines.

THE GLOBAL INSTITUTIONALIZATION OF INTERNATIONAL DEVELOPMENT

In the decades immediately preceding and following World War II, the world witnessed hitherto inconceivable advances in medicine, which led to the global eradication of several major diseases, such as smallpox, as well as the control of dozens of others, including typhus, typhoid, yellow fever, and polio. Later, in the 1960s, high-yielding hybrid varieties of cereals, new fertilizers, and more powerful pesticides led to dramatic increases in agricultural production in some of the most famine-prone areas of the world. These successes generated confidence that conscientious generation and application of science-based innovations might be used to accelerate progress, or in other words, development, all over the world. At the same time, the popularity of comprehensive, governmental economic planning prompted by Keynes and like-minded economists before, during, and after World War II convinced many that governments, guided by well-trained economists, were in a unique position to plan and promote development on a national scale.

By the 1970s, the responsibility of all governments to promote science-based progress was universally recognized and the scope of development expanded from economic growth to improving the welfare of citizens. Similarly, the responsibility of governments of high-income or "developed" countries to provide "international-development assistance" to low-income or "developing" countries became evident in an increase in the number of IGOs[2] established to broker that assistance. As shown in Table 9.1, these organizations today include bilateral governmental development agencies or ministries in industrialized countries and intergovernmental development banks. In addition, operating under the "principle of participatory equality" (UNITR 1984), at least 30 UN agencies evolved into de facto development organizations as the number of "developing" member-states came to exceed the "developed" member-states.[3]

Despite this emphasis on governmental action and responsibility, many scientific breakthroughs demonstrating the scientific and operational feasibility of international development, such as the Green Revolution and the vaccine for smallpox, in fact were sponsored by private organizations. Furthermore, government support for development in foreign countries, for the benefit of individuals who shared few direct ties with citizens of the donor country, did not spring up spontaneously at the end of World War II. Rather, the norm for international-development assistance developed incrementally over the course of more than a hundred years, fed by several trends. Two of these trends were the legitimation of both the activist state (Noel and Thérien 1995) and the growth of internationalism, both of which owe much to nongovernmental humanitarian movements of the nineteenth and early twentieth centuries (Lumsdaine 1993).

By the late twentieth century, many of these humanitarian movements, along with many other types of NGOs, appeared in directories of international-development organizations (see, for example, East et al. 1990; Korsmeyer 1991; and OECD-DC 1990). The criteria used for inclusion in these

TABLE 9.1
Types of International Development Organizations

Type, with roles	Source of funds	Funding, in millions of 1991 U.S. dollars	Number of organizations
Multilateral agencies (intergovernmental organizations)			
Development banks and funds	Government contributions, interest on loans	7,227	< 40
United Nations agencies	Assessments, government and private contributions	5,364	< 70
Regional development organizations	Assessments, government contributions	3,630	< 140
Bilateral agencies (governmental organizations with international mandates)			
Development assistance agencies	Taxes, government surplus	50,926	< 40
International nongovernmental organizations			
Research, training, and professional organizations	Private and public grants, dues, fees	?	< 2,000
For-profit firms with governmental contracts	Fees	N/A	< 1,200
Non-profit agencies in high-income countries	Private and public grants, dues, fees	5,403+	> 2,500
Non-profit groups based in low-income regions	Private and public grants, dues, fees	?	< 300

SOURCES: Organization data: East, Smith-Morris, and Wright 1990 (approx. 850 organizations); Eurofi 1988 (approx. 75 governmental organizations); Korsmeyer 1991 (739 U.S. and Canadian organizations); OECD-DC 1990 (2,542 INGOs only), 1991, 1992, 1993; Union of International Associations 1993/94, 3: 1754 (1,710 INGOs/IGOs); World Bank, Operations Policy Research and Planning Group, Operations Policy Department, NGO Unit 1996 (approx. 10,000 organizations, including national NGOs). For more details see Chabbott 1996.

Funding data: OECD, Development Assistance Committee, 1994.

directories are quite broad; the OECD, for example, simply required that the INGOs be (1) nonprofit, (2) have spent funds on development activities in Third World countries or on awareness-raising activities in the First World within their home country within the last twelve months, and (3) respond to the OECD's questionnaire. By 1995, over 2,500 INGOs in OECD countries claimed to be advocating increased support for international development or operating development programs in low-income countries, thus outnumbering all other types of development organizations (OECD-DC 1995). For the purposes of this chapter, which uses the activities of INGOs to track both the precursors and the changing definition of international development over time, self-declaration is the sole criterion for identifying development INGOs.

By 1991, 25 percent of the official development assistance of some bilateral donors flowed through INGOs, and almost all bilateral and multilateral donor agencies had established permanent units to act as liaisons with development INGOs (Smillie and Helmich 1993). Moreover, in 1994 INGOs together raised more funds for development purposes than all UN agencies combined (see Table 9.1).

The size and special role of development INGOs in the international-development community is the subject of a large, predominantly practitioner-based literature (see Bolling 1982; Clark 1991; Dichter 1988; Drabek 1987; Fisher 1993 and 1997; Korten 1990; Lissner 1977; and Smillie and Helmich 1993). This literature is chiefly policy oriented, exploring appropriate roles of governmental and nongovernmental organizations in achieving desired development outcomes and assessing the degree to which these roles are complementary or conflictual. In contrast, my analysis focuses not on outcomes but on the process by which these generally underresourced, non-state actors played an important role in both shaping the dominant rationalizing discourse about international development and implementing the global-development enterprise. Realist concerns such as the Cold War and the gap between UN mandates and resources are factors in this process. Yet the thesis here is that world culture at the end of the twentieth century, essentially rational Western individualism, provides the overarching framework within which both state and non-state actors operate (Meyer, Boli, and Thomas 1987).

THE ORIGIN AND GROWTH OF DEVELOPMENT INGOS

Figure 9.1 plots the foundings of 2,152 self-declared development INGOs based in OECD countries, by year, from 1900 to 1985 (OECD-DC 1995).

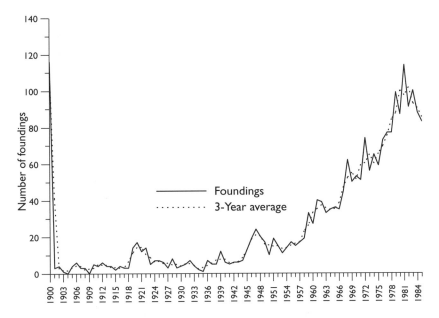

FIGURE 9.1. International nongovernmental development organizational foundings, 1900–1985 (actual and three-year running average).

The dotted line represents 1,620 INGOs that are engaged in operational development activities, or in other words, provide funds, personnel, and materials for actions undertaken in low-income countries. The dashed line shows the 532 organizations that confine their activities to development advocacy, that is, educating the public in high-income countries about the importance of development.

The foundings fall into three periods: the prewar period, until 1913, with slowly increasing but steady foundings; the war period, 1914–45, with more frequent foundings, bracketed by dramatic growth at the beginning and end of the period; and the postwar period, 1946–85, during which more than 80 percent of all development INGOs were founded.[4]

Establishing the Moral Basis for International Development

The founding of INGOs prior to World War I predates modern concepts of "international-development assistance" or "international development." The three types of organizations founded during this period—missionary organizations, specialized humanitarian organizations, and professional, labor, and political solidarity groups—all shared more general religious or moral aims. In fact, over two-thirds of the development INGOs with founding dates prior to 1900 and surviving to the early 1990s mention a religion explicitly in their titles.

The oldest extant development INGO, for example, is the Moravian Mission in Switzerland (founded 1734). Although many of the earliest mission activities overseas focused on direct proselytization in Africa, Asia, the Middle East, and Latin America, many gradually developed schools and hospitals, both to attract potential converts and to serve new Christian communities. Many early missions raised funds directly and continuously from churches and individuals with whom they maintained personal contact. Each missionary thus communicated regularly with dozens, if not hundreds, of individuals about conditions in Africa, Asia, or Latin America. Over time, as missions became organized under mission boards, their fund-raising campaigns emphasized a personal responsibility to general humanity. Regular contributors received newsletters, expanding the funders' relations with significant others outside traditional collectivities of family, race, class, and nationality. While these relations were often paternalistic, they carried, nonetheless, the stirrings of a global consciousness.

One of the oldest INGOs that does not mention religion in its name was nonetheless created by individuals, many of them Quakers, motivated by a common moral framework. The British and Foreign Anti-Slavery Society (founded 1839), now known as Anti-Slavery International (ASI), is the oldest INGO to focus on a specialized humanitarian task. The World ORT Union (United Kingdom, founded 1880) supported vocational education for Jews in Europe and other newer areas of settlement.

Likewise, the best-known "secular" humanitarian INGO listed in development directories, the International Committee of the Red Cross (founded 1863; see Chapter 6), reflects its religious origins in its symbol. The Red Cross's work with war-wounded, refugees, and prisoners of war was made possible by an intergovernmental agreement, the Geneva Convention, which declared certain categories of persons officially neutral. Maggie Black (1986) argues that the Geneva Convention's principle of neutrality for the wounded, prisoners, and relief workers paved the way for a later conferral of neutrality on children and noncombatants in general, spurring, in turn, the later creation of INGOs to rescue noncombatants in time of war or natural disaster. Although the early work of the Red Cross was entirely oriented to wartime relief, it spurred the founding of eleven national committees in the following fourteen years, principally for peace-time purposes such as disaster relief.

Unlike the missionary NGOs, most professional, labor, and political organizations lack historic links in low-income countries and, unlike humanitarian organizations, most did not begin providing funds, carrying out activities, or promoting the concept of development in their own countries until
late in the twentieth century. These include organizations such as the Finnish
Rubber and Leather Workers' Union (founded 1897) and the Norwegian
Confederation of Sport (founded 1861). Therefore, although they represent
a significant proportion of the development INGOs formed prior to World
War I, their contribution to development does not begin until after World
War II. They are discussed in a later section.

*Establishing the Scientific and Operational Basis for
International Development*

Three new types of INGOs appeared in the period encompassing World
Wars I and II: private philanthropies, specialized sectoral organizations, and
emergency relief organizations. Relative to the total number of development
INGOs, there are very few INGOs of these types, but their contribution to
the conceptualization of international development far exceeds their numbers. They become the most visible operational development INGOs after
World War II in terms of the financial/geographic scope of their resources,
the generation of research that gave international development its claim to
scientific validity; their ability to project their activities as scientific; and their
use of professionals.

Private Philanthropies

Many of the earliest private philanthropists were American industrialists
with strong Christian sectarian leanings. Nonetheless, the Carnegie Foundation (founded 1911) and the Rockefeller Foundation (founded 1913), unlike
earlier missionary organizations, focused not on saving souls, or on tem-
porarily relieving human suffering, but on using science to attack what they
perceived to be the physical and intellectual causes of human misery. Carnegie specialized in higher education in the former British empire; Rockefeller's medical research programs played a major role in controlling malaria,
typhus, tuberculosis, rabies, yaws, and schistosomiasis, and produced the vaccine for yellow fever. After World War II, Rockefeller, in collaboration with
the Ford Foundation and other U.S.-based philanthropies, set up the International Agricultural Research Centers that helped to produce the Green
Revolution.

Although founded in 1936, it was not until the late 1940s that the Ford Foundation became involved in international philanthropy in a major way. Throughout the 1950s and 1960s, its budget for overseas activities exceeded those of all other private and many UN and bilateral development organizations. With Rockefeller, Ford gave early attention to global population growth, providing funds for research centers, such as Princeton's Office of Population Research, and for the Population Council, to raise public awareness; moreover, the Ford Foundation sent representatives to discuss the implications of up-to-date population research with governments all over the world (see Chapter 8). In the early 1970s, the Foundation's president told the *New York Times* he felt confident in phasing out large-scale support for population control programs because it was now well-established on the "world agenda" (Bolling 1982: 74).

As of 1945, the philanthropies' main contribution to the rationalization of international-development discourse had been twofold: on a technological level, the production of well-funded, science-based approaches to social problems; on a more cognitive level, the idea that capitalism entailed a sense of voluntary social responsibility. Their third contribution does not appear until the postwar period. Rockefeller and Ford were the initial funders for dozens of development economics departments, development policy research institutes, and development education programs in U.S. universities and abroad (Berman 1983), which served to create a critical mass of literature and professionals to justify development as an area of scientific expertise.

Specialized Sectoral Organizations

Although specialized health organizations, usually associated with Christian missions, were among the earliest bodies working in low-income countries (for example, the Leprosy Mission [United Kingdom, founded 1874] and the Swedish Federation of the Visually Handicapped [founded 1889]), few organizations specializing in other technical areas appeared until the early twentieth century. The earliest include the International Tree Planting Committee (United Kingdom, founded 1922), the Population Reference Bureau (United States, founded 1929), and the Water Pollution Control Federation (United States, founded 1928). While the founding dates of these INGOs provide no hint to when they actually started work in or on behalf of low-income countries, we know some were funded by the private philanthropies described above to produce both the basic science underlying new approaches to agriculture and health and technological innovations relevant to low-income countries.

Emergency Relief Organizations

Building on the precedent set by the Red Cross, Eglantyne Jebb, the founder of Save the Children (United Kingdom, founded 1919), declared during World War I that there was no such thing as an enemy child. In defiance of British courts, Jebb carried food collected in England through the British blockade to German children. Jebb's principle carries over to the present day in the fund-raising campaigns and child-sponsorship programs of many successful development INGOs. In a less confrontational manner, engineering magnate, Quaker, and future U.S. president Herbert Hoover, resident in London, set up the Committee for the Relief of Belgium (CRB, founded 1914) and secured permission from the combatant governments to transport food to starving noncombatants in Belgium.

The first jump in development INGO foundings shown on Figure 9.1 corresponds to the creation of emergency relief organizations like the CRB and Save the Children during and after World War I, many of them staffed by volunteers. During this period, quasi-NGOs, such the American Relief Administration run by Herbert Hoover, blurred the line between governmental and nongovernmental organizations in their efforts to address simultaneous epidemics and famines in devastated Europe. IGOs, such as the Office International d'Hygiène Publique, the predecessor to the World Health Organization, gained credibility through their relief efforts as well. "After the First World War, no crisis, no invasion, no aggression between the countries of a still-colonial world took place without eliciting a reaction from the forces of modern humanitarianism" (Black 1986: 22).

World War II brought famine and pestilence on an unprecedented scale and prompted the creation of a host of new governmental and nongovernmental organizations. These included private groups that would later become some of the largest development INGOs: Oxfam (founded 1943), Catholic Relief Services (founded 1943), World Relief (founded 1944), CARE (founded 1945), Church World Service (founded 1946), and Lutheran World Relief (founded 1946). CARE, by far the largest and best known of these, was formed as a temporary, nonsectarian agency by representatives of more than a dozen sectarian NGOs. The scope and neutrality of CARE's original program, which involved delivering packages personally assembled by donors in the United States to friends or relatives in both Allied and Axis areas, plus the success of its sophisticated advertising campaigns, set new standards for emergency relief operations.

These INGOs broke new ground in publicizing the widespread existence of suffering and convincing the public that the means existing to alleviate it constituted a responsibility to respond. "Morality must march with ability" (Toynbee 1947) became a mantra for a generation of relief and development promoters. More subtly, with the commitment to pacifism of such prominent INGOs as the Nobel Peace Prize-winning American Friends' Service Committee (founded 1917) and the British Friends' Committee, the ideas of world peace and the alleviation of human suffering became linked. Alleviating human suffering, always difficult during war, now began to represent the means to work toward world peace, a way of staving off war.

The United Nations Relief and Rehabilitation Administration (UNRRA, founded 1943), created before the UN itself was established, served as the first relief IGO in the postwar period and set precedents for funding that later development IGOs never managed to replicate. UNRRA collected a one-percent assessment of national income from each country that had not been invaded during the war, closing down its operations after three years with a surplus to hand on to its successor organizations. But the Cold War undermined the UNRRA's efforts, and its demise set the stage for increasing IGO/NGO collaboration throughout the postwar era.

Supporting the Postwar Development Regime

Most of the prominent development INGOs active in the postwar period, both in terms of funding levels and name recognition, have already been introduced: the Ford Foundation, CARE, Church World Service, and so on. Despite their continuing prominence, however, the types of INGOs described thus far account for less than 20 percent of the organizations included in the OECD's 1995 database. Rather, five new types of INGOs account for most foundings[5] in the postwar period: (1) UN support organizations, (2) development support organizations, (3) issue-based organizations, (4) geographically based solidarity organizations, and (5) regional organizations in Africa, Asia, and Latin America. Of these new types, four appear to be responses to increased IGO development activities. A fifth type, perhaps the most numerous, may represent a reaction to the professionalism that was a result of increased IGO and INGO development activity. The following subsections highlight how the needs of the development IGOs emerging at the end of World War II fostered the growth of both older and newer types of INGOs.

Older INGO Types

Building on many of the rallying ideas of World War II, such as Roosevelt's Freedom from Want construct, education and health were integrated into the

UN Charter and Declaration of Human Rights as fundamental principles essential for human welfare and a lasting peace. In 1949 President Truman introduced the Point Four program to support "underdeveloped nations." Britain followed suit with the Colombo Plan to strengthen the social and economic structure of its soon-to-be-former colonies, and other announcements of support for newly independent nation-states issued forth from various European countries. This work was sometimes envisioned as prevention of what seemed an imminent World War III, as the capitalist core (the First World) set about saving the periphery (the Third World) from the Communist Second World. In realist terms, the Cold War provided a rationale for deeming virtually any country as vital to U.S. or Western core interests, thereby qualifying it for economic assistance. Alternatively, some European states less engaged in the Cold War, such as Sweden, became advocates of economic and social equity on an international level, which they considered necessary for international peace and harmony.

In the early 1950s, the organizational infrastructure to deliver large-scale development programs could not be created overnight, and many postwar relief and rehabilitation INGOs stepped forward to fill the gap. With a dramatic drop-off in donations toward the end of the postwar reconstruction period, CARE, for example, defying several founders who did not want more competition for scarce contributors, became a permanent organization. Shifting the focus of its fund-raising to low-income countries, CARE appealed for cash, not in-kind donations of used clothing and warm blankets. Along with other relief organizations, it also began using government surplus food commodities more intensively.

In contrast, many smaller INGOs already working in low-income countries but with little previous history of working with states were recruited by governments in high-income countries to deliver bilateral development assistance. Likewise, the U.S. government, which until the 1990s supported the largest bilateral development program of any donor country, was the largest contributor to several UN specialized agencies and also channeled millions of dollars of development assistance through U.S.-based operational development NGOs. Other bilateral programs based in high-income countries, such as Japan, having few NGOs overseas, or less experience with collaboration between governmental and nongovernmental agencies in the delivery of public services, warmed more slowly to the idea of collaboration with INGOs.

In 1958 the World Council of Churches set the first target for official development assistance at one percent of GNP for each high-income country and suggested that churches set aside 2 percent of their income for development aid, above and beyond what they provided to churches in low-income countries. Vatican encyclicals issued in 1963 and 1967 defined individuals, not nation-states or national economies, as the agents and goals of development (OECD 1988), at the same time articulating motivations based on self-reliance and solidarity (Sommer 1977). By the 1970s, many mainline denominations of Christianity represented in the World Council of Churches argued that the disproportionate share of resources controlled and consumed by the "northern" high-income countries was perpetuating, if not causing, poverty in the "southern" low-income countries.

Meanwhile, in the new era of independence, even among the most conservative, non-WCC member churches, missions around the world were rapidly upgraded to national churches, their administration handed over to local members, and new, more equal relationships with aid recipients were initiated. In this way, secular organizations, mainline Western churches, and even small independent missions were all exposing, however imperfectly, larger and larger segments of the Western public to a Third World that was in some sense equal to the First, inhabited by individuals with universal needs and rights.

NGO Support for UN Organizations

At the end of World War II, a U.S. review of the state of the UNRRA's global operations determined that while the Western alliance contributed most of UNRRA's funding, Eastern Europe received most of its assistance. With the Cold War looming, the review suggested that U.S. contributions to UNRRA were being used to prop up puppet Communist regimes in Eastern Europe and recommended that the bulk of future U.S. foreign aid be channeled not through multilaterals, where its destination was difficult to control, but through bilateral programs, such as the Marshall Plan, and through U.S.-based INGOs. At U.S. insistence, UNRRA was dissolved in 1946, and its functions were divided among several UN agencies, most notably UNICEF (founded 1946), an organization whose ability to weather the storms of the Cold War and later anti-UN sentiment rests to a large extent on its association with a highly legitimate, nonpolitical ("there is no such thing as an enemy child") target group.

With the legacy of UNRRA leading to consistent shortfalls between multilateral funding and mandates, UNICEF, UNESCO, and other UN organizations set about establishing nationally based fund-raising campaigns in high- and middle-income countries. In 1948, the UN persuaded many nationally based NGOs to participate in the United Nations' Appeal for Children, passing on the bulk of the proceeds to UN organizations and retaining a share. By the 1970s almost every OECD member country had a nongovernmental, fund-raising-oriented UNICEF National Committee as well as an annual nongovernmental Freedom from Hunger campaign to raise funds for the Food and Agriculture Organization. All of these committees and campaigns recruited national NGOs, such as the Swedish Girl Guides, that previously might not have considered themselves involved in international development but now routinely appear as development advocacy NGOs in international-development directories.

Coordination, Training, Research, and Professional Organizations

The largest coordinating group for development INGOs was created in 1962, when several existing conferences for relief and refugee organizations formed the International Council for Voluntary Agencies. Among its 89 current members are national coordinating councils for development NGOs and INGOs in both high- and low-income countries, as well as international federations representing national chapters of emergency relief and child-sponsorship agencies. The International Council and all the associated national coordinating councils publish newsletters, provide a convenient mechanism for IGOs to communicate with INGOs, and set both explicit and implicit norms for the development INGO community.

Volunteers staffed many of the emergency relief INGOs founded in the first half of the twentieth century. Since that time, a few INGOs, such as World University Service (founded 1920), the Mennonite Central Committee (founded 1920), and the International Voluntary Service (founded 1934), have remained mainly volunteer, but most have professionalized. INGOs such as World Learning (formerly the Experiment in International Living, founded 1932) provide professional training and support, from pre-service orientation for volunteers to degree-level training for career program officers in large IGOs. As Table 9.1 shows, these organizations represent a major segment of the development sector but most are not included in the OECD's database and do not appear in Figure 9.1. Increasing professionalism in both IGOs and INGOs is also reflected in the creation of the Society for International Development (founded 1957), a professional membership association with chapters in over 100 countries and over 6,000 members in 1995, and in the many research institutes and university-based programs that appeared as development INGOs in the 1980s.

Issue-Based Organizations

Issue-based INGOs, such as Friends of Temperance (Finland, founded 1853), have existed for over 100 years. There has been, however, a dramatic increase in the number of INGOs working on specific issues in recent decades. Consistent with the findings in other chapters in this volume, OECD-DC (1981, 1990) reports the number of organizations engaged in population and environmental issues increasing from a base of 9 and 4 to 40 and 37, respectively, between 1981 and 1990. Furthermore, among the titles of OECD-based INGOs founded at ten-year intervals between 1945 and 1985 (OECD-DC 1995), no titles mention women until 1985. Likewise, environmental concerns do not appear in the titles of OECD-based INGOs founded in 1945, 1955, or 1965; the first two appear in 1975, two more in 1985. Nonetheless, specific issue NGOs do not account for the bulk of the increase in the number of development INGOs appearing in international-development directories in the last two or three decades. INGOs including population, women, disarmament, and the environment in their titles together accounted for only 7 percent of OECD-based development INGO foundings in 1975 and just under 10 percent in 1985.

Geographically Based Solidarity

More of the increase in foundings in OECD-based countries may be accounted for by solidarity or friendship societies linking small groups in high- and low-income countries (e.g., the Philippines Solidarity Group of the Netherlands [founded 1975] and the Danish-Gambian Friendship Society [founded 1975]). The factors prompting the growth of these organizations are not entirely clear, but formalization is probably in part responsible. For example, as large emergency relief and development INGOs, such as CARE, moved away from volunteers toward professionals and from in-kind contributions to cash, contributors desiring more personal involvement may have promoted the growth of these smaller INGOs.

Regional Development INGOs Based in Africa, Asia, and Latin America

The fastest growing set of development NGOs appear to be those founded by and for individuals in low-income countries (Fisher 1993). However, less than 600 of the NGOs based in low-income countries, and perhaps as few as 200, work in more than one country and may be considered true INGOs (World Bank 1996). Among these, the General Arab Women's Federation (founded 1944), the Inter-American Planning Society (founded 1956), and the Afro-Asian People's Solidarity Organization (founded 1957) are some of the oldest.

Similar to the pattern described above regarding IGOs and NGOs based in high-income countries, some of the growth of regional INGOs in low-income regions is closely related to the mandates and initiatives of IGOs. For reasons described in greater detail below, IGOs have encouraged domestic NGOs in low-income countries to undertake "development" activities, to create national consortia of development NGOs, and to federate into regional-level INGOs. Promoting domestic NGOs in low-income countries is sometimes referred to as promoting the development of "civil society" and "democratization" (Clark 1991; Fisher 1993; Smith 1990), both presumed to be necessary elements of well-functioning nation-states.

As a result, IGOs routinely fund the compilation of directories of development NGOs and sponsor national and regional NGO development conferences. For example, the UNESCO-sponsored *African Development Sourcebook* (UNESCO 1991) documents 174 networks of development NGOs, of which fewer than 70 are clearly regional or international. In fact, many of the NGOs listed in the *Sourcebook* are the direct products of INGO/IGO donor-funded conferences or ongoing projects. A good example is the Forum of African Women Educators (FAWE, founded 1990), which was first convened by the Donors to African Education to provide senior women policy-makers in education in Africa with a setting to discuss girls' education issues of pressing concern to the donors.

Summary

The growth in development INGOs since 1945 is related to the conceptualization of international development as an essential global undertaking, which created, in turn, a demand on the part of governments and IGOs for INGOs and NGOs able to operationalize that concept. The process started more than a century ago with charity and relief bodies, organized strictly voluntarily and motivated by Christian concepts and missionary zeal. In the twentieth century, the success of the philanthropies in devising scientific approaches to relieving human suffering, and of the emergency relief organizations in responding to crises with modern organizational science, impressed on Europe the feasibility of national and international campaigns. Immediately following World War II, the emphasis of the Western alliance on development as a way of securing the peace, and of fighting the Communist threat, provided compelling reasons for government support of development in low-income countries. At the same time, the broadening fund-raising campaigns of various preexisting emergency relief INGOs and emerging development INGOs and IGOs elicited substantial private support for international development as well.

The growing global acceptance of the idea of international development and the functional needs of the international-development community together explain the rapid growth in the number of development INGOs in the post–World War II period. They do not, however, explain the abrupt increase in organizational foundings beginning in the late 1960s and culminating, in my data, in the early 1980s.[6] The following section tracks the changing themes in the dominant development discourse, particularly since the early 1970s, that legitimated an increased role for development INGOs and NGOs in international development and supported the upsurge in organizational foundings in the 1970s and 1980s.

SHIFTS IN INTERNATIONAL-DEVELOPMENT DISCOURSE

The discourse of development IGOs placed increasing emphasis on the role of external factors in national development, simultaneously constraining nation-state autonomy and creating space for non-state actors in development. Table 9.2 highlights the most prominent themes in dominant development discourse for each decade from 1950 to 1990, as articulated in the mainstream practitioner literature (Arndt 1987; Lewis and Kallab 1986; Lewis 1988; Lipton and Maxwell 1992; Meier 1995). Note that new themes do not entirely replace older ones. Rather, they merge with older themes to create increasingly complex definitions of development and more diffuse responsibilities for nation-states and development organizations.

As shown in column 1, the "comprehensive economic development planning" approach used in the 1950s by both Marxist and capitalist donors assumed that each developing nation-state was a relatively autonomous unit. In this conception, every nation-state could achieve modernization through prudent management of domestic resources; foreign technical assistance and technology could speed up the process. By the 1960s, the evolving development discourse emphasized the central importance of foreign investment in helping low-income countries reach the "take-off" level for sustained "economic growth," measured in terms of GNP, agricultural production, and industrial output growth rates. Critics of this dominant strain of discourse ar-

TABLE 9.2
International Development Approaches, 1950–1990

Decade	Development approaches	Status of low-income nation-states	Role for INGOs/NGOs
1950s	Comprehensive economic planning Industrialization and community development	Sovereign and autonomous	Minor: emergency relief
1960s	Economic growth Dependency	Sovereign but dependent on foreign trade and investment	Limited: technical assistance, schools, and hospitals
1970s	Equitable growth Micro/domestic: Poverty alleviation Basic human needs (BHN) Macro/international: New International Economic Order (NIEO)	Sovereign but dependent on foreign trade and investment and liable to outside scrutiny relative to the welfare of citizens	Limited: small-scale rural social service delivery pilots and development advocacy
1980s	Structural adjustment and social dimensions of adjustment	Sovereign but dependent on foreign trade and investment and liable to outside scrutiny relative to the welfare of citizens and financial solvency	Significant: social service delivery to the poor
1990s	Sustainable development	Sovereign but dependent on foreign trade and investment and liable to outside scrutiny relative to the welfare of citizens and financial solvency and global environmental concerns	Major: development and dissemination of environmentally sound innovations and modern contraceptives

NOTE: Trends over time: Nation-state autonomy decreases. International nongovernmental organization legitimacy increases.

gued that underdevelopment was the result of economic dependencies created by Western imperialism and investment, and that an alternative, "real"
development in low-income countries was contingent on a more equitable
("new") international economic order. Both these avenues of discourse, emphasizing foreign investment, foreign imperialism, and external dependencies, undercut earlier images of low-income nation-states as autonomous and
largely in control of their own development. At the same time, both discourses retained the earlier idea that the state is nonetheless largely account-
able for prudent management of domestic resources.

Similarly, in the 1970s, the dominant discourse retained the idea of ultimate state accountability and, simultaneously, the conviction that the state
was constrained by external factors. However, a new imperative was added:
the state must ensure that development does not exacerbate existing inequalities among nation-states or subnational groups. Much concern emerged
about the potential negative repercussions of economic growth on lower-in-
come and historically disadvantaged groups within countries. Many Western
bilateral and multilateral donors began to condition continued support of
low-income countries on the ability of their governments to demonstrably alleviate poverty. In addition to measuring overall GNP growth rates and dis-
aggregated industrial and agricultural growth rates, the Overseas Development Council, for example, began to rank countries using a Physical Quality
of Life Indicator. Donors began to describe levels of development using measures such as under-five mortality rates for children in addition to GNP
growth rates.

The alternative discourse stressed the need for measures to counteract the
effects of external dependencies on the development prospects of most low-
income countries. A coalition of low-income countries focused attention on
measuring international inequality and restructuring the trade and foreign
aid systems that allegedly fostered such inequality. Again, for all their disagreements, both the dominant and alternative discourses implied that the
larger world community had a major role to play in the development of low-
income countries, whether as the definer and arbiter of "real" national development or as the guarantors of a new international economic order.

In the 1980s, although again shifting, the dominant discourse continued
to emphasize, simultaneously, the central role of low-income governments
and the importance of external factors. The World Bank imposed structural
adjustment programs in many low-income countries on the brink of bank-
ruptcy after decades of failed development efforts. External factors such as
trade and the establishment of healthy foreign exchange reserves figured

strongly in all structural adjustment programs. Later, to soften the social effects of these austerity packages, the World Bank incorporated various activities. Sometimes called Social Dimensions of Adjustment packages, these activities focused on improving the governments' ability to monitor the effects of the adjustment program on the poor and to promote NGO programs to mitigate those effects.

Likewise, in the 1990s, the emphasis on "sustainable development" focuses attention on the global impact of development and continuing population growth on the environment. Nonetheless, as broader global concerns compel governments to incorporate environmental impact studies into their development project designs, these same studies routinely identify the potential negative effects of these projects on various subnational groups. Building on the special status of the poor and the marginalized established in earlier decades, the studies help create an identity and voice for new groups whose specialized needs governments are expected to address. Along with the newly discovered importance of "governance" to development (World Bank 1997), all the development themes of the 1990s provide a broader mandate for development IGOs to scrutinize low-income country governments, further eroding their autonomy.

To the extent that the United States was indisputably the largest international-development donor from the end of World War II until the end of the 1980s, a worldwide expansion of discourse around human rights might make sense in purely realist terms. However, although the United States played a major role in producing the Declaration of Universal Human Rights, throughout the postwar period it consistently restricted its international human rights concerns to that subset of rights dealing with civil and political liberties. Moreover, that concern was more often used in international forums to bludgeon its Cold War opponents than to support efforts to improve civil and political rights in Third World countries. The United States remains firmly opposed to social or economic entitlements at either the national or global level and is one of the few countries yet to ratify the Convention on Economic, Social, and Cultural Rights, an act which would codify the Declaration of Universal Human Rights into international law. The types of social and economic rights embodied in the expanded international-development discourse by the end of twentieth century go far beyond the point indicated by a narrow, realist construction of U.S. interests.

Over time, then, development discourse has elaborated not only a reduction of nation-state autonomy but an increase in the interest and responsibility of the larger international community for development in general. It has also entailed a simultaneous shift away from national economic indicators as the preferred measure of development toward more individually based indicators of development. Following the early shift from GNP to GNP per capita, non-economic measures such as the under-five mortality rate were added, to be joined by indicators focused on historically disadvantaged groups within nation-states. This concern with generating development indicators and servicing disadvantaged groups opened a niche in the development discourse for INGOs and NGOs, as described in the last column of Table 9.2.

In the 1950s and 1960s, the role of INGOs in low-income countries was mainly limited to the running of schools and hospitals and ad hoc disaster relief. Several bilateral donors nonetheless established channels for development assistance through INGOs based in one or more low-income countries, either as a precursor to a formal aid program or to give access to "technical assistance" available from the INGOs. By the late 1970s, however, as poverty alleviation came into vogue, INGOs' potential to carry out small-scale pilot projects for service delivery to disadvantaged groups was recognized and the INGOs were recruited to work with bilateral, if not always multilateral, IGOs. This coincides with a sharp increase in the founding of development INGOs at this time (Figure 9.1).

This trend continued in the 1980s, as donor organizations became less sanguine about the administrative capacity of low-income states to manage structural adjustment programs and, at the same time, deliver services to disadvantaged groups. By the late 1980s, therefore, the INGOs, as well as national development NGOs emerging in the low-income countries, became the social service delivery agents of choice for many donors. This has been even more the case in the 1990s, when the discourse on sustainable development—combining concerns for population control, the environment, and respect for micro-communities—called for the development and grassroots dissemination of environmentally sound technologies and appropriate contraceptives.

In summary, although nation-states formally remain the most highly legitimated actors in international relations, followed by IGOs, the dominant development discourse elevated INGOs from a relatively insignificant to a relatively central role in international development during these last two decades of the twentieth century. The turning point for this discourse occurred in the 1970s, when the object of development shifted from a unique focus on national economic growth toward individual welfare improvement.

The timing of this shift in discourse corresponds to and, indeed, may well have generated the dramatic increase in development INGO foundings shown in Figure 9.1, beginning in the late 1960s and early 1970s.

PROFESSIONALS AND PROFESSIONALIZATION

What was the source of the dominant and alternative discourses that justified the expansion in the types of legitimate actors and purposes and foci of concern in the global-development sector of the late twentieth century? Reflecting on the education sector within the international-development field, Robert Arnove (1980) and Edward Berman (1983, 1992) argue that capitalist organizations, such as the Ford, Carnegie, and Rockefeller Foundations, in founding and supporting most of the research, policy, and higher education programs in educational development, essentially fabricated the dominant neoliberal discourse about educational development. However, while this may explain the pro-market bent of the dominant discourse, it does not explain the concern of the discourse for the poor and its willingness to impose restrictions on the nation-state. To understand these themes we must look to more institutional factors.

When the development IGOs began recruiting personnel at the end of World War II, the individuals with the most relevant experience included former colonial officers, military personnel, and veterans of INGOs. In the 1960s and 1970s, master's and doctoral development studies programs at the London School of Economics, Harvard, and Princeton—all funded by private philanthropies that certainly placed a liberal stamp on the programs—produced candidates for high-level jobs in IGOs. Volunteer experience in emergency relief and grassroots-oriented development INGOs also provided entry-level experience and on-the-job training for a career in the larger development INGOs and IGOs.

Since the 1960s, this combination of schooling and work experience has produced a specialized cadre of international-development professionals who spend the bulk of their working lives in a series of assignments in global metropolises and low-income country capitals. Development professionals often become somewhat detached from their countries of origin; their perspectives and concerns may be quite different from those of legislators and ordinary citizens who fund international-development organizations. Given their distance from the funders, they face significant opportunities and temptations to exercise personal and professional prerogatives. The policies and actions of international-development organizations run by international-development professionals therefore should not be assumed to represent the intentions of their nation-state or individual funders, as demonstrated in the annual struggles between the U.S. Senate's Foreign Affairs Committee and the population office of the U.S. Agency for International Development.

To date, international development remains a relatively informal profession. Within the workplace, international-development professionals recognize each other but they lack both legal and public recognition (Abbott 1988). Membership in the Society for International Development is open to all comers and is too diverse in its causal beliefs and objective tasks to constitute an "epistemic community" (see Haas 1992).[7] Nonetheless, I suggest that international-development professionals have contributed to the rise in legitimacy of INGOs in the development discourse in at least two ways.

First, over time, it has been professionals, rather than national politicians or diplomats, who have generated the international-development discourse. Professionals write UN reports, draft conference statements, design conference follow-up strategies, and help new nation-states draft national development policies. A common career path in humanitarian-oriented, public service organizations, both governmental and nongovernmental; a common task environment; the standardizing effects of professionalization and increased interdependence among development IGOs and INGOs described above—all these contribute to the shaping of a common culture and belief system among development professionals. This system includes a belief in the centrality of development to human progress, in the responsibility of governments to promote it, in the imperative for international-development assistance to support it, in the definition of development in "human" rather than strictly economic terms, and so on.

Among the planners and policy analysts in the profession, economists hold a privileged position by virtue of their discipline's claim to "scientific" rigor, that is to say, quantitative sophistication. Part of the World Bank's influence derives not just from the size of its budget but from its roster of the largest concentration of development economists in the world and its publication of more scientific reports on international development than any other organization. Although some of the early development theorists and promoters, such as Nobel Prize winners W. Arthur Lewis, Theodore Schultz, and Gunnar Myrdal, were economists, in recent years the neoclassical economists employed by the World Bank tend to follow rather than lead trends in international-development discourse and practice. As the rest of the international-development profession has come to value activities with less clear economic returns, the Bank has devoted much effort to calculating "internal rates of return" for development activities as diverse as contraception, child immunization, and girls' schooling.

The belief system of international-development professionals also places persistent emphasis on individualism. In the 1950s and 1960s, a "modern" society was distinguished from a traditional one by the proportion of its members who actively participated in society (Inkeles and Smith 1974; McClelland 1961): more active individuals exercising individual preferences added up to a more modern society. Individualism and individual preferences also fit well into mainstream neoclassical economics as practiced by the development banks.

Individualism also appears as a recurring theme in the practitioner-oriented literature on development NGOs and INGOs, in the emphasis on "participation" by the intended beneficiaries of development (Rahnema 1993). In the 1970s and 1980s, many liberal critiques attributed the failures of the First and Second Development Decades (the 1960s and 1970s) to "top-down" projects that failed to incorporate grassroots input (Montgomery 1988). The failures of many subsequent "bottom-up" development efforts since that time are similarly explained by inadequate participation/ownership by the intended beneficiaries (Korten 1990). There are hints of this same reasoning in the rediscovery of the neglect of "civil society" in earlier development theories (Frantz 1987), and in the now fashionable use of the terms "empowerment" and "democratization" (Clark 1991). The practitioner literature including these themes has, not surprisingly, produced consistent calls for greater incorporation of INGOs and NGOs in all levels of development work.

Second, one of the pervasive activities of professions is the establishment and maintenance of jurisdiction over an area of social activity (Abbott 1988). Throughout most of the 1950s and 1960s, many professionals in IGOs tried to maintain a strict distinction between their scientifically based development activities and the supposedly more "amateur," "do-gooder" relief activities of INGOs. By the early 1970s, however, the perceived debacle of the First Development Decade and the subsequent rejection of many aspects of modernization theory undermined the legitimacy of international development as "science." This challenge pushed the professionals in development IGOs back toward the more objective, humanitarian qualities of their mandate— meeting "basic human needs"—and the rationalization of a whole new range of related development activities. Perceiving many of these new activities as beyond the scope of many governments in low-income countries, inappropriate for bilateral IGOs, and beyond the funding constraints of multilateral IGOs, the development profession began to co-opt and recruit INGOs and NGOs into the international-development field. The roles constructed for INGOs and NGOs, however, remained subordinated to the larger role of IGOs (though not always subordinate to low-income governments), hence the emphasis in the development practitioner literature on the "complementary" roles of governmental and nongovernmental organizations. In this way, consciously or unconsciously, international-development professionals retained jurisdiction over their expanded definition of development.

In summary, professionals in international-development organizations are primarily responsible for generating the practitioner discourse described in the preceding section. The increased emphasis in that discourse, beginning in the 1970s, on the important role of NGOs in international development is consistent with the long-term emphasis on individualism within the professionals' belief system and the tendency within professions to expand and maintain jurisdiction over a particular activity.

CONCLUSIONS AND AREAS FOR FUTURE RESEARCH

International-development assistance has been described by some international relations scholars as a regime (Lumsdaine 1993). According to Thérien (1991: 266), "The aid regime is . . . a political institution which is gaining in importance because it fits with dominant hard core interests and ideology [of nation-states] at the international level." Yet there is much that occurs in the international-development community that is difficult to understand in terms of "hard core" political interests and ideology. Why the expansion and reification of individual human rights to a degree far beyond the capacity or willingness of most nation-states—both aid donors and recipients—to fulfill?

I have argued that non-state actors, mostly drawing on liberal humanitarian traditions (and, to be sure, on funds provided by Cold-War "realists"), played a critical role in legitimating international development as an arena of international activity. INGOs in the nineteenth and early twentieth centuries impressed on the world polity both the moral imperative and the practical feasibility of addressing human needs on an international basis. The "needs" have always existed; poverty, disaster, and war in faraway places are hardly nineteenth-century inventions. What changed was the sense of obligation to help the poor and the suffering. This moral imperative strengthened as INGOs in the first half of the twentieth century created the scientific knowledge, the technological innovations, and the mass delivery mechanisms that made rapid development in former colonies appear possible.

The sense of global-development obligation contributed to the establishment of a host of development IGOs after 1945. IGOs, however, lacking adequate resources and supposedly excluded from lobbying nation-states, turned to INGOs for help in both operational development programs and development advocacy in high-income countries. The IGOs encouraged existing INGOs to redefine at least some of their activities as development, and they promoted the founding and strengthening of many NGOs in low-income countries. The postwar development enterprise called forth a sizable amount of resources, underwent considerable professionalization, and supported a growing number of IGOs and INGOs, all of which served to reinforce the importance and the rationality of international development itself. The rationalizing discourse of development, in turn, institutionalized new roles for INGOs and NGOs in the world polity.

The complex and vital institutional connections described in this chapter among development IGOs, INGOs, and NGOs in both low- and high-income countries suggest that increases in the number of development INGOs and NGOs should be interpreted cautiously. The degree to which development INGOs and NGOs have proliferated in response to government initiatives and mandates, rather than popular interest, remains to be explored, but it is certainly substantial. Furthermore, it is important to note that the UN organizations, staffed for the most part by non-Americans (United Nations Development Programme 1993), tend to take a much less sanguine view of NGOs than the OECD's Development Assistance Committee (Smillie and Helmich 1993) or the World Bank (Paul and Israel 1991), both of which have a higher proportion of Americans on staff. Thus, the extent to which the expanding role of NGOs and INGOs in the 1970s and 1980s simply reflects the dominance of Tocquevillian models of social action during a period of U.S. hegemony in the international-development industry is an important issue for study.

Certain indicators, however, suggest otherwise. Since 1989 the United States has been eclipsed by the Japanese as the largest donor of concessional foreign assistance. Japan is not generally considered as much an associational society as the United States, and the history of its NGOs in international work is very limited in comparison to U.S. NGOs. Nonetheless, in Japan, the rhetoric regarding the important role of development INGOs and NGOs has, if anything, escalated in the last eight years.

In conclusion, the emergence of development INGOs in the last half of the twentieth century follows a pattern familiar to readers of other chapters in this volume. Since the end of World War II, the growing Western tendency to define human progress in international terms has called forth new types of international organizations. The rationalizing discourse of these new organizations, drawing heavily on both humanitarian and scientific ideals in world culture, elaborates and expands a new domain of activity at the international level, requiring new forms of IGO and INGO cooperation and coordination. All this goes on essentially outside the world economy, creating a structure by which younger nation-states may be integrated into the world economy faster, and perhaps more humanely, than otherwise might be possible. The capitalist core benefits from this arrangement, by trade and perhaps increased international political stability, but one can imagine far more efficient ways to secure larger benefits, were nation-states not constrained and individuals motivated by a vision of progress that reifies both science and individual welfare.

Chapter Ten Science Associations in the
International Sphere, 1875–1990:
The Rationalization of Science
and the Scientization of Society

EVAN SCHOFER

European science has had a transnational character throughout its history.
Scientific societies, while tied to specific nations or city-states, have supported
an international network of communication since the seventeenth century
(Ornstein 1928). Journals, personal correspondence, emigration, and travel
linked scientists from London to Milan and beyond. The very emergence of
science was clearly a Europe-wide phenomenon with deep cultural roots in
visions of universalism and rationalism (Wuthnow 1980; Toulmin 1989).
Furthermore, the modern scientific concerns with community, organization,
and communication were, in part, already present in the formative period
(McClellan 1985). Yet it was not until the latter part of the nineteenth century that scientists and people concerned with science came together to form
international associations—that is, associations not based solely in one city or
nation, and with members from several other countries (Crawford 1992).[1]

In the contemporary world, however, international nongovernmental organizations devoted to science ("science INGOs") are commonplace. Several
hundred science INGOs exist, and new ones are being created at an increasing pace. Much international scientific activity is professional in character, supporting international communication and collaboration among scientists. Associations such as the International Union of Biological Sciences
produce journals and hold meetings bringing together scientists from around
the world. More recently, collaborative laboratories have been created to aggregate the resources of many nations, supporting scientific projects of immense scale.

However, not all science INGOs are oriented toward the scientific profession. The International Organization for Chemical Sciences in Development is a collection of scientists, research consortia, development professionals, and individuals who support chemistry not for its own sake, but for the purpose of improving the economies of developing countries. Similarly, the International Network of Engineers and Scientists for Global Responsibility focuses on issues of peace, environmental protection, and development. These organizations are related to science but their goals are fundamentally social.

The varied forms of international science associations are an indication of the complex, transnational nature of modern science. In addition, these international associations reflect and embody world culture (see Chapter 1). Thus, by examining the emergence, proliferation, and changing character of science INGOs, we gain insight into the evolving cultural and organizational role of science in world society.

The rationalization and professionalization of scientific activity occurring in core (developed-economy) nations has directly supported the creation of professional science INGOs. However, professionalization has also helped pave the way for the routinized application of science to social problems. As such views were taken up by science professionals, nation-states, and intergovernmental organizations (IGOs), new cognitive models arose linking scientific activity to societal development. Such models proliferated with the postwar intensification of the liberal world polity, leading to unprecedented levels of international organization around science. The rise of these organizational populations has important implications for the overall expansion of scientific authority and the "scientization" of many domains of social activity.

SCIENCE INGOS: DESCRIPTION OF THE POPULATION

In 1994, there were approximately 350 active international science associations. The earliest organization was founded in the mid-nineteenth century, though such early organizations were relatively rare; over 95 percent of the associations were founded in this century, over 70 percent of them after 1945. Like most sectors of international activity, science organizations have been growing in number at an accelerating rate.

Figure 10.1 shows the cumulative number of science INGOs founded in the world over the period 1870 to 1990. From this simple graph it is clear that organizational activity began in the mid 1800s, accelerated in the 1920s only to be interrupted by World War II, and grew rapidly in the postwar era. However, the appearance of smooth, continuous expansion shown in the

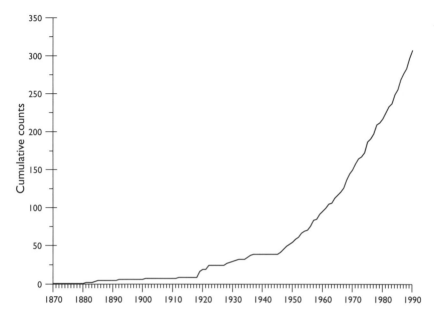

FIGURE 10.1.   Cumulative foundings of all science INGOs, 1870–1990.

figure is misleading. When one examines the characteristics of individual science INGOs—such as their stated goals, activities, and structure—it becomes clear that the population of international science organizations is comprised of two related but separate types of organizations.

Professional science organizations were the first type to appear. Here I use the term "professional" broadly to include organizations focused on: (1) the professional interests of a specific scientific field, or science professionals in general (e.g., International Union of Geological Sciences), (2) scientific standards and nomenclature (e.g., the International Commission on Zoological Nomenclature), and (3) the production of scientific knowledge (e.g., the International Statistical Institute). Essentially, these are associations of scientists working to benefit either their research or their profession. Indeed, many such associations emerged directly out of professional activities, such as annual meetings or congresses. A typical example, the International Union of Biological Sciences, publicly states the following aims: "[To] promote the study of biological sciences; initiate, facilitate, and coordinate research and other scientific activities that require international cooperation; ensure the discussion and dissemination of the results of cooperative research; promote

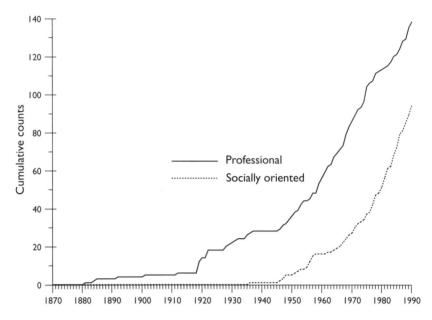

FIGURE 10.2.   Cumulative foundings of professional and socially oriented science INGOs.

the organization of international conferences and assist in the publication of their reports" (UIA 1994–95: 1076).

Figure 10.2 shows the cumulative number of professional science INGOs founded over time, showing much activity well before World War II. In addition to their early origins, professional organizations as a group share many of the same characteristics. They tend to be small organizations, their memberships consisting of active scientists, national branch associations, and some interested amateurs. Larger bodies have memberships in the thousands, while associations based on obscure scientific subfields may have only a few dozen members. Another shared characteristic of professional science INGOs is their relative isolation from other organizations in the international sphere. They rarely establish formal relations with other associations, with the exception of other science associations of related subfields. Similarly, they rarely have formal relations with intergovernmental organizations such as the United Nations.[2] Finally, they tend not to directly advise nation-states on matters related to their expertise. In short, they are associations of and for scientists.

In contrast, the recent period is typified by increasing numbers of international science associations focused primarily on issues outside the narrow professional interests of scientists (Figure 10.2). These associations support science in order to address social problems such as economic development, environmental degradation, war, nuclear weapons, ethics, and so on. I will refer to such organizations as "socially oriented" science INGOs. Activities frequently include (1) bringing scientific information to the citizenry or policymakers (e.g., The International Network for the Availability of Scientific Publications), (2) promotion of science or science policy that directly ameliorates social problems (e.g., the Research and Development Forum for Science-Led Development in Africa), and (3) promotion of ethics in the application of science (e.g., the International Network of Engineers for Global Responsibility).

The character of these organizations is evident upon examination of their professed aims, activities, and membership. For example, the stated goals of the International Organization for Chemical Sciences in Development are "[to] encourage cooperation among chemists . . . ; endeavor to harness chemical sciences to work towards solutions of socio-economic problems; . . . assist in the determination of priorities for development with respect to the chemical sciences in less developed countries; focus attention, effort, and resources from developed countries onto the needs and problems of developing countries by enlisting the help of selected specialists and institutions" (UIA 1994–95: 983). These goals clearly extend beyond the narrow professional interests of scientists. Rather, this organization hopes to utilize the expertise of chemists to help solve a particular social problem—economic underdevelopment.

These socially oriented science associations differ from professional associations not only in their aims but also in their memberships and linkages to other international organizations. Scientists are not always the sole or even dominant members of socially oriented science associations. These organizations typically include policy professionals and interested citizens, sometimes even to the exclusion of scientists. Also, while professional organizations are relatively isolated, socially oriented science INGOs tend to have many links to other international organizations—particularly intergovernmental organizations such as the United Nations Development Programme and the United Nations Education, Science, and Cultural Organization (UNESCO). Finally, socially oriented science INGOs are almost exclusively a postwar phenomenon. They were quite rare before 1945 and were founded in significant numbers starting only in the 1960s. However, their rate of growth has accelerated and continues to accelerate up to the present (Figure 10.2).

The dramatic rise of two such different populations of science organization suggests long-term historical changes in the nature of science in the international sphere. To understand these changes, we must look both to historical changes in science itself and to the changing characteristics of the international sphere.

THE RATIONALIZATION AND PROFESSIONALIZATION OF SCIENCE AND THE RISE OF PROFESSIONAL SCIENCE INGOS

When one hears the term "science," one cannot help but think of highly rationalized activities—the Baconian experimental ideal, Popper's logic of hypothesis testing, the image of a team of researchers methodically searching for a cure for cancer. It is easy to forget that the organization of science into a clearly defined set of activities to be practiced by professionally trained personnel is, in fact, a historically recent development. The modern scientific profession was a product of the nineteenth century (Bates 1965). Even as late as the early twentieth century, science remained an activity often performed as entertainment by or for the wealthy gentlemen of society. The subject of a scientific study was often an interesting curiosity, rather than a systematically planned experiment designed to augment scientific knowledge. In scientific journals of the late nineteenth century it is not uncommon to see articles about chemical experiments juxtaposed with ones concerning newly invented farming tools, a recently sighted meteor, a debate about whether or not humans are innately aggressive, and even reports of oddities such as the birth of a two-headed goat on a farm near London (*Nature* 1876).

In other words, exactly what constituted science was not well established—indeed, the word "scientist" was not coined until 1840 (McClellan 1985). There are those whom we look upon with hindsight as scientists, such as Kelvin or Huygens, because their work conformed, more or less, to modern conceptions of scientific activity. However, there were also hundreds of tinkerers, collectors, and observers of nature whose work was routinely included in scientific discourse of the time but has since been relegated to the realm of "invention," "amateur observation," or, most harshly of all, "pseudo-science" and "quackery" (Russell 1983; Slotten 1994). In other words, while some very "modern" scientific activity went on before the nineteenth century, science as a whole was not a modern, rational enterprise (Ellul 1964).

The historical process that yielded "modern" science was a complex one, involving worldwide historical movements toward modernity, secularization, and rationalization (Ellul 1964; Habermas 1987; Toulmin 1989). At the same time, these broad trends were paralleled by local struggles of scientists hoping to increase their status, share their findings, or improve the quality of scientific research (Bates 1965; Slotten 1994). The rationalization and professionalization of science involved several related phenomena: (1) the establishment of refined methodologies and practices that were "scientific"—that is to say, the rationalization and, to some extent, routinization of scientific practice; (2) the creation and strengthening of professional identities and credentials (professional boundaries), establishing a formal scientific community; and (3) the creation of organizational infrastructure to support routine scientific practice—for example, the rise of the research university, industrial research labs, and so on (Russell 1983; Slotten 1994; Abbott 1988; Ben David 1971).

A rationalized professional infrastructure in developed nations provided a strong base for the transition of scientific professional activity and practice to the international sphere, especially compared to the weaker, less professional scientific societies of earlier centuries. However, this factor by itself is not sufficient to account for the expansion of science into the international arena. Local or national-level activity can become highly rationalized and organized without necessarily leading to organization at the international level.[3]

The reason that science organization made the transition to the international sphere lies in the culture of science itself, which can be described as rooted both in universalism and a strong community of practitioners (Merton 1942). The essence of the modernist scientific project is the search for knowledge that is universal rather than embedded in local context (Toulmin 1989). This universality is cognitively "built into" modern science and is evident in the attitudes of individual scientists (Zuckerman 1989) and in professional discourse. Consequently, the work of scientists in any part of the world is seen as relevant to scientists everywhere. Such a culture provides the impetus and legitimation for efforts to organize beyond national boundaries.

This discussion leads to the following proposition:

> 1. The expansion of professional science activity (which is rationalized, universalistic, and communitarian in character) within core nations increases the founding rate of professional science INGOs in the international sphere.

However, I do not expect the population of professional science INGOs to grow without bound. The same universalistic impulse that initially led scientists to organize internationally also makes their associations inherently competitive or preemptive in nature. By this I do not mean that they literally compete to undermine each other. Rather, they compete in the sense that professional science associations claim to offer universal, abstract knowledge over a particular domain of science. Once the International Union of Analytical Chemistry was founded, scientists had little incentive to found additional associations of analytical chemistry. Instead, analytical chemists would typically join the existing organization. In fact, historical evidence suggests that in areas where multiple organizations exist in the same scientific field, mergers commonly occur (UIA 1986). Thus, the very expansion of professional science INGOs limits subsequent growth, suggesting the following proposition:

> 2. An increase in the number of professional science INGOs has a negative effect on the rate at which new ones are founded.

In addition, the rise of science INGOs was influenced by a series of historical processes that have affected all international activity. The most straightforward of these factors are the world wars and economic depression, which disrupted international activity and reduced the rate of formation of science INGOs. Another factor was the rising number of nation-states in the world. The creation of new nations provides additional bases for generating international organization, either around newly created regional identities (e.g., physicists in Asia, ecologists in the Caribbean) or as the result of regionally specialized scientific interests (e.g., studying African fauna). For example, virtually no African science associations existed prior to the decolonization of Africa, whereas several now exist.

Furthermore, science organization would be rare in a time when any form of international association was difficult to arrange or hard to imagine. On the one hand, factors such as the difficulty of international travel and slowness of long-distance communication inhibit transnational organizing. On the other hand, without the models and experiences of a wide array of international organizations that could be copied or used as guides, and in the absence of cognitive cultural models of "the world" as an important unit of activity and social progress, even imagining an international science association becomes unlikely. Since the late nineteenth century, however, both of these inhibiting factors gave way to conditions fostering the creation of new international organizations.

An obvious indicator of the increase in facilitating technical means and motivating cognitive structures for international science organization is the cumulative number of existing international associations. This variable captures the aforementioned processes, including raw growth in international communication, legitimation of INGOs as an organizational form, and expansion in the number of governmental organizations that fund INGO activity, all of which support the creation and survival of science INGOs. Thus, a series of control variables are suggested:

> 3. Periods of war and economic depression decrease the founding rate of professional science INGOs, but increases in the number of independent nations and in the number of INGOs in general increase the founding rate of professional science INGOs.

MODELS OF SCIENCE AND SOCIETY AND THE INSTITUTIONALIZATION OF THE LIBERAL WORLD POLITY

Along with the professionalization of the sciences, new links were being formed between science, the state, and wider society. As long as science remained an inchoate set of activities practiced by amateurs, it was implausible that scientific activity might systematically benefit society. The rationalization and professionalization of science paved the way for new visions of science as deeply valuable to all members of society, a view promoted earliest and most vigorously by scientists themselves.

Many early scientists were also social reformers who saw science and the scientization of society as the solution to many of society's ills (Mackenzie 1981; Russell 1983). In the late 1870s science professionals first gained significant financial support from the state in Britain and the United States. That support was dramatically augmented in the 1910s and after World War II (Alter 1987). Active science professionals proclaimed that they, rather than inventors, entrepreneurs, or engineers, held the keys to progress and economic growth. Furthermore, they argued that the rational application of scientific logic to many domains of social life (e.g., the workplace, management, production) would solve social ills ranging from labor disputes to social anomie to war (Alter 1987).

This model of science as a primary source of progress and social development was incorporated into many nation-states, as well as many intergovernmental organizations (IGOs), in the years around World War II (Finnemore 1991; Haraway 1989; Drori 1993). A variety of factors prompting this trend have been cited, among them functional (Merton 1970 [1938]; Ben David 1971), organizational (Russell 1983), and cultural (Ramirez and Lee 1995;

Haraway 1989). Functional and organizational perspectives typically presume that the "obvious" social utility of science, along with the strength of professional science organizations, led to the general acceptance of science as the source of social progress. Cultural perspectives depict the "science-for-society" model as contingently emergent from interwar and postwar liberal, democratic cultural discourse—either preoccupied with the war experience, the bomb, decolonization, and progress (Haraway 1989), or as a product of the triumph of liberal models and the expansion of the UN system (Finnemore 1991; Ramirez and Lee 1995).

While the causes may be disputed, it is clear that liberal nations such as the United States and Britain, as well as science IGOs, became crucial carriers of the "science-for-society" vision. UNESCO is the consummate example of the process. Its primary activities include encouraging scientific activity and the diffusion of scientific knowledge not for its own sake, but rather for the benefit of society as a whole (UNESCO 1972; Finnemore 1991).

By the postwar period, nation-states, scientific professionals, and central IGOs all viewed science as socially valuable. Scientists were urged to address topics of social import, while other social actors were encouraged to adopt more scientific approaches. This environment supported the founding of socially oriented science INGOs.

At a basic level, the existence of socially oriented science INGOs depends crucially upon, and in fact presumes, the existence of organized, professionalized scientific activity. If science were not coherently organized, the task of pursuing "science for development," or of forging links between science and policymakers, would be problematic at best. However, as science was organized around consistent, rationalized field categories (e.g., physics or hydrology) with professional identities, it became possible to consult appropriate scientists routinely for advice on problems of social import, such as nuclear radiation or environmental degradation. Furthermore, professional organizations themselves were the strongest supporters of this conception. Their increasing presence in the international sphere provided support for the creation of socially oriented science INGOs. This suggests the following proposition:

> 4. The rise of professional science INGOs increases the founding rate of socially oriented science INGOs.

Unlike professional science INGOs, these socially oriented science INGOs are not inherently preemptive or competitive. Scientists are bound by a universalistic discourse that encourages them to organize collectively but monopolistically: one organization in a given domain is sufficient. Socially oriented science INGOs, in contrast, organize around social problems and social action. There is no expectation that any single organization will or can hegemonically devise solutions to a given social problem. For example, a social problem such as environmental degradation generates a tremendous amount of organization with varying substantive foci (pollution, deforestation, ozone depletion), varying regional focus (Brazilian rain forests, Mediterranean marine dumping), and varying methodologies (grassroots mobilization, local projects, lobbying organizations). This logic applies directly to socially oriented science INGOs, which organize around many substantive areas, emphasize different regions, and employ varied methodologies. Indeed, rather than competing, new associations serve to legitimate the application of science to social problems and thus promote the creation of additional science INGOs. This suggests the following proposition:

> 5. The number of socially oriented science INGOs in existence will not negatively affect the rate at which new ones are founded.

However, socially oriented science INGOs do experience certain forms of competitive pressure. It has been observed that the creation of IGOs with jurisdiction in a given substantive area can outcompete or preempt INGO activity in that area. In the case of environmental INGOs, for example, the expansion of IGO activity and the founding of a single dominant environmental IGO (the UN Environment Programme) reduced the founding rate of environmental INGOs (see Chapter 3 herein and Meyer, Frank et al. 1997). By that same logic, "official" socially oriented science IGOs might have sufficient status and resources to undercut their unofficial INGO counterparts.[4] Hence the last proposition:

> 6. The formation of socially oriented science IGOs has a negative effect on the founding rate of socially oriented science INGOs.

Finally, I expect that socially oriented science INGOs will be affected by the same factors (described above) that affect professional science INGO foundings: periods of war and economic depression, the increasing number of nation-states in the world, and the general expansion of INGO activity.

A QUANTITATIVE ANALYSIS OF THE RISE OF SCIENCE INGOS

Using data on the foundings of international associations, I modeled the historical expansion of professional and socially oriented science INGOs as separate organizational populations. My source for organizational foundings data was the 1995 *Yearbook of International Organizations* (*YIO*), which attempts to catalog all international organizations that have ever existed. International INGOs are defined in the *YIO* as organizations with members from at least three different nations. I used the categories employed in the *YIO* to select the superset of all science-related organizations and examined the description of each organization to determine which organizations fit the concepts employed in this study.[5] I also used the organizational description to determine whether an organization was professional or socially oriented in character. The data encompass the full population of professional and socially oriented science INGOs currently active.[6]

The event of interest in this analysis is the founding of a new science INGO. The rate of such events over time (the hazard rate) can be modeled using event history analysis methods (Tuma and Hannan 1984; models were estimated using RATE [Tuma 1992]). I employed a constant rate (exponential) model because it assumes a constant rather than time-dependent hazard rate. Any time-dependence is of fundamental substantive interest and will be accounted for by independent variables, rather than being specified in the model itself.

Independent variables for these analyses are collected at yearly intervals. I used two variables to test hypotheses regarding foundings of professional science INGOs: first, the rationalization and professionalization of scientific activity in core nations, as measured by the cumulative number of professional scientific associations in the United States;[7] second, competitive and preemptive pressures among professional science INGOs, as measured by the cumulative number of professional science INGOs that have previously been founded.

I used three variables to test hypotheses regarding the founding of socially oriented science INGOs. Professional scientific activity in the international sphere is measured by the cumulative number of professional science INGOs in the world. Competition among socially oriented science INGOs is indicated by the cumulative number of socially oriented science INGOs previously founded. Finally, competition and preemption caused by science IGOs is measured by the cumulative number of socially oriented science IGOs in the world.

Additionally, the following control variables are included in both models: wartime and economic depression are indicated by dummy variables reflecting the years of World War I, World War II, and the Great Depression. To conserve degrees of freedom, these three time-period dummy variables

TABLE 10.1

Constant-Rate Model Showing the Effects of Covariates on
the Founding Rate of Professional Science INGOs, 1875–1980
(*N*=114 events)

Variable	Parameter	Standard error
Constant	-1.61	2.23
Professionalization of science in core nations	.0035*	.002
Competition: Density of professional science INGOs	-.003*	.002
Expansion of the international system: Nation-state/ INGO factor	.289	1.43
Periods of wartime and world economic depression	-.953**	.407

Chi-square compared to constant-rate model, no covariates, 93.48***
* *p* < .1, ** *p* < .05, *** *p* < .01

were combined into a single variable.[8] Measures for increasing numbers of nation-states and increasing INGO activity are simply the cumulative numbers of those in existence. Because the latter two variables are highly collinear and reflect related underlying processes, they were combined into a single index using factor analysis.

Table 10.1 shows results from a constant-rate model predicting the founding rate of professional science INGOs. The model strongly supports the propositions outlined above. Professionalization of science at the national level has a significant positive effect on the founding of professional INGOs. The density of existing professional INGOs has a strong negative effect on the rate of new organizational foundings, suggesting preemption or competition among professional science INGOs. Increases in the number of nations in the world and the total number of INGOs increase the founding rate for professional science INGOs. Finally, the combined wartime and world economic depression variable has a negative but nonsignificant impact.

Table 10.2 shows results of a model predicting the founding rate of socially oriented science INGOs. International professional activity has a significant positive effect on foundings, while the insignificant effect of cumulative density of socially oriented science INGOs suggests that competition and preemption are not occurring. However, the existence of socially oriented science IGOs does have a significant negative effect on new foundings, sug-

TABLE 10.2

Constant-Rate Model Showing the Effects of Covariates on the Founding
Rate of Socially Oriented Science INGOs, 1875–1980
(*N*=48 events)

Variable	Parameter	Standard error
Constant	-2.57	2.26
International professional activity: Cumulative density of professional science INGOs	.124*	.0736
Competition: Cumulative density of socially oriented science INGOs	.005	.006
Competition from IGOs: Cumulative density of socially oriented science IGOs	-.370***	.125
Expansion of the international system: Nation-state/ INGO factor	1.33	1.84
Periods of wartime and world economic depression	-2.08*	1.12

Chi-square compared to constant-rate model, no covariates, 101.29***
* $p < .1$, ** $p < .05$, *** $p < .01$

gesting clear preemption by these more official science organizations. Finally, the war/economic depression dummy has a significant negative effect, but the factor variable combining expansion of the nation-state form and total INGO creation has a nonsignificant positive effect.

These results support the description of the rise of science INGOs developed above. In the nineteenth century, science professionalized in the dominant core nations, producing local organizations with strong international linkages. Combined with the expansion of the international system, this professional activity emerged at the international level in the form of professional science INGOs. This process, in turn, legitimated the application of science to society, yielding socially oriented science INGOs.

IMPLICATIONS AT THE NATION-STATE LEVEL

Within core countries, the impact of professional science INGOs is eclipsed by the strength of national-level science organizations. In the United States, for example, professional science associations are typically larger, wealthier, and support more prestigious conferences and journals than their international counterparts. In the periphery the situation could not be more different, because national scientific infrastructure is often weak or absent. Professional science INGOs, in conjunction with elite journals, become a peripheral scientist's primary link to current activity in his or her field.

For scientists in peripheral nations, then, participation in professional science INGOs is likely to be more important to their research than participation in local science organizations. Local organization is typically poorly funded in the periphery, and in some fields it does not even exist. A nonsystematic comparison of the number of national-level professional science societies to the number of memberships in science INGOs suggests the following pattern: individual scientists in a given peripheral nation are typically connected to dozens of international science associations, yet national-level organizations are often rare—sometimes nations have fewer than five (UIA 1989; Sachs 1990). Whether or not such participation in science INGOs actually precipitates national-level organizations cannot be determined without a rigorous longitudinal analysis. Nevertheless, it is clear that peripheral scientists often participate in INGOs in a given scientific field prior to any significant organization of that field in their home countries.

Thus, for the periphery, the transnational network of professional science associations is likely to be very consequential. Such a network may help scientists keep up on developments in their respective fields even in the absence of local scientific communities. At the same time, science associations facilitate communication and participation by peripheral scientists—potentially reducing the massive inequalities in world scientific research output that exist today.

The impact of socially oriented science INGOs is harder to gauge, in part because they are a rather heterogeneous group of organizations. Some focus on scientific ethics and primarily affect the work of scientists themselves. Other socially oriented science INGOs focus on specific social issues like environmental protection. As international lobbyists, they have the potential to affect policy in nation-states around the world. However, many socially oriented science INGOs focus specifically on economic development or the support of science in underdeveloped nations. They typically bring resources, technologies, training, and policy advice to developing nations, intervening via programs, conferences, and grassroots efforts. One result is that peripheral nations almost certainly have more scientific activity and infrastructure than they would in the absence of socially oriented science INGOs.

BROADER IMPLICATIONS: THE "SOCIALIZATION" OF SCIENCE AND "SCIENTIZATION" OF SOCIETY

The most important impact of science INGOs is on both nation-states and intergovernmental organizations alike. The rise of socially oriented science INGOs, as well as their counterparts at the national level, is indicative of a broad social trend, namely, the advent of science and rationality as a dominant model for organizing social activity. By this I mean the following: (1) scientists increasingly shape and define social issues and the identification of problems worth solving; (2) scientific expertise and information is increasingly integrated into governmental organization and decision-making; (3) scientific discourse increasingly infuses policy discussion and debate.

As I have argued above, this trend toward the "scientization" of social activity is particularly pronounced at the international level, where world-polity values of rationality and universalism are strong (see Chapter 1). John Meyer (1994) speaks of "rationalized others"—professional or scientific bodies that have no formal power but offer information and policy advice to nation-states and bodies of international governance. Socially oriented science INGOs are one organizational embodiment of this phenomenon. Peter Haas (1992) summarizes the notion of "epistemic communities," collections of like-minded scientists and policy professionals operating at the international level to provide information to nation-states and thereby influence or even shape state goals and interests. The many linkages that socially oriented science INGOs form among themselves and with IGOs suggests that they form a network and are part of the organizational basis for epistemic communities. If the rapid, continuing growth of socially oriented science INGOs is any indication, "rationalized others" and "epistemic communities" are proliferating.

The increasing authority and dominance of science in social decision-making has another important effect: nation-states and IGOs begin demanding scientific input and information in decision-making processes. They increasingly invite scientists and science INGOs to serve as advisers and consultants. More recently, IGOs and nation-states have encouraged the creation of new science associations, in part to gain policy information. As of 1994, over twenty science INGOs had been founded by IGOs such as UNESCO, the European Union, and the UN. One example is the European Pollution Science Society, an INGO concerned with the effects of pollution on the world ecosystem, founded by the European Union in 1988. The founding of this organization *preceded* the professionalization of "pollution science" as a field. Science has become such a routine solution to social problems among intergovernmental organizations and states that it is encouraged and even demanded, irrespective of the amount of scientific knowledge available. This circumstance, the hyper-demand for rational action plans, is described in detail in this volume for one arena, development, in Chapter 9, but it likely exists in many areas where pressure for governmental action is acute but no existing structures provide routinized strategies or solutions.

There is a tendency in both lay and academic discussion to treat the scientization of social planning and governance as a purely instrumental response to the efficacy of science. While this is certainly the case in many domains, it is hardly the whole story. Much scientization takes place in domains where there is little scientific consensus or the efficacy of science is questionable—e.g., complex environmental problems such as global warming, or issues of economic underdevelopment (Chapter 9 herein; Schofer et al. 1997). The fact that science "works" in many contexts is not sufficient to account for the intense and often unrealistic level of scientization observed. It makes more sense to view scientization as driven, in part, by the rationalized culture of the Western-derived world polity. Moreover, scientific rationality was a foundational ideology that coevolved with and justified modern forms of organization and governance (Shapin and Shaffer 1985). As a consequence, it is unsurprising that states and branches of international governance tend to organize activities and solutions in terms of rationalized, scientized policy solutions.

Finally, science is not left unchanged by its increasing role in social policy formation. There is evidence that both IGOs and science INGOs are working to support new scientific fields that can cope with the social problems of society. As resources are increasingly allocated to these new types of scientific activity, the very disciplinary structure of science may be transformed. Many new or rapidly expanding scientific fields have clear socially oriented components: environmental sciences, genetic engineering research, and so on. At the same time, "Big Science" is losing support now that governments are less willing to spend billions to support arcane research with little social utility. Thus, there is evidence to argue that science itself is "socializing," that is, becoming more organized around social issues and problems.

CONCLUDING THOUGHTS

The increasing presence of science in policy and governance is becoming apparent. However, it is less clear exactly how science is being incorporated into governance and what implications it will have. One could imagine science being directly incorporated by a strong central world state. However, this seems unlikely given the highly decentralized nature of the world polity. Research on "rationalized others" and "epistemic communities" has begun to theorize the process, but much work remains. At this point even very basic knowledge is lacking. How often do decision-makers use or cite scientific knowledge? Does this vary across substantive domains? What sort of scientific organizations provide policy information? With which governments do they interact? Further study of science INGOs would provide insight into some of these questions.

Conclusion: World Authority Structures and Legitimations

JOHN BOLI

World polity, world culture, world authority: these are the primary foci of the chapters in this book. Yet except in Chapter 1, world authority has received little explicit attention. Here it takes center stage. The key puzzle can be stated rather simply: in a world in which global governance processes are becoming increasingly prominent (Diehl 1996; Weiss, Gordenker, and Watson 1996; Murphy 1994), how can international nongovernmental organizations exercise authority? Clearly they are not, by and large, powerful organizations. The resources of even the largest INGOs, which number their members in the millions, pale in comparison to the capital, incomes, and personnel of other world actors, especially states and transnational corporations. Why are INGOs not simply ignored as global actors, as they are ignored by most scholars studying world political, economic, and cultural processes?

Many readers will object that this question places a rickety cart before a powerful horse: INGOs matter little, because states and TNCs dominate the world. The chapters of this book do not demonstrate that INGOs exercise authority; at best, they hint or suggest that INGOs influence state behavior and national policy in some domains at some times under ill-specified conditions. INGOs are simply interest groups operating at a high level, no different from the many interest groups that influence national or local legislation and administration.

This objection derives from an inadequate analysis of the nature of authority in the contemporary world, especially of the authority that is exercised by interest groups. The purpose of this chapter is to explore the nature of global authority so that a more fully theorized understanding of the role and effectiveness of INGOs will be forthcoming.

AUTHORITY IN INGO OPERATIONS

From the analyses presented in Chapters 3 through 10, we can usefully distinguish three modes of INGO operation that reflect distinct forms of the exercise of authority. I designate these autonomous, collateral, and penetrative forms of authority.

Autonomous INGO Authority

For a wide range of social sectors, INGOs and their associated national and local counterparts operate with virtually complete autonomy. Autonomy is most evident in the chapters on Esperanto, standardization, and science.

In fashioning a global identity through Esperanto (Young Kim's Chapter 5), the organizations that have appeared at a fairly steady rate throughout the century have not looked to states, IGOs, or other governmental units for direction or guidance. Rather, they have relied solely on their members, constructing their own rules and managing their sphere of global culture and organization with essentially no external interference. Esperanto enthusiasts have founded new bodies in a variety of areas very much as they pleased, writing by-laws and procedural rules that at most are subject to the minimal regulation imposed by states in whose territories the organizations are legally incorporated. Of course, internal authority disputes have arisen over the years in Esperanto INGOs, particularly regarding the issue of whether the language should be allowed to change, as living languages do, or remain fixed for all time. However, these and other disputes have been debated and adjudicated solely by the Esperantists themselves. For this sector, autonomy is virtually complete.

In the standardization sector (Chapter 7), Thomas Loya and John Boli show that much of the ethos of ISO and the IEC has been directed against state involvement and against legislation that would make standards compulsory. Structures and procedures were established to prevent considerations of power from deflecting the standards bodies from their commitment to purely technical considerations, and states have been only marginally involved in the sector throughout the period. Until the 1950s, the sector was composed almost entirely of voluntaristic national standards associations that kept states and IGOs at arm's length. With the rise of quasi-state national standards bodies and the practice of limited compulsory standards for some safety and consumer areas, states became indirectly involved, but almost exclusively on the implementation end. Here, then, the autonomy of the sector's authority has been high, but it has become somewhat mixed with state authority more recently.

A third sector of generally expanded autonomy is that of science. Evan Schofer's INGOs in Chapter 10 are of two types: purely scientific bodies whose goals and activities focus solely on the accumulation and dissemination of knowledge, and socially oriented science organizations that seek to influence social policy. Both types are internally autonomous, like virtually all INGOs; states and IGOs have no role in their decision-making, internal governance structures, or scientific and social policy formulation. On the other hand, only the first of these types deliberately resists state authority with respect to its goals (the expansion of scientific knowledge). Their involvement with states consists mainly of lobbying for state support of scientific research, and they strongly resist any effort by states to shape the scientific enterprise as such. But socially oriented bodies actively engage in the political process, urging states to develop policies and programs that will reshape their respective national societies. In this respect they are attempting to exercise collateral authority.

As indicated, with respect to their internal operations virtually all INGOs operate with a high degree of autonomy. The broad and important role of states in global and national governance means, however, that INGOs in many sectors must work with or through states to achieve their objectives. This consideration leads to the second type of INGO authority.

Collateral INGO Authority

In those sectors in which states are active, particularly by means of well-established intergovernmental organizations, INGOs recognize the inherent limits on their ability to shape global development autonomously. They therefore devote much of their energies to influencing IGOs and, thus, state policies.

As Nitza Berkovitch shows in Chapter 4, women's groups initially targeted individual states, particularly with regard to political structures restricting suffrage to men (other issues included deregulating prostitution and halting trafficking in women and children). With the establishment of the International Labor Organization after World War I, women's INGOs at once understood that body's potential to influence the labor policies of many states simultaneously. In the 1930s, they lobbied successfully in favor of ILO conventions to protect women (and children) from harsh working conditions and long working hours; later, as their ideology shifted to more purely egalitarian universalism, they pushed the ILO to dismantle protective policies in favor of women's full equality with men. Further expansion of "official" global governance structures (the establishment of the United Nations and its agencies) found women's INGOs regularly lobbying for policies and programs on a broad front. All this culminated in the UN Decade for Women (1976–1985), during which women's groups held massive international conferences parallel to, and largely directed toward, the official conferences comprised of state representatives. The results were both global, in action programs adopted by UN bodies to improve the status and life chances of women, and state-specific, as a large proportion of states created national ministries or agencies concerned with women's issues.

A more direct example of collateral INGO authority, striking in its apparent simplicity, is that of the International Committee of the Red Cross analyzed by Martha Finnemore in Chapter 6. In this early case, moral suasion by a small but prominent group of individuals deeply committed to basic principles of what would later become codified as "human rights" was able to induce states to change their behavior in that most nakedly power-dominated activity, war-making. This small INGO had as its weapons only eloquent arguments built around legitimated ideologies of the worth of individuals and their rights to respect and decent treatment. Finnemore shows, though, that the ICRC successfully established the groundwork for the Geneva Conventions despite the fact that rational state interests dictated rejection of these humanitarian practices. Remarkably enough, this Geneva framework has continued to temper the worst excesses of warring parties, though it obviously has not eliminated them entirely.

The population-policy sector (Chapter 8) looks very much like the women's INGO arena. Deborah Barrett and David Frank show that INGOs strove to influence states from the very beginning, initially by pronatalist ideology depicting population growth as linked to national strength. With the rise of nationalism, social Darwinism, and doctrines of racial or genetic purity, eugenics enjoyed a brief flurry of popularity, pushed by many INGOs and adopted by a number of states in specific legislative measures regarding the sterilization of criminals and the insane. Strongly delegitimated by the horrifying practices of fascist regimes, eugenics gave way after World War II to neo-Malthusianism, an ideology that always had adherents but had never earlier been prominent. What made neo-Malthusian INGO discourse and lobbying effective was the rise of individual-based models of national development, themselves promoted by a variety of international and national NGOs (see Chapter 9), that convinced states that their interests lay not in ever larger or purer populations but in better educated, more productive, more broadly capable citizens. Tellingly, however, it was only when neo-Malthusianism was effectively theorized as beneficial to state and national goals that the population-policy INGOs were able to persuade UN agencies, other IGOs, and separate states to adopt systematic population-control policies and family planning programs. Here the IGOs became essential agents of INGO authority: population-policy groups exercised collateral authority via their influence on IGOs, but by themselves they likely would not have been able to shift so many states to neo-Malthusian policies.

Turning to the development sector, the problems faced by population-policy INGOs in directly effecting global change become even more evident. Development requires enormous resources, and INGOs are generally resource-poor. Hence, Colette Chabbott's development INGOs (Chapter 9) were initially only bit-players in the international development aid sector. They may have been active and important in the shaping of global discourse about development, but most aid was bilaterally arranged and administered by donor and host state agencies. Partly because of changes in global ideology regarding development—changes that development INGOs themselves helped engender—these INGOs have gradually expanded their role as conduits for and administrators of aid programs. They interact extensively with IGOs and states to target recipients, shape the nature of the aid projects to be undertaken (moving away from the massive, technology-intensive projects of the 1950s and 1960s to appropriate-technology and sustainable development efforts more recently), and provide on-the-ground direction to increase the chances that aid will actually reach its intended beneficiaries.

Penetrative INGO Authority

The third form of INGO authority, distinguished from autonomous authority by the fact that states are also engaged in these sectors, operates through individual states or directly on subnational units. It depends on successful INGO penetration of the boundary-maintenance mechanisms shielding national and local polities from outside influence, as well as on the conscious effort by lower-level units to connect with INGO discourse and programs. Penetrative authority may be indirect, via state policy and program implementation: INGOs effect change within countries by inducing states to move in desired directions. In this sense it resembles collateral authority, except that IGOs are not involved in the relevant sectors. More often, penetrative authority comprises direct effects of INGOs on non-state individuals and organizations, shaping their worldviews, values, commitments, and action.

The analysis of environmental organizations by Frank and colleagues in Chapter 3 constitutes a good example of penetrative INGO authority, though collateral authority is also clearly involved. INGOs helped develop the cultural shift from conceptions of humanity as strictly separated from a seemingly inexhaustible nature to ideologies of humanity as a product of nature and therefore heavily immersed in and interdependent with a finite natural world. Their rationalizing activity yielded powerful models of nature as a domain governed by scientific principles and sensitive to human activity. Different types of INGOs emerged (resource-oriented, sentimental or preservationist, and ecosystemic-scientific), and the different perspectives they promoted were embraced by national and local organizations on an increasingly broad front.

Of course, this process involved bottom-up as well as top-down developments. Individuals, communities of scholars, and local or national organizations produced lines of thinking and acting with respect to the environment that were incorporated into global environmental discourse. However, the global propagation of this discourse—its penetration into arenas where it did not arise independently—has been largely the result of INGO activity, which has helped generate environmental organizations and movements in many countries that otherwise might yet not be engaged in the sector.

Frank and colleagues also uncover collateral INGO effects, beginning with the 1972 Stockholm conference (itself prompted in large part by the agitation of environmental INGOs) that found IGOs and, hence, states taking a newfound interest in environmental questions. Once environmentalism landed on the global IGO agenda, especially signified by the establishment of the UN Environment Programme, state creation of environmental protection agencies became a routine event. INGOs could hardly coerce states into establishing EPAs, but their collateral influence in this regard was considerable.

Penetrative INGO authority is also evident in several of the other sectors studied in this volume. Women's INGOs have helped generate new women's organizations and movements in countries where such activity was dormant or previously unknown, and their lobbying in specific countries has promoted the creation of state agencies intended to improve the status of women. Global standardization bodies have helped states and business sectors organize quasi-state national standards associations that can qualify for ISO and

IEC participation, thereby also bringing numerous companies and industry associations into the standardization process. State action to implement family planning and reproductive control policies, in response to INGO/IGO action at the global level, has prompted the formation of local and national bodies both for and against these policies, thereby expanding total global participation in the sector. Thus, for any given sector, all three forms of authority—autonomous, collateral, and penetrative—may be operating simultaneously, with varied effectiveness at different times and in different places.

This summary provides the background of my analysis of global authority; now for the foreground.

ON THE NATURE OF AUTHORITY

The dominant conception of authority, shared by both the public at large and most social scientists, is what Max Weber (1968) described as legal-rational authority: the authority that inheres in formally rationalized systems of legislation and judicial procedure characteristic of the modern state. Weber identified such authority as one of the three essential types of domination, along with traditional (patriarchal or patrimonial) and charismatic authority. His emphasis is on the capacity to dominate that is associated with these forms.

As the chapters in this volume indicate, however, authority cannot always be equated with domination. A fourth type, of which Weber no doubt was aware[1] but to which he seems to have attributed little general significance, is that of rational-voluntaristic authority, a concept introduced in Chapter 1. This is authority not of domination but of freely exercised reason, in which fundamentally equal individuals reach collective decisions through rational deliberations that are open to all. In this model, not power or interests but Weber's value or substantive rationality determines the outcome. The model assumes that the interests of the individuals involved are not ultimately irreconcilable, that the rational process itself can lead to a shared understanding of the coincidence of interests once the latter are properly conceived. It does not rule out self-interested action, but it contextualizes self-interest by recognizing the importance of collective interests as essential to the successful pursuit of self-interest.

Rational voluntarism has emerged in world culture as the morally superior form of authoritative organization, an ideal to which all societies should aspire. What gives it this moral virtuosity? To answer this question, we need to begin with fundamental elements of our socially constructed world. In the modern conceit, the sovereign individual has become both the primordial building-block of society and the ultimate source of value, meaning, and purpose. Individuals have the absolute right to be, to will, to do; to manage their own existence, with due respect for the right of other individuals to do likewise. No external party can justifiably rule the individual against his or her will. If there is to be collective authority, it must be built up from the authority that inheres in free, self-directed individuals, with due recognition of the basic equality that reigns among sovereign individuals.

This conception of egalitarian individualized society, now well institutionalized in world culture, was central to those much belabored moral philosophies that have been identified as so formative for modern Western culture: the social contracts of Hobbes, Locke, and Rousseau. The social contract is grounded in the sovereignty of individuals as citizen members of the body politic. These sovereign beings may freely choose Leviathan, granting authority to the state to direct affairs autonomously (Hobbes); they may insist on a minimal state that leaves social arrangements, as much as possible, to rational individuals in control of their own affairs (Locke); they may submerge themselves in a transcendental general will that subordinates individual interests to the collective good (Rousseau). In any case, authority is based on the individual, and it is self-justifying because the free, egalitarian individual is of ultimate value.

In recent times one finds the principal elements of this conception—the ultimate sovereignty of free, equal individuals—underlying such prominent philosophical constructs as Jürgen Habermas's (1981, 1989) ideal of the public sphere of rational discourse, John Rawls's (1971) theory of justice, and Lawrence Kohlberg's (1983) theory of morality. Habermas imagines a polity in which self-authorized individuals, acting with informed competence and concerned commitment to both societal and individual interests, make collective decisions needing no other justification for their propriety than the procedures by which they are reached. Individualized liberty and equality lead to truth and justice[2] as long as genuine liberty and equality are at work, so that every sovereign individual has the capacity and opportunity to participate in the public realm in which rational discourse takes place.

Rawls makes justice the only criterion of the good, while he proclaims that the discernment of justice is an entirely individual property: justice is revealed in the judgment an individual would make if presented with a decision whose consequences for particular individuals were hidden by a "veil of ignorance." Such an approach, Rawls insists, would yield ultimately and absolutely just decisions. Meanwhile, Kohlberg's morality similarly enthrones the individual as the "measure of all things," his moral stages proceeding from simple self-interest or unthinking obedience to authority to, at the highest level, the use of self-chosen principles applied and interpreted rationally by the individual actor. In Kohlberg's analysis, only the self-directed individual applying reasoned principles to make self-authorized judgments is truly moral.

Hence the principle of voluntarism, based on the conception that sovereignty lies with free and equal individuals, is absolutely foundational in these analyses. The other half of this authority model, rationality, is compelled both by perceptions of the functional requirements of social order and by the quest for mechanisms that can produce the good (rational) society. In prevailing ideology, order requires predictability, which requires principles, which require disciplined reason. Value rationality requires knowledge of the structure and operations of society, understanding of the causal processes that shape societal structure and operations, and knowledge of the consequences of proposed collective decisions. This knowledge must be at the disposal of the individuals who participate in collective policy formulation, and they must apply it rationally if the decisions they reach are to produce genuine social improvements.

Despite its enthroning of the individual as the ultimate source of both sovereignty and rationality, the rational-voluntarism model is decidedly institutional and collective. The model depicts individuals as ultimately responsible for the moral order, but they can create a just and value-enhancing moral order only by behaving in accordance with broad cultural principles of rational and proper action. Further, the model obliges individuals to do so. To be a properly functioning individual, one must orient one's action toward sustaining the good society. Even extreme libertarian doctrine has this collective character: each individual is authorized to act out of self-interest, but action must stay within the law and respect the equal rights and legitimate self-interests of others. The result, goes the story, will be a society that maximizes the welfare of all. The ultimate moral justification for libertarianism (especially, the minimalist state) is thus a kind of individualized collective good: the free, just, and wealthy nation comprised of free, just, and wealthy individuals. The doctrine would falter badly if it admitted that it necessarily entails steep stratification and the disempowerment of most individuals.

Individual-based rational voluntarism is thus not quite the bottom-up vision of society that it pretends to be. It relies clandestinely on general cultural prescriptions of propriety and value that are to be enacted by all purportedly self-directed individuals, and it implicitly assumes that these prescriptions are well institutionalized at the broadest level. Alexis de Tocqueville's (1966 [1836]) observation remains apt: nothing produces conformity like thorough individualism, and no model of society depends more on willing conformity if the model is to function well.

STRUCTURES OF RATIONAL VOLUNTARISM

The modern model of rational-voluntaristic authority came to fruition in Western thought but has now been incorporated into world culture as the dominant ideological form. It is the backbone of virtually all national constitutions (Boli 1987a), which delineate democratic political institutions and procedures that are more or less faithfully realized in practice. Where practice is less than perfect, it energizes recurrent waves of democratic social movements (Diamond and Plattner 1993). Within firms, professions, and churches in all sorts of countries it appears in the gradual shift from paternalistic forms of authority to collegial and team models (Kunda 1992). Within social movements in general, and in associations in general, it is the habitual model employed. Even within the family it has made serious inroads in many places (Skolnick 1992), as children, too, have become individuals endowed with a good measure of sovereignty and participatory rights.

The model does not go unchallenged. Critics of "cold reason" argue that rationality alone is too limited a basis for authority or morality; it must be complemented by, for example, caring or compassion (Gilligan 1982; Noddings 1984). Religious traditions, notably some variants of Islam and Christianity, still insist on the sovereignty of a divine being and necessary subordination of human will to the divine. These and other challengers to the dominant form are not without import, but they exhibit strikingly little strength in comparison to the rational-voluntarism model, which excludes divinity almost entirely and incorporates compassion mainly as a source of motivation for the commitment to rational purposes (when it is not seen as a hindrance to rationality).

Among both INGOs and IGOs the rational-voluntaristic authority model is by far the most common ideal enacted in organizational structure and ethos. Rare indeed is the organization that describes itself as explicitly inegalitarian, deliberately authoritarian, or subject to the will of God or Allah. In contrast, global organizations whose goals or means include something like compassion (world peace, harmony, fellowship, mutual understanding, tolerance) are not at all rare, but few of these allow compassion to play a major role in their internal structures or operations. Most are much too rationalized for that.

STRUCTURES OF WORLD AUTHORITY

This conceptual elaboration opens the way to an analysis of the structure of world authority and its legitimation mechanisms.

World Legal-Rational Authority

Legal-rational authority in the world polity is reserved exclusively for states. The principle of sovereignty holds that each state constitutes the locus of ultimate authority in its associated polity. No state has authority over any other; states and other organizations may influence a given state, but they cannot command that state and expect that the command will be obeyed (James 1986; Hinsley 1986). By the same token, no state may exercise authority over any aspect of the polity associated with another state. Jurisdiction over a polity is reserved to its sovereign state as regulated by the constitutional and legal framework that underpins the state.

Formal authority over social policy is thus strictly a state matter, though aspects of policymaking may be delegated to subordinate authorities. With the expansion of the state everywhere in the world in the twentieth century (Boli 1987b), states have assumed the authority to determine policy across an enormous range of activities. Exercise of that authority is tempered, however, by the demand that it operate "with the consent of the people," as the rational-voluntarism model of authority stipulates. The people's consent is signified in the social contract presumed by the constitution and in judicial interpretations that define the limits of state authority. Where a constitutional court does not exist or has only weak powers, the limits of state authority are determined by the legislature, whose accord with the consent of the people is presumed by virtue of the democratic institutions that elect legislators and shape the content of legislation.

Because states are the only loci of formalized sovereignty and "the people" are the ultimate source of that sovereignty, the only form of citizenship that has reified meaning and formal structuration in the world polity is national citizenship. National citizenship entails a relationship of mutual authority (i.e., the social contract) between citizens and the state: the state derives its authority from the sovereignty of citizens, who are entitled to participate in the formulation of state policy, while citizens are obligated to comply with the authority exercised by the state. Similarly, citizens can demand protection by the state while the state can demand action by citizens to protect the state.

The upshot of the citizen-state sovereignty relationship is that collectively generated decisions about the regulation and restructuring of society are seen as the province of national states. States therefore are the focus of citizen political action, and states are held responsible for the condition of their polities. Thus, in assessments of the developmental success of different countries, the focus of evaluation is the state: Is it adequately supporting education? Do its policies encourage investment? Does it properly embody the ideology of democracy? Are its efforts on behalf of public health sufficient? Has it ensured that working conditions are safe? Does it show proper concern for environmental preservation? Evaluations in these dimensions are made both by residents of the respective polities and by others who concern themselves with problems of international development, justice, equality, environmental protection, and the like.

Like citizens, non-state organizations are subject to the authority of the state, be they corporations, small businesses, associations, schools, unions, or parties. Like citizens, sometimes they act as agents of the state, while they also can demand that the state act as their agent (to settle disputes, provide protection, maintain order). They exercise certain forms of citizenship, though not in formal institutions: they lobby, propagandize, support candidates, and wield influence to affect public policy at various levels, but they may not vote, hold office, fill civil service positions, or join the judiciary.

For the most part, non-state organizations are seen as not responsible for the collective dimensions of societal development. In pure market theory, no single actor can shape the market; in oligopolistic theory, a few actors can dominate a given market and steer that aspect of societal development; in instrumentalist visions of the state, major capitalist organizations can even dominate the state. But in none of these theories are non-state actors seen as obligated to put collective interests before individual maximization. Classes, unions, parties, firms, interest groups, professions, ethnic groups—for all such collective actors, rational purpose means the promotion of self-interest, tempered, perhaps, by concerns for reciprocity and general social order but nonetheless subordinating societal goods to a secondary place. Only the state must and can ensure that self-interested action does not harm collective interests. Though voluntary associations typically act as self-appointed guardians of collective interests and providers of public goods, they cannot enforce policies to promote the common weal and are therefore, in the final analysis, also not responsible.

In short, where collective societal management is concerned, the state is the only structure that is both responsible and presumably capable. Such is the dominant world-polity ideology of legal-rational authority, and it is deeply institutionalized in most national polities.

World Rational-Voluntaristic Authority

To understand rational-voluntaristic authority at the world level, it is useful to begin by considering the national level. National voluntary associations take it upon themselves to organize activities for a variety of purposes: alleviating social problems, providing meaning, offering entertainment, facilitating interaction. Generally, they neither need nor desire outside authority for their actions. They work largely autonomously, organizing sports leagues, running soup kitchens, holding national chess tournaments, hiring lobbyists to promote agricultural subsidies. In the process, they make internal rules, develop industry standards, promulgate codes of ethics, and identify social problems. Their members are expected to abide by these rules, standards, codes, and definitions, and those who do not are subject to penalties established and enforced by the associations themselves.

While it is certainly the case that national-level associations are ultimately subject to state authority and must act within the law, many states expressly refuse to regulate or direct associations except in the most general terms. They are left free to manage their own affairs "between states and markets" (Wuthnow 1991), and they obtain a high degree of compliance with their internal rules and operating procedures. From the point of view of individual members, such compliance only makes sense. It is rational to abide by the rules, standards, and codes of ethics of the groups to which they belong because such prescriptions have been established by noncoercive procedures established and controlled by the members themselves. Not to abide by and promote the policies they have helped formulate would be a senseless self-contradiction.

World-level organizations operate almost entirely analogously. They are constructed in accordance with the rational-voluntarism model, and their members find it rational, even natural, to comply with the authority they exercise. Explicitly or implicitly, members see themselves as parties to a genuine social contract, where membership signifies both willingness to accept the authority structure and authorization to attempt to influence or reshape that structure. This model applies, in the main, to both IGOs and INGOs, though the former sometimes incorporate explicitly inegalitarian elements, such as weighted voting or veto powers for powerful countries (as in the UN Security Council).

The analogy to national-level associationism is not perfect, however. For world-level bodies, no overarching state acts as the final arbiter of propriety, dispute resolution, and penalty assessment for violations of formal rules. Far from weakening associationism, however, the absence of higher authority intensifies world voluntary rationalism (Meyer, Boli et al. 1997). If there is no world state, world actors must rely absolutely on self-generated structures of authority and action; the deus ex machina of the state is not available. If they cannot rely on coercive capacity, they must base their authority on theorized legitimation. They must, then, embody prevailing value-imbued conceptions of legitimate authority as fully as possible.

To some extent, INGOs remain subject to, and can draw on, legal-rational state authority to back up their decisions or rules. Every INGO is legally incorporated in some national polity and therefore subject to the jurisdiction of a national state. In practice, however, states treat INGOs much like they treat national and local associations, leaving them largely autonomous. Only very rarely does a dispute internal to an INGO, or between two INGOs, become a formal legal issue adjudicated in a state court, not least because the ideology of voluntary rationalism strongly discourages INGOs from turning to a state forum for dispute resolution.

For IGOs the situation is rather different. IGOs are assemblies of states operating under the still underanalyzed notion of "shared sovereignty," that is, voluntary accession to arrangements that involve collective state jurisdiction over particular domains. While rational voluntarism is the basic principle underlying such arrangements (each state is a voluntary participant, purportedly acting primarily to promote its interests and in theory free to withdraw at any time), the ideology of "self-help" (Waltz 1979) constantly keeps power differentials among states just under the surface (or sometimes glaringly above the surface) in IGO negotiations. Thus, more powerful states often can work their will in IGOs despite the formal egalitarianism of IGO structures, through influence and quid pro quo deal-making. In addition, of course, the latent threat of force (economic as well as military) encourages smaller and weaker states to tread lightly when powerful states take strong positions on issues.

Remarkably, however, states almost never come to blows over IGO negotiations. Further, very few states ever withdraw from IGOs or are ejected by their members, even though dissatisfaction among states with IGO decisions is routine. State managers are usually wont to convince themselves that their interests lie in continuing participation in global governance structures despite their displeasure with particular outcomes. In IGOs, then, a sort of disgruntled rational voluntarism is the basic principle of authority, though it is likely to be limited by considerations of power politics.[3]

Organized Legitimations of World-Level Authority

The general legitimation structure based on rational voluntarism becomes effective when it is translated by transnational bodies into specific structures and procedures. These bodies also draw on other organized forms of authority that inhere in their memberships. These elements constitute the core of world-level authority.

Structure and Procedures

Despite the inegalitarianism of some IGOs, the vast majority of INGOs and IGOs operate in close correspondence with the rational-voluntarism model. Membership is open to all interested parties, members stand on an equal footing with one another, procedures are formalized and public, decision-making is an open process, and the one-member one-vote principle is followed religiously in both the selection of officers and the determination of policy. For any given member, then, the requirements of rational voluntarism are well met, even though "politics" (attempts to build power bases and thereby exert inordinate influence) certainly comes into play in their daily operations. Tellingly, politicking is typically seen as a subversion of the legitimate model and is normally resented.

The openness of world-level bodies is not absolute, in many cases, but by and large any restrictions on membership eligibility are themselves rationally justified. For example, ISO has rather strict requirements for the structure and operations of any national standards body that applies for membership. These requirements are justified as necessary to ensure that the applying body can meaningfully participate in ISO activities (its members have the technical competence to do so) and adequately represent its associated national polity (the national body must have internal authority to develop and implement standards; see Chapter 7). Similarly, regional IGOs limit their membership to states in the relevant region, and some umbrella professional INGOs limit membership to national associations (or their members) in the relevant profession. The bases of exclusion still accord well with the logic of rational voluntarism in that all those (but, perhaps, only those) with true competence in the social domain at issue are eligible for membership.

That said, it is nevertheless the case that maximum inclusiveness endows the greatest authority on any particular world body. If the International Olympic Committee, always somewhat suspect because of the reputed authoritarian tendencies of some of its high officials, were to exclude arbitrarily a particular category of countries, it would be the target of constant criticism and the Olympics would generate much less enthusiasm. Similarly, because Greenpeace has grown from a small, tightly managed group of activists to a membership of millions from virtually every corner of the globe, its authority to speak and act on behalf of nature has been greatly enhanced. Rational voluntarism is universalistic because it is based on concepts of universal human rights, obligations, and capacities; for that reason, the greatest legitimacy is enjoyed by organizations that involve "all" of humanity, and most of the INGOs involved in the sectors studied in this volume have this all-inclusive character.

Member Identities as Sources of Authority

The authority imbued in transnational organizations via their conformity to overarching world-cultural legitimation theories is complemented by the authority embodied by their members. Member-based authority derives from national and local authority structures that are aggregated, in a loose sense, in transnational structures, yielding legitimation structures that endow IGOs and INGOs with authority both from "above" and from "below."

For IGOs, the situation is seemingly quite simple: their members are states, and states are the primary loci of legal-rational authority for their respective territories and citizens. Ergo, the authority of states as members endows IGOs with considerable collective authority. Even here, however, the particular properties of the separate states affect the legitimacy accorded to IGOs. States that glaringly depart from world-cultural standards regarding, say, the treatment of their citizens—for example, the South African state during the apartheid era, or Cambodia under the Khmer Rouge—may be castigated as oppressive and therefore illegitimate. If they are allowed to become or remain active members in a given IGO, that organization risks its own legitimacy (whence South Africa's exclusion from many IGOs, and numerous INGOs as well). IGO authority thus depends to some extent on the proper constitution of member states, though the realpolitik of interstate relations tempers these effects.

INGOs, on the other hand, rely heavily on the characteristics of their members as sources of authority. Though their members usually are individuals, they are hardly disconnected or isolated individuals. Rather, they bring to INGOs combinations of the following sources of legitimacy:

(1) Credentials. Degrees, certificates, and licenses issued by educational institutions, states, professional organizations, and quasi-state associations identify individuals as products or agents of these bodies. The individuals thereby absorb a measure of the authority wielded by the certifying organizations. When INGOs promoting women's equality, family planning, or research into global warming speak, the voices of hundreds of universities, dozens of states, and scores of professional associations are murmuring in the background. Each of these local or national bodies is itself legitimated through various social theories and structures, so that INGOs are, as it were, perched atop multiple pillars of legitimation deeply set in the bedrock of local reality.

(2) Professional standing and expertise. Of course, some individuals are more equal than others in the highly egalitarian structures that INGOs construct. Leaders of professional associations, prominent scholars or scientists, noted authorities on particular issues, widely published intellectuals, experts of world renown—all these types of members lend not only prestige but enhanced voluntary-rationalist authority to the INGOs to which they belong. Merely famous members, on the other hand, make a more dubious contribution: a Brigitte Bardot opposing the fur trade may evoke a good deal of ridicule because she lacks the structured standing of a "true" expert or professional.

(3) Organizations and organizational position. Beyond professional certification and standing, individual members bring to INGOs a measure of the authority lodged in the organizations to which they belong. The engineers and managers from DEC, Sony, Philips, and Ericsson who participate in ISO Working Groups carry the expertise and clout of these corporations into the world arena (Chapter 7). The same logic holds for officers of national Red Cross and Red Crescent associations who belong to their international counterparts (Chapter 6), for foundation officials and professors of economics who participate in development INGOs (Chapter 9), and for executive officers of national family-planning organizations who belong to the corresponding international bodies (Chapter 8). It holds as well for those INGOs that admit organizations as members: INGO authority is enhanced by their members' national or global prominence, which derives mainly from their knowledge, expertise, and exemplary performance.

(4) Moral and spiritual charisma. INGO members often bring authority

based on a more intangible characteristic: the moral fervor and spiritual virtuosity made famous by Weber as charisma. What makes Bardot not merely laughable as a champion of furry friends is her long-term, dedicated commitment to her cause. What made Henry Dunant and his fellow ICRC members difficult to ignore (Chapter 6) was their unwavering insistence on the moral propriety of their proposals. Greenpeace gradually won worldwide respect in part because its core members were willing to face considerable danger (e.g., virtual acts of war by the French government) while carrying out guerrilla protests (Chapter 3). If the cause means more to them than their lives, goes the logic of this mechanism, there must be something to it. Thus, the intensity of the "human spirit" that is evident in the members of many INGOs gives a further boost to the legitimacy of these bodies.

(5) The new clergies. Finally, many INGOs benefit from the tremendous authority and value associated with the purposes they activate in their respective domains. INGO members are, as it were, priests of the world polity, mediating between the authority lodged in grand collective human projects and the mundane world of everyday action. This is a highly differentiated priesthood, reflecting the elaborate differentiation of social organization (Luhmann 1982) of the past several centuries. Highly specialized clergies link various realms of the sacred to profane endeavors. The members of world scientific organizations are conduits for the authority of the rationalized investigation of nature and the cosmos (Chapter 10); the members of world economics associations embody the authority of the "dismal science" in assessing development programs (Chapter 9); the members of INGOs concerned with medicine and health, engineering disciplines, and humanistic fields are incorporations of the virtually unchallengeable authority, prestige, and value associated with their respective domains.

These clergies most often exercise institutionalized charisma, usually quite different from that of morally fervent visionaries. They speak in sober, rational, measured tones, but their words carry weight because they represent the pinnacles of human endeavor in the great rationalizing projects that are the essence of the world polity.

The Authority of Legitimated Purposes

This final source of authority combines the abstract, high-level legitimation that derives from conformity to world cultural principles with the more concrete, local authority of organizational structure and position. IGOs and INGOs gain legitimacy through their organized commitment to legitimated purposes of human action: progress, development, order, democracy, and justice at the societal level; comfort, security, self-development, freedom, moral rectitude, and equality at the individual level. To these can be added such global purposes as peace, order, harmony, justice, and environmental preservation. These lists are by no means exhaustive, but they indicate the range of purposes that are legitimated both globally and at lower levels of social organization. In contrast, human purposes that are deemed out of bounds include warfare, destruction, anarchy, authoritarianism, slavery and torture, genocide, depravity, and so on.

While legitimated purposes are frequently expressed in general, abstract terms, they also translate into highly specific measures reflecting the organizational structures that are supposed to be necessary for their realization. Thus, the goal of progress is measured as GDP per capita or the infant mortality rate (cf. Chapters 8 and 9); equality is measured as women's income compared to that of men (cf. Chapter 4); standardization is measured in terms of the number of standards produced and the sales of standards documents (Chapter 7); science development is captured by research and development expenditures as a proportion of GDP (cf. Chapter 10); individual development is measured as school enrollment or completion rates. All of these measures imply comprehensive and systematic rationalized organization. Meaningful infant mortality figures cannot be reported unless births and deaths are universally recorded. The recording system thus must reach into every place where births and infant deaths occur. To achieve this, birth attendants (doctors, midwives) are licensed, hospitals are required to file vital statistics reports, registration offices are established, statisticians are employed. Similarly, meaningful science expenditure data require comprehensive reporting systems reaching into universities, corporations, and research institutions to apply standard definitions of scientific work, scientific personnel, relevant expenses, and so on.

The pursuit of abstract rationalized purposes thus implies the promotion of thoroughly rationalized means. INGOs and IGOs neglect these purposes and means at great peril to their authority, and few subject themselves to such peril. Some INGO sectors are notable exceptions: transnational bodies promoting such "irrational" or arational activities as religion, humanistic philosophy, and spiritualism are hardly rare (though they comprise only a small proportion of the INGO population). As discussed in Chapter 1, the rational/irrational dialectic guarantees the production and viability of a good deal of such activity. Most such organizations nonetheless pursue standard

FIGURE C.1.   Heuristic representation of world authority structures and legitimations.

rationalized purposes, such as individual development, righteousness, world peace, and social justice, through increasingly rationalized means. They thereby enhance their authority.[4]

The Voluntary Rationalism of World Citizenship

Figure C.1 represents the elements of world authority outlined in the preceding analysis. The figure is a heuristic device intended only to bring these elements together in easily surveyable form. It should not be read as a causal diagram of or set of assertions about the relative importance of IGO and INGO authority.

Figure C.1 indicates that the most widely legitimated models of authority begin with the individual as the ultimate locus of sovereignty. By virtue of their capacity for freely exercised rational interaction, sovereign individuals (or their representatives) can arrive at collective decisions that are proper, just, and therefore inherently binding. This is the ideal-typical image of individualistic, egalitarian citizenship, which is seen as the foundation for state legal-rational authority. In world-level organizations, this is the image of world citizenship.

World citizenship involves the self-authorized action of equal and sovereign individuals who form collectivities to organize global social sectors. The authority of these collectivities varies with the extent to which they implement rational-voluntaristic structures and procedures, pursue legitimated purposes through rationalized means, and attract members who are credentialed, professional, expert, organizationally prominent, and impassioned. Because INGOs do all of these things rather well, they enjoy considerable authority at the world level. Ironically, IGOs often embody less pure authority than their nongovernmental counterparts. They less fully implement egalitarian rational voluntarism, they allow much less room for individual participation, and they rely on states' coercive capacities to implement the policies and programs they develop. The implications of this difference emerge when we examine the practical operations of world authority.

WORLD AUTHORITY IN OPERATION

As indicated, the principal structures by which world authority is formally organized are two: IGOs, or assemblies of states; and INGOs, or assemblies of individuals and, sometimes, organizations, most often of associational form.

IGOs: Compulsory Rational Voluntarism in the Context of Power Politics

Most analyses of IGOs assume that states are strictly voluntary participants exercising their sovereign authority (Krasner 1983a; Young 1989; Groom and Taylor 1990; Rosenau and Czempiel 1992). Their collective action thus represents little more than cooperatively shared sovereignty, overlapping jurisdictions, or voluntary limitations on sovereignty.

In practice, the voluntary aspect of state membership in IGOs or compliance with IGO decisions and policies is a good deal more hypothetical than actual. The literature that assumes state voluntarism in IGOs itself shows that states often feel compelled to join IGOs for a variety of reasons: to ensure that they have input into decisions that will affect global markets, resources, technical development, communications, and transportation; to hasten national development by "plugging in" to global structures that promise access to knowledge, expertise, and resources; to ensure that competitors do not dominate global governance structures to their own detriment. Beyond these "functional" factors, states also need the legitimacy conferred by IGO participation, which helps constitute them as properly functioning actors duly promoting national progress and citizen welfare (Meyer, Boli et al. 1997).

From the point of view of any particular state, then, IGO participation is much more compulsory than the notion of the rational voluntaristic exercise of sovereignty suggests. Even the most powerful states are hesitant to refrain from IGO participation. The United States withdrew from UNESCO when it became clear that it would not be able to prevent UNESCO's Third-World majority from promoting policies that seemed to challenge U.S. hegemony (Imber 1989), but that action is notable primarily for its rarity.

Hence, though states exercise considerable autonomy in many domestic domains, increasingly they find it "in their interests" (i.e., necessary, by a variety of logics) to join IGOs and abide by the decisions reached by the latter. The necessity factor is strongest with respect to IGOs that manage technical systems and economic relations, such as the International Air Transport Association, the World Trade Organization, the International Telecommunications Union, the International Postal Union, and the World Maritime Organization. As many of these have become virtually universal bodies exercising effective collective authority over their respective domains, states have learned that globalization entails the necessary subordination of their national polities to a single, larger entity: the world polity.

This process is now well enough institutionalized that most states consider it quite routine. Few worry much about their sovereignty because the theory of rational voluntarism underlying most IGOs convinces states that their participation is discretionary: no IGO can command cooperation or compliance from any particular state.[5] Power politics certainly shapes the outcomes of many IGO negotiations, but the outcomes are not coercively enforceable even though compliance may be unwilling or only partial. Further, states are remarkably restrained with respect to undertaking uninvited action to enforce IGO decisions within the territory of other states. Ultimately, compliance remains theoretically voluntary even though state managers may feel they have little choice but to "decide" to comply.

INGOs: Three Forms of Rational-Voluntaristic Authority

INGO authority resembles IGO authority in that it also involves informal but powerful logics of compulsion that are masked by the theory of rational voluntarism. Where INGOs differ most is in their lack of legal-rational sovereignty: they have no formal jurisdiction over specified domains. If they are to be effective, INGOs must either sidestep state authority or devote considerable effort to influencing states and other social entities to act in line with INGO purposes and goals. At this point, then, I return to the three forms of INGO authority identified in the review at the beginning of this chapter: (1) autonomous INGO authority, in social sectors over which states make little or no effort to exert control; (2) collateral INGO authority, in sectors where states have formed IGOs as the center of global governance structures; and (3) penetrative INGO authority, in "domestic" sectors subject to state jurisdiction, where INGOs can be effective by influencing states and, through state policies, local actors as well, or, alternatively, by bypassing states to influence local organizations directly (Meyer, Boli et al. 1997).

As indicated, autonomous authority is most pronounced in this volume's sectoral studies of Esperanto (Chapter 5), standardization (Chapter 7), and science (Chapter 10). This form of INGO authority appears to be more typical than exceptional. In a great many sectors, INGO-based global governance, usually reaching down to national and local levels of action, operates largely outside the aegis of states. This form appears to be activated in most technical and knowledge domains; most professions and humanistic disciplines; most sports, hobby, and leisure activities; some industry and trade domains; most religious and cultural identity sectors; many charity and relief activities; and a good number of explicitly world-polity related domains, particularly those concerned with buttressing global identities and one-worldness.

Autonomy means that states are at most weakly involved in the activities and discourse organized by INGOs and their national and local counterparts, whether at the world level or at lower levels. As mentioned earlier, most states make little effort to regulate associational life, except by requiring conformity with accounting principles and procedures and, of course, abiding by the law in general. Here the pure form of rational voluntaristic authority holds sway to an extraordinary degree.

How much INGOs actually shape the activities of local and national actors in these autonomous sectors varies considerably, however. One type of variation is sectoral, as a comparison of sports organizations and the professions illustrates. Most international sport federations establish rules that are definitive for the entire world and sponsor world championships that (contra the "World Series" of American baseball) include all of the premier competitors in the world. Here rational voluntarism is at its most universal. The game of football (soccer) is virtually identical no matter where it is played, and the World Cup produces the undisputed world champion every four years. In contrast, many INGO professional associations have only limited success in promulgating such rule systems as codes of ethics or guidelines for the study of human subjects. National professional bodies often develop codes and guidelines reflecting distinct national circumstances and traditions, so their prescriptions may not fully accord with INGO doctrine.

A second type of variation derives from country characteristics. Smaller, less developed, less powerful countries are apt to find conformity with INGO rules and principles especially attractive, especially during the initial stages of their INGO involvement. Chapter 2 supports this assertion: growth rates in the breadth of INGO membership are highest among smaller and weaker countries, indicating their eagerness to plug in to world culture and structure. Nascent professional organizations in, say, African countries, are thus likely to look to their international counterparts for guidance. Larger, richer, more powerful countries, on the other hand, can sometimes be stubbornly contrary. A good example is the American National Standards Institute (ANSI), which seems to be unique among national standards bodies in its competitive attitude and attempts to dominate the standardization sector. Yet ANSI also serves as an object lesson for other standardization bodies. Its go-it-alone attitude has had negative consequences for American firms, the prime example in recent years being the slowness of ANSI to encourage compliance with the ISO 9000 standards that are formally mandatory for many products aimed at the European market (Chapter 7).

Systematic research into the extent of INGO influence on national and local activity, and the factors that affect INGO influence, has yet to be conducted. Investigations into this topic would be most welcome.

Where IGOs are clearly engaged, INGOs cannot govern autonomously but must rely on collateral authority by attempting to influence IGO policies, as we saw in Barrett and Frank's chapter on population-policy INGOs, Berkovitch's work on women's INGOs, and Chabbott's study of the development sector. More generally, we can expect to find collateral authority at work in economic development, technical, military, and political domains, since the bulk of IGOs are concentrated in these areas (Jacobson, Reisinger, and Mathers 1986; Shanks, Jacobson, and Kaplan 1996). How does this collateral authority succeed?

Several mechanisms appear to be at work. First, while IGOs have coercive jurisdiction over the domains at issue, they often lack relevant knowledge, expertise, and technical competence. More often than not, INGOs are superior repositories of such knowledge and competence (for numerous examples, see Charnovitz 1997). Population INGOs assemble the world's foremost demographers; environmental INGOs assemble outstanding experts on ozone depletion, tropical deforestation, and acid rain; educational INGOs assemble leading educators and educational economists. IGOs are therefore at a disadvantage in developing policy decisions in these domains, and they often find themselves relying on INGO studies and consultants to lay the groundwork. Even more, when INGOs lobby IGOs they can invoke the prestige and expertise of their members to convince IGO staffs that their views are not to be ignored.

Second, because INGOs constitute the primary public sphere within which world-cultural discourse is developed and presented, they often take the initiative in generating items for the world agenda and propagating the cultural framework (conceptions of value, problems, progress, desiderata) used to address these items. As Berkovitch (Chapter 4) documents, women's INGOs shifted from a conception of women as fundamentally different from men to a fully egalitarian conception, in line with the general shift to strongly universalistic egalitarianism after World War II. By promoting this conception, women's INGOs were able to change the orientation of the ILO with regard to women's work and thereby evoke the abolition of various protective (i.e., inegalitarian) provisions in a number of states.

Similarly, in the population debate, INGO discourse and theorizing laid the foundation for reconceptualizing population as a potential threat to national development rather than a measure of national strength (Chapter 8). Universal egalitarianism was again at work, as the concept of development shifted from a collective property (aggregate size or wealth) to an individualized measure (wealth per capita; Chabbott also discusses this process in Chapter 9). Population INGOs' adoption of this conceptual change, and their efforts to educate states about this new conception, had striking consequences.

Third, the moral stature of INGOs and the moral fervency of their individual members help them influence IGOs. This mechanism appears to be at work in Finnemore's account (Chapter 6) of the ICRC's success in promoting rules for the humane treatment of prisoners, and it probably applies quite generally. For example, women's INGOs convincingly present themselves as representing all women everywhere; when they gather in Nairobi or Beijing, tens of thousands strong and coming from practically every country in the world, they constitute the moral voice of women *tout court*. They care deeply about the issues and plead their case passionately, speaking as "half of humanity" whose worth cannot be denied and whose well-being is not to be neglected. Diffuse though this moral-virtuosity factor may be, it does seem to influence the views and decisions of IGO delegates, even if some delegates hope that symbolic gestures without much practical import will suffice to appease INGO groups.

A related point is, fourth, the rational voluntarism of IGOs themselves. Because they must rely on (purportedly) voluntary compliance by member states, and because member states are legitimated as agents of the democratically expressed will of their citizens, IGOs seek the legitimacy provided by INGOs as representatives of the same constituencies that states represent. If IGOs can present their actions as promoting individual welfare and collective justice, that is, as actions serving "the people" (global or national) rather than the interests of states as such, they improve their chances of obtaining compliance by member states and by national and local organizations affected by those actions. This mechanism may not apply well to issues where "national security" is at stake, such as military matters, but it can be important in many sectors of global governance.

Collateral INGO authority thus amounts to a fusion of rational-voluntaristic and legal-rational authority in the interplay between INGOs and IGOs. IGOs gain legitimacy by incorporating INGO knowledge and views in their reports and policy proposals, because INGOs represent informed "world public opinion" and are buttressed by the ultimate sovereignty that inheres in their individual members as world citizens. INGOs enhance their prestige by collaborating with the IGOs that are formally responsible for the domains in question, thereby improving their chances of exercising greater influence in future policy debates.

As noted in Chapter 1, this collaborative process is much more than casual. IGOs and INGOs have formal ties, numbering into the hundreds for many UN agencies, and IGOs often co-opt INGO experts to aid or staff IGO technical committees and study groups.[6] All this is part of the process, often noted in recent years at the national level (Habermas 1989; Seligman 1992), by which the distinction between public and private, between the state and the many interest groups that practice institutionalized lobbying, has become blurred. World governance is conducted by INGOs and IGOs in a give-and-take interplay in which, to a large extent, the framework and issues to be addressed are established by the nongovernmental organizations, and the two types of bodies jointly hammer out policy decisions based on that framework.

This sketch of INGO/IGO relations is obviously oversimplified in that INGOs often speak with conflicting voices on particular issues. Among women's INGOs, for example, sharp disagreements have arisen about such issues as female circumcision and women's role in child-rearing. Among environmental INGOs, experts disagree about global warming and the causes of ozone depletion. Among socially oriented science INGOs, some factions favor a complete ban on nuclear power while others insist on its continued expansion. INGO influence can be difficult to assess because of such disagreements. The point is that INGOs are fully engaged in IGO global governance structures, and their arguments, both pro and con, help shape the terms of debate and the possible policy outcomes. INGO effectiveness may be more discernible when a consensually accepted view reigns in the relevant INGO sector (as with women's INGOs with respect to many issues), but even when dissensus is palpable, INGOs are often important participants in the global governance process.

The third form of INGO authority—penetrative authority—operates through individual states or directly on subnational units, in domains where states are decidedly engaged. Many of the mechanisms involved in penetrative authority are similar to those of collateral INGO authority, but the sectors involved are rather different. Most IGOs deal with military matters, economic relations, and technical management issues, and the power and interests involved limit INGO influence in these sectors. In sectors where IGOs are uncommon but INGOs cannot operate autonomously because state interests and programs are activated, INGOs attempt both to influence states and, bypassing states, to influence associations, corporations, and local governments directly.

The sector in which penetrative INGO authority most commonly operates is probably that of human rights, in which INGOs directly appeal to states to end political repression and violence against individuals or groups. Amnesty International and Human Rights Watch are prominent examples. Their effectiveness depends absolutely on their moral fervor and political nonpartisanship, which combine with their rational voluntaristic character to make them a sort of "voice of humanity" to which states must listen. Listen and ignore, many times, to be sure, for moral suasion by itself is hardly determinative. Still, as the example of South Africa shows, sustained moral suasion, particularly when combined with even dubiously effective economic and political sanctions, can eventually effect quite radical change in domestic arrangements.

This example reveals an important aspect of penetrative INGO authority: led by a variety of INGOs and their national counterparts, the global movement against apartheid was able to mobilize not only states but also corporations and local governments to act against South Africa. For the most part, corporate participation was mandated by states, though some companies (and other entities, notably universities) responded voluntarily. On the other hand, sometimes INGOs act quite directly on corporations, especially TNCs. Exxon has been a favorite INGO target since its oil spill in Alaska, Nestlé for its undermining of breast-feeding in Africa, Shell for its cooperation with the

Nigerian government. Notably, however, these efforts rarely accomplish much unless they bring states into play.

Beyond the mobilization of states and corporations, a common mechanism peculiar to penetrative INGO authority processes is the role INGOs play in engendering or supporting domestic movements that attempt to influence state policy. At one level, this mechanism is characteristic of INGOs almost by definition: they encourage broad participation and are especially eager to see their reach extend to individuals or associations in countries that have not previously been involved with their activities. Thus, environmental INGOs help local chapters form in new places, and those chapters may become the nuclei for new national environmental movements.

INGOs also reach out to existing organizations (social movement, professional, technical, scientific, and many other types). They establish network ties to strengthen the INGO field, mobilize sympathetic organizations for particular causes or campaigns, and help organizations whose purposes mesh well with their own. Hence, women's INGOs aid women's movements struggling against "patriarchal" regimes, and they help prepare reports on the status of women in countries without strong women's organizations. Development INGOs send advisers and consultants to help organize and activate the rural poor in less developed countries. Sports INGOs supply aid to establish national sports federations, while knowledge INGOs give assistance for the improvement of library organization and information technology. Some such actions are directed at influencing state policy, while others are motivated by the failure of states to meet their presumed responsibilities or by the perceived weakness of civil-society institutions in poorer nations.

Systematic information about the effectiveness of INGO authority, be it autonomous, collateral, or penetrative, is not available and would be, in the nature of the case, quite difficult to gather. Though the chapters in this book point to some striking effects, and case studies of particular INGOs often convincingly imply that collateral and penetrative effects are substantial, much work is needed to understand the conditions under which INGOs act effectively via these three forms of authority. Perhaps the analysis here can help guide such research in coming years.

AGENCY AND INTERESTS: MAKING INGO AUTHORITY EFFECTIVE

The preceding review of world authority structures and processes underscores the embeddedness of INGOs, IGOs, and states in the global cultural and moral order. The meaning of world-level action emerges as it is interpreted within and against the contours of this cultural order, and such interpretation frequently raises the issue of agency (Wendt 1992; Onuf 1989). A useful way to address this issue is through the following question: When global actors become engaged, as whose agents do they act? What agency options are available to INGOs, IGOs, states, TNCs, and individuals in contemporary world culture?

INGOs operate in a world in which actors are expected to be self-interested; they are agents of the self. Prevailing political, economic, and social theories assume that states, organizations, and individuals—the dominant, most highly reified social entities in world culture—both can and do act rationally to advance their interests. Of all the conceivable possibilities, their primary interests actually cover a rather narrow range: wealth, prestige, prominence, power, development. Promotion of these interests is not only expected but wholly legitimate in world culture, as long as the means used to promote them accord with rational-legal and moral prescriptions. Indeed, self-interested action is seen as an integral element in progress and value-creation, for it reflects the freedom and sovereignty of individuals whose combined efforts are theorized as leading to the good society.

Self-interested action is thus constructed as morally proper—but only within limits.[7] "Naked" self-interest, in the global moral order, goes too far; self-interest must at least be "enlightened." The self-interested actor must recognize the legitimate interests of others and such collective interests as order, stability, and the rule of law. Self-agency thus must be tempered by collective agency: to be successful as an agent of the self, the actor must also be an agent of the whole. However, even enlightened self-interest is regarded as morally dubious in many quarters because it permits (and fosters) exploitation, inequality, intolerance, and related ills. In this view, quite widespread in world culture, enlightened self-interest is uncertainly bounded and can easily become destructive of all that makes human dignity possible.

In the world moral order, then, actors acting solely as agents of themselves are morally questionable (Boli 1996). The burden of proof lies on self-interested actors to demonstrate that more than self-aggrandizement animates their action, even though their action promotes important purposes like progress or growth. Just as medieval merchants met this burden of proof by paying for masses in the town cathedral, even quintessential self-interested actors feel compelled to demonstrate their collective concerns: Mobil sponsors public broadcasting productions, George Soros supports numerous charitable organizations. Higher virtue is reserved for those who act as agents of others, subordinating personal gain to broader concerns.

The grandest virtue of all, in this reading of world culture, is enacted by actors who serve as agents of all others, that is, of humanity as a whole. This other-orientation is what defines so many voluntary associations as the "do-gooders" of national societies and the world polity: based on strict principles of rational voluntarism, they charge themselves with putting collective interests above their own or those of their members. John Meyer (1994) describes INGOs in this respect as disinterested "rationalized others." INGOs adopt the posture of the (often unpaid) consultant or adviser whose sole interest is the welfare of the client, be the client a less developed country, working women, world health, the rural poor of Asia, or the world economy. This posture embodies high moral virtue, rendering the INGOs that adopt it particularly valuable as sources of advice, rules, models, systems, and methods.

INGOs thus act as agents of those they advise and aid, including both the organizations that rely on INGO expertise and the beneficiaries of projects sponsored by those organizations. Conversely, as critics of states and corporations that do not abide by established world-cultural models and standards for behavior, INGOs are agents of more diffuse entities and concepts. They act on behalf of justice, equality, science, truth, freedom, progress; on behalf of children, the animal kingdom, people of color, Africa.

Such diffuseness carries a distinct liability, however. Rational actors concerned primarily for their own interests are not easily persuaded to act on behalf of truth or animals or Africa in the abstract. This is why INGO effectiveness increases when the discourse, models, and methods INGOs propagate are translated into concrete, interest-optimizing prescriptions. To illustrate, consider again Barrett and Frank (Chapter 8) on population policy. When states learned from world discourse that population growth would inhibit national development, that it was "in their interest" to worry about overpopulation, they quickly climbed aboard the family planning train. Similarly, when the environmental movement convinced states that pollution and large-scale climatic change threatened national well-being and viability, states began to realize that environmental protection ministries make a great deal of sense (Chapter 4). On the other hand, Young Kim has shown that the Esperanto movement (Chapter 5) has been unable to engender official interest because the distance between the goals it espouses (world harmony and mutual understanding) and the means it proposes (a common language) is too great and the contribution of Esperanto to specific actor interests is too vague.

Because national development (progress and power) is the key concern of the state, rationales for state acceptance of INGO prescriptions are most convincing if they directly link these prescriptions to development. But prevailing theories of development that depict it as a complex, multidimensional phenomenon make a broad range of rationales effective. For example, the influence of women's groups has increased as the importance of women for development has become an increasingly self-evident element of world discourse. However, because "women are people too" in world culture, the kinds of changes seen as necessary to promote women as contributors to development extend well beyond economic concerns. For example, women should be competent citizens, so they "need" and "have a right to" comprehensive and empowering education, not just occupational training. States thus find it in their interests to incorporate women in secondary and tertiary schooling, with all that such education entails of extra-economic socialization (Bradley and Ramirez 1996).

The general broadening and individualization of the concept of development (Chapter 9) indicate that, indeed, states now find it in their interests to promote all sorts of programs and policies that have little to do with national progress or power as such. International psychology associations can argue for nationally subsidized psychological counseling because a psychologically stable population will be more productive. International travel and tourism bodies can advise expansion of paid-vacation periods because a rested and "leisured" workforce will be more productive. In effect, by such logic almost any state policy or program that works to the benefit of individuals, or corporations, or unions, or even voluntary associations can be justified as a state interest.

Hence, INGOs affect the behavior and policies of self-interested actors by couching their discourse in terms that fit with prevailing cultural understandings of how these actors are defined and motivated. They lead states, individuals, and organizations to incorporate new purposes and goals in their constellations of interests and to abandon older purposes and goals that fall out of favor in world culture. By continuing to act as agents of themselves, under the guidance of INGOs that are conceptualized as disinterested agents of collective goods and entities, actors discover new interests, come to appreciate links between their own interests and those of other actors, and even redefine their interests as quite contrary to what they once supposed they were (as shown in this volume's chapters with respect to population policy, warfare, and the unconstrained exploitation of nature). All the while actors keep alive the myth of their self-directed autonomy because they are not compelled to comply with INGO prescriptions and need not acknowledge INGO influence on their conceptions of self-interest. Furthermore, they enhance their legitimacy by incorporating world-cultural conceptions of proper constitution and action, aligning themselves with up-to-date definitions of valued, rational, progressive behavior.

No zero-sum game, this; both self-interested actors and disinterested INGO advisers gain in their give-and-take interaction. The more that states become indirect agents of broad collective goods and purposes while remaining committed to the myth of self-direction, the more rational and adequate they appear to be, both internally and externally. Similarly, the more that INGOs act as agents of state self-interest by helping states increase their societal management capabilities in line with evolving world-cultural models, the more effective they become.

Once again, the temptation to suppose that this process is in any way smooth, harmonious, or functionally beneficial in an unambiguous sense must be strongly resisted. Disagreement, conflict, and struggle are endemic to every aspect of the process, precisely because the actors presumed to be the driving forces of the world polity are defined as profoundly self-interested. Clashes and oppositions are the central concerns of most of the literature on relationships among INGOs, IGOs, states, and corporations. The literature may exaggerate the degree of conflict that prevails, since conflict is what gets observers' attention, but conflict is certainly widespread. In any case, as John Meyer and colleagues (in Meyer, Boli et al. 1997) argue, global structures in which INGOs and IGOs jointly develop and propagate world-cultural models are bound to be riven by many forms of conflict that would not occur in a truly anarchic world.

CULTURAL INGO AUTHORITY AND THEORIES OF GLOBAL CHANGE

The research projects reported in this volume suggest that INGOs exercise a surprising degree of authority in the contemporary world. This authority is neither coercive nor commanding; above all, it is cultural. It depends on widely and deeply legitimated theories of the ultimate sources of sovereignty, the proper constitution of rational action, the worthwhile ends of human endeavors, and the proper organization of collective structures to solve social problems.

As an essentially cultural process, the exercise of INGO authority is difficult to observe directly. The contemporary world-cultural frame so prizes purportedly primordial, interest-driven, bounded rational actors as the engines of social development and change that INGO authority is often practically invisible. This volume demonstrates, however, that it can be identified and revealed through careful analysis.

Much of what we have tried to establish runs counter to, or considerably complicates, dominant theoretical perspectives on global governance and change. Any perspective that takes states for granted as largely rational actors with relatively well defined interests—and such is the assumption of all of the dominant perspectives, including neorealism, regime theory and neoliberal institutionalism, functionalism, and world-system theory—begins to reach its limits when it becomes apparent that state interests change in sudden, dramatic, and even contradictory ways. States switch wholesale from pronatalist to neo-Malthusian population policies; states and corporations discover that they want to, and even must, develop environmental policies and programs that are costly and difficult to administer; states pass protective legislation for women and children in one era and then reverse course to dismantle such legislation a decade or two later. Such changes sweep through the state system, through populations of organizations, and through civil society, in all sorts of countries—rich and poor, central and peripheral, democratic and totalitarian, Western and non-Western—in what by historical standards must be considered the blink of an eye. Such changes are, indeed, global, not the somehow synchronous results of "domestic" developments occurring independently in a hundred different countries.

Certainly, rational states would learn from one another, look to each other for models and examples by which to pursue their missions, and copy the successes of leading states (Meyer, Boli et al. 1997). State-centric rational-actor perspectives can accommodate such behavior, hesitant though their advocates may be to do so. As soon as we begin to recognize the prevalence of such processes, however, and especially when we recognize that such processes involve the development and acceptance of abstract but increasingly institutionalized world models rather than the activation by autonomous states of interests that inhere in "the nature of things," rational-actor models are seriously compromised.

To understand global governance, we need to understand where interests come from, how new sources of purpose and value emerge, why actor identities change, how definitions of "rational behavior" evolve. This volume's studies indicate that attention to global cultural development, organized and elaborated chiefly by INGOs as the main structural loci of universalistic discourse and debate, can take us a considerable way in addressing such issues. Sectoral INGO studies can trace the crystallization and evolution of global ideologies, chart the embodiment of these ideologies in organizations and movements, and uncover the links between global structures and national and local actors. They can, therefore, provide us with means of understanding how sweeping, simultaneous global change becomes not only possible but, with ongoing world integration, rather routine.

All this by no means implies that neorealism, neoliberal institutionalism, functionalism, and world-system theory have only marginal explanatory value. States compete fiercely for control of resources and comparative advantage; major powers habitually try to use IGOs to further their own interests; perceived technical imperatives certainly prompt states to build international regimes; transnational corporations routinely enlist state aid in pursuing new markets and investment opportunities. Fundamentally, world-polity theory has only minor quarrels with many of the substantive claims of rational-actor theories centered on states and capitalist enterprises. The primary failing of such theories is that their ignorance of the encompassing cultural frame within which political, military, and economic competition takes place leads them both to ignore many dimensions of global development and to have little to offer with respect to explaining far-reaching systemic shifts in the self-understanding and behavior of the purportedly rational actors who are subject to that frame. World-polity theory is both complement and corrective to these more widely employed perspectives, but the latter are nonetheless crucial in accounting for many aspects of global development.

Speaking for the many authors in this volume, I hope that, like all fruitful lines of inquiry, the world-polity institutionalism that guides these investigations raises more questions than it answers. We do not claim to have shown that INGOs are the dominant force in global governance and development. We do hope, however, that our work demonstrates the importance of bringing INGOs into the analysis of global governance in a systematic and open-minded way. Our further hope is that these studies will stimulate discussion, debate, and further research by highlighting new issues and arenas that scholars should address if we are to develop a satisfactory understanding of the contemporary world polity.

Reference Matter

Notes

Chapter 1

1. A much reduced version of this chapter appeared as "World Culture in the World Polity: A Century of International Non-governmental Organization," *American Sociological Review* 62, no. 2 (April 1997): 171–90. Permission from the American Sociological Association to reprint portions of that version is thankfully acknowledged. We also gratefully acknowledge the support of the Swedish Social Science Research Council and the Emory University Research Council (Boli), and the Evangelical Scholarship Initiative for a year-long research fellowship (Thomas). Opinions expressed are those of the authors, not of the granting agencies. Our thanks go to Young Kim and Tom Loya for research assistance, the World Culture Research Group at Arizona State University for data coding and constructive criticism, and the many readers of earlier versions, especially Al Boskoff, Terry Boswell, David Frank, Ron Jepperson, Frank Lechner, John Meyer, Chiqui Ramirez, and Roland Robertson. Special thanks to Anthony Judge and the Union of International Associations, without whom this research would not have been possible.

2. Often designated simply "nongovernmental organizations," or NGOs, we emphasize the international focus of the organizations in our study by using the "INGO" acronym.

3. Western-originated world culture spread through colonization, economic expansion, and evangelization, and the Western core countries continue to be major contributors to world-cultural development. There is little evidence, however, that world culture is simply the latest phase of core domination of the capitalist world-system (cf. Chase-Dunn 1989). Tomlinson (1991) has shown the weakness of cultural imperialism arguments; Krasner (1985) demonstrates that even intergovernmental organizations regularly develop anti-core agendas. More to the point, many INGOs oppose core interests by promoting human rights ideology, critiquing world inequality, promoting the protection of indigenous peoples, and so on. In addition, the assumption that core elites have the capacity to shape world culture to their liking ignores the stubbornly de-

centralized character of the world polity and the complexity, inclusiveness, and ubiquitous character of contemporary world culture.

4. Because of its rationalistic assumptions, this perspective is also referred to as rational institutionalism (Keohane 1993; Cupitt, Whitlock, and Whitlock 1996), a label consistent with our choice of "reductionist rationalism" to describe it and its kin. In trying to account for the emergence of higher orders of social reality, sociological rational-choice theories (e.g., Coleman 1990) similarly rely on processes of norm formation and second-order sanctions that seem to emerge spontaneously when egoistic actors cannot attain social optima via first-order exchange (see also the evaluation of such arguments in March 1994). We think neoliberal institutionalists would do well to build on their evident interest in international institutions by relaxing their rationalist assumptions rather than formalizing them.

5. The social psychology of this "neo-institutionalist" perspective is normally dramaturgical (Goffman 1959, 1974; Mills 1940; Scott and Lyman 1968), but substantial disagreement persists among neo-institutionalists about the interplay between structure and agency (Zucker 1988; Powell and DiMaggio 1991).

6. Social reality is irremediably circular in this sense; Berger and Luckmann (1966) call this the sociological dialectic. The issue is not "which comes first"— actor or structure—but how actors and structures are reciprocally constitutive. What agency is, who can exercise it, and the degree to which it can be exercised are not a priori universals but historical-cultural constructs (Lechner and Boli 1995).

7. Many actions clearly violate prescriptions of world culture. Violations per se tell us little about the strength of cultural definitions or norms; what is most revealing in this regard is how violations are treated (Durkheim's insight). When violations of world-cultural prescripts occur, quite routinely they evoke outrage, indignation, mobilization, and attempts at sanctioning; further, violators know such reactions are likely (Weber's insight). If violations were treated by both violators and others as nothing but reflections of differing values or fatalistic occurrences, our analysis would lose considerable credibility. Much work is needed to clarify the meaning of world-cultural sins and to distinguish such sins from cases of clashing alternative cultural models, or from cases where dialectical tensions rule among incompatible world-cultural principles.

8. The sharedness and similarity required for the existence of categories (a category constituting a thing comprised of similar particulars) are themselves social constructions that have yet to be thoroughly analyzed in the sociology of culture (see Douglas 1966, 1986; Douglas and Hull 1992). It is easier to say what sharedness and similarity are not. By "shared," we do not mean that everyone everywhere has a common "lifeworld" (Habermas 1984) or "habitus" (Bourdieu 1977); even less do we see world culture as consisting of normative

or value consensus. Rather, in the world context, "shared" means that institutional structures are socially constructed throughout the world and are held to be applicable everywhere in the world. Hence, it is not the case that every single individual holds to, uses, or even has heard of these structures, but no dimension of social distinction has been able to prevent their penetration. World institutions are salient across geographic regions, classes, educational levels, genders, ethnic identities, types of settlement, political ideologies, and every other line of social demarcation. No matter how we divide up the world, we can no longer identify a barrier that is impermeable to world-cultural institutions.

9. The UIA traces its origins to the Central Office of International Associations, founded in Brussels in 1907. It was active in the founding of the League of Nations and the International Institute of Intellectual Cooperation (the predecessor of UNESCO), and it founded the first international university in the 1920s. Its official abbreviation is UAI, based on the French version of its name.

10. Earlier quantitative analyses of INGOs (Speeckaert 1957; Feld 1971; Kriesberg 1981; Archer 1983), while more limited in the range of data employed, show similar descriptive patterns. The UIA *Yearbook* has also been used as a source of data on IGOs (e.g., Jacobson, Reisinger, and Mathers 1986).

11. In these analyses we treat all organizations as equivalent regardless of size. Too few organizations report membership numbers to make size a useful variable, though about three-fourths report the countries in which members reside. Analysis of 1994 country-of-residence data kindly provided in electronic form by the UIA suggests that this measure of size (or scope) is rather uniformly distributed across organizational aims. The inferences we make here likely would apply if we were to select only large organizations.

12. In 83 percent of cases, dissolution means cessation of activities or formal disbanding; 15 percent involve merger with or absorption by another INGO. Only 2 percent represent organizations contracting to less than international scope.

13. Many of the following analyses were conducted using both primary and secondary aims, with similar results.

14. The *Yearbook* lists only 37 organizations founded before 1875, but the growth of INGOs hardly marks the beginning of the contemporary world polity. It is rooted in Christendom and Western law (Collins 1986; Mann 1986; Hall and Ikenberry 1989), the Enlightenment (Watson 1992), and, at least through the nineteenth century, the Roman Catholic Church and its religious orders. Its growth and integration have depended greatly on the development of the world economy, European imperialism, and global transportation and communication systems, among other factors. See Charnovitz 1997 for a detailed description of INGO development from the late eighteenth century through World War II.

15. Sources include Banks 1975, IBRD (various years), UNESCO 1965–

90, United Nations (various years), and Boli[-Bennett] 1976. Some of the Banks data include interpolations between observations at irregular intervals, for the early part of the period.

16. Aggregation may account for some of the high covariation at the world level, but national-level correlations are so much lower (in the .6–.7 range) that it likely is not a major problem. In any case, several of these variables are not aggregates but measures of world properties.

17. An increase in the coherence and coordination of world authority would likely intensify these processes, but only in the absence of a bureaucratic world state. By contrast, if our analysis is correct, the absorption of IGOs by a world state bureaucracy would be associated with a parallel absorption of INGOs because the nature of world authority would shift from diffuse universalism to formal legal rationalism, which would allow neither states nor individuals to organize at will. Similarly, a general transformation of INGOs into IGOs, without the emergence of a central world state, would seriously challenge world-polity theory.

18. IGOs and INGOs nevertheless conflict, often bitterly, but the fact that they do so supports our analysis: If INGOs were irrelevant, states would hardly be so concerned about their "interference." Moreover, it is likely that, in some sectors under some conditions, a zero-sum relation between INGOs and IGOs obtains. In technical and infrastructure sectors, for example, the formation of an effective universal INGO might well preclude the formation of a corresponding IGO, and vice versa. More work is needed to understand the conditions and characteristics of INGO/IGO conflict and competition (see Chapters 3 and 9).

19. Note that we do not follow the classification contained in the *Yearbook*, which distinguishes universal, intercontinental, and regional bodies. The UIA's scheme is based solely on membership dispersion: Universal bodies have members from at least 60 countries (or 30 countries from several continents), intercontinental bodies require at least ten countries and at least two countries on each of two continents. Our categories are more substantive, classifying numerous "regional" bodies as universalistic if they do not explicitly limit themselves to a particular region or sub-world polity.

20. Organizations that have particularistic goals or target populations—such as women's rights or religious social service bodies—are not considered regional unless they confine their membership or activities to a particular geographical arena. The arena in question need not be contiguous, however. For example, francophone organizations are regional even though francophone countries are found on two separate continents and in scattered island locations.

21. Regionalism also increased among IGOs after World War II, largely along the lines of the Cold War divisions between NATO, the Warsaw Pact, and the "Third World" (Jacobson, Reisinger, and Mathers 1986). Not surpris-

ingly, regional IGO growth has diminished with the collapse of Communism after 1989 (Shanks, Jacobson, and Kaplan 1996). INGO regionalism has never had much to do with ideological blocs of this sort, so INGO regionalism likely will not be affected similarly.

22. Recent work associates world citizenship mainly with human rights and ecological movements (Turner 1993; van Steenbergen 1994). This work tends to infer from the high levels of individual engagement that world citizenship develops "from below" (Turner 1986), ignoring the importance of world culture in making world-citizenship conceptions meaningful and significant to individuals. Falk's (1994) image of the "global management" citizen, more technical than political in orientation, is especially important in light of our findings below on the sectoral distribution of INGOs.

23. The reluctance of most analysts to give much credence to world citizenship reflects both the absence of a bureaucratic world state and the world-cultural presumption that citizenship must involve a state-individual relationship. Our analysis suggests that a broader cultural sense of the concept of the state is in order if this presumption is to apply to world citizenship.

24. Before World War II a substantial number of INGOs had the explicit goal of forging universal harmony or social-cultural-knowledge integration. Examples include World Conscience, the International Anti-War Medical Association, the World Union for Human Progress, and *Pro Gentillezza*: Association for the Spreading of Good and Human Feeling. Many of these bodies attempted to (re-)organize the entirety of world culture, proposing new schemata for human knowledge and consciousness and new syntheses of the sciences and humanities. Such organizations were highly prone to failure, and new bodies of this sort are rare; they have not kept pace with the rapid cultural and technical differentiation of the twentieth century. Note, though, that a large proportion of INGOs across all substantive categories mention world or international cooperation, solidarity, or harmony as elements in their statements of purpose. These goals are taken for granted in most of the discourse of world organizations.

25. One caveat about this finding: The UIA handles many religious organizations separately because of their "unconventional" organizational forms. Thus, these data suggest not a decline in transnational religious organization but the divergence of such organizations from standard INGO forms.

26. In the labor et al. category, labor is the only declining component: Labor organizations were over 9 percent of all INGOs founded by 1910 but just over 2 percent of those founded after 1945. Labor organizations are somewhat more likely than other types to disappear via merger rather than failure, but this tendency is too small to account for much of their decline. Similarly, religion is the major declining portion of its category, dropping from 8 percent of all INGOs before 1910 to 4 percent since 1945. The UIA's special treatment

of religious organizations (note 25) makes interpretation of this decline difficult, however.

Chapter 2

1. We gratefully acknowledge the support of the Swedish Social Science
Research Council and the Emory University Research Council at various
stages in this research. Thanks are also especially due to Anthony Judge of the
Union of International Associations for making data available in electronic
form. Opinions expressed are those of the authors, not of the granting agencies.

2. While it would be preferable to have INGO-specific membership data
on a longitudinal basis, we have not had the resources to code this information
from the *Yearbook* at regular intervals. We had hoped to obtain it in electronic
form from the UIA but the Union has not kept files of historical data. Hence
membership or secretariat information about failed organizations cannot be
obtained either.

3. Plugging in to world culture obviously involves a good deal of ambivalence. World culture is decried as Western or capitalist imperialism, decadence,
domination, and distortion of authentic local values. Such rhetorical resistance
is rampant, and organized resistance in some corners is at times fairly effective.
Usually, though, resistance is highly selective and superficial, focusing on issues
of lifestyle and personal morality rather than the fundamental core of world
culture: science, information, technique, organization, monetarization, accounting and control systems, professionalization, and so on. See Meyer, Boli
et al. 1997 for a fuller discussion.

4. Shanks, Jacobson, and Kaplan (1996) report similar results for regressions of 1992 IGO memberships on independent variables measured in 1981
(without the lagged dependent variable), using a broad definition of IGOs
($N = 1147$). In their fully specified equation, total GDP had only a small effect,
whereas GDP per capita, literacy, and a political-freedom index had no effects.
The most notable factors affecting IGO memberships were dummy variables
showing that Asian countries were especially low, European countries especially high, and "newly chaotic countries" (recently independent countries with
unsettled regimes) especially low compared to all other types of regimes
(ranging from dictatorships to multiparty democracies). These results are considerably at variance with the cross-sectional findings in Jacobson, Reisinger,
and Mathers 1986, for 1,075 IGOs in 1981, probably because the latter study
used a much less fully specified regression model.

Chapter 3

1. Direct correspondence to David John Frank, Department of Sociology,
Harvard University, Cambridge MA 02138 (frankdj@wjh.harvard.edu). The

research was supported by a grant from the National Science Foundation (SES 9213258) to Nancy Brandon Tuma and John W. Meyer. Work on the paper was aided by suggestions from Henrich Greve, Francisco O. Ramirez, and project colleagues in Stanford's Comparative Workshop.

2. Our data are from the 1995 edition of the *Yearbook* and certainly underestimate the number of environmental INGOs formed between 1980 and 1990 (see the discussion in Chapter 1 on how long it takes newly formed INGOs to appear in the *Yearbook*). In spite of this, note the dramatic rise of INGO formation in preparation for the 1992 UN Conference on Environment and Development.

3. These twenty INGOs are a subset of those described above and have a disproportionate number of old and large associations. They were chosen because they had membership data available over a long period of time. We believe comparable information for the entire set of INGOs would demonstrate a similar trend, although we lack the data to show this.

4. Once again, these INGOs were drawn from the larger set, based on available data. They demonstrate trends found in virtually all of the organizations, although our current data are insufficient to show this systematically.

5. Note that here the definition of INGOs and IGOs is broadened to include regional organizations (members from two countries) and internationally oriented national organizations. See UIA 1965, 1995.

6. By "official," we do not mean to imply that intergovernmental organizations have authority *over* states, but rather that their authority derives *from* states. Even amid globalization, states retain sovereignty, and may even exaggerate its ritual display. In deriving their authority from sovereign states, IGOs differ importantly from INGOs, which derive authority from the participation of universalized world citizens (see Chapter 1).

7. The continuity between the three types of organizations is demonstrated by the fact that the results for the event-history analysis summarized in Table 3.1, which include all types of environmental INGOs, are similar for each of the three types when the environmental INGO population is divided.

8. The relationship between science INGOs and environmental INGOs could be spurious, since virtually all kinds of INGOs increased over the twentieth century (see Chapter 1). Thus, it is important to point out that other measures of the rationalized discourse around nature, such as the cumulative number of unions associated with the International Council of Scientific Unions, produce effects similar to those produced by science INGOs.

9. Other measures of consolidation, such as the number of nation-states with environmental ministries, work similarly (Frank 1997b; Meyer, Frank et al. 1997).

10. The dependent variable may be underestimated in the later years, because of the lag between founding dates and appearance in the data source. To

ensure that this did not change the analysis, we set the cutoff date at 1980 and reestimated the model in Table 3.1. The results were quite similar to those reported.

11. Alternative measures of rationalized discourse, including the cumulative number of environmental INGOs and a discourse factor score (cumulative number of unions in the ICSU, cumulative number of environmental INGOs, log of the cumulative number of national parks) work similarly.

12. We see the same effects for other indicators of consolidation, such as the cumulative number of environmental IGOs multiplied by time and a measure of UNEP staff size.

Chapter 4

1. Said by Josephine Butler, leader of the International Abolitionist Federation, a movement that aimed at abolishing police regulation of prostitution and was involved in the suffrage campaign as well.

2. The section titled "Place of Women Workers in the Economic System," in the ILO yearbooks for the years 1930–1937, documents the measures taken by various countries.

3. That is, they are in consultative status category "A," permitting greater participation than categories "B" and "C."

4. I have identified founding dates for 195 organizations, using the *Yearbook of International Organizations* (UIA 1950–93) and other sources. Deborah Stienstra (1994) reports a larger number of organizations, especially for the Decade period. She includes many more of the network type that were not included in the UIA list.

Chapter 5

1. I would like to thank John Meyer, Francisco Ramirez, John Boli, and George Thomas for their comments on earlier drafts. One version of this chapter was presented at the meetings of the MacArthur Consortium for Democracy and Empowerment, Minneapolis, April 1994.

2. Esperanto INGOs (80 in all) founded by 1984 include the following: from 1905 to 1913, the Esperanto Academy, the International Esperantist Scientific Association, the World Esperantist Vegetarian Association, the Universal Medical Esperanto Association, and the Christian Esperanto International Association; from 1918 to 1938, the Scout's Esperanto League, the Quaker Esperanto Society, the Association of Nationless Esperanto Workers, and the World Organization of Young Esperantists; from 1945 to 1984, the World Association of Esperanto Journalists, the International League of Blind Esperantists, the International Esperanto Association of Jurists, the International Esperantist Chess League, the Esperantist Ornithologists' Association,

the Philatelic Esperanto League, the International Society of Esperantist Architects and Builders, International Association of Esperantist Mathematicians, the League of Homosexual Esperantists, the International League of Agricultural Specialists-Esperantists, and the International Esperanto Society for Nature Conservation.

3. The contrast with English as the de facto lingua franca of the world polity is revealing in that English was not a deliberately constructed language and it was not promoted explicitly as a world-integrating force (except, perhaps, by British imperialists bent on "civilizing" the non-European world). Its proliferation has derived from the fact that it is the language of the two hegemonic powers of recent centuries, Britain and the United States, with which the Esperanto movement was ill equipped to compete.

4. The first schism took place in 1887 when Emile Dormy started a variant named "Balta," which was followed by others such as Nuvo-Volapük (1887 by Auguste Kerckhoffs), Spelin (1888 by Juraj Bauer), Dil (1893 by Fieweger), Veltparl (1896 by Arnim), and Dilpok (1898 by Marchand).

5. The most widely used model is based on a loglinear relationship between the expected number of events and the covariates: $E(Y_t) = \rho_t = \exp(\chi_t\beta)$. This ensures that ρ_t is not negative and contingent on changes in χ_{it}, the covariates.

6. In other words, the probability of an event occurring in an observation period is not affected by the previous history of the series of events. In addition, it does not depend on the length of time since the previous event, primarily because the occurrence event is considered purely random. For more information on problems with the original Poisson method, see Johnson, Kotz, and Kemp 1992 and Barron 1992.

7. Most organizational ecologists include the secondary effect of the density (N^2) in the model to show that density effects change over time. However, based on Hypothesis 1, I test models using constant density effects throughout the period.

Chapter 6

1. This chapter is adapted from Finnemore 1996: chap. 3.

2. It should be emphasized that while the claims of sovereignty and human rights are in tension, they are not diametrically opposed. States gain legitimacy by claiming to serve the welfare of individuals within them. One of the classic moral justifications given by realist statesmen for their policies is that protection of the national interest is the best way to protect the individual within the state (Morgenthau 1973). This attempt at reconciliation does not completely solve the problem, however. The realist view still sets the welfare of citizens above that of aliens and even justifies abuse of the latter to protect the former. Humanitarians, by contrast, are concerned primarily with individuals and

would argue that the good of the state should be pursued only within the context of humane treatment of individuals.

3. Surprisingly little historical work has been done on the International Committee of the Red Cross. By far the best single source is the Committee's own two-volume history (Boissier 1985; Durand 1984). The Committee's monthly serial publication, *Revue internationale de la Croix-Rouge*, occasionally contains historical pieces; it published a larger-than-average number of these around the time of the organization's centennial in 1963–64 (ICRC 1963–64). Other sources used to construct the following account include Gumpert 1938, François 1918, and Coursier 1961.

4. For background on Dunant prior to his involvement in the ICRC, see Boissier 1985: 7–16 and Gumpert 1938: 3–31.

5. Total casualties from the battle at Solferino have been estimated at 6,000 dead and 42,000 wounded. That would make it the bloodiest battle since Waterloo. The number of those wounded brought into the town of Castiglione, whose peacetime population was about 5,000, was estimated at 9,230 by the physician in charge. Gumpert gives a figure of 6,000 wounded to be treated by only two doctors. By contrast, there were roughly four veterinarians per thousand horses in the French army (Boissier 1985: 20–23; Gumpert 1938: 46).

6. Reviews of the first and third editions of *A Memory of Solferino*, which appeared in the *Journal de Genève*, are reprinted in *Revue internationale de la Croix-Rouge* (ICRC May 1954: 370–73). The influential *Journal des Débats* (February 15, 1863) also gave the book high praise. Discussions of *A Memory of Solferino* appearing in other publications are noted in François 1918: 117.

7. Not all of this correspondence was laudatory. Randon, for example, was incensed and viewed the account as an attack on France and the French military. Nightingale, while supportive of Dunant's exposé of medical conditions in the military, was not enthusiastic about his proposed solution. She shared the view of her government that care for the war wounded was a government responsibility (Boissier 1985: 41–42). The grand-duke actually sent money, as well as a letter, to help Dunant set up his relief societies (ICRC, May 1954). For more detail on Dunant's contacts in the *salons* of Paris and elsewhere, see Gumpert 1938: chap. 6.

8. The change in name occurred in 1880 (ICRC 1963–64: 56–72).

9. The Committee's invitation to the Congress is reprinted in Pictet 1964: 384–85.

10. The military man on the Committee, General Dufour, proposed the requirement that societies be closely linked to national militaries and serve at their pleasure (ICRC 1863–64). The anticipation of military objections to the societies was well founded. The French minister of war, Marshall Randon, viewed Dunant's book as an attack on the French military command, since

many of the horrors documented were due to the inadequacies of French military medicine (Boissier 1985: 41).

11. It should be noted, though, that the activities of the Committee received regular press coverage in a number of publications, thereby bringing the Committee's project to the attention of a wider public (ICRC 1954).

12. Dunant's letters to Moynier during this Congress are explicit discussions of networking strategy in which Dunant reports his progress and assigns to Moynier the job of securing representation from countries not yet contacted (Dunant 1954 [1863]: 424–28). While attending this conference Dunant added the notion of neutrality to his proposal for volunteer relief societies. He did this without the knowledge and consent of the rest of the Committee, causing considerable consternation when reports of his activities reached Geneva (Gumpert 1938: 114–16; Boissier 1985: 61–67; Dunant 1954 [1863]: 424–28).

13. Dunant also traveled to France before the conference, primarily to help set up a French relief society but also to persuade various French elites to use their influence on hesitant potential participants (ICRC 1863–64; Pictet 1964: 381).

14. For a complete list of participants and their titles, see ICRC 1954.

15. One of the recommendations of the conference was that governments should "extend their patronage" to the new societies and "facilitate as far as possible the accomplishment of their task" (quoted in Boissier 1985: 81). This opened the door to government contributions to the new organizations, but government funding was never expected to constitute a large portion of the societies' resources.

16. The inclusion of neutrality among the proposals was particularly controversial. Dunant got it on the conference agenda against the wishes of the other four members of the Committee, who felt that states would never agree. As it turned out, delegates to the 1863 conference were much more concerned about the proposed relief societies as such than about neutral status. It was not until the negotiations over the drafting of the 1864 Geneva Convention that neutrality again emerged as controversial, states agreeing only to accord neutral status to military medical personnel and the wounded, not to relief society volunteers. Although the 1874 Brussels Declaration accorded neutral status to volunteers, the Declaration did not have the force of law, since it was never ratified. Volunteers were not formally granted neutral status until the 1949 revision of the Convention. See Boissier 1985: 61–83, 112–21, 293.

17. The Patriotic Society proved impotent in the face of actual war responsibilities. Among the difficulties it encountered was lack of communication with other relief societies or the Austrian military, as would have been afforded a Red Cross society. Consequently, following the Austro-Prussian War (1866), a Red Cross society was formed in Vienna and granted recognition by the ICRC.

18. For more on Dunant's efforts to found the French relief society, see ICRC 1963–64: 260–66.

19. Lists of attendees vary slightly among sources. The official list from ICRC archives is Baden, Belgium, Denmark, Spain, France, Great Britain, Hesse, Italy, the Netherlands, Portugal, Prussia, Saxony, Sweden, Switzerland, and Württemberg (Pictet 1964: 385–86). Only Austria, Bavaria, and the Vatican refused the invitation outright, Austria because it considered its Patriotic Society adequate for all requirements, the latter two because of Catholic distaste for the Geneva location of the conference. Brazil, Mexico, Greece, and Turkey did not attend but sent messages of endorsement, while the Russian delegate arrived after the conference was over (Gumpert 1938: 154). Both Gumpert (1938) and Boissier (1985) note the presence of the United States, although Gumpert says that the United States was there only in informal status. In fact, the U.S. delegate, Charles Bowles, represented only the U.S. Sanitary Commission, which was busily revolutionizing military medicine among the Union forces in the American Civil War. Gumpert provides an extensive reprinting of Bowles's fascinating report on the conference (pp. 157–70).

Boissier denies that Dunant and later Moynier were influenced by foreign models, American or otherwise, in their original conception of the Red Cross and the earliest meetings of the Committee. I have found no evidence to the contrary. Given the backgrounds and experience of the two, who were neither military nor medical men, Boissier's claim seems plausible. However, the importance of models from previous European or foreign experiences clearly rose as the movement matured and more people with wider experience became involved. Bowles certainly believed that he and the Sanitary Commission's example were having an effect on the 1864 Geneva Conference (Gumpert 1938: 157–70; Boissier 1985: 163–65).

20. As suggested earlier, one source of controversy at the conference was whether the volunteers of the relief societies should enjoy neutral status. The treaty does not mention them. The Prussian delegates pushed strongly for explicit recognition of volunteers in the treaty, while the French had been instructed (by Marshall Randon) not to sign anything conferring neutrality on volunteers. The vague language about "medical personnel" in the treaty was designed to placate both parties.

21. A list of signatory states and the dates of signings through 1907 can be found in Pictet 1964: 401–2. During this period a second conference made additions to the original Geneva Convention. The most notable of these were the extension of Geneva principles to naval warfare and provisions that parties to the Convention would compile lists of dead, wounded, and prisoners for exchange with other belligerents.

22. Gustave Moynier, president of the ICRC, noted that the Austrian refusals showed a complete lack of comprehension of what the Convention was

about, since they focused on Austria's perceived self-sufficiency to handle her own war wounded rather than on issues of neutrality (Boissier 1985: 178).

23. The Sino-Japanese War was also the first application of the Geneva Conventions to naval warfare, as required by the 1867 amendments to the Convention.

24. The ICRC has always said that it considers public opinion to be the only tool of enforcement of the Geneva Conventions. It would be worth studying this global "public" to explore whose opinions matter on what issues in what ways. In the early days of the Red Cross movement, elite opinions and support were essential. Later, as the relief societies expanded and public awareness of the Conventions grew, a broader spectrum of opinion probably became important.

25. The earlier Carlist insurrection in Spain provided some precedent for this decision. In that case, the national Spanish Red Cross Society decided that foreign combatants should not be receiving greater protection than the country's own citizens (Boissier 1985: 298).

26. This step was particularly important in light of the strongly Christian revivalist motivations of Dunant (Gumpert 1938: chap. 1). Note, too, that Moynier, president of the ICRC for 48 years, described the Red Cross as a product of progressive "Christian civilization" and attributed the success of the Red Cross movement to the growing influence of Christianity (Boissier 1985: 34).

27. It became apparent during this conflict that the Red Cross flag was sufficiently provocative to Turkish troops that it was drawing fire rather than protecting Red Cross personnel. Boissier quotes some rather horrific accounts of treatment of Red Cross personnel during the conflict at the hands of Muslim Turks (Boissier 1985: 303–12).

28. The only qualifications mentioned are "sincerely philanthropic motives" (Dunant 1986: 117).

29. The small number of scholars interested in ethics and "principled issues" in international politics is an exception. For a discussion of how international moral norms are constructed by "issue networks" of philosophers, lawyers, religious leaders, educators, and government officials, see Keck and Sikkink 1998, and McElroy 1992: chap. 2. A related but less specific argument can be found in Walzer 1977. For more on the role of individuals in international politics see Girard 1994.

30. The epistemic community literature is beginning to make inroads in this direction. However, the group of elites active in the founding of the ICRC would not qualify under Haas's (1992: 3) definition of epistemic community as "a network of professionals with recognized expertise and competence in a particular domain and an authoritative claim to policy-relevant knowledge within that domain or issue-area" because the ICRC lacked both specialized knowl-

edge and competence of any obvious kind. Their main qualification was a set of principled beliefs that created an agenda for action.

Given the similarity of both process and outcome between this case and many of those documented by scholars of epistemic communities, it seems worth questioning the uniqueness of the epistemic-community phenomenon. Moral authority appears to act in ways similar to knowledge; it guides policymakers' actions both by giving them new goals and by providing legitimacy for those goals. If this is the case, proponents of the epistemic-community approach need to distinguish more clearly their communities from the myriad of others vying for access to governments.

31. One indicator of Dunant's altruistic commitment to his cause is the fact that he bankrupted himself in the service of the Red Cross. He virtually disappeared from the organization after 1867 and was believed dead until a Swiss journalist discovered him in a hospice in Heiden in 1895 (Gumpert 1938: chaps. 14, 19).

32. The contrasting notions of a "logic of consequences" versus a "logic of appropriateness" come from March and Olsen 1989. For a fuller discussion of the implications of this contrast for theories in international politics, see Finnemore 1996.

Chapter 7

1. This research was supported in part by a grant from the Emory University Research Committee. We thank Terry Boswell, Cliff Brown, Frank Lechner, Tien-Lung Liu, Denis O'Hearn, and Regina Werum for thoughtful comments on earlier drafts. David Clifton, Harry Wadsworth, and Holly Lawe of the Georgia Institute of Technology's Center for International Standards and Quality (CISQ) also provided valuable insight into key issues. Janet Maillard, at ISO's Infocentre, generously arranged for the generation of a data file giving a quantitative snapshot of ISO's organizational structure. We especially thank Pete Perkins, the convener of IEC TC74/WG5 ("Safety Pilot Subcommittee on Measurement of Leakage Current"), for extensive "insider" information on how standardization works, and Frank Loya, the first author's father and a U.S. delegate to IEC TC 77 for ten years, for frequent and in-depth reflection on his experience in light of his careful reading of earlier drafts.

2. General Electric was founded in 1892 with the backing of J. P. Morgan for the organized, large-scale research of Thomas Alva Edison, following the merger of the largest American electrical firms. It was the world's leading electrical corporation.

3. The ISO council is comprised of five principal officers and eighteen member bodies elected by a majority of the general assembly to a three-year term. The current council members are France, the United States, India, Philippines, the United Kingdom, Germany, Egypt, Chile, Tunisia, Japan,

Netherlands, Australia, South Africa, Canada, Israel, Malaysia, Sweden, and Slovenia.

4. The rationalized accounts of national bodies vary in revealing ways. The United States' ANSI reviews a year of accomplishments in the global arena with hegemonic and self-congratulatory phrases: "strengthened strategic standardization interests," "advanced U.S. leadership," "launched new services," and "secured recognition" (ANSI 1993: 1). Compare this to the much more modest British approach emphasizing service and accountability to its members: "We use up-to-date technology to deliver the widest collection of the world's national, European and international standards to you, our customer" (BSI 1994b: 1). France's AFNOR lives up to the reputation of the birthplace of Chauvin by repeatedly claiming to "promote the French point of view" in European and global standards organizations (AFNOR 1994: 1). Finally, although Sweden is an important player in the standards sector, it places its activities in the broadest possible framework, as though its own existence were historically epiphenomenonal: "Since ancient times standardization has facilitated human activities . . . this is part of an ancient and continuous project." The document goes on to make references to the standardization of carpets in the Ottoman Empire, the development of alphabets, Roman weights and measures, and Venetian shipbuilding (SIS 1993: 1). We hope to make a systematic exploration of these differing cultural accounts of participation in the global standardization sector in a later phase of the project.

5. Membership fees vary among national bodies, based on economic indicators of gross national product (GNP) and the value of imports and exports.

6. Regional and national bodies are funded similarly, though many of the latter receive state support and some (such as Norway) get most of their revenue from the sale of standards.

7. Comparable operations and procedures are employed by CEN and CENELEC.

8. CEN is also unique in that it weights its members' votes along European Union lines and the implementation of standards by members is mandatory.

9. A survey conducted by Mobil Europe (1995) found the following illustrative data: By March, 1995, U.S. firms accounted for only 6.2 percent of the 95,476 ISO 9000 certificates issued worldwide, while European firms held about 75 percent of the total. While the survey does not provide figures for the number of firms in the "at-risk" populations for ISO 9000 procedures, the proportion of eligible U.S. firms that had obtained certification was evidently much lower than for European countries.

10. Delegates typically make three to four distant excursions yearly and are in constant communication with their standardizing colleagues, in total devoting perhaps several months a year to their responsibilities in ISO or the IEC. ISO and the IEC bear no costs of member participation.

11. For example, a soon to be published IEC standard will require that power supply components of all electrical devices meet a new higher capacity to filter out "pollution" found in the AC power grids that cover the world. However, this "pollution" (referring to effects of sine wave degradation of AC power caused by high-resistance power lines and heavy power drains caused by large appliances) is primarily a problem for Europe, whose 240 volt system has allowed it to use higher resistance wiring throughout. The imminent publication of this global standard has imposed tremendous cost on American industries, because they must design and produce new power supplies for every electrical device, even if it is to be used in the United States where such pollution is minimal. U.S. resistance to this standard, however, has no technical grounds and is thus invalid, so they have been forced to comply even if it diminishes their competitive edge vis-à-vis European industries and cuts into profits.

12. Neither ISO nor the IEC bear or remunerate any costs associated with maintaining a TC secretariat. Considering that even medium-sized TCs involve hundreds of individuals and extensive administrative tasks, these costs are not insignificant.

Chapter 8

1. Direct correspondence to Deborah Barrett, Carolina Population Center, 123 W. Franklin St., Chapel Hill NC 27516 (dbarrett@email.unc.edu). During different stages of this research, Barrett was supported by a fellowship from the Morrison Institute at Stanford University and the Carolina Population Center at the University of North Carolina, Chapel Hill. Frank was supported by a MacArthur Fellowship from the Center for International Security and Arms Control at Stanford University. For comments on earlier drafts, we thank John Boli, George M. Thomas, and John W. Meyer.

2. By population control, we refer only to ideas about controlling fertility, not migration or mortality. The term "population control" is no longer considered acceptable terminology; it has been replaced by "unmet need in family planning." We use it here because it represents the language that popularized neo-Malthusian thinking in the 1960s.

3. Dr. Jacques Bertillon, in *Revue Politique et Parlementaire*, June 10, 1897, quoted in Beale 1911: 135.

4. For details, see Barrett 1995a.

5. These are housed at the Stanford Libraries, which include Government Documents (a United Nations repository), the Hoover Library, Lane Medical Library, and an interlibrary loan service connected to all U.S. university libraries. In England, archives are located at the State House Library and the Wellcome Institute History of Medicine Collection.

6. E.g., *The Malthusian, The IPPF News, Milbank Reports*.

7. *Eugenical News* (1916–1953) and *The Eugenics Review* (1909–1968).

8. Eldridge 1954; United Nations 1987, 1989a, 1989b, 1989c; UNFPA 1988.

9. These lines of thought are described in more detail in Barrett 1995a.

10. Herr Hausmeister in *The Malthusian* 28, no. 4 (May 1904).

11. Charles Hooper, M.D., "A Denunciation of Birth Control," *Medical World*, June 1931, p. 243.

12. Newton J. Hunsberger, M.D., "Artificial Childlessness and Race Suicide," *Journal of the American Medical Association*, 1907.

13. See Ferguson 1990 and Chapter 9 on the rise of national development.

14. At the meeting on international security in 1937, eugenics was mentioned in the discussion of how to define a population optimum.

15. We are confident about the completeness of the list up to World War II, which includes about 20 percent of the total meetings. After World War II, the proliferation of population-control conferences was so rapid that a few are undoubtedly missing. We are certain that their addition would only reemphasize, rather than change, the patterns we find below.

16. Then called the International Conference on Hybridisation and the Cross-Breeding of Varieties.

17. The main example of a general-purpose intergovernmental organization is the United Nations, founded in 1945, although the earlier League of Nations served some of the same functions.

18. The League's Institute of Intellectual Cooperation held a conference titled "Peaceful Change: Procedures, Populations, Raw Materials, and Colonies," in Paris, June 28–July 3, 1937.

19. For evidence along these lines, see Meyer et al. 1995.

20. In response to the creation of international population-control conferences and organizations, national-level nongovernmental organizations proliferated. World-level organizations provided legitimacy for national-level organizations, which may not otherwise have survived under repressive regimes. World-level organizations also provided organizational and financial resources to national-level organizations. For example, the International Planned Parenthood Federation (IPPF), which was formed at an international conference in 1952, gave rise to national and regional Planned Parenthood Federation organizations worldwide.

21. These sterilization laws are clearly based on eugenics principles. Other policies such as immigration and marriage policies would also be indicative (e.g., 29 U.S. states prohibited racial intermarriage, punishable with fines and imprisonment), but we had less systematic data, and they more likely exist for a broader range of reasons.

Chapter 9

1. The research summarized in this chapter was completed as part of a broader study of the ties between society, education, and development sup-

ported by the National Science Foundation (RED 9254958). In addition, the Development Centre of the Organization for Economic Cooperation and Development and the NGO Unit of the Operations Division of the Operations and Policy Research Group of the World Bank provided access to their databases of international development NGOs. All views expressed in this chapter are, however, those of the author and do not necessarily reflect the views of the OECD, the World Bank, or any other organization.

2. For the purposes of this chapter, the term "international" organization indicates an organization working in more than one nation-state, even though it may only be funded by one. Other chapters in this volume use a narrower definition, implying greater international breadth.

3. Almost all terminology attempting to distinguish "developed" from "developing" countries is problematic. The terms "high-income" and "low-income" countries will be used throughout the rest of the chapter.

4. The founding rate drops off after 1982, which probably reflects underreporting of newer organizations.

5. Part of the apparent "growth" in foundings may be an artifact of the absence of data on many small INGOs that "died" and therefore do not appear in the OECD's directory. Indeed, most of the organizations appearing in OECD-DC 1995 that were founded after 1970 are relatively small in terms of funding and staff level.

6. UIA analyses in 1983–84 and 1993–94 show that the unusual increase in growth in development continued into the 1990s. Between 1984 and 1993, the total number of conventional international organizations grew only 2 percent, but the number of international organizations in the "development" category grew 94 percent.

7. Note, however, that many subgroups of development professionals do share beliefs, interests, and an internationally recognized knowledge base in a bounded "scientifically based" domain or issue-area—such as the environment, population, or women's issues—and do indeed make an "authoritative claim to policy-relevant knowledge within that domain or issue area" (Haas 1992: 3).

Chapter 10

1. Work on this paper was supported by National Science Foundation grant SES 9213258 to Nancy Brandon Tuma and John Meyer, and grant NSF RED 92-54-958 to John Meyer and Francisco Ramirez. The advice and comments of John Meyer, Francisco Ramirez, Ann Hironaka, John Boli, George Thomas, and the members of the Stanford Comparative Workshop are greatly appreciated.

2. The notable exception is the International Council of Scientific Unions, a central professional association that forged tight links with many intergovernmental associations, such as UNESCO.

3. Examples include labor unions (e.g., Chapter 1) and patent organizations (Hironaka and Schofer 1994), which are highly organized in many nations but remain relatively weak in the international sphere.

4. Such processes do not affect professional science INGOs for the simple reason that very few professional science IGOs exist.

5. The *YIO* categories used were Science, Fundamental Science, Research, and Research Standards. Organizations only tangentially related to science (based on their description) were excluded.

6. Inactive organizations are not included in these analyses. The analysis of socially oriented science INGOs is not likely to be affected because they have had an extremely low mortality rate. The analysis of professional science INGOs should be interpreted with more caution, however, as the absence of inactive organizations may bias the sample. Preliminary examination indicates, though, that inactive science INGOs do not appear to be very different in character or founding pattern from their active counterparts. Thus, indications are that bias is minimal.

7. A more comprehensive measure reflecting scientific organization in all core nations would be preferable. However, historical evidence suggests that professionalization occurred at nearly the same time in core nations (McClellan 1985). Thus, the use of data for one nation as a proxy for the others seems appropriate.

8. Results with this aggregated variable are virtually unchanged compared to results in which these dummy variables were introduced individually.

Conclusion

1. See, for example, the discussion of "confraternity" in medieval cities (Weber 1968: chap. 16).

2. Note the inversion here from the moral order dominant earlier in the West: the Christian ideal that "the truth shall set you free." When sovereignty lies outside humanity, human organization is the "realm of necessity" (Ellul 1976) in which autonomous efforts to construct authority are only forms of (self-)enslavement.

3. The disgruntled include powerful states as well as weak ones. The United States has been the odd man out in many an episode of IGO negotiations and policymaking, most recently with respect to the World Trade Organization. Yet the United States has rarely withdrawn from IGOs (UNESCO is the major exception, during the Reagan years), and it often "chooses" to comply with IGO decisions that it finds distasteful.

4. In a study of standardization and accounting INGOs, Tamm Hallström (1997) notes that conflicts may arise between these different forms of legitimation; for example, the expertism of credentialed members or the drive for the legitimated goal of efficiency may create tensions with efforts to promote

democratic egalitarianism. The main purpose of these bodies may be "harmonization," but there is no reason to expect their internal operations to be entirely harmonious.

5. The most advanced form of compulsorily voluntary submission to transnational authority is, of course, the European Union. In this case, however, state authorities much more openly acknowledge the cession of sovereignty to collective institutions, and enforcement mechanisms are relatively well institutionalized and respected.

6. UNAIDS has even gone so far as to put NGO representatives on its governing board, becoming the first IGO to make this formal fusion between INGO and IGO authority (UNAIDS Programme 1996).

7. Some extreme versions of individualism recognize no limits to the moral virtue of self-interest. Their absolutist reductionism and obsession with simpleminded notions of freedom virtually obliterate any sense of collective value. Of course, they also ignore the inevitable straitjackets on individual freedom that a completely atomized society generates, in the form of steep hierarchies of control and irresistible Tocquevillian horizontal pressures toward conformity.

References

Abbott, Andrew. 1988. *The System of Professions*. Chicago: University of Chicago Press.

Abbott, Andrew, and Stanley DeViney. 1992. "The Welfare State as Transnational Event: Evidence from Sequences of Policy Adoption." *Social Science History* 16, no. 2: 245–74.

Alter, Peter. 1987. *The Reluctant Patron: Science and the State in Britain, 1850–1920*. New York: St. Martin's Press.

Alund, Aleksandra. 1991. "Modern Youth and Transethnic Identities." *European Journal of Intercultural Studies* 2, no. 2: 49–62.

American Eugenics Society. 1916–1953. *Eugenical News: Current Record of Human Genetics and Race Hygiene*. New York: American Eugenics Society.

American National Standards Institute (ANSI). 1992, 1993. *Annual Report*. New York: American National Standards Institute.

Amin, Samir. 1977. *Imperialism and Unequal Exchange*. New York: Monthly Review Press.

Anderson, Benedict. 1983. *Imagined Communities*. London: Verso.

Archer, Clive. 1983. *International Organizations*. London: George Allen & Unwin.

———. 1992. *International Organizations*. Rev. ed. London: Routledge.

Archer, Margaret S. 1988. *Culture and Agency: The Place of Culture in Social Theory*. Cambridge: Cambridge University Press.

Armstrong, David. 1982. *The Rise of the International Organization: A Short History*. New York: St. Martin's Press.

Arndt, H. W. 1987. *Economic Development: The History of an Idea*. Chicago: University of Chicago Press.

Arnove, Robert F., ed. 1980. *Philanthropy and Cultural Imperialism: The Foundations at Home and Abroad*. Boston: Hall.

Aron, Raymond. 1984 [1962]. *Paix et guerre entre les nations*. 8th ed. Paris: Calmann-Lévy.

Ashley, Richard. 1992. "Imposing International Purpose: Notes on a Problematic of Governance." In Ernst Otto Czempiel and James Rosenau, eds.,

Governance Without Government: Order and Change in World Politics, pp. 251–90. Cambridge: Cambridge University Press.

Ashworth, Georgina. 1982. "The UN 'Women's Conference' and International Linkages in the Women's Movement." In Peter Willetts, ed., *Pressure Groups in the Global System: The Transnational Relations of Issue-Oriented Non-Governmental Organizations*, pp. 125–47. London: Frances Pinter.

Association Française de Normalisation (AFNOR). 1994. *General Brochure*. Paris: AFNOR Communication Department.

"Au temps du 'Congrès de Genève.'" 1954. Reprint from *Journal de Genève*, March 19, 1863, in *Revue internationale de la Croix-Rouge*, no. 425 (May): 373–74.

Axelrod, Robert, and Robert O. Keohane. 1993. "Achieving Cooperation Under Anarchy: Strategies and Institutions." In David A. Baldwin, ed., *Neorealism and Neoliberalism: The Contemporary Debate*, pp. 85–115. New York: Columbia University Press.

Badie, Bertrand, and Pierre Birnbaum. 1983. *The Sociology of the State*. Chicago: University of Chicago Press.

Bainbridge, William Sims. 1985. "Utopian Communities." In Phillip E. Hammond, ed., *The Sacred in a Secular Age*, pp. 21–35. Berkeley: University of California Press.

Baldwin, David A., ed. 1993. *Neorealism and Neoliberalism: The Contemporary Debate*. New York: Columbia University Press.

Banks, Arthur S. 1975. *Cross-National Time Series Data Archive*. Binghamton: Center of Comparative Political Research, State University of New York.

Banks, Michael, ed. 1984. *Conflict in World Society: A New Perspective on International Relations*. Brighton, Eng.: Wheatsheaf.

Barrett, David B. 1982. *World Christian Encyclopedia*. Nairobi: Oxford University Press.

Barrett, Deborah. 1995a. "Global Quality: Eugenics as an International Social Movement." Paper presented at the Joint Meeting of the Society for the History of Technology and Society for Social Studies of Science, Charlottesville, Va., October 18–22.

———. 1995b. "Reproducing Persons as a Global Concern: The Making of an Institution." Ph.D. diss., Stanford University.

Barron, David N. 1992. "The Analysis of Count Data: Overdispersion and Autocorrelation." In Peter V. Marsden, ed., *Sociological Methodology*, 22: 179–220. Washington, D.C.: American Sociological Association.

Basch, Linda, and Gail Lerner, eds. 1986. "The Spirit of Nairobi and the UN Decade for Women." Special issue of *Migration World Magazine* 14, no. 1–2: 7–59.

Bates, Ralph S. 1965. *Scientific Societies in the United States*. Cambridge, Mass.: MIT Press.

Beale, Octavius Charles. 1911. *Racial Decay: A Compilation from World Sources*. London: A. C. Fifield.

Bell, Susan Groag, and Karen M. Offen, eds. 1983. *Women, the Family, and Freedom: The Debate in Documents*. Stanford, Calif.: Stanford University Press.

Ben David, Joseph. 1971. *The Scientist's Role in Society*. Englewood Cliffs, N.J.: Prentice-Hall.

Berger, Peter, Brigitte Berger, and Hansfried Kellner. 1973. *The Homeless Mind: Modernization and Consciousness*. New York: Random House.

Berger, Peter, and Thomas Luckmann. 1966. *The Social Construction of Reality*. Garden City, N.Y.: Anchor Books.

Berkovitch, Nitza. 1995. "From Motherhood to Citizenship: The Worldwide Incorporation of Women into the Public Sphere in the Twentieth Century." Ph.D. diss., Stanford University.

———. 1995. "Women and Development: Emergence of a Global Agenda." Paper presented at the Social Science History Association Meetings, Chicago, November 16–19.

———. Forthcoming. *From Motherhood to Citizenship: Women's Rights and International Organizations*. Baltimore: Johns Hopkins University Press.

Berman, Edward H. 1983. *The Ideology of Philanthropy: The Influence of the Carnegie, Ford, and Rockefeller Foundations on American Foreign Policy*. Albany: State University of New York Press.

———. 1992. "Donor Agencies and Third World Educational Development, 1945–85." In Robert F. Arnove, Philip G. Altbach, and Gail P. Kelly, eds., *Emergent Issues in Education: Comparative Perspectives*, pp. 57–74. Albany: State University of New York Press.

Berman, Harold J. 1988. "The Law of International Commercial Transactions." *Emory Journal of International Dispute Resolution* 2, no. 2: 235–310.

Black, Maggie. 1986. *The Children and the Nations: The Story of UNICEF*. Potts Point, Sydney, Australia: P.I.C.

Blanc, Cristina Szanton, Linda Basch, and Nina Glick Schiller. 1995. "Transnationalism, Nation-States, and Culture." *Current Anthropology* 36, no. 4: 683–86.

Boissier, Pierre. 1985. *From Solferino to Tsushima: History of the International Committee of the Red Cross*. Geneva: Henry Dunant Institute.

Boli, John. 1987a. "Human Rights or State Expansion?" In George M. Thomas, John W. Meyer, Francisco O. Ramirez, and John Boli, *Institutional Structure: Constituting State, Society, and the Individual*, pp. 133–49. Beverly Hills, Calif.: Sage.

————. 1987b. "World-Polity Sources of Expanding State Authority and Organization, 1870–1970." In George M. Thomas, John W. Meyer, Francisco O. Ramirez, and John Boli, *Institutional Structure: Constituting State, Society, and the Individual*, pp. 71–91. Beverly Hills, Calif.: Sage.

————. 1996. "The Moral Order of World Culture and the Operation of World Authority." Paper presented at the Institutional Analysis conference, Tucson, Ariz., March.

————. 1998. "Rights and Rules: Constituting World Citizens." In Connie L. McNeely, ed., *Public Rights, Public Rules: Constituting Citizens in the World Polity and National Policy*. New York: Garland. In press.

————. 1999a. "Sovereignty from a World-Polity Perspective." In Stephen D. Krasner, ed., *Problematic Sovereignty*. Forthcoming.

————. 1999b. "World Polity Dramatization via Global Events." In Roland Robertson and William Garrett, eds., *Religion and Global Order: The Contemporary Circumstance*. Forthcoming.

Boli, John, and George M. Thomas. 1994. "The World Polity Under Construction: A Century of International Non-Governmental Organizing." Emory University, Department of Sociology.

————. 1997. "World Culture in the World Polity: A Century of International Non-Governmental Organization." *American Sociological Review* 62, no. 2: 171–90.

Boli[-Bennett], John. 1976. "The Expansion of Nation-States: 1870–1970." Ph.D. diss., Stanford University.

Bolling, Landrum Rymer. 1982. *Private Foreign Aid: U.S. Philanthropy for Relief and Development*. Boulder, Colo.: Westview.

Bornschier, Volker, and Christopher Chase-Dunn. 1985. *Transnational Corporations and Underdevelopment*. New York: Praeger.

Boswell, Terry. 1995. "Hegemony and Bifurcation Points in World History." *Journal of World-System Research* 1, no. 1, item 15.

Boulding, Elise. 1977. "Women and Peace Work." In Elise Boulding, *Women in the Twentieth Century World*, pp. 167–83. Beverly Hills, Calif.: Sage.

————. 1990. "Building a Global Civic Culture." *Development* 2: 37–40.

————. 1991. "The Old and New Transnationalism: An Evolutionary Perspective." *Human Relations* 44, no. 8: 789–805.

————. 1992. *The Underside of History: A View of Women Through Time*. Rev. ed. Newbury Park, Calif.: Sage.

Bourdieu, Pierre. 1977. *Outline of a Theory of Practice*. Cambridge: Cambridge University Press.

Boxer, Marilyn, and Jean H. Quataert. 1978. "The Class and Sex Connection: An Introduction." In Marilyn Boxer and Jean H. Quataert, eds., *Socialist Women: European Socialist Feminism in the Nineteenth and Early Twentieth Century*, pp. 1–18. New York: Elsevier North-Holland.

Bradley, Karen, and Francisco O. Ramirez. 1996. "World Polity and Gender Parity: Women's Share of Higher Education, 1965–85." *Research in Sociology of Education and Socialization* 11: 63–91.

Braverman, Harry. 1975. *Labor and Monopoly Capital: The Degradation of Work in the Twentieth Century.* New York: Monthly Review Press.

Brennan, Katherine. 1989. "The Influence of Cultural Relativism on International Human Rights Law: Female Circumcision as a Case Study." *Law and Inequality* 7: 367–98.

British Standards Institute (BSI). 1994a. *Profits From Standards.* Milton Keynes, Eng.: British Standards Institute.

———. 1994b. *Raising Standards for British Industry.* Milton Keynes, Eng.: British Standards Institute.

Brock, Gerald. 1975. "Competition, Standards and Self-regulation in the Computer Industry." In Richard E. Caves and Marc J. Roberts, eds., *Regulating the Product: Quality and Variety*, pp. 75–96. Cambridge, Mass.: Ballinger.

Bulbeck, Chilla. 1988. *One World's Women's Movement.* London: Pluto Press.

Bull, Hedley, and Adam Watson, eds. 1984. *The Expansion of International Society.* Oxford: Oxford University Press.

Bunch, Charlotte, ed. 1987. *Passionate Politics.* New York: St. Martin's Press.

Burton, John W. 1972. *World Society.* Cambridge: Cambridge University Press.

Bussey, Gertrude, and Margaret Tims. 1980. *Pioneers for Peace: Women's International League for Peace and Freedom, 1915–1965.* London: Women's International League for Peace and Freedom, The British Section.

Butora, Martin, and Zora Butorova. 1993. "Slovakia: The Identity Challenges of the Newly Born State." *Social Research* 60, no. 4: 705–36.

Cagatay, Nilufer, Caren Grown, and Aida Santiago. 1986. "The Nairobi Women's Conference: Toward Global Feminism?" *Feminist Studies* 12, no. 2: 401–11.

Caldwell, Lynton Keith. 1990. *International Environmental Policy.* 2d ed. Durham, N.C.: Duke University Press.

Carden, Maren Lockwood. 1969. *Oneida: Utopian Community to Modern Corporation.* Baltimore: Johns Hopkins University Press.

Castermans, Alex Geert, Lydia Schut, Frank Steketee, and Luc Verhey, eds. 1991. *The Role of Non-Governmental Organizations in the Promotion and Protection of Human Rights.* Leiden: Stichting NJCM-Boekerij.

Chabbott, Colette. 1996. "Constructing Educational Development: International Development Organizations and the World Conference on Education for All." Ph.D. diss., Stanford University.

Chadwick, Douglas H. 1995. "The Endangered Species Act." *National Geographic*, March, 2–41.

Chang, Patricia, and David Strang. 1990. "Internal and External Sources of the Welfare State: A Cross-National Analysis, 1950–1980." Paper presented at the annual meeting of the American Sociological Association, Cincinnati, Ohio, August.

Charnovitz, Steve. 1997. "Two Centuries of Participation: NGOs and International Governance." *Michigan Journal of International Law* 18, no. 2: 183–286.

Chase-Dunn, Christopher. 1989. *Global Formation: Structures of the World-Economy*. Cambridge, Mass.: Blackwell.

Clark, John. 1991. *Democratizing Development: The Role of Voluntary Organizations*. West Hartford, Conn.: Kumarian Press.

Coale, Ansley J., and Edgar M. Hoover. 1958. *Population Growth and Economic Development in Low-Income Countries: A Case Study of India's Prospects*. Princeton, N.J.: Princeton University Press.

Coleman, James S. 1990. *The Foundations of Social Theory*. Cambridge, Mass.: Belknap Press.

Collins, Randall. 1986. *Weberian Sociological Theory*. Cambridge: Cambridge University Press.

Comité Européen de Normalisation (CEN). 1993. *Annual report 1992*. Brussels: Comité Européen de Normalisation.

Council on Environmental Quality. 1991. *Environmental Quality: 22nd Annual Report*. Washington, D.C.: U.S. Government Printing Office.

Coursier, Henri. 1961. *The International Red Cross*. Geneva: International Committee of the Red Cross.

Cowhey, Peter F. 1990. "The International Telecommunications Regime: The Political Roots of Regimes for High Technology." *International Organization* 44, no. 2: 169–99.

Cox, David R., and Valeris Isham. 1980. *Point Process*. London: Chapman & Hall.

Crane, Barbara. 1993. "International Population Institutions: Adaptation to a Changing World Order." In Peter M. Haas, Robert O. Keohane, and Marc A. Levy, eds., *Institutions for the Earth*, pp. 351–92. Cambridge, Mass.: MIT Press.

Crane, Rhonda J. 1979. *The Politics of International Standards: France and the Color TV War*. Norwood, N.J.: Ablex.

Crawford, Elisabeth. 1992. *Nationalism and Internationalism in Science, 1880–1939*. Cambridge: Cambridge University Press.

Croce, Paul Jerome. 1993. "Erosion of Mass Culture." *Society* 30, no. 5: 11–16.

Cupitt, Richard T., Rodney L. Whitlock, and Lynn Williams Whitlock. 1996. "The (Im)mortality of International Governmental Organizations." *International Interactions* 21, no. 4: 389–404.

Czempiel, Ernst Otto, and James Rosenau, eds. 1992. *Governance Without*

Government: Order and Change in World Politics. Cambridge: Cambridge University Press.

Diamond, Larry, and Marc F. Plattner, eds. 1993. *The Global Resurgence of Democracy.* Baltimore: Johns Hopkins University Press.

Dichter, Thomas W. 1988. "The Changing World of Northern NGOs: Problems, Paradoxes, and Possibilities." In John P. Lewis, ed., *Strengthening the Poor: What Have We Learned?* pp. 177–88. New Brunswick, N.J.: Transaction Books.

Diehl, Paul F., ed. 1996. *The Politics of Global Governance: International Organizations in an Interdependent World.* Boulder, Colo.: Lynne Rienner.

Directory of National Machinery for the Advancement of Women. 1991. Vienna: Division for the Advancement of Women, CSDHA, United Nations.

Docksey, Christopher. 1987. "The European Community and the Promotion of Equality." In Christopher McCrudden, ed., *Women, Employment and European Equality Law*, pp. 1–23. Oxford: Eclipse Pub.

Donnelly, Jack. 1986. "International Human Rights: A Regime Analysis." *International Organization* 40, no. 3: 599–642.

Douglas, Mary. 1966. *Purity and Danger.* London: Routledge & Kegan Paul.

———. 1986. *How Institutions Think.* Syracuse, N.Y.: Syracuse University Press.

Douglas, Mary, and David Hull, eds. 1992. *How Classification Works: Nelson Goodman Among the Social Sciences.* Edinburgh: Edinburgh University Press.

Drabek, Anne Gordon. 1987. "Development Alternatives: The Challenge for NGOs." *World Development* 15: 261. New York: Pergamon.

Drori, Gili. 1993. *The National Science Agenda as a Ritual of Modern Nation-Statehood: The Consequences of National "Science for Development" Projects.* Ph.D. diss. prospectus, Stanford University.

DuBois, Ellen Carol. 1991. "Woman Suffrage and the Left: An International Socialist-Feminist Perspective." *New Left Review* 186: 20–45.

Dunant, Henry. 1986 [1862]. *A Memory of Solferino.* Geneva: International Committee of the Red Cross.

———. 1954 [1863]. "Lettres de J. Henry Dunant à Gustave Moynier." *Revue internationale de la Croix-Rouge*, no. 425 (May): 424–28.

Dunlap, Riley E., and Angela G. Mertig. 1992. "The Evolution of the U.S. Environmental Movement from 1970 to 1990." In Riley E. Dunlap and Angela G. Mertig, eds., *American Environmentalism*, pp. 1–10. Philadelphia: Taylor & Francis.

Durand, André. 1984. *From Sarajevo to Hiroshima: History of the International Committee of the Red Cross.* Geneva: Henry Dunant Institute.

East, Roger, Miles Smith-Morris, and Martin Wright, eds. 1990. *World Development Directory.* Essex: Longman.

Egan, Michelle, and Anthony R. Zito. 1995. "European Standards Networks and the Integration of Global Markets." Paper presented at the annual meeting of the International Studies Association, Chicago, Illinois, March.

Eisenstadt, S. N. 1963. *The Political Systems of Empires*. New York: Free Press.

Eisler, Riane, and David Loye. 1985. "Will Women Change the World?" *Futures* 17, no. 5: 550–55.

Eldridge, Hope Tisdale. 1954. *Population Policies: A Survey of Recent Developments, Committee on Investigation of Population Policies*. Washington, D.C.: The International Union for the Scientific Study of Population.

Ellul, Jacques. 1964. *The Technological Society*. New York: Knopf.

———. 1973. *Les nouveaux possédés*. Paris: Arthème Fayard. Published in English under the title *The New Demons* (New York: Seabury, 1975).

———. 1976. *The Ethics of Freedom*. Grand Rapids, Mich.: Eerdmans.

———. 1980. *The Technological System*. New York: Continuum.

Epstein, Barbara Leslie. 1981. *The Politics of Domesticity: Women, Evangelism, and Temperance in Nineteenth-Century America*. Middletown, Conn.: Wesleyan University Press.

Eugenics Education Society. 1909–1968. *The Eugenics Review*. London: Eugenics Education Society.

———. 1913. *Problems in Eugenics*. Vols. 1–2. Papers communicated to the First International Eugenics Congress, University of London, July 24–30, 1912. London: Kingsway House.

Eurofi, Ltd. 1988. *Development Aid: A Guide to National and International Agencies*. New York: Eurofi (UK).

European Academy for Standardization (EURAS). 1994. "Information Brochure." Hamburg: EURAS.

Evans, Peter. 1995. *Embedded Autonomy: States and Industrial Transformation*. Princeton, N.J.: Princeton University Press.

Evans, Peter, Dietrich Rueschemeyer, and Theda Skocpol, eds. 1985. *Bringing the State Back In*. Cambridge: Cambridge University Press.

Evans, Richard. 1977. *The Feminists: Women's Emancipation Movements in Europe, America and Australia, 1840–1920*. London: Croom Helm.

Falk, Richard. 1994. "The Making of Global Citizenship." In Bart van Steenbergen, ed., *The Condition of Citizenship*, pp. 127–40. London: Sage.

Falk, Richard A., Friedrich Kratochwil, and Saul H. Mendlovitz, eds. 1985. *International Law: A Contemporary Perspective*. Boulder, Colo.: Westview.

Farer, Tom J. 1988. "The UN and Human Rights: More Than a Whimper, Less Than a Roar." In Adam Roberts and Benedict Kingsbury, eds., *United Nations, Divided World: The UN's Role in International Relations*, pp. 95–138. Oxford: Clarendon Press.

Featherstone, Michael. 1990. *Global Culture: Nationalism, Globalization and Modernity*. Special issue of *Theory, Culture, and Society* 7, nos. 2 and 3.

Feld, W. 1971. "Non-Governmental Entities and the International System: A Preliminary Quantitative Overview." *Orbis* 15: 879–922.

Fels, Xavier, ed. 1992. "La télévision à haute définition: l'Europe dans la compétition mondiale." *Revue du Marché Commun et de l'Union Européenne*, February, pp. 99–192.

Ferguson, James. 1990. *The Anti-Politics Machine: "Development," Depoliticization, and Bureaucratic Power in Lesotho*. Cambridge: Cambridge University Press.

Finnemore, Martha. 1991. *Science, the State, and International Society*. Ph.D. diss., Stanford University.

———. 1993. "International Organizations as Teachers of Norms: UNESCO and Science Policy." *International Organization* 47, no. 4: 565–97.

———. 1996. *National Interests in International Society*. Ithaca, N.Y.: Cornell University Press.

First Convention of International Congress of Working Women. November 3, 1919. Shorthand reports. National Museum, Washington D.C.

Fisher, Julie. 1993. *The Road from Rio: Sustainable Development and the Non-governmental Movement in the Third World*. Westport, Conn.: Praeger.

———. 1997. *Nongovernments: NGOs and the Political Development of the Third World*. West Hartford, Conn.: Kumarian.

Foggon, George. 1988. "The Origin and Development of the ILO." In Paul Taylor and A. J. R. Groom, eds., *International Institutions at Work*, pp. 96–113. London: Pinter.

Foner, Philip S. 1980. *Women and the American Labor Movement*. Vol. 2. New York: Free Press.

For the Record, Forum '85. The Non-Governmental World Meeting for Women, Nairobi, Kenya, September. Prepared by Caroline Pezzullo for the NGO Planning Committee. New York: International Women's Tribune Center.

Forster, Peter G. 1982. *The Esperanto Movement*. Paris: Mouton.

Forsythe, David P. 1991. *The Internationalization of Human Rights*. Lexington, Mass.: Lexington Books.

Fox, Barry. 1992a. "CD Makers Perform in Unison to Stop the Rot." *New Scientist* 134, no. 1815: 19.

———. 1992b. "Interference as Usual After Brussels Bungle." *New Scientist* 134, no. 1818: 18.

———. 1993. "Big Squeeze for Video (MPEG standard for digital coding)." *New Scientist* 139 (August 28): 21–23.

François, Alexis. 1918. *Le Berceau de la Croix-Rouge*. Genève: Librairie A. Jullien.

Frank, David John. 1995. "Global Environmentalism: International Treaties in World Society." Ph.D. diss., Stanford University.

———. 1996. "The Globalization of the Environment, 1870–1990." Working paper, Department of Sociology, Harvard University.

———. 1997a. "The Social Bases of Environmental Treaty Ratification, 1900–1990." Working paper, Department of Sociology, Harvard University.

———. 1997b. "Science, Nature, and the Globalization of the Environment, 1870–1990." *Social Forces* 75 (December): 411–37.

Frantz, Telmo Rudi. 1987. "The Role of NGOs in the Strengthening of Civil Society." *World Development* 15 (Supplement): 121–28.

Freeman, John, and Michael T. Hannan. 1983. "Niche Width and the Dynamics of Organizational Populations." *American Journal of Sociology* 88, no. 6: 1116–45.

Freudenberg, William R. S., Scott Frickel, and Robert Gramling. 1995. "Beyond the Nature/Society Divide: Learning to Think About a Mountain." *Sociological Forum* 10: 361–92.

Friedman, Jonathan. 1992. "The Past in the Future: History and the Politics of Identity." *American Anthropologist* 94, no. 4: 837–59.

Genschel, Philipp, and Raymund Werle. 1993. "From National Hierarchies to International Standardization: Modal Changes in the Governance of Telecommunications." *Journal of Public Policy* 13, no. 3: 203–25.

Gibson, John. 1991. *International Organizations, Constitutional Law, and Human Rights*. New York: Praeger.

Giddens, Anthony. 1985. *The Nation-State and Violence: Volume Two of a Contemporary Critique of Historical Materialism*. Los Angeles: University of California Press.

———. 1992. *The Transformation of Intimacy*. Stanford, Calif.: Stanford University Press.

Giele, Janet Zollinger. 1995. *Two Paths to Women's Equality: Temperance, Suffrage, and the Origins of Women's Feminism*. New York: Twayne.

Gilliam, Angela. 1991. "Women's Equality and National Liberation." In Chandra T. Mohanty, Ann Russo, and Lourdes Torres, eds., *Third World Women and the Politics of Feminism*, pp. 215–36. Bloomington: Indiana University Press.

Gilligan, Carol. 1982. *In a Different Voice: Psychological Theory and Women's Development*. Cambridge, Mass.: Harvard University Press.

Gilpin, Robert. 1987. *The Political Economy of International Relations*. Princeton, N.J.: Princeton University Press.

Giorgis, Belkis Wolde. 1981. "Female Circumcision in Africa." ST/ECAA-TRCW/81/02. Addis Ababa: UN Economic Commission for Africa; ATRCW and Association for African Women for Research and Development.

Girard, Michel, ed. 1994. *Les individus dans la politique internationale*. Paris: Economica.

Goffman, Erving. 1959. *The Presentation of Self in Everyday Life*. Garden City, N.Y.: Doubleday Anchor Books.

———. 1974. *Frame Analysis*. Cambridge, Mass.: Harvard University Press.

Goldstone, Jack A. 1991. *Revolution and Rebellion in the Early Modern World*. Berkeley, Calif.: University of California Press.

Gordon, Elizabeth P. 1924. *Women Torch-Bearers: The Story of the Woman's Christian Temperance Union*. Evanston, Ill.: National Woman's Christian Temperance Union.

Grew, Raymond. 1984. "The Nineteenth-Century European State." In Charles Bright and Sandra Harding, eds., *Statemaking and Social Movements*, pp. 83–120. Ann Arbor: University of Michigan Press.

Grieco, Joseph M. 1993. "Anarchy and the Limits of Cooperation: A Realist Critique of the Newest Liberal Institutionalism." In David A. Baldwin, ed., *Neorealism and Neoliberalism: The Contemporary Debate*, pp. 116–40. New York: Columbia University Press.

Groom, A. J. R., and Paul Taylor, eds. 1990. *Frameworks for International Cooperation*. London: Pinter.

Gruber, Max von, and Ernst Rudin, eds. 1911. *Fortpflanzung, Vererbung, Rassenhygiene*. Katalog der Gruppe Rassenhygiene der Internationalen Hygiene-Ausstellung 1911 in Dresden. Munich: J. F. Lehmanns Verlag.

Guillen, Mauro F. 1994. *Models of Management*. Chicago: University of Chicago Press.

Gumpert, Martin. 1938. *Dunant: The Story of the Red Cross*. New York: Oxford University Press.

Gurr, Ted Robert. 1990. *Polity II: Political Structures and Regime Change, 1800–1986*. ICPSR data set 9263. Ann Arbor, Mich.: Inter-University Consortium for Political and Social Research.

Haas, Ernst B. 1964. *Beyond the Nation State*. Stanford, Calif.: Stanford University Press.

Haas, Peter M. 1992. "Introduction: Epistemic Communities and International Policy Coordination." *International Organization* 46, no. 1: 1–35.

Haas, Peter M., Robert O. Keohane, and Marc A. Levy, eds. 1993. *Institutions for the Earth*. Cambridge, Mass.: MIT Press.

Habermas, Jürgen. 1981. *The Theory of Communicative Action*. Vol. 1: *Reason and the Rationalization of Society*. Boston: Beacon.

———. 1984. *The Theory of Communicative Action*. 2 vols. Boston: Beacon.

———. 1987. *The Philosophical Discourse of Modernity*. Cambridge, Mass.: MIT Press.

———. 1989. *The Structural Transformation of the Public Sphere*. Cambridge, Mass.: MIT Press.

Hall, John. 1985. *Powers and Liberties: The Causes and Consequences of the Rise of the West*. Oxford: Blackwell.

Hall, John A., and G. John Ikenberry. 1989. *The State*. Minneapolis: University of Minnesota Press.

Hannan, Michael T., and John Freeman. 1989. *Organizational Ecology*. Cambridge, Mass.: Harvard University Press.

Hannerz, Ulf. 1987. "The World in Creolisation." *Africa* 57, no. 4: 546–59.

———. 1992. "Cosmopolitans and Locals in World Culture." *Theory, Culture and Society* 7, no. 2–3: 237–51.

Hannerz, Ulf, and Orvar Löfgren. 1994. "The Nation in the Global Village." *Cultural Studies* 8, no. 2: 198–207.

Haraway, Donna. 1989. *Primate Visions*. New York: Routledge.

Harmsen, Hans, and Franz Lohse, eds. 1936. *Bevölkerungsfragen. Bericht des Internationalen Kongresses für Bevölkerungswissenschaft. Berlin, 26. August–1. September 1935*. Munich: J. F. Lehmanns Verlag.

Hartmann, Betsy. 1995. "Building a 'Consensus' for Cairo and Beyond." In Betsy Hartmann, ed., *Reproductive Rights and Wrongs: The Global Politics of Population Control*, pp. 131–55. Rev. ed. Boston, Mass.: South End Press.

Hayden, Sherman Strong. 1942. *The International Protection of Wild Life*. New York: Columbia University Press.

Heater, Derek. 1990. *World Citizenship and Government*. New York: St. Martin's Press.

Hechter, Michael. 1975. *Internal Colonialism: The Celtic Fringe in British National Development*. London: Routledge & Kegan Paul.

Held, David. 1989. *Political Theory and the Modern State*. Stanford, Calif.: Stanford University Press.

———. 1991. "Democracy, the Nation-State and the Global System." In David Held, ed., *Political Theory Today*, pp. 197–236. Stanford, Calif.: Stanford University Press.

Hinsley, F. H. 1986. *Sovereignty*. 2d ed. Cambridge: Cambridge University Press.

Hironaka, Ann. 1996. "The Institutionalization and Organization of a Global Environmental Solution: The Diffusion of Environmental Impact Assessment Legislation." Working Paper, Department of Sociology, Stanford University.

Hironaka, Ann, and Evan Schofer. 1994. "The Globalization of Invention: The International Diffusion of the Patent System." Paper presented at the American Sociological Association meetings, Los Angeles, Calif., August.

Hobsbawm, Eric J. 1990. *Nations and Nationalism Since 1780*. Cambridge: Cambridge University Press.

Honeycut, Karen. 1981. "Clara Zetkin: A Socialist Approach to the Problem of Women's Oppression." In Jane Slaughter and Robert Kern, eds., *European Women in the Left*, pp. 29–49. Westport, Conn.: Greenwood Press.

Huefner, Klaus, Jens Naumann, and John Meyer. 1987. "Comparative Education Policy Research: A World Society Perspective." In Meinolf Dierkes, Hans N. Weiler, and Ariane Berthoin, eds., *Comparative Policy Research*, pp. 188–243. Aldershot, Eng.: Gower.

Hunsberger, Newton J. 1907. "Artificial Childlessness and Race Suicide." *Journal of the American Medical Association*, August 10, p. 458.

Ibrahim, Saad Eddin. 1995. "Liberalization and Democratization in the Arab World: An Overview." In Rex Brynen, Bahgat Korany, and Paul Noble, eds., *Political Liberalization and Democratization in the Arab World*, 1: 29–57. Boulder, Colo.: Lynne Rienner.

Imber, Mark F. 1989. *The USA, ILO, UNESCO and IAEA: Politicization and Withdrawal in the Specialized Agencies*. New York: St. Martin's Press.

Inkeles, Alex, and David H. Smith. 1974. *Becoming Modern: Individual Change in Six Developing Countries*. Cambridge, Mass.: Harvard University Press.

Inter-American Commission of Women. 1974. *Inter-American Commission of Women, 1928–1973*. Washington, D.C.: General Secretariat, Organization of American States.

International Bank for Reconstruction and Development (IBRD; World Bank). Various years. *World Tables*. Washington, D.C.: IBRD.

International Committee of the Red Cross (ICRC). 1863–64. "Minutes of 17 Feb., 17 March, 25 August 1863, 13 March 1864 meetings." Reprinted in ICRC, "La Fondation de la Croix-Rouge," *Revue internationale de la Croix-Rouge*, May 1954, pp. 58–66.

———. May 1954 [1863], 1963–64. *Revue internationale de la Croix-Rouge*. Geneva: ICRC.

———. 1963. "Le Premier Effort Moderne de Codification du Droit de la Guerre: Francis Lieber et l'Ordonnance Générale no. 100." *Revue internationale de la Croix-Rouge*, nos. 532–33.

International Council of Women. 1966. *Women in a Changing World: The Dynamic Story of the International Council of Women Since 1888*. London: Routledge & Kegan Paul.

International Council on Scientific Unions (ICSU). 1954–90. *Year Book*. Paris: ICSU Secretariat.

International Electrotechnical Commission (IEC). 1993a. *Annual Report 1992*. Geneva: International Electrotechnical Commission.

———. 1993b. *Make World Trade a Reality*. Geneva: IEC.

———. 1993c. *Statutes and Rules of Procedure*. Geneva: IEC.

International Labour Conference (ILC). 1919. 1st Session, *Record of Proceedings*. Geneva: International Labour Office.

————. 1944. 26th Session, *Record of Proceedings*. Geneva: International Labour Office.

————. 1947. 30th Session, *Record of Proceedings*. Geneva: International Labour Office.

————. 1951. 34th Session, *Record of Proceedings*. Geneva: International Labour Office.

————. 1958. 42d Session, *Record of Proceedings*. Geneva: International Labour Office.

————. 1992. 79th Session, *List of Ratification by Convention and by Country* (as of 31 December 1991), report III(5). Geneva: International Labour Office.

International Labour Organization (ILO). 1935–36. *Yearbook*. Geneva: International Labour Office.

————. 1936. *Yearbook*. Geneva: International Labour Office.

————. 1937. *Official Bulletin* 22, no. 3. Geneva: International Labour Office.

————. 1939. *Official Bulletin* 24, no. 3. Geneva: International Labour Office.

International Organization for Standardization (ISO). 1985. *ISO Constitution, 12th Edition*. Geneva: ISO.

————. 1993. *Compatible Technology Worldwide*. Geneva: ISO.

International Research Council. 1922–52. *Reports of Proceedings of the General Assembly*. London: International Research Council.

Jacobson, David. 1996. *Rights Across Borders: Immigration and the Decline of Citizenship*. Baltimore: Johns Hopkins University Press.

Jacobson, Harold K. 1979. *Networks of Interdependence: International Organizations and the Global Political System*. New York: Knopf.

————. 1982. "The Global System and the Realization of Human Dignity and Justice." *International Studies Quarterly* 26, no. 3: 315–32.

————. 1984. *Networks of Interdependence: International Organizations and the Global Political System*. 2d ed. New York: Alfred Knopf.

Jacobson, Harold K., William M. Reisinger, and Todd Mathers. 1986. "National Entanglements in International Governmental Organizations." *American Political Science Review* 80, no. 1: 141–59.

Jacobson, Roberta. 1992. "The Committee on the Elimination of Discrimination Against Women." In Alston Philip, ed., *The United Nations and Human Rights*, pp. 444–72. Oxford: Clarendon Press.

James, Alan. 1986. *Sovereign Statehood: The Basis of International Society*. London: Allen & Unwin.

James, Stephen A. 1994. "Reconciling International Human Rights and Cultural Relativism: The Case of Female Circumcision." *Bioethics* 8, no. 1: 1–26.

Jang, Yong Suk. 1995. "Diffusion of the Ministry of Science and Technology, 1950–1990." Paper presented at the annual meeting of the Pacific Sociological Association, San Francisco, Calif., March.

Janton, Pierre. 1993. *Esperanto: Language, Literature, and Community*. New York: State University of New York Press.

Jepperson, Ronald L. 1991. "Institutions, Institutional Effects, and Institutionalization." In Walter W. Powell and Paul J. DiMaggio, eds., *The New Institutionalism in Organizational Analysis*, pp. 143–63. Chicago: University of Chicago Press.

———. 1992. *National Scripts: The Varying Construction of Individualism and Opinion Across the Modern Nation-States*. Ph.D. diss., Yale University.

Jepperson, Ronald L., and John W. Meyer. 1991. "The Public Order and the Construction of Formal Organizations." In Walter W. Powell and Paul J. DiMaggio, eds., *The New Institutionalism in Organizational Analysis*, pp. 204–31. Chicago: University of Chicago Press.

Johnson, George W., and Lucy Johnson. 1909. *Josephine Butler: An Autobiographical Memoir*. London: J. W. Arrowsmith.

Johnson, Norman L., Samuel Kotz, and Adrienne W. Kemp. 1992. *Univariate Discrete Distributions*. 2d ed. New York: John Wiley & Sons.

Johnson-Odim, Cheryl. 1991. "Common Themes, Different Contexts: Third World Women and Feminism." In Chandra Talpade Mohanty, Ann Russo, and Lourdes Torres, eds., *Third World Women and the Politics of Feminism*, pp. 314–27. Bloomington: Indiana University Press.

Johnston, George Alexander. 1924. *International Social Progress: The Work of the International Labour Organization of the League of Nations*. London: George Allen & Unwin.

Journal des Débats. 15 February 1863.

Kaganas, Felicity, and Christina Murray. 1994. "The Contest Between Culture and Gender Equality under South Africa's Interim Constitution." *Journal of Law and Society* 21, no. 4: 409–33.

Kant, Immanuel. 1963 [1795]. "Perpetual Peace." In Lewis White Beck, ed., and Lewis White Beck, Robert E. Anchor, and Emil L. Fachenheim, trans., *On History*, pp. 85–135. Indianapolis: Bobbs-Merrill.

Kates, Robert W., B. L. Turner II, and William C. Clark. 1990. "The Great Transformation." In B. L. Turner II, W. C. Clark, R. W. Kates, J. F. Richards, J. T. Matthews, and W. B. Meyer, eds., *The Earth as Transformed by Human Action*, pp. 1–17. Cambridge: Cambridge University Press.

Keck, Margaret, and Kathryn Sikkink. 1998. *Activists Without Borders: Advocacy Networks in International Politics*. Ithaca, N.Y.: Cornell University Press.

Keeling, C. D., R. B. Bacastow, A. F. Carter, S. C. Piper, T. P. Whorf, M. Heimann, W. G. Mook, and H. Roeloffzen. 1989. "A Three Dimensional Model of Atmospheric CO_2 Transport Based on Observed Winds." *Geophysical Monograph* 55: 165–236.

Keohane, Robert O. 1984. *After Hegemony: Cooperation and Discord in the World Political Economy*. Princeton, N.J.: Princeton University Press.

———. 1989. *International Institutions and State Power*. Boulder, Colo.: Westview.

———. 1993. "Institutional Theory and the Realist Challenge After the Cold War." In David A. Baldwin, ed., *Neorealism and Neoliberalism: The Contemporary Debate*, pp. 269–300. New York: Columbia University Press.

———, ed. 1986. *Neorealism and Its Critics*. New York: Columbia University Press.

Kim, Young S. 1995. "Increasing Complexity of Government Structure and the Contemporary World Polity." Paper presented at the annual meeting of the Pacific Sociological Association, San Francisco, Calif., March.

Koch, Gary G., Susan Atkinson, and Maura Stokes. 1986. "Poisson Regression." In Samuel Kotz and Norman Lloyd Johnson, eds., *Encyclopedia of Statistical Sciences*, pp. 32–41. New York: John Wiley & Sons.

Kohlberg, Lawrence, with Charles Levine and Alexandra Hewer. 1983. *Moral Stages: A Current Formulation and a Response to Critics*. Basel: Karger.

Kohn, Hans. 1962. *The Age of Nationalism*. New York: Harper.

Korsmeyer, Pamela, ed. 1991. *The Development Directory 1991: A Guide to the International Development Community in the United States and Canada*. 3d ed. Detroit, Mich.: Omnigraphics.

Korten, David C. 1990. *Getting to the 21st Century: Voluntary Action and the Global Agenda*. West Hartford, Conn.: Kumarian.

Kraditor, Aileen S. 1981. *The Ideas of the Woman Suffrage Movement, 1890–1920*. New York: Columbia University Press.

Krasner, Stephen, ed. 1983a. *International Regimes*. Ithaca, N.Y.: Cornell University Press.

———. 1983b. "Structural Causes and Regime Consequences: Regimes as Intervening Variables." In Stephen Krasner, ed., *International Regimes*, pp. 1–21. Ithaca, N.Y.: Cornell University Press.

———. 1985. *Structural Conflict: The Third World Against Global Liberalism*. Berkeley: University of California Press.

Kratochwil, Friedrich, and John Gerard Ruggie. 1986. "International Organization: the State of the Art on the Art of the State." *International Organization* 40 (Autumn): 753–75.

Kriesberg, Louis. 1981. "Varieties of ISPAs: Their Forms and Functions." In William M. Evan, ed., *Knowledge and Power in a Global Society*, pp. 49–68. Newbury Park, Calif.: Sage.

Kunda, Gideon. 1992. *Engineering Culture: Control and Commitment in a High-Tech Corporation*. Philadelphia: Temple University Press.

Lapid, Yosef, and Friedrich Kratochwil, eds. 1996. *The Return of Culture and Identity in IR Theory.* Boulder, Colo.: Lynne Rienner.

Large, Andrew. 1985. *The Artificial Language Movement.* Oxford: Basil Blackwell.

League of Nations. 1931. *Official Journal.* February. Geneva: League of Nations.

———. 1933. "Bulletin of Information of the Work of International Organizations." Geneva: League of Nations.

———. 1935a. *Official Journal* (February). Geneva: League of Nations.

———. 1935b. "Statements Presented by International Women's Organizations." A.19.V. Geneva: League of Nations.

———. 1937a. "Status of Women." A.54.V. Geneva: League of Nations.

———. 1937b. *Work of the League.* Geneva: League of Nations.

———. 1938a. *Official Journal* (July). Geneva: League of Nations.

———. 1938b. *Work of the League.* Geneva: League of Nations.

Lechner, Frank. 1989. "Cultural Aspects of the Modern World-System." In W. H. Swatos, ed., *Religious Politics in Global and Contemporary Perspective,* pp. 11–28. New York: Greenwood Press.

Lechner, Frank, and John Boli. 1995. "Actors in Order: Notes Toward a Constructive Theory of Culture." Paper presented at the annual meetings of the Southern Sociological Society, Atlanta, Ga., April.

Lévi-Strauss, Claude. 1966. *The Savage Mind.* Chicago: University of Chicago Press.

Lewis, John P., ed. 1988. *Strengthening the Poor: What Have We Learned?* New Brunswick, N.J.: Transaction Books.

Lewis, John P., and Valleriana Kallab, eds. 1986. *Development Strategies Reconsidered.* New Brunswick, N.J.: Transaction Books.

Lipton, Michael, and Simon Maxwell. 1992. *The New Poverty Agenda: An Overview.* IDS Discussion Paper 306. Brighton, Eng.: Institute for Development Studies, University of Sussex.

Lissner, Jörgen. 1977. *The Politics of Altruism.* Geneva: World Lutheran Federation.

Livi-Bacci, Massimo. 1994. "Population Policies: A Comparative Perspective." *International Social Science Journal* 46, no. 3 (141): 317–30.

Lowenthal, David. 1990. "Awareness of Human Impacts: Changing Attitudes and Emphases." In B. L. Turner II, William C. Clark, Robert W. Kates, John F. Richards, J. T. Matthews, and W. B. Meyer, eds., *The Earth as Transformed by Human Action,* pp. 121–35. Cambridge: Cambridge University Press.

Lubin, Carol Riegelman, and Anne Winslow. 1990. *Social Justice for Women: The International Labor Organization and Women.* Durham, N.C.: Duke University Press.

Luhmann, Niklas. 1982. *The Differentiation of Society*. New York: Columbia University Press.

———. 1989. *Ecological Communication*. Chicago: University of Chicago Press.

Lumsdaine, David H. 1993. *Moral Vision in International Politics: The Foreign Aid Regime, 1949–1989*. Princeton, N.J.: Princeton University Press.

Mackenzie, Donald A. 1981. *Statistics in Britain, 1865–1930: The Social Construction of Scientific Knowledge*. Edinburgh: Edinburgh University Press.

Mahoney, Francis X., and Carl G. Thor. 1994. *The TQM Trilogy: Using ISO 9000, the Deming Prize and the Baldrige Award to Establish a System for Total Quality Management*. New York: American Management Association.

Malthus, Thomas. 1803. *An Essay on the Principles of Population*. London: J. Johnson.

Malthusian League. 1879–1916. *The Malthusian: A Crusade Against Poverty*. Vols. 1–40.

Mann, Michael. 1986. *The Sources of Social Power*. Vol. 1: *A History of Power from the Beginning to A.D. 1760*. Cambridge: Cambridge University Press.

Marcel, Henchoz. 1949. *Yearbook of International Organizations 1949*. New York: Hafner.

March, James G. 1994. *A Primer on Decision Making: How Decisions Happen*. New York: Free Press.

March, James G., and Johan P. Olsen. 1989. *Rediscovering Institutions: The Organizational Basis of Politics*. New York: Free Press.

Marchand, Marianne H., and Jane Parpart, eds. 1995. *Feminism/Postmodernism/Development*. London: Routledge.

Marsh, George P. 1965 [1864]. *Man and Nature*. Edited by David Lowenthal. Cambridge, Mass.: Belknap Press.

Matsunawa, T. 1986. "Poisson Distribution." In Samuel Kotz and Norman Lloyd Johnson, eds., *Encyclopedia of Statistical Sciences*, pp. 20–25. New York: John Wiley & Sons.

Mauldin, William P., and Robert Lapham. 1985. "Measuring Family Program Effort in Developing Countries in 1972 and 1982." In Nancy Birdsall, ed., *The Effects of Family Planning Programs on Fertility in the Developing World*, pp. 7–39. World Bank Working Papers, Number 677. Washington, D.C.: World Bank.

McClellan, James E. 1985. *Science Reorganized: Scientific Societies in the Eighteenth Century*. New York: Columbia University Press.

McClelland, David C. 1961. *The Achieving Society*. Princeton, N.J.: Van Nostrand.

McCormick, John. 1989. *Reclaiming Paradise*. Bloomington: Indiana University Press.

———. 1993. "International Nongovernmental Organizations: Prospects for a Global Environmental Movement." In Sheldon Kamieniecki, ed., *Environmental Politics in the International Arena*, pp. 131–42. Albany: State University of New York Press.

McCoy, Michael, and Patrick McCully. 1993. *The Road From Rio: An NGO Action Guide to Environment and Development*. Utrecht: International Books.

McElroy, Robert. 1992. *Morality and American Foreign Policy*. Princeton, N.J.: Princeton University Press.

McIntosh, Robert P. 1976. "Ecology Since 1900." In B. J. Taylor and T. J. White, eds., *Issues and Ideas in America*, pp. 353–72. Norman, Okla.: University of Oklahoma Press.

McMichael, Philip. 1996. *Development and Social Change: A Global Perspective*. Thousand Oaks, Calif.: Pine Forge Press.

McNeely, Connie. 1995. *Constructing the Nation-State: International Organization and Prescriptive Action*. Westport, Conn.: Greenwood.

McPherson, J. Miller, Pamela Popielarz, and Sonja Drobnic. 1992. "Social Networks and Organizational Dynamics." *American Sociological Review* 57: 153–70.

Meier, Gerald M., ed. 1995. *Leading Issues in Economic Development*. 6th ed. New York: Oxford University Press.

Melko, Matthew. 1995. "The Nature of Civilizations." In Stephen K. Sanderson, ed., *Civilizations and World Systems*, pp. 25–45. Walnut Creek, Calif.: Altamira Press.

Merton, Robert K. 1942. "The Normative Structure of Science." In Norman W. Storer, ed., *The Sociology of Science: Theoretical and Empirical Investigations*, pp. 267–78. Chicago: University of Chicago Press.

———. 1970 [1938]. *Science, Technology, and Society in Seventeenth Century England*. New York: Howard Fertig.

Meyer, Alfred. 1977. "Marxism and the Women's Movement." In Dorothy Atkinson, Alexander Dallin, and Gail W. Lapidus, eds., *Women in Russia*, pp. 85–112. Stanford, Calif.: Stanford University Press.

Meyer, John W. 1987a. "The World Polity and the Authority of the Nation-State." In George M. Thomas, John W. Meyer, Francisco O. Ramirez, and John Boli, *Institutional Structure: Constituting State, Society and the Individual*, pp. 41–70. Beverly Hills, Calif.: Sage.

———. 1987b. "Self and the Life Course: Institutionalization and Its Effects." In George M. Thomas, John W. Meyer, Francisco O. Ramirez, and John Boli, *Institutional Structure: Constituting State, Society and the Individual*, pp. 242–60. Beverly Hills, Calif.: Sage.

———. 1994. "Rationalized Environments." In W. Richard Scott and John W. Meyer, *Institutional Environments and Organizations: Structural Complexity and Individualism*, pp. 28–54. Thousand Oaks, Calif: Sage.

———. Forthcoming. "The Changing Cultural Content of the Nation-State." In George Steinmetz, ed., *New Approaches to the State in the Social Sciences*. Ithaca, N.Y.: Cornell University Press.

Meyer, John W., John Boli, and George M. Thomas. 1987. "Ontology and Rationalization in the Western Cultural Account." In George M. Thomas, John W. Meyer, Francisco O. Ramirez, and John Boli, *Institutional Structure: Constituting State, Society, and the Individual*, pp. 12–37. Beverly Hills, Calif.: Sage.

Meyer, John W., John Boli, George M. Thomas, and Francisco O. Ramirez. 1997. "World Society and the Nation-State." *American Journal of Sociology* 103, no. 1: 144–81.

Meyer, John W., David Frank, Ann Hironaka, Evan Schofer, and Nancy B. Tuma. 1994. "The Rise of an Environmental Sector in World Society." Paper presented at the American Sociological Association meetings in Los Angeles, Calif., August.

———. 1995. "The Structuring of World Society, 1870–1990: The Case of the Environment." Working Paper, Department of Sociology, Stanford University.

———. 1997. "The Structuring of a World Environmental Regime, 1870–1990." *International Organization* 51: 623–51.

Meyer, John W., and Michael T. Hannan, eds. 1979. *National Development and the World System: Educational, Economic, and Political Change, 1950–1970*. Chicago: University of Chicago Press.

Meyer, John W., and Ronald L. Jepperson. Forthcoming. "The 'Actors' of Modern Society: The Cultural Construction of Social Agency." In Walter W. Powell and David Jones, eds., *Remaking the Iron Cage: Institutional Dynamics and Processes*. Chicago: University of Chicago Press.

Meyer, John W., David Kamens, Aaron Benavot, Yun-Kyung Cha, and Suk-Ying Wong. 1992. *School Knowledge for the Masses*. London: Falmer Press.

Meyer, John W., Francisco O. Ramirez, and Yasemin Soysal. 1992. "World Expansion of Mass Education, 1870–1980." *Sociology of Education* 65, no. 2: 128–49.

Meyer, John W., and Brian Rowan. 1977. "Institutionalized Organizations: Formal Structure as Myth and Ceremony." *American Journal of Sociology* 83, no. 2: 340–63.

Milbank, Dana. 1994. "New Competitor: East Europe's Industry Is Raising Quality and Taking on the West." *Wall Street Journal*, September 21, p. A1.

Miller, Carol. 1994. "Geneva—the Key to Equality." *Women's History Review* 3, no. 2: 219–45.

Mills, C. Wright. 1940. "Situated Actions and Vocabularies of Motive." *American Sociological Review* 5: 904–13.

Mitchell, Robert Cameron, Angela G. Mertig, and Riley E. Dunlap. 1992. "Twenty Years of Environmental Mobilization." In Riley E. Dunlap and Angela G. Mertig, eds., *American Environmentalism*, pp. 11–26. Philadelphia: Taylor & Francis.

Mitrany, David. 1943. *A Working Peace System: An Argument for the Functional Development of International Organization*. London: Royal Institute of International Affairs.

Mobil Europe, Ltd. 1995. "The Mobil Survey of ISO 9000 Certificates Awarded Worldwide (Fourth Cycle)." *Quality Systems Update* 5, no. 9: 8–12.

Mohanty, Chandra Talpade. 1991. "Under Western Eyes and Colonial Discourses." In Chandra Talpade Mohanty, Ann Russo, and Lourdes Torres, eds., *Third World Women and the Politics of Feminism*, pp. 51–80. Bloomington: Indiana University Press.

Mongardini, Carlo. 1988. "Contradictions in Social Change: Reflections on the Ideological Transformation of Present-Day Europe." *Research in Social Movements, Conflicts and Change* 10: 213–23.

Montgomery, John Dickey. 1988. *Bureaucrats and People: Grassroots Participation in Third World Development*. Baltimore: Johns Hopkins University Press.

Morgenthau, Hans. 1960. *Politics Among Nations: The Struggle for Power and Peace*. 3d ed. New York: Knopf.

———. 1973. *Politics Among Nations*. 5th ed. New York: Knopf.

Morse, David. 1969. *The Origin and Evolution of the ILO and Its Role in the World Community*. Ithaca: New York School of Industrial and Labor Relations, Cornell University.

Murphy, Craig N. 1994. *International Organization and Industrial Change: Global Governance Since 1850*. New York: Oxford University Press.

Myrdal, Gunnar. 1957. *Economic Theory and Under-Developed Regions*. London: Duckworth.

Myres, Denys. 1935. *Handbook of the League of Nations: A Comprehensive Account of Its Structure, Operation and Activities*. New York: World Peace Foundation.

Nadelmann, Ethan A. 1990. "Global Prohibition Regimes: The Evolution of Norms in International Society." *International Organization* 44, no. 4: 479–526.

Nature. 1876. London: MacMillan Journals.

Nelkin, Dorothy, and Michael Pollak. 1981. *The Atom Besieged*. Cambridge, Mass.: MIT Press.

Nettl, J. P., and Roland Robertson. 1968. *International Systems and the Modernization of Societies: The Formation of National Goals and Attitudes*. London: Faber & Faber.

Noddings, Nel. 1984. *Caring: A Feminine Approach to Ethics and Moral Education.* Berkeley: University of California Press.

Noel, Alain, and Jean-Philippe Thérien. 1995. "From Domestic to International Justice: The Welfare State and Foreign Aid." *International Organization* 49: 523–53.

Northedge, Frederick S. 1976. "Transnationalism: The American Illusion." *Millennium* 5: 21–28.

———. 1988. *The League Of Nations: Its Life and Times. 1920–1946.* Leicester, Eng.: Leicester University Press.

Offen, Karen. 1987. "Liberty, Equality, and Justice for Women: The Theory and Practice of Feminism in Nineteenth-Century Europe." In Renate Bridenthal, Claudia Koonz, and Susan Stuard, eds., *Becoming Visible: Women in European History*, pp. 335–73. Boston: Houghton Mifflin.

Olson, Mancur. 1965. *The Logic of Collective Action.* Cambridge, Mass.: Harvard University Press.

Onuf, Nicholas Greenwood. 1989. *World of Our Making: Rules and Rule in Social Theory and International Relations.* Columbia: University of South Carolina Press.

Open Door Council. 1929. *Report of the Conference Called by the Open Door Council.* Berlin: Open Door Council.

Organization for Economic Cooperation and Development (OECD). 1988. *Voluntary Aid for Development: The Role of Non-Governmental Organisations.* Paris: OECD.

Organization for Economic Cooperation and Development, Development Assistance Committee (OECD-DAC). 1994. *Development Cooperation: Efforts and Policies of the Development Assistance Committee, 1993 Report.* Paris: OECD.

Organization for Economic Cooperation and Development, Development Centre (OECD-DC). 1991. *Directory of Development Research and Training Institutes in Europe.* Paris: OECD.

———. 1981. *Directory of Non-Governmental Organizations in OECD Member Countries Active in Development Cooperation.* Paris: OECD.

———. 1990. *Directory of Non-Governmental Development Organizations in OECD Member Countries.* Paris: OECD.

———. 1992. *Directory of Research and Training Institutes in Africa.* Paris: OECD.

———. 1993. *Directory of Research and Training Institutes in Latin America.* Paris: OECD.

———. 1995. *Database of Non-Governmental Development Organizations in OECD Member Countries.* Paris: OECD.

Ornstein, Martha. 1928. *The Role of Scientific Societies in Seventeenth Century Europe.* Chicago: University of Chicago Press.

Otto, Dianne. 1996. "Nongovernmental Organizations in the United Nations System: The Emerging Role of International Civil Society." *Human Rights Quarterly* 18: 107–41.

Papanek, Hanna. 1975. "The Work of Women: Postscript from Mexico City." *Signs* 1, no. 1: 215–26.

Parsons, Talcott. 1964. "Evolutionary Universals in Society." *American Sociological Review* 29: 339–57.

Parzybok, William. 1994. "ISO 9000." *Industry Week*, June 6, p. 35.

Paul, Samuel, and Arturo Israel, eds. 1991. *Nongovernmental Organizations and the World Bank: Cooperation for Development.* Washington, D.C.: World Bank.

Pepper, David. 1984. *The Roots of Modern Environmentalism.* London: Croom Helm.

Perrow, Charles. 1979. *Complex Organizations.* 3d ed. New York: McGraw-Hill.

Peterson, Martin. 1993. "Cultural Identity and the Formation of Sub-National, National and Trans-National Ideologies." *Scandinavian Journal of Development Alternatives* 12, no. 4: 5–31.

Petras, James, with Morris H. Morley, Peter DeWitt, and A. Eugene Havens. 1981. *Class, State and Power in the Third World, with Case Studies on Class Conflict in Latin America.* Montclair, N.J.: Allanheld, Osmun.

Pfister, Ulrich, and Christian Suter. 1987. "International Financial Relations as Part of the World System." *International Studies Quarterly* 31, no. 3: 239–72.

Pictet, Jean. 1964. "Centième anniversaire de la première convention de Genève." *Revue internationale de la Croix-Rouge*, August: 380–414. Geneva: ICRC.

Pierpoint, Raymond. 1922. *Report of the Fifth International Neo-Malthusian and Birth Control Conference.* Kingsway Hall, London, July 11–14. London: William Heinemann.

Pietila, Hilkka, and Jeanne Vickers. 1990. *Making Women Matter: The Role of the United Nations.* London: Zed Books.

Pitt-Rivers, G. H. L. F., ed. 1932. *Problems of Population: Being the Report of the Proceedings of the Second General Assembly of the International Union for the Scientific Investigation of Population Problems held at the Royal Society of Arts, London, June 15–18, 1931.* London: George Allen & Unwin.

Powell, Walter W., and Paul J. DiMaggio, eds. 1991. *The New Institutionalism in Organizational Analysis.* Chicago: University of Chicago Press.

Power, Michael. 1997. "Standardizing Management Control." Paper presented at the SCANCOR/SCORE Seminar on Standardization, Arild, Sweden, September 18–20. London: London School of Economics and Political Science.

Rahnema, Majid. 1993. "Participation." In Wolfgang Sachs, ed., *The Development Dictionary*, pp. 116–31. London: Zed.

Ramirez, Francisco O. 1987. "Global Changes, World Myths, and the Demise of Cultural Gender." In Terry Boswell and Albert J. Bergesen, eds., *America's Changing Role in the World-System*, pp. 257–73. New York: Praeger.

Ramirez, Francisco O., and John Boli. 1987a. "Global Patterns of Educational Institutionalization." In George M. Thomas, John W. Meyer, Francisco O. Ramirez, and John Boli, *Institutional Structure: Constituting State, Society, and the Individual*, pp. 150–72. Beverly Hills, Calif.: Sage.

———. 1987b. "On the Union of States and Schools." In George M. Thomas, John W. Meyer, Francisco O. Ramirez, and John Boli, *Institutional Structure: Constituting State, Society, and the Individual*, pp. 173–97. Beverly Hills, Calif.: Sage.

———. 1987c. "The Political Construction of Mass Schooling: European Origins and Worldwide Institutionalization." *Sociology of Education* 60 (January): 2–17.

Ramirez, Francisco O., and Molly Lee. 1995. "Education, Science, and Economic Development." In Gerard Postiglione and Lee Wing-On, eds., *Social Change and Educational Development in Mainland China, Taiwan, and Hongkong*, pp. 15–39. Hongkong: University of Hongkong, Center for Asian Studies.

Ranger-Moore, James, Jane Banaszak-Holl, and Michael T. Hannan. 1991. "Density-Dependent Dynamics in Regulated Industries: Founding Rates of Banks and Life Insurance Companies." *Administrative Science Quarterly* 36: 36–65.

Rawls, John. 1971. *A Theory of Justice*. Cambridge, Mass.: Harvard University Press.

Razak, Victoria. 1995. "Culture under Construction: The Future of Native Arubian Identity." *Futures* 27, no. 4: 447–59.

Reanda, Laura. 1992. "The Commission on the Status of Women." In Philip Alston, ed., *The United Nations and Human Rights: A Critical Appraisal*, pp. 265–303. Oxford: Clarendon Press.

Restivo, Sal. 1988. "Modern Science as a Social Problem." *Social Problems* 35 (June): 206–25.

Robbins, Bruce. 1992. "Comparative Cosmopolitanism." *Social Text* 31/32: 169–86.

Robertson, Roland. 1992. *Globalization: Social Theory and Global Culture*. Newbury Park, Calif.: Sage.

———. 1994. "Globalization or Glocalization." *Journal of International Communication* 1, no. 1: 33–52.

Rogers, Hudson P., and C. M. Kochunny. 1994. "Assessing Worldmindedness

Among Students: An Exploratory Study." *Journal of Teaching in International Business* 5: 17–33.

Rosenau, James, and Ernst Otto Czempiel. 1992. *Governance Without Government: Order and Change in World Politics*. Cambridge: Cambridge University Press.

Rubinson, Richard. 1978. "Political Transformation in Germany and the United States." In Barbara H. Kaplan, ed., *Social Change in the Capitalist World Economy*, pp. 39–74. Beverly Hills, Calif.: Sage.

Russell, Colin A. 1983. *Science and Social Change, 1700–1900*. New York: MacMillan Press.

Sachs, Michael, ed. 1990. *World Guide to Scientific Associations and Learned Societies*. 5th ed. Munich: K. G. Saur.

Salter, Liora, ed. 1993. "Have We Reached the Information Age Yet? The Political Economy of Information Standards." *International Journal of Political Economy* 23 (Winter): 3–133.

Sanger, Margaret, and Hannah Stone, eds. 1931. *The Practice of Contraception: An International Symposium and Survey*. From the Proceedings of the Seventh International Birth Control Conference, Zurich, Switzerland, September 1930. Baltimore: Williams & Wilkins.

Schofer, Evan, Francisco O. Ramirez, and John W. Meyer. 1997. "The Effects of Science on National Economic Development." Presented at the American Sociological Association meetings, Toronto, Ontario, August.

Schreiber, Adele, and Margaret Mathieson. 1955. *Journey Towards Freedom*. Written for the Golden Jubilee of the International Alliance of Women. Copenhagen: International Alliance of Women.

Schultz, Theodore W., ed. 1945. *Food for the World*. Chicago: University of Chicago Press.

Scott, Marvin B., and Stanford M. Lyman. 1968. "Accounts." *American Sociological Review* 33 (February): 46–62.

Scott, W. Richard, and John W. Meyer. 1991. "The Organization of Societal Sectors." In Walter W. Powell and Paul J. DiMaggio, eds., *The New Institutionalism in Organizational Analysis*, pp. 108–40. Chicago: University of Chicago Press.

Seligman, Adam B. 1992. *The Idea of Civil Society*. New York: Free Press.

Sen, Gita, and Caren Grown. 1987. *Development, Crises, and Alternative Visions: Third World Women's Perspective*. New York: Monthly Review Press.

Sewall, May Wright, comp. 1914. *Genesis of the International Council of Women and the Story of Its Growth, 1888–1893*. Indianapolis: International Council of Women.

Sewell, William H., Jr. 1992. "A Theory of Structure: Duality, Agency, and Transformation." *American Journal of Sociology* 98 (July): 1–29.

Shanks, Cheryl, Harold K. Jacobson, and Jeffrey H. Kaplan. 1996. "Inertia and Change in the Constellation of International Governmental Organizations, 1981–1992." *International Organization* 50, no. 4: 593–627.

Shapin, Steven, and Simon Schaffer. 1985. *Leviathan and the Air-Pump: Hobbes, Boyle and the Experimental Life.* Princeton, N.J.: Princeton University Press.

Sikkink, Kathryn. 1993. "Human Rights, Principled Issue-Networks, and Sovereignty in Latin America." *International Organization* 47 (Summer): 411–41.

Skocpol, Theda. 1979. *States and Social Revolutions: A Comparative Analysis of France, Russia, and China.* Cambridge: Cambridge University Press.

———. 1985. "Bringing the State Back In: Strategies of Analysis in Current Research." In Peter Evans, Dietrich Rueschemeyer, and Theda Skocpol, eds., *Bringing the State Back In*, pp. 3–43. Cambridge: Cambridge University Press.

Skolnick, Arlene S. 1992. *The Intimate Environment: Exploring Marriage and the Family.* 5th ed. New York: HarperCollins.

Slotten, Richard H. 1994. *Patronage, Practice, and the Culture of American Science.* Cambridge: Cambridge University Press.

Smillie, Ian, and Hans Helmich. 1993. *Non-Governmental Organisations and Governments: Stakeholders for Development.* Paris: OECD Development Centre.

Smith, Anthony. 1980. *The Geopolitics of Information: How Western Culture Dominates the World.* London: Faber & Faber.

Smith, Brian H. 1990. *More than Altruism: The Politics of Private Foreign Aid.* Princeton, N.J.: Princeton University Press.

Smith, Jackie. 1997. "Characteristics of the Modern Transnational Social Movement Sector." In Jackie Smith, Charles Chatfield, and Ron Pagnucco, eds., *Transnational Social Movements and Global Politics: Solidarity Beyond the State*, pp. 42–58. Syracuse, N.Y.: Syracuse University Press.

Smith, Jackie, Charles Chatfield, and Ron Pagnucco, eds. 1997. *Transnational Social Movements and Global Politics: Solidarity Beyond the State.* Syracuse, N.Y.: Syracuse University Press.

Smith, Jackie, Ron Pagnucco, and Winnie Romeril. 1994. "Transnational Social Movement Organisations in the Global Political Arena." *Voluntas* 5: 121–54.

Snow, C. P. 1959. *The Two Cultures.* Cambridge: Cambridge University Press.

Sommer, John G. 1977. *Beyond Charity: U.S. Voluntary Aid for a Changing Third World.* Washington, D.C.: Overseas Development Council.

Sorokin, Pitirim. 1957. *Social and Cultural Dynamics.* Boston: Porter Sargent.

Sowerwine, Charles. 1987. "The Socialist Women's Movement from 1850 to 1940." In Renate Bridenthal, Claudia Koonz, and Susan Stuard, eds.,

Becoming Visible: Women in European History, pp. 399–426. Boston: Houghton Mifflin.

Soysal, Yasemin Nuhoglu. 1994. *The Limits of Citizenship: Migrants and Postnational Membership in Europe.* Chicago: University of Chicago Press.

Speeckaert, Georges Patrick. 1957. "The 1,978 International Organizations Founded Since the Congress of Vienna." In *Documents for the Study of International Nongovernment Relations*, no. 7. Brussels: Union of International Associations.

Spencer, Anna Garlin. 1930. *The Council Idea: A Chronicle of Its Prophets and a Tribute to May Wright Sewall.* New Brunswick, N.J.: J. Heidingsfeld.

Spengler, Oswald. 1932. *The Decline of the West.* London: Allen & Unwin.

Spiro, Peter J. 1995. "New Global Communities: Nongovernmental Organizations in International Decision-Making." *The Washington Quarterly* 18, no. 1: 45–56.

Stanley, Edith Kirkendall. 1983. *Ten Decades of White Ribbon Service, 1883–1983.* Cincinnati: Revivalist Press.

Staunton, Dorothy. 1956. *Our Goodly Heritage: A Historical Review of the World's Woman's Christian Temperance Union, 1883–1956.* N.p.: n.p.

Stein, Arthur. 1993. "Coordination and Collaboration: Regimes in an Anarchic World." In David A. Baldwin, ed., *Neorealism and Neoliberalism: The Contemporary Debate*, pp. 29–59. New York: Columbia University Press.

Steinberg, Stephen. 1989. *The Ethnic Myth: Race, Ethnicity, and Class in America.* Boston: Beacon Press.

Stern, Paul C., Oran R. Young, and Daniel Druckman, eds. 1992. *Global Environmental Change.* Washington, D.C.: National Academy Press.

Stetson, Dorothy McBride, and Amy G. Mazur, eds. 1995. *Comparative State Feminism.* Thousand Oaks, Calif.: Sage.

Stienstra, Deborah. 1994. *Women's Movements and International Organizations.* New York: St. Martin's Press.

Stinchcombe, Arthur L. 1968. *Constructing Social Theories.* New York: Harcourt, Brace & World.

Strang, David. 1990. "From Dependence to Sovereignty: An Event History Analysis of Decolonization." *American Sociological Review* 55: 846–60.

Swedish Standards Institute (SIS). 1993. *Standardization in Sweden, 1922–1992: Summary and Guide.* Stockholm: SIS.

Swidler, Ann. 1986. "Culture in Action." *American Sociological Review* 51 (April): 273–86.

Tamm Hallström, Kristina. 1997. "The Authority of Two International Standard Setters." Presented at the SCANCOR/SCORE Seminar on Standardization, Arild, Sweden, September 18–20. Stockholm: Stockholm Center for Organizational Research.

Taubenfeld, Rita Falk, and Howard J. Taubenfeld. 1983. *Sex-Based Discrimi-*

nation: International Law and Organizations. Part 4. Dobbs Ferry, N.Y.: Oceana.

Tax, Meredith. 1980. *The Rising of the Women: Feminist Solidarity and Class Conflict, 1880–1917.* New York: Monthly Review Press.

Taylor, Peter J. and Frederick H. Buttel. 1992. "How Do We Know We Have Environmental Problems? Science and the Globalization of Environmental Discourse." *Geoforum* 23: 405–16.

Teich, Mikuláš. 1989. "Electrical Research, Standardization and the Beginnings of the Corporate Economy." In Alice Teichova, Maurice Lévy-Leboyer, and Helga Nussbaum, eds., *Historical Studies in International Corporate Business,* pp. 29–42. Cambridge: Cambridge University Press.

Thayer, Ann. 1994. "Chemical Companies See Beneficial Results From ISO 9000 Registration." *Chemical Engineering News,* April 25, pp. 10–26.

Thérien, Jean-Philippe. 1991. "Non-Governmental Organizations and International Development Assistance." *Canadian Journal of Development Studies,* 12, no. 2: 263–80.

Thomas, George M. 1989. *Revivalism and Cultural Change: Christianity, Nation-Building, and the Market in the Nineteenth-Century United States.* Chicago: University of Chicago Press.

————. 1993. "U.S. Discourse and Strategies in the New World Order." In David Jacobson, ed., *Old Nations, New World: Conceptions of World Order,* pp. 143–72. Boulder, Colo.: Westview.

Thomas, George M., and Pat Lauderdale. 1987. "World Polity Sources of National Welfare and Land Reform." In George M. Thomas, John W. Meyer, Francisco O. Ramirez, and John Boli, *Institutional Structure: Constituting State, Society, and the Individual,* pp. 198–214. Beverly Hills, Calif.: Sage.

————. 1988. "State Authority and National Welfare Programs in the World System Context." *Sociological Forum* 3, no. 3: 383–99.

Thomas, George M., and John W. Meyer. 1984. "The Expansion of the State." *Annual Review of Sociology* 10: 461–82.

Thomas, George M., John W. Meyer, Francisco O. Ramirez, and John Boli. 1987. *Institutional Structure: Constituting State, Society, and the Individual.* Beverly Hills, Calif.: Sage.

Thränhardt, Dietrich. 1992. "Globale Probleme, globale Normen, neue globale Akteure." *Politische Vierteljahresschrift* 33, no. 2: 218–34.

Tilly, Charles. 1978. *From Mobilization to Revolution.* Reading, Mass.: Addison-Wesley.

————. 1985. "War Making and State Making as Organized Crime." In Peter Evans, Dietrich Rueschemeyer, and Theda Skocpol, eds., *Bringing the State Back In,* pp. 169–91. Cambridge: Cambridge University Press.

———. 1992. *Coercion, Capital, and European States, A.D. 990–1992*. Rev. ed. Cambridge, Mass.: Blackwell.

———, ed. 1975. *The Formation of National States in Western Europe.* Princeton, N.J.: Princeton University Press.

Timbers, Michael J. 1992. "ISO 9000 and Europe's Attempts to Mandate Quality." *Journal of European Business* 3 (March–April): 14–25.

Tinker, Irene, and Jane Jacquette. 1987. "UN Decade for Women: Its Impact and Legacy." *World Development* 15 (3): 419–27.

Tocqueville, Alexis de. 1966 [1836]. *Democracy in America.* New York: Doubleday.

Tomlinson, John. 1991. *Cultural Imperialism: A Critical Introduction.* London: Pinter.

Toulmin, Stephen. 1989. *Cosmopolis.* New York: Free Press.

Toynbee, Arnold Joseph. 1947. "The Present Point in History." In Arnold Joseph Toynbee, ed., *Civilization on Trial*, pp. 16–28. Oxford: Oxford University Press.

Trzyna, Thaddeus C., and Roberta Childers. 1992. *World Directory of Environmental Organizations.* 4th ed. Sacramento: California Institute of Public Affairs.

Tuma, Nancy B. 1992. *Invoking Rate.* Palo Alto, Calif.: DMA Corporation.

Tuma, Nancy B., and Michael T. Hannan. 1984. *Social Dynamics: Models and Methods.* Orlando, Fla.: Academic Press.

Turner, Bryan S. 1986. *Citizenship and Capitalism: The Debate over Reformism.* London: Allan & Unwin.

———. 1993. "Outline of the Theory of Human Rights." In Bryan S. Turner, ed., *Citizenship and Social Theory*, pp. 162–90. London: Sage.

Tyrrell, Ian. 1991. *Woman's World / Woman's Empire: The Woman's Christian Temperance Movement in International Perspective, 1880–1930.* Chapel Hill: University of North Carolina Press.

Union of International Associations (UIA). 1950–95. *The Yearbook of International Organizations.* Munich: K. G. Saur.

———. 1994. Extract of database on international non-governmental organizations supplied to John Boli, Emory University. Brussels: UIA.

United Nations (UN). 1947–48, 1975, 1976, 1980, 1981, 1985. *Yearbook of the United Nations.* New York: Office of Public Information, United Nations.

———. 1987. *Global Population Policy Database.* New York: UN Department of International Economic and Social Affairs.

———. 1989a. *Global Review and Inventory of Population Policies.* New York: UN.

———. 1989b. *World Population Policies.* Vols. 1–3. New York: UN Department of International Economic and Social Affairs, Population Studies No. 102.

———. 1989c. *Case Studies in Population Policy.* New York: UN Department of International Economic and Social Affairs.

———. 1990. *International Trade Statistics Yearbook: 1991.* New York: UN.

———. Various Years. *Population Policy Compendium: Country Reports.* New York: UN.

———. Various years. *Statistical Yearbook.* New York: UN.

UNAIDS Programme. 1996. "Fact Sheet: UNAIDS." Geneva: World Health Organization.

United Nations Development Programme. 1993. *Human Development Report.* New York: Oxford University Press.

United Nations Educational, Scientific, and Cultural Organization (UNESCO). 1965–90. *UNESCO Statistical Yearbook.* Louvain: UNESCO.

———. 1991. *African Development Sourcebook.* 1st ed. Paris: UNESCO.

United Nations Environment Programme (UNEP). 1991. *Environmental Data Report.* 3d ed. Oxford: Basil Blackwell.

United Nations Fund for Population Activities (UNFPA). 1988. *Population Profiles.* Vol. 2: *Law and Population.* New York: UN.

United Nations Institute for Training and Research (UNITR). 1984. *The Principle of Participatory Equality of Developing Countries in International Economic Relations: Analytical Paper and Supplementary Notations and Amendments to Analytical Compilation of Texts of Relevant Instruments* (Progressive Development of the Principles and Norms of International Law Relating to the New International Economic Order No. UNITAR/ DS/6/Add.1). New York: UN.

Universal Esperanto Association (UEA). 1979. *Translation in International Organizations.* Esperanto Documents, vol. 20. Rotterdam: UEA.

———. 1981a. *Esperanto and the Universal Esperanto Association.* Esperanto Documents, vol. 23A. Rotterdam: UEA.

———. 1981b. *Constitution of the Universal Esperanto Association.* Esperanto Documents, vol. 25A. Rotterdam: UEA.

Van de Veer, Peter. 1994. *Religious Nationalism: Hindus and Muslims in India.* Berkeley: University of California Press.

Van Steenbergen, Bart. 1994. "Towards a Global Ecological Citizen." In Bart van Steenbergen, ed., *The Condition of Citizenship*, pp. 141–52. London: Sage.

Ventresca, Marc. 1990. "Counting People When People Count: Global Establishment of the Modern Population Census, 1820–1980." Paper presented at the Asilomar Conference on Organizations, Asilomar, Calif., September.

———. 1995. *When States Count: Institutional and Political Dynamics in Modern Census Establishment, 1800–1993.* Ph.D. diss., Stanford University.

Voss, Bristol. 1994. "Mexico Will Use ISO 9000 to Raise Trade Barriers." *Journal of Business Strategy* 15, no. 3: 6.

Waggaman, Mary T. 1919. "First International Congress of Working Women, Washington, D.C." *Monthly Labor Review* 9, no. 6: 280–98.

Walgenbach, Peter. 1997. "Show Biz Hype or Rowing on the Galley: On the Use of the ISO 9000 Standards in Companies." Paper presented at the SCANCOR/SCORE Seminar on Standardization, Arild, Sweden, September 18–20. Mannheim: Fakultät für Betriebswirtschaftslehre.

Wallace, Michael, and J. David Singer. 1970. "Inter-Governmental Organization and the Preservation of Peace, 1816–1965: Some Bivariate Relationships." *International Organization* 24: 520–47.

Wallerstein, Immanuel. 1974. *The Modern World-System: Capitalist Agriculture and the Origins of the European World Economy in the Sixteenth Century.* New York: Academic Press.

———. 1979. *The Capitalist World-Economy.* Cambridge: Cambridge University Press.

———. 1990. "Culture as the Ideological Battleground of the Modern World-System." In Mike Featherstone, ed., *Global Culture: Nationalism, Globalization and Modernity,* pp. 31–55. London: Sage.

———. 1991. *Geopolitics and Geoculture: Essays on the Changing World-System.* Cambridge: Cambridge University Press.

Wallerstein, Immanuel, and Terrence Hopkins. 1980. *Processes of the World-System.* Beverly Hills, Calif.: Sage.

Waltz, Kenneth M. 1979. *Theory of International Politics.* Reading, Mass.: Addison-Wesley.

Walzer, Michael. 1977. *Just and Unjust Wars: A Moral Argument with Historical Illustrations.* New York: Basic Books.

Wapner, Paul. 1996. *Environmental Activism and World Civic Politics.* Albany: State University of New York Press.

Warwick, Donald P. 1979. "Cultural Values and Population Policies: Cases and Contexts." In John Montgomery, Harold Lasswell, and Joel Migdal, eds., *Patterns of Policy: Comparative and Longitudinal Studies of Population Events,* pp. 295–337. New Brunswick, N.J.: Transaction Books.

Watson, Adam. 1992. *The Evolution of International Society: A Comparative Historical Analysis.* London: Routledge.

Weber, Max. 1946. *From Max Weber.* Translated by Hans H. Gerth and C. Wright Mills. New York: Oxford University Press.

———. 1968. *Economy and Society: An Outline of Interpretive Sociology.* 2 vols. Edited by Guenther Roth and Claus Wittich. Translated by Ephraim Fischoff et al. New York: Bedminster.

Weiss, Edith Brown. 1989. "Legal Dimensions of Global Change: A Proposed Research Agenda." *International Social Science Journal* 41, no. 3 (121): 399–412.

Weiss, Thomas G., Leon Gordenker Jr., and Thomas J. Watson. 1996. *NGOs, the UN, and Global Governance*. Boulder, Colo.: Lynne Rienner.

Wendt, Alexander. 1992. "Anarchy Is What States Make of It: The Social Construction of Power Politics." *International Organization* 46, no. 2: 391–425.

Wendt, Alexander, and Raymond Duvall. 1989. "Institutions and Order in the International System." In Ernst Otto Czempiel and James Rosenau, eds., *Global Changes and Theoretical Challenges*, pp. 51–73. London: Lexington.

Weston, Burns H., Richard A. Falk, and Anthony A. D'Amato. 1980. *International Law and World Order: A Problem-Oriented Coursebook*. St. Paul, Minn.: West Publishing.

Whittick, Arnold. 1979. *Woman into Citizen*. Santa Barbara, Calif.: ABC-Clio.

Willets, Peter, ed. 1982. *Pressure Groups in the Global System: The Transnational Relations of Issue-Oriented Non-Governmental Organizations*. London: Frances Pinter.

Wiseberg, Laurie S. 1991. "Human Rights NGO's." In Alex Geert Castermans, Lydia Schut, Frank Steketee, and Luc Verhey, eds., *The Role of Non-Governmental Organizations in the Promotion and Protection of Human Rights*, pp. 23–44. Leiden: Stichting NJCM-Boekerij.

Woman Suffrage in Practice. 1913. *The International Woman Suffrage Alliance*. Compiled by Chrystal Macmillan et al. London: National Union of Women's Suffrage Societies.

World Bank. Operations Policy Research and Planning Group. Operations Policy Department. NGO Unit. 1996. *Development NGO Database*. Washington, D.C.: World Bank.

World Bank. 1997. *World Development Report 1997: The State in a Changing World*. New York: Oxford University Press.

Wuthnow, Robert. 1980. "The World-Economy and the Institutionalization of Science in Seventeenth-Century Europe." In Albert Bergesen, ed., *Studies of the Modern World-System*, pp. 25–55. New York: Academic Press.

———. 1987. *Meaning and Moral Order: Explorations in Cultural Analysis*. Berkeley: University of California Press.

———. 1989. *Communities of Discourse*. Cambridge, Mass.: Harvard University Press.

———, ed. 1991. *Between States and Markets: The Voluntary Sector in Comparative Perspective*. Princeton, N.J.: Princeton University Press.

Young, Oran R. 1989. *International Cooperation: Building Regimes for Natural Resources and the Environment.* Ithaca, N.Y.: Cornell University Press.

Zucker, Lynne G. 1988. *Institutional Patterns and Organizations: Culture and Environment.* Cambridge, Mass.: Ballinger.

Zuckerman, Harriet. 1989. "The Sociology of Science." In Neil Smelser, ed., *Handbook of Sociology*, pp. 511–74. Newbury Park, Calif.: Sage.

Index

In this index an "f" after a number indicates a separate reference on the next page, and an "ff" indicates separate references on the next two pages. A continuous discussion over two or more pages is indicated by a span of page numbers, e.g., "57–59." *Passim* is used for a cluster of references in close but not consecutive sequence.

Agency, 4, 35, 40, 163f, 295, 304n6; of actors, 3ff, 13, 18, 29–30, 37, 295–98. *See also* Enactment
American National Standards Institute (ANSI), 176, 290
Anarchy, global, 15, 27
Anthony, Susan B., 104
Anti-slavery, 108, 228
Appia, Louis, 155, 161
Austria-Prussia war (1866), 159–60
Authority: charismatic, 193, 273, 283–84; cultural, 37, 298; of INGOs, 37, 48, 116f, 176, 193–97 *passim*, 267–73 *passim*, 283, 288–94, 298–99, 309n6; of nation-states, 43–48 *passim*, 114, 130, 142, 152, 190, 277; rational-legal, 14, 48, 193, 273, 277–82 *passim*, 286, 292; rational voluntarist, 17, 35–38 *passim*, 45, 47, 194, 273, 277–83 *passim*, 289, 292; traditional/patriarchal, 193, 273; world, 46, 48, 267, 277–94, 306n17
Autonomous authority, *see under* Authority, of INGOs

Balkan Wars (1875–78), 160–61
Birth control, 208f, 213
Britain, 153, 157, 233, 257f
British Standards Institute (BSI), 176f, 181, 183
Bureaucratization, 39

Capitalism, 41, 71f, 184–85, 188, 230

CARE, 231, 233, 236
Carnegie Foundation, 229, 243
Catholic Church, 305n14
Charity and relief INGOs, 46, 228, 231, 235, 242
Chase-Dunn, Christopher, 184, 189, 196
Choice, and population policy, 203, 208–10, 211
Christendom, 305n14
Christianity, 53, 160, 228, 234, 315n26. *See also* Missionary organizations; Religion
Citizenship: national, 34, 40, 61, 209, 277; world, 17, 28, 34f, 39–41, 45, 61, 73–77 *passim*, 86, 123, 127–30 *passim*, 146, 150, 286–87, 292, 307nn22,23
Civil society, 17, 75, 237, 245
Clitoridectomy, 123
Cold War, 223, 232ff, 241, 246
Collateral authority, *see under* Authority, of INGOs
Colombo Plan, 233
Colonies, 32–34, 61
Comité Européen de Normalisation (CEN), 175
Community, world, 36, 101f, 241
Constitutions, national, 14, 276
Constructivism, 3
Contraception, 204f, 208
Convention for the Elimination of All Forms of Discrimination Against Women (CEDAW), 121
Core countries, of world-system, 53, 62–65

Library of Congress Cataloging-in-Publication Data

Constructing world culture : International nongovernmental
organizations since 1875 / edited by John Boli and George M. Thomas.
    p. cm.
    Includes bibliographical references and index.
    ISBN 0-8047-3421-6 (cloth) — ISBN 0-8047-3422-4 (pbk.)
    1. International relations—History.   2. Non-governmental
organizations—History.   3. Internationalism—History.
I. Boli, John.   II. Thomas, George M.
JZ1249.c66   1999
327.1'7'09—dc21   98-35017
                                                 CIP

∞ This book is printed on acid-free, recycled paper.

Original printing 1999
Last figure below indicates year of this printing:
08   07   06   05   04   03   02   01   00   99